Eustress and Distress: Reactivation

Polish Contemporary Philosophy and Philosophical Humanities

Edited by Jan Hartman

Volume 17

PETER LANG

Jan Felicjan Terelak

Eustress and Distress: Reactivation

PETER LANG

Bibliographic Information published by the Deutsche Nationalbibliothek
The Deutsche Nationalbibliothek lists this publication in the Deutsche Nationalbibliografie; detailed bibliographic data is available in the internet at http://dnb.d-nb.de.

Library of Congress Cataloging-in-Publication Data
A CIP catalog record for this book has been applied for at the Library of Congress.

This publication was financially supported by
the Cardinal Stefan Wyszyński University in Warsaw.

ISSN 2191-1878
ISBN 978-3-631-77534-9 (Print)
E-ISBN 978-3-631-78503-4 (E-PDF)
E-ISBN 978-3-631-78504-1 (EPUB)
E-ISBN 978-3-631-78505-8 (MOBI)
DOI 10.3726/b15414

Peter Lang – Berlin · Bern · Bruxelles · New York · Oxford · Warszawa · Wien

This publication has been peer reviewed.

www.peterlang.com

This monograph is dedicated to *the memory of Hans Selye, known as "Doctor Stress", whose book entitled: "The stress of life" initiated the interest in stress issues in Polish psychology*

Preface

Relatively quick exhaustion of circulation of the 2017 academic textbook entitled: "Stres życia: Perspektywa psychologiczna" (Life stress: psychological perspective) has led me to publish a new edition in the form of a monograph addressed to a wide range of readers, not only psychologists. The present publication is mainly aimed at increasing the awareness of readers that "there is no life without stress" and at pointing out two aspects of it, which H. Selye (1974) named: "Eustress" (good motivational stress) and "Distress" (bad destructive stress).

Therefore, the recipients should certainly be, first of all, employees of various professional orientations, who are interested in the so-called stress factors in the physical and social environment of work or in the challenges posed by contemporary 21st-century civilization.

The title of the previous book *The stress of life,* to which I refer in my dedication, refers to the 58th anniversary of the translation into Polish of Hans Selye's book entitled *The stress of life*, which for the first time in Polish psychology proposed a new term: "stress" (used by the translator in the original version - spelled with two "s")[1]. The book provoked a lively discussion among Polish physiologists. For example, Polish physiologist Stanisław Kozłowski (1986) pointed out the important fact that the concept introduced by Selye did not correspond to the English physiological terms *stress* and *strain.* It should be noted that Selye (1936, p. 32) was aware of this fact, as he had not used the term before, as can be seen in the article entitled *A syndrome produced by diverse noxious agent.* The terms *noxius agents* and *stress* are essentially neologisms in scientific terminology, which however, for pragmatic reasons, have become popular, especially with non-specialists in physiology, including psychology and sociology, as evidenced, inter alia, by the fact that more than six thousand jobs a year have begun to appear after the

---

1 It is worth noting here the difficulties related to the Polish translation of this English term. Translators of the book by Sely - Jan W. Guzek and Roman Rembiesa translated its title literally, introducing the original form of the notation into Polish terminology. After some time this term was further polished in Polish literature and assumed the spelling "stres" (with one "s"), which caused a turbulent discussion amongst the then-small group of experts on the subject. Other proposals of the equivalent of the word stress, such as "tension" or "pressure". However, these equivalents, as contrary to Sely's intentions, have not been accepted in Poland, as well as in other countries.

publication of *The stress of life* (Appley, Trumbull, 1967). Subsequent concepts by Selye (1974, 1975) - drew attention, on the one hand, to the so-called omnipresence of stress and, on the other hand, to its dual meaning: “stress” vs “distress”. In this way, Selye broadened the understanding of stress by shifting the focus from harmful factors *(noxious agents)* to all destructive requirements (*distress)*, on the one hand, and to positive functions motivating to deal with life’s challenges *(eustress)*, on the other hand. Janusz Reykowski (1966), one of the first to refer to this new understanding of stress in Polish psychology, identified two antagonistic areas on the basis of the continuum of the concept of stress: “Stress load” vs “stress overload”. Although traces of knowledge about stress can be found both in ancient philosophy and in medicine, where it was defined in three meanings: *load* - understood as an external force; *stress* - as an internal reaction caused by external force; *strain* - as a disturbance or deformation of the subject, these are basically three aspects of the same phenomenon, covered by a common, conventional name “stress”.

Since the Second World War until now, there has been an increasing interest in extreme stress research. The interest includes a wide range of representatives of social and medical sciences, dealing on the one hand with *Post Traumatic Stress Disorder* (local wars, terrorism, catastrophes) and on the other hand with *Traumatic Stress* in its new forms of causes related to civilizational requirements at the turn of the 20th and 21st centuries, resulting from the globalization of information and communication processes (e.g. stress of loneliness in cyberspace or information overload), intercontinental and space transport (weightlessness, social isolation and chronobiological stress) and migration processes (acculturative stress).

The message of this book is based on the thesis that stress, apart from the discomfort aspects (disorganization of action), is also an important motivational factor in resurrecting the effort and reaching for energy reserves of the body, sometimes in order to survive, but most of all for one’s own development and ambitious achievements.

Jan F. Terelak
Warsaw, 2018.

Contents

Introduction

One of the precursors of stress from the 19th century, the outstanding French biologist Claude Bernard, speaking the language of contemporary man, drew attention to the skillful management of one's "inner environment" (French: *milieu intérieur*). As a biologist and philosopher, he used the cell structure model and drew attention to the semipermeable membrane, which is responsible for maintaining the internal stability of the cell environment. His intuition regarding the biochemical mechanism responsible for maintaining this relative stability of the cell's inner environment, despite external threats, was only confirmed after more than 100 years by three 2013 Nobel Prize winners in the field of physiology and medicine - James E. Rothman from Yale University (New Haven), Randy W. Schekman from University of California (Berkeley) and Thomas C. Südhof from Stanford University (Palo Alto) for "discovering the organization of the main cellular transport system that uses bubble-like vesicles surrounded by lipid membranes" as well as the 2016 Nobel Prize winner, Yoshinori Ohsumi from Tokyo University, for his discoveries regarding the autophagy process.

This model became the basis of the Theory of Homeostasis by American physiologist Walter B. Cannon, who at the turn of the 19th and 20th century developed it in relation to people, colloquially calling it the "wisdom of life". Both models are referred to by psychological concepts of stress, using terms: "adaptation" or "adjustment", bearing in mind, however, their limitations due to the complexity of mental processes, which, unlike animals', are not based on passive adaptation based on the innate image of the enemy species, which is synonymous with the threat triggering the 'fight' or 'flight' reaction. Although *homo sapiens* no longer has an enemy species at the cognitive level, if a situation is defined as a threat, there are still some atavistic reactions to stress, observed at the physiological level, causing the "mobilization of energy", which are generally redundant and inadequate to the situation that a person can perceive in three dimensions: past, present or future. The cognitive mechanisms of dealing with dangerous situations are addressed by the R. Lazarus's and S. Folkman's cognitive theory of stress, which understands adaptation to a stressful situation as a transaction between humans and danger, which is active coping.

Concepts such as stress, coping with stress or adaptation and adjustment are related to individual human problems described mainly by psychologists, pedagogues, doctors and sociologists. It is therefore possible to write about stress from many points of view, which exceeds the competence of a single author.

Sticking to the psychological point of view, it should be emphasized that man has a rich repertoire of natural systems of adaptation to stress. On the one hand, a preventive system that takes into account the ability to learn, to regulate the level of stimulation or organization of the conceptual system, and on the other hand, a pathological system that manifests itself in learning disorders, neuroses or psychoses. However, the point is to prevent the activation of pathological adaptive systems. All these issues form the basis of monographs presenting contemporary knowledge of stress theories, sources of danger and responses to them, as well as coping. It is worth noting that if from the turn of the 19th and 20th century to the middle of the 20th century individual biological mechanisms of homeostasis and cognitive concepts of assessment of stressful situations and own resources were more emphasized, in the second half of the 20th century and in the early 21st century the focus of research interests shifted towards clinical symptoms of extreme stress (e.g. PTSD) due to the global threat.

As early as during World War II, Roy R. Grinker and John P. Spiegel (1945) drew attention to "war neurosis" as a typical reaction to extreme existential trauma. The authors described in great detail the immediate and long-term effects of combat stress, from demobilization reactions and panic to neurotic reactions and mental illnesses. After the atomic bombing of Hiroshima and Nagasaki, after the Korean and Vietnam wars, many new researches on the delayed psychological effects of war trauma have emerged (Rahe, 2007a). Nowadays, since the First Gulf War, and during the permanent Israeli-Palestinian conflict, especially in the situation of the war on terrorism in Iraq and Afghanistan and the so-called Islamic State, as well as the Russian aggression against Crimea, much attention has been paid primarily to chronic stress and social support in extreme situations (Bronstein, Montgomery, Dobrowolski, 2012; Solomon, Mikulincer, 2007).

Difficult issues related to the taxonomy of sources of danger include multilateral relations between man and the broadly understood environment: physical, biological, social and spiritual environment. Therefore, the division into four categories - environmental (climate, noise, lighting, ionizing and microwave radiation, vibrations, hypoxia, gravity - acceleration vs weightlessness), chronobiological (circadian rhythm, sudden change of time zone), psychological (deprivation vs overload, disruptions, wrongdoings, threats, challenges etc.), social (social status, social roles, management styles, competition, awards vs penalties, career, work/house relations etc.) - adopted in this monograph is for illustrative purposes only. Content identification is difficult due to the variety of non-specific and specific (in particular) reactions that need to be diagnosed from the point of view of their harmfulness to the comfort of life and/or health. Four perspectives of stress response characteristics have been adopted: physiological (EEG, ECG, heart rate, breath rate, sweating, temperature, etc.), emotional (stimulation, expression, speech, etc.), cognitive (memory disorders, mental impairment, etc.), behavioral (psychomotor response time, visual-motor coordination, etc.).

Dealing with stress is described in psychology in two terms that differ significantly: *resistance to stress* and *coping with stress.* In the monograph it is assumed that "resistance to stress" has no scientific status in psychology, and if it is sometimes applied it is only an analogue of immunological resistance, defined in biology as the insensitivity of an organism to pathogenic microorganisms or their venom (toxins). In psychological practice there are two notions of *resistance to stress:* microanalytical, describing it as a feature of temperament and intelligence, and macroanalytical, defining it as a style of action conditioned by certain natural mechanisms of temperament. On the basis of this temperament-related understanding, three basic ways of coping with stress are assumed: (a) by a change of temperament, (b) by avoiding or preferring stressful situations according to one' s temperamental characteristics, (c) one's individual style of action.

Scientific status is, however, given to the term *coping with stress*, the essence of which is not only the ability to passively adapt to stressful environmental conditions, but above all to learn various ways of dealing with stress throughout one's life. Remedial skills in stressful situations depend not only on the type of situation and strategies of coping with stress, but also on various personality traits, age, gender, education, current health condition, etc. The most frequently mentioned in the subject literature are problem-solving (task-oriented) strategies, emotion-oriented strategies, as well as avoidance strategies. One of the important ways of dealing with stress is social support, which is defined, among other things, as relationships between people, allowing a person to feel and perceive that they have people to rely on around them. Support can be of a certain nature: emotional (experiencing empathy, being able to trust someone, being surrounded by care, friendship, feeling), instrumental (experiencing help in different areas of life and in a specific way, e.g. borrowing money, doing part of a task), information support (receiving information that can help in dealing with certain tasks or problems). There are no clear opinions on the positive or negative role of social support, as it sometimes leads to learned helplessness. Apart from individual forms of social support, various forms of institutional support, including in the first place service-minded institutions grouping government administration, as well as non-governmental institutions, are listed. The forms and quality of institutional support depend to a large extent on the political system of a given country and the political culture of its administration.

An institutional form of social support is particularly useful in global crisis situations (wars, disasters, catastrophes, epidemics, migration, unemployment, etc.). Nowadays, thanks to universal access to the Internet and television, social media are a new form of support.

1 Theoretical foundations of stress

The theoretical foundations of stress have a rich history, which we use as a criterion to organize our deliberations on the various concepts of stress. Looking for the beginnings of modern history of stress we come across a 17th century engineering model of Robert Hooke's bridge structure, in which the author distinguished such physical components of the bridge as: *load*, *stress* and *strain*, which three centuries later found their application in describing various aspects of stress both in biological and psychological terms.

A model of the structure of the R. Hooke's bridge was in a sense a forerunner of the 19th century model of "milieu intérieur" by French biologist Claude Bernard and the 20th century model of "homeostasis" by American physiologist Walter Cannon, as well as the model of "General Adaptation Syndrome" by Hans Sely, a Canadian doctor of Hungarian origin, and a number of psychological models using the term "adaptation to stress", among which two models by American psychologists are at the forefront: "frustration model" by J. Dollard and N.A Miller and the "cognitive" model of Richard S. Lazarus and Susan Folkman. We will discuss selected models of stress, because the detailed history of this issue is the subject of the *Encyclopedia of Stress* and many other studies (Fink, ede., 2007).

1.1 Biological take on stress

The biological concepts of risk were based on the knowledge of the adaptation of living organisms to the external environment and attempts to explain the mechanisms of dealing with harmful factors, as well as on the question regarding individual differences in terms of adaptation to different environmental conditions: aquatic, terrestrial and aerial, and climatic: tropical vs polar. Biologists are in agreement that adaptability is the most important feature that distinguishes the world of living beings from inanimate nature. It should be stressed that the adaptation of living organisms to a changing environment is not passive, as most of the adaptation mechanisms, apart from some pathological reactions, are connected with *feedback systems.* Detailed knowledge of adaptation mechanisms begins with the outstanding 19th century French physiologist Claude Bernard and his American epigone Walter B. Cannon.

1.1.1 Claude Bernard's law on the relative stability of the internal environment

Biologists are in agreement that the ability to adapt to the environment is relatively stable and that it is a prerequisite for independent living. The detailed knowledge of the mechanisms of stability of adaptation dates back to the 19th century times of the outstanding French physiologist Claude Bernard, creator of the law of *stability of the internal environment*". (French: *milieu intérieur*). The author of this law drew attention to the fact that the cell, as the basic unit of life of organisms, lives in its own, isolated from the world environment, in which constant changes take place, often disturbing the body's functions or threatening its life. This internal environment, which guarantees relative stability, is at the same time a condition for the independent existence of the system. At the intercellular level, this internal environment is the extracellular fluid that fills all intercellular gaps, blood vessels, lymphatic vessels and others. Bernard's merit is not only the claim that the stability of the internal environment is preserved thanks to the physiological and biochemical processes of the system, but also the reference to the semipermeable membrane of the cell as a hypothetical basic mechanism explaining the processes of information exchange between the cell interior and the external environment. It is extremely interesting from a methodological point of view, as theory is far ahead of empirical evidence. An example of this is the case of Bernard, whose hypothesis on the role of the semipermeable membrane of a cell was empirically confirmed only after about one hundred years by three scientists, 2013 Nobel Prize laureates in the field of physiology and medicine - James E. Rothman from Yale University (New Haven), Randy W. Schekman from University of California (Berkeley) and Thomas C. Südhof from Stanford University (Palo Alto) for "discovering the organization of the main cellular transport system that uses bubble-like vesicles surrounded by lipid membranes".

Let us recall the operating mechanism of a semipermeable cell membrane. The activity of cells of living organisms depends on the proper transport of tiny bubbles. The question answered by the 2013 Nobel Prize winners concerns the mechanism of biochemical opening of these bubbles to information carried by calcium ions. Schekman's contribution to explaining this mechanism consists in empirical verification (he experimented on yeast cells), which genes are responsible for the proper functioning of the transport system. Rothman answered the question: how do the protein chains on the transporting bubbles connect with the corresponding proteins on the surface of the cell membrane? This allows the material to reach its destination. Finally, the very biochemical mechanism of triggering the process of bubbles sticking to the cell membrane, the opening and release of calcium ions as carriers of transport necessary for the cell information was described by Südhof. This mechanism is responsible for the time and logic aspects of semipermeable membrane. New details concerning mysterious bubbles surrounding the lipid membrane were provided by Prof. Yoshinori Ohsumi from the University of Tokyo - the 2016 Nobel Prize winner in the field of medicine for his discoveries concerning the autophagy process. The discovery concerning the autophagy process (Greek: *auto*, and *phagein*), a method by which cells clean their interior of dead or damaged elements (e.g. proteins and organella) by first chopping them up and then digesting them, is of great importance for understanding the mechanism of preserving the stability of cell life. This mechanism is in fact based on the disposal of unnecessary waste which is surrounded by a film, forming a bubble similar to a bag (autophagosome), transported to a lysosom, which is a specific waste processing plant. Here, its content is decomposed into simpler components, used by the cell as recyclable materials - a building material and/or fuel (energy source). Ohsumi also identified the genes that are responsible for this process. Autophagy takes place both in healthy cells, guaranteeing them a long life, as well as in pathological cells, helping them cope with diseases.

1.1.2 Walter Bradford Cannon's homeostasis model

Walter B. Cannon (1932), an American physiologist, neurologist and psychologist, introduced the concept of *homeostasis* (Greek: *homoios* – similar and *stasis* – state), referring to the concept of Claude Bernard on the stability of the internal environment of an organism. By calling homeostasis colloquially "the wisdom of the body", he drew attention to the system of regulatory mechanisms that allow the body to respond favorably to environmental stimuli, the graphical model of which is presented in Fig. 1.1.

Cannon is both the founder of homeostasis theory and the one who introduced this concept into physiology for the first time. Homeostasis can be translated as constant power, i.e. as the ability to remain the same, and concerns different regulatory processes based on the principle of negative feedback. The concept of Cannon's homeostasis has become one of the main principles of any theory of self-regulation and internal organization in complex open systems (cf. McEwen, 2007). The biological graphic model of the homeostat itself is extremely simple, as it reflects a constant level of a number of physical (e.g. body temperature, osmotic blood pressure) and chemical (e.g. sugar, carbon dioxide, hemoglobin in blood) parameters. In order to obtain the effect of homeostasis, it is necessary

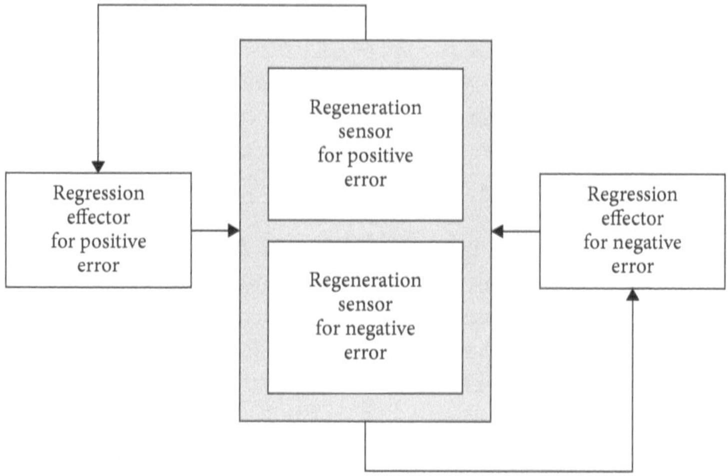

Fig. 1.1: Graphical model of homeostasis (Source: own elaboration based on: Cannon, 1932)

to have measuring devices and effector devices working against each other. Effects of homeostasis can also be found in many technical devices intended for common use, the most famous of which is the thermostat (Greek: *therme* - hot and *stasis* - state), used to maintain a relatively constant temperature by automatically switching off heating when the set temperature is exceeded and vice versa (e.g. in refrigerators, automatic washing machines). In biological organisms, especially highly organized ones, regulatory mechanisms based on homeostasis are very complex. We will follow the model of homeostasis on the example of physiological processes responsible for maintaining a constant body temperature (the so-called *set point*).

Blood temperature-sensitive cells (acting as a measuring device) in the hypothalamus receive information about the body temperature through the blood that flows through the hypothalamus. If the body temperature rises, the so-called heat receptors (cells sensitive to excessive heat) are activated. Through the vegetative system they affect the sweat glands (the sympathetic part), which produce sweat. Sweating absorbs a large amount of heat, which reduces body temperature. After some time, the lower-temperature blood reaches the hypothalamus and stimulates the so-called cold receptors (cells sensitive to too low a temperature). They act through the vegetative system on the skin vessels, narrowing them down and thus reducing the loss of heat by the body surface. At the same time as the blood, adrenaline is thrown away, which causes an increase in metabolism and, consequently, an increase in heat production. With longer cooling, another mechanism is activated: the hypothalamus - pituitary - thyroid gland, responsible for the production of thyroxine, which has a much greater metabolic effect.

Without going further into the complex physiological mechanisms of homeostasis, which are the domain of physiology, it should be generally said that homeostasis assumes that a system can function properly only within the limits within which it is capable of rapid adaptation, so as to preserve its internal environment, within a framework strictly defined for each organism. However, each system's response to changes in the environment must be such as to enable it to function properly under the changed conditions. The permanent existence of the homeostasis system, whether simple or extremely complex, provides biological evidence that it has the mechanisms to maintain its distinctiveness despite the constant pressure of *thermal stress* and that it is capable of adapting to this type of stress. Although homeostasis is only an ideal concept and therefore it should be remembered that after reacting to the stimulus the organism does not always return exactly to its initial state (e.g. disease), complementary concepts of homeostasis, adaptation and stress (the term *homeostasis* correlates with English physiological terms: *stress* and *strain*) are important for explaining life mechanisms at all levels of biological (single- or multicellular systems), psychological and social organization.

The theory of homeostasis is developed in physiology and psychology by the theory of adaptation, which, referring to the former, at the same time deprives it of its seemingly static character by drawing attention to the dynamic aspect of homeostasis. This means that the balance once achieved is not maintained by the force of inertia, but requires constant activity of the body in order to maintain it.

It is also worth noting that the somewhat static character of homeostasis has been replaced today by other terms, namely homeodynamics or allostasis (Latin *alius* - different, and Greek *stasis* - state) (Goldstein, 2004), which are not only of a semantic nature, but above all have evolutionary character, because thanks to overcoming decades of attachment to homeostasis and the limitations resulting from it we can now explain such phenomena as: development of the body both in ontogenetic and filogenetic aspect, regulatory processes occurring after brain injuries, self-fulfillment, spontaneous creativity and any cultural activity, any irrational human behavior, etc. (McEwen, Wingfield, 2007).

1.1.3 Hans Selye's General Adaptation Syndrome (GAS)

The term "adaptation" was used by H. Selye (1956) to describe the main mechanisms of the disease and gained the greatest publicity and special interpretation under the term *General Adaptation Syndrome*. This syndrome is the main element of stress theory viewed from a physiological perspective, although its creator himself was an endocrinologist and pathophysiologist. The author of *GAS* is an outstanding expert on stress, as evidenced, among other things, by the fact that for his scientific, journalistic and organizational activities he was nominated to the Nobel Prize ten times, and called the "Father of stress" or "Doctor of Stress" in the literature of the subject.

It is worth noting the genesis of H. Selye's interest in stress issues. From Selye's biographical memoirs, it can be concluded that the beginning of his interest in non-specific aspects of stress dates back to his student years, when, as a medical student at Charles University in Prague and participating with doctors in the so-called routine ward rounds, he noticed that apart from the specific symptoms of individual diseases, medical teams generally ignored the so-called non-specific symptoms typical for all diseases, regardless of their genesis. The future physician believed that information important for the understanding of the disease was omitted (after: Tuchweber, Bois, 2007). Further medical experience and research at McGill University of Montreal's biochemical laboratory led to the crystallization of stress theory. The author himself admits that the use of the phrase *biological stress*, and then *stress,* met with violent opposition from physiologists who criticized the use of the word *stress* to describe the body's reactions, because in common English it means nervous effort.

According to Selye (1956), an important argument for the non-specificity of stress reactions is the mechanism of activation of the endocrine system, or more precisely the adrenal cortex. The stress control mechanism can be described as follows. A stressor stimulates the hypothalamus, a substance indicating that the pituitary gland should release more adrenocortic-cotropic hormone (ACTH) into the blood. Under the influence of ACTH, the external adrenal part of the adrenal gland releases corticosteroids. This in turn leads to the reduction and disappearance of the thymus and other associated changes, such as lymphadenopathy, inhibition of inflammatory reactions and sugar production. The second typical feature of the stress response is the formation of gastrointestinal ulcers (of stomach and intestines), which is associated with high levels of corticosteroids in the blood and the functioning of the autonomic nervous system. The described set of changes, caused by harmful factors (stressors) such as injury, infection, high temperature, noise, etc. on the body, is of an adaptive nature and manifests itself in two ways:

- *Local Adaptation Syndrome (LAS*), covering specific changes occurring in the stressor area (e.g. in the area of burns);
- *General Adaptation Syndrome* - GAS, covering non-specific, generalized changes, the schema of which is shown in Fig. 1.2.

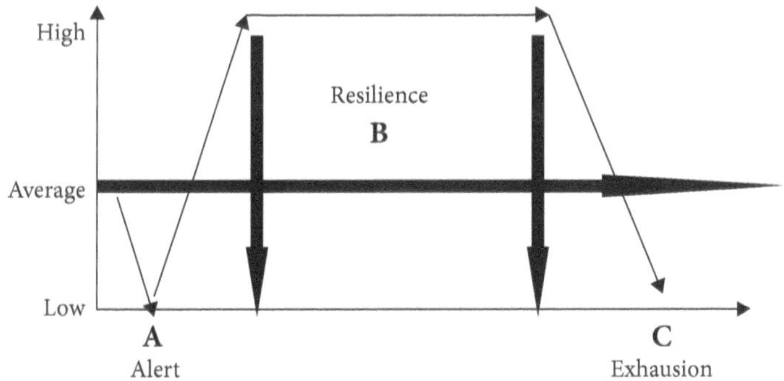

Fig. 1.2: General Adaptation Syndrome - GAS of H. Selye (Source: own elaboration based on: Selye, 1956).

Note: (A - Alarm response stage; B - Immunity stage; C - Exhaustion stage)

The latter group of any non-specific physiological changes, i.e. not directly related to nature and harmful stimuli, is the essence of stress in Selye's concept. A stress response understood in this way develops in three stages: alarm response, immunity and exhaustion.

A *Alarm response stage* - is an expression of the general mobilization of the body's defensive forces. At this stage, two phases are distinguished: (a) *shock phase*, consisting of the initial direct effect of a noxious agent on the body, characterized by the occurrence of first signs of stimulation of the body to defend itself (e.g. a decrease in blood pressure or a decrease in temperature) or of injury indicators; (b) *shock response phase*, consisting of defensive reactions accompanied by changes in physiological functions (e.g. an increase in blood pressure, an increase in body temperature) (Mccarty, Pacak, 2007).

B *Immunity stage* - is a stage of relative adaptation characterized by the fact that the body is able to tolerate the noxious agents that have been active for some time relatively well, and less able to tolerate other stimuli that were previously harmless.

C *Exhaustion stage* - occurs when the noxious agents act too intensively or for too long, and the general stimulation of the body no longer serves to fight stress, but is characterized by a loss of defensive abilities, which is indicated by the dysregulation of physiological functions. In this stage relatively permanent pathological reaction may occur, which could lead to death if the stressor continues to act.

The endocrine-neuronal model of physiological stress mechanisms developed by Sely has received contemporary criticism from many physiologists, who have focused primarily on the enigmatic definition of stress, which explains the relationship between stress and disease, but its universality from the physiological point of view is not empirically justified. Regardless of the criticism of the detailed mechanisms of physiological stress in Sely's theory, it was undoubtedly his merit to draw attention to the anatomical and physiological mechanisms of stress. Nowadays they can be described not only on the basis of the hormonal system (hypothalamic–pituitary–adrenal axis), but also on the basis of the neural system (cf. Werka, 1997). The very essence of stress in Sely's approach, namely its non-specificity, is also called into question. Indeed, in such different situations as heavy muscle workload, exposure to low ambient temperature or hemorrhage, a seemingly similar - one would like to say - non-specific reaction as increased adrenal cortex secretion activity (increased secretion of glucocorticoids and increase in their concentration in blood) can be observed. However, a closer analysis of these phenomena may lead to a different conclusion. It turns out that in each of these different situations the mechanisms of adrenal cortex activation are different and the effects of their action are different. The action, on the other hand, is closely related to the conditions under which the organism operates, contributes to the exposure to these particular conditions, and is therefore as much as possible a "specific adaptive response". (Kozłowski, op. cit., p. 25). It is typical that the popularity of the concept of stress in the social sciences is the result of Selye's (1974) distinction between *distress* (*bad stress*) and *eustress* (*good stress*),[2]as illustrated by Fig. 1.3.

The basis of this distinction between two types of stress is the philosophical reflection and substantive context of the stressor, which are more typical for psychotherapists than physiologists' competences (Matthews, 2007). This is confirmed by Selye himself, admitting that he formulated this view on the basis of clinical observations collected during medical and therapeutic practice, as well as under the influence of existential philosophy, preferring a holistic approach to the description of social phenomena. No wonder, therefore, that in later works he modified his definition, treating stress as "a non-specific reaction of the organism to all the requirements that are imposed on it" (Selye, 1974).

---

2 It is worth noting that Selye's belief regarding the bivalent meaning of stress in human life has accompanied his interests in stress from the very beginning, and this was already signaled in the first edition of the book "The Stress of Life" dedicating it"*...to those who are not afraid to enjoy the stress of a full life, and at the same time do not think naively that they could do so without an intellectual effort*" (Selye, 1956).

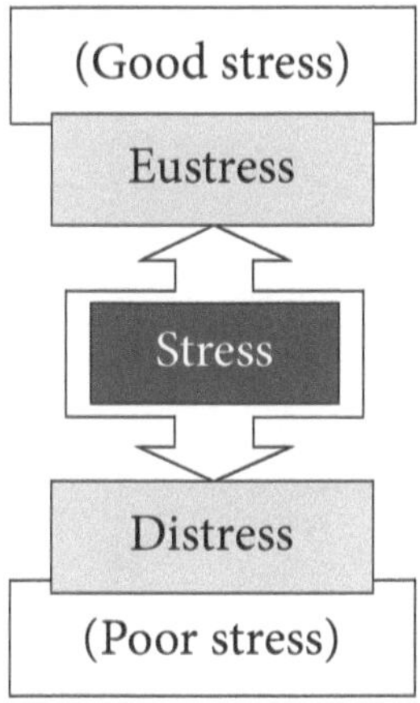

Fig. 1.3: Evaluative aspects of stress (Source: own elaboration based on: Selye, 1975)

Finally, at the end of his professional life, Selye has become a strong supporter of positive psychology, referring to human and the so-called biological codes of ethics, on the basis of which he formulated the so-called ethical commandments: 1) To find a proper level of resistance to stress; 2) To be guided by the principles of altruistic selfishness; 3) To earn the love of the fellow human beings. Selye has therefore undergone a certain evolution of his views, from purely biological to psychological and philosophical ones (Selye, 1980a, b).

Returning to the already traditional GAS model, it should be stressed that susceptibility to stress, both in the phase of adaptation to stress and general exhaustion, is characterized by high individual variability. In some cases it manifests itself in an increase in the level of adrenal hormones and general exhaustion (pathological aspects), while in others it only mobilizes the body to act (motivational aspects). The motivational aspects of *eustress* are studied by psychologists and therapists. Brain mechanisms of stress and treatment of the effects of stress associated with exhaustion of the body and preventive healthcare are dealt with by medical concepts of stress.

1.1.4 Neuropsychological model of optimal activation by Donald O. Hebb

Donald O. Hebb (1965), followed by Clarence Leuba (1965), proposed an idealistic model of stress, based on the physiological mechanism of normal distribution, according to the Gaussian Curve, of the level of *activation (or arousal)* or

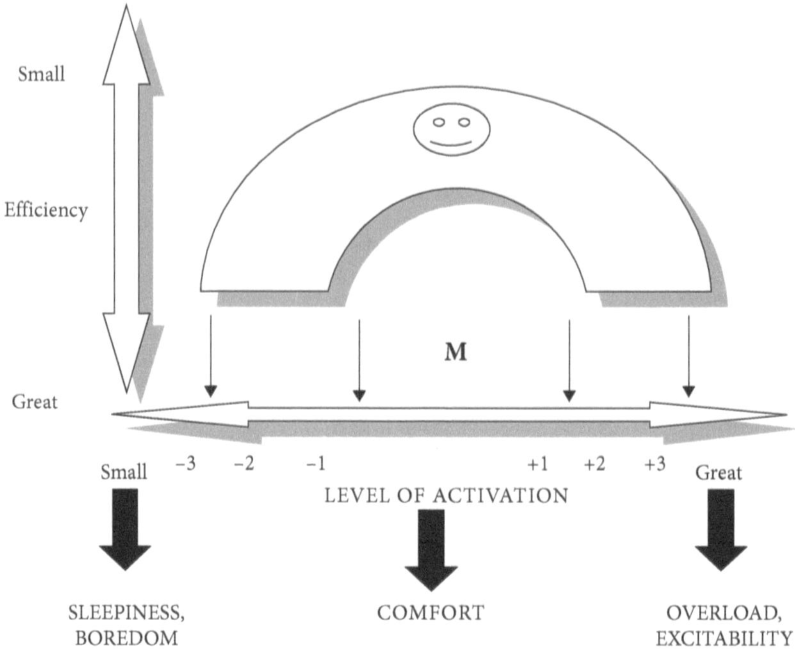

Fig. 1.4: Psychometric model of optimal activation. (Source: own elaboration based on: Hebb, 1965).

stimulation. The complementary use of this model is justified by the fact that the optimal activation reflects at the same time both the formal aspects (strength, intensity) of the stimulus, as well as its content aspects, reflecting its psychological meaning, which significantly modifies the stress response.

Stress is of an aversial nature and results from exceeding the optimal area of activation distribution in both suboptimal and superoptimal directions, accompanied by efficiency of action and deterioration of mood (boredom, monotony or hyperactivity, overload). Changes in the activation level, associated with the function of the brainstem reticular formation and other subcortical structures (the so-called emotional part of the nervous system), have two aspects. One aspect, the so-called activation aspect, refers to changes in the level of activation of the cerebral cortex. An indicator of this activation level is the bioelectrical brain activity recorded in the EEG.

The characteristic electroencephalographic image of cortical activation consists, among other things, in the appearance of high frequency and low amplitude waves (so-called beta waves) in the cerebral cortex, i.e. desynchronization of the basic bioelectrical activity related to the activity of brain processes. During the state of relaxation and rest we observe the opposite phenomenon, the so-called synchronization of *alpha* rhythm. Then the high amplitude and low-frequency waves (so-called *alpha* waves) appear. The second aspect of activation refers to changes in the emotional part of the brain (limbic system), characterized, among others, by increased level of stimulation, which in the peripheral nervous system manifests itself in various physiological reactions that can be observed, such as: galvanic skin response (GSR), overall muscle tone increase (EMG), heart activity (ECG), respiratory rate etc. These changes indicate a general mobilization of the energy resources of the entire organism in stressful situations and we are talking about the level of *arousal* rather than, as in the case of changes in the central nervous system, about the level of *activation*. Psychologists use the above mentioned indicators of activation (Terelak, 1976) and stimulation as physiological correlates of emotions (Sosnowski, Zimmer, ed., 1993).

1.2 Medical concepts for stress

It is important for the physician to determine the causes of the disease, among which stressful life events are important. Stress theorists draw attention to the methodological difficulties of studying qualitative descriptions of life events, which significantly weakens their exploratory value. However, concepts explaining their importance in the selection of methods of disease therapy can be found in the literature of the subject.

1.2.1 Model of stress antecedents as precursors of disease

Analyzing the resumes of individual people, one can indicate significant or critical life events (e.g. death of loved ones, divorce, marriage, personal harm, loss of job), influencing bad mood, neurosis, depression, etc. These observations became the basis for the concept of stressful life events as predictors of so-called civilization diseases.

1.2.1.1 Daily stressful life events

This concept is based on the stress-disease model, although according to literature it does not sufficiently explain the disease, as it was created on the basis of socioepidemiological data, which are difficult to quantify. One of the models of *stressful life events* is presented in Fig. 1.5.

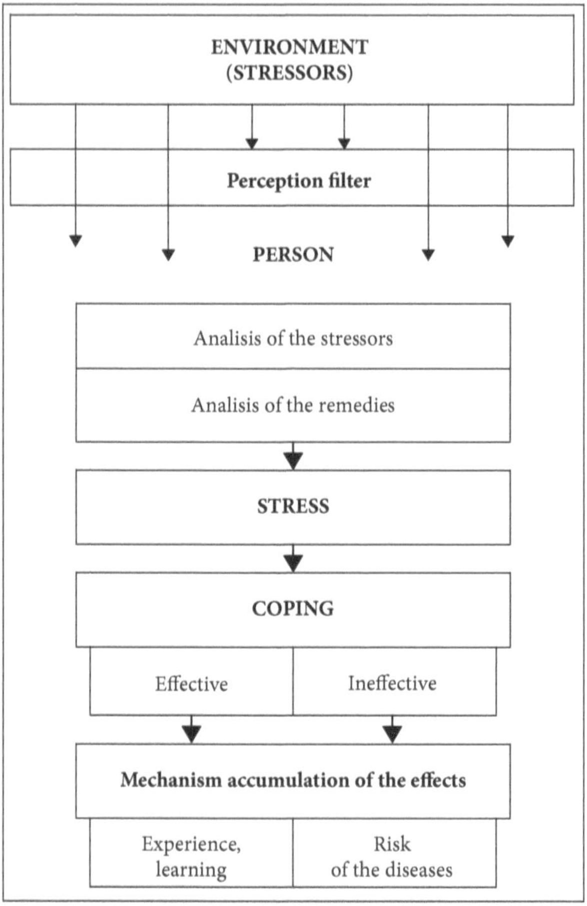

Fig. 1.5: A model of stressful events as precursors of disease. (Source: own elaboration based on: Dohrenwend and Dohrenwend, 1982)

As it appears from the above Fig. 1.5, this model is based on the assumption that stressful life events can be caused both by objective environmental factors (climate, noise, hypoxia, weightlessness, etc.), as well as by subjective personal factors (type of temperament, personality attributes, intelligence, appearance, etc.). Daily stress events can lead to a state of stress that reflects the impact of the environmental and personal contexts. The context can modify both the size of a stress condition and its negative (likelihood of illness) and positive (personality development) effects. If the assessment of daily stress events is possible for one person, it is not suitable for averaging it in the case of group studies. The weakness of this concept is the dubious assumption that stressful life events accumulate on a daily, weekly or other basis and that they can be quantified. This is confirmed by various more or less successful attempts to standardize their measurement (Holmes, Rahe, 1976), based on the assumption of accumulation of individual stress events, introducing a special *life chart* into medical diagnosis. It contains biographical data taking into account significant events in one's life, which are to prove the accumulation of life events in some period of life and prediction of disease. Studies on the standardization of stress measurement are of an epidemiological nature. The collected symptoms of patients were subjected to quantitative analysis using the weight estimation method, which made it possible to identify a certain number of events-dimensions, which were then identified arbitrarily by competent judges. These identified critical *stressful life events* to which a certain rank has been assigned, e.g. 100 discretionary points for the most stressful event ("spouse's death"). Evaluation based on an criterion which is arbitrary as to the importance of an event for human life and development is of little use for scientific research, which does not diminish its usefulness in individual clinical trials with the use of structured medical history (such as *The Life Events and Difficulties Schedule* - LEDS) (cf. Surtees, Wainwright, 2007). An alternative method is the narrative technique based on *The Structured Event Probe and Narrative Rating* - SEPRATE, analyzed from the perspective of their relationship with the disease (Dohrenwend, Dohrenwend, 1982). Despite criticism from so-called methodological purists, it should be stressed that the concept of stressful life events, based on their treatment as precursors to so-called stress illnesses, has highlighted two important issues that have been developed in psychological stress concepts (e.g. Lazarus), namely that there are stress incidents that tend to have a delayed response over time, which sometimes leads to chronic stress and ultimately to an illness, and that there are quite significant individual differences both in stress responses and in the dynamics of illness changes.

Summarizing the theoretical and methodological aspect of the concept of stressful life events, it should be stated that in the normative sense life events are defined in terms of external stressors. This approach is dominated by the sociological-epidemiological orientation, which constitutes the basis for the formulation of laws concerning the relationship between life stress and illnesses. The individual approach focuses on measuring life events according to psychological concepts of stress, which pay attention to the cognitive evaluation of stress events.

The concept of stressful life events is popular especially among physicians, because it is treated as a predictor of psychosomatic disorders, although, according to the literature, it does not adequately explain the illness. Furthermore, the very measurement of stressful life events is controversial.

1.2.1.2 Occasional crisis events

Knowledge about crisis situations in human life, which have a significant impact on one' s fate, is the subject of research mainly of psychiatrists and therapists. The so-called crisis theories that have been emerging since the 1940s try to put this knowledge in order.

1.2.1.2.1 Incidental life crises according to Gerard Caplan

Among many authors of the crisis theories, the most famous is the theory of the American psychiatrist Gerard Caplan (1964), the essence of which is its developmental aspect, because it is based on the assumption that the human personality is formed under the influence of stress not gradually, but in leaps and bounds, that is from crisis to crisis. Caplan understands crisis as a state of emotional stress that forces the body to resist stressors by mobilizing countermeasures. Thus, a characteristic aspect of this theory is the positive role of crisis situations in the development of a human personality, and not just focusing on the negative effects of stress. Although Caplan, as a psychiatrist, was aware of the fact that the crisis can also lead to chronic illness or even death (e.g. suicide attempt), he emphasizes that positive adaptation is a more frequent assumption. This essentially therapeutic approach is based on the belief in human adaptive abilities and is typical for American psychiatry of the post-war years, which, under the influence of humanistic psychology, sought justifications for the reduction of the psychological effects of World War II and the search for meaning of human life. In the light of this theory, crises represent a natural phase in the process of adaptation to new life challenges.

1.2.1.2.2 Cyclical life crises according to Erik H. Erikson

Using the developmental life cycles proposed by Erik H. Erikson (1968), concerning the search for one's own identity, they are credited with crises adequate to the developmental age. These crises occur in transition periods between the different phases of development and are of a stressful nature, requiring social support from a parent, psychologist, pedagogue or physician. Thus, taking as a starting point the stages of human development: infancy - early childhood - pre-school period - middle childhood - adolescence - early adulthood - middle adulthood - old age, we can attribute them with accompanying psychosocial crises such as: trust vs. lack of trust (infancy), autonomy vs. shame and uncertainty (early childhood), initiative vs. guilt (pre-school period), diligence vs. inferiority (middle childhood), identity vs. dispersion (youth), intimacy vs. isolation (early adulthood), productivity vs. stagnation (middle adulthood), integration vs. loss of hope (old age). Each stage of development is associated with its own specific crisis situations, which man has to solve himself on the basis of current possibilities determined by the level of biological, psychological and social maturity or should seek social support.

Moreover, there are accidental crisis situations that can be experienced not only by individuals but also by entire communities, such as formal groups (e.g. family, nation, followers of a particular religion, political party, army) or informal situations (e.g. cliques, fractions, hobby clubs, etc.). An example of a crisis situation for formal groups can be: divorce, unemployment, war, religious or political intolerance, etc., while for informal groups - e.g. change of leader in a group, law, moral norms, police intervention, etc.

Although the aim of the theory of crisis is to point to positive aspects of stress, from a psychological point of view the most difficult are the periods between crisis situations, because they distort (disorganize) important cognitive and emotional functions. Stress caused by a crisis situation leads not only to mobilization of human defense forces, but also to a qualitatively new situation, reorganization of adaptation mechanisms, the concept of which, in Polish psychiatry, was developed by Kazimierz Dąbrowski (1964) as the so-called positive disintegration.

1.2.1.2.3 Existential life crises according to Kazimierz Dąbrowski

K. Dąbrowski, a doctor, philosopher and existential psychologist by education, within his concept of transcendental personality, assuming that the essence of its development is "movement" towards not only physical, but also metaphysical existence, developed a mechanism of personality development and coping with stress called "positive disintegration". The author assumes that in situations of existential stress (e.g. threats of war, border states, suffering, loneliness or death) it is possible and justified to conduct psychotherapy based on the so-called projective transfer, focused on finding oneself in a "Me - another person (e.g. eminent people, creators, saints and heroes)" relation, as well as in relation to the personal God. This makes it possible to better understand why the personality can be disintegrated at all and have an existential benefit from it.

As a neuropsychologist, Dąbrowski refers in his concept of positive disintegration to the negative aspects of evolution, i.e. the transition from well-organized,

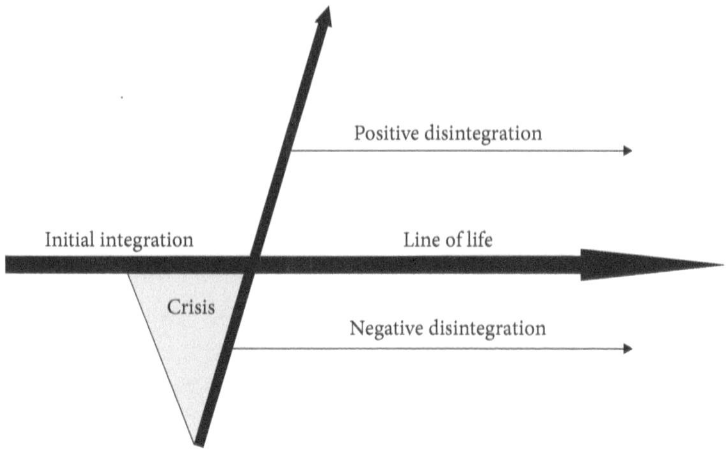

Fig. 1.6: Model of positive disintegration in a crisis situation. (Source: own elaboration based on: Dąbrowski, 1964)

simple and more automated mechanisms to mechanisms with a lesser degree of organization, more complex and non-automated and to the mechanism of dissection, i.e. the disruption of the nervous system, psyche. In his model of psychotherapy based on the model of positive disintegration, Dąbrowski gives both concepts a new meaning.

Mental evolution is understood as the process of loosening the primary cohesiveness of the entity (the so-called primary integration), and then integrating its elements at a higher level. This is a positive disintegration, because this new organization is as compact and efficient as the previous one, but at a higher level of development, as illustrated in the Fig. 1.6.

A human development crisis may be of the following nature: stagnant, in the case of return (after a crisis) to the same level of development, regressive, in the case of retreat to a lower level of development (e.g. diseases disrupting development processes), or progressive, in the case of moving to a higher level of individual development (positive disintegration).

Integrated structures can be found mainly among normal people, where moments of disintegration are relatively brief, play a secondary role and pass quickly. However, in life crisis situations (incidental or developmental) longer lasting states of negative disintegration also occur. However, when the cause of these integration disorders disappears, they re-adapt to the surrounding reality and reach the right level of integration. This process is more or less conscious, and sometimes the very consciousness of one's own state of disintegration is an impulse to eliminate this state. But if the very awareness of one's own inner disintegration does not lead to an effort to get out of this state, crisis intervention by e.g. a pedagogue, psychiatrist, or psychologist is required, because otherwise the ineffective from the point of view of own development, psychosomatic diseases, self-destructive behavior (alcoholism, drug addiction, suicide) or social deviations may become entrenched.

Dąbrowski considers both these aspects of the process of positive or negative disintegration in two forms: one-level (connected with some more important periods of human life cycle and its temperamental properties) and multi-level (connected with the development of self-awareness and self-knowledge). In practice, it is not possible to make a strict distinction between the two types of disintegration processes.

This psychological and therapeutic resonance of the theories discussed above, namely Caplan's theory of crises and Dąbrowski's theory of positive disintegration, emphasizes the possibility of human ontogenetic development despite the existence of high-intensity stress.

In almost all of the biological and medical concepts cited so far, stress is defined in two aspects. One aspect takes into account the description of stress through external factors, the other - takes into account internal processes or states occurring in the individual. The differences between the various concepts consist in accentuating one of them and the methods in which they are characterized. Both approaches assume, more or less indirectly, the existence of interactions between external and internal factors. This interaction is emphasized by psychosomatic medicine, which is a bridge between biological-medical concepts of stress and psychological theories. It is based on two assumptions: 1) there are physiological correlates of emotions; 2) there is a link between intense and prolonged emotions and somatic health.

1.3 Psychological theories of stress

Unlike the descriptive concepts of stress presented so far, which describe stress in biological and medical terms, psychological theories of stress focus to a large extent, in addition to the description of psychological responses to stress, on the formulation of mechanisms explaining the relationship between stress stimulus and response.

1.3.1 John Dollard's frustration–aggression model

Undoubtedly, the first concise psychological theory of stress fulfilling the methodological requirement of the explanatory function is the model of the

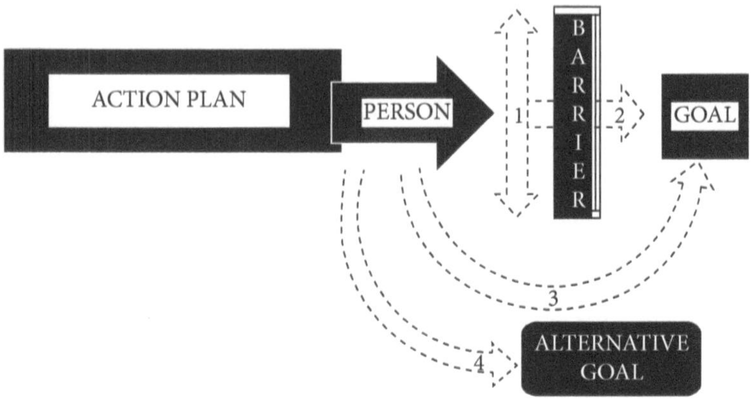

Fig. 1.7: Frustration model (Source: own elaboration based on: Dollard et al., 1939)
Note: (Legend: 1. submissive resignation; 2. overcoming an obstacle; 3. bypassing an obstacle; 4. searching for a replacement goal)

frustration process, understood as a reaction to an emerging obstacle on the way to achieving the goal/by John Dollard et al. (1939) presented in Fig. 1.7. The basic hypotheses have been best documented experimentally in terms of the relationship between frustration and aggression. The first hypothesis saying that frustration leads to a tendency to aggression is illustrated by the authors with a description of the fact that a hungry dog reacts more aggressively (crawling, baring teeth) than a dog that is not hungry, when the food is taken away from it. The second hypothesis, which refers to the relationship between the size of the obstacle and tendency towards aggression, is represented by statistical data, which shows that as the economic living conditions of the population deteriorate, the number of anti-social acts and crimes increases.

The third hypothesis, which states that the tendency towards aggression depends on the anticipation of punishment, is illustrated by popular observations concerning the so-called phenomenon of summation of aggressive behaviors (irritation, bad humor) along with experiencing successive failures (conflicts) in short intervals, each of which is trivial separately. The consequences of frustration in the form of aggressive reactions, exposed by Yale psychologists, do not completely cover their entire range.

The significance of the theory of frustration stems from the fact that it is part of a more general theory of behavior trying to explain some mechanisms of human behavior in situations of appearance of obstacles impeding or making impossible the "normal" course of behavior. Individual authors or interpreters of the theory of frustration define the concept of frustration differently, emphasizing either the obstacle itself (an external fact affecting the mental state) or the reaction to an obstacle (a state of emotional tension, usually unpleasant, associated with an unsatisfied need). The first case emphasizes the causes and sources of frustration, while the second one - the direct and distant consequences and effects of frustration. The causes of frustration can be categorized into four basic categories, using two criteria: passivity vs. activity and internality vs. externality:

1. Passive external obstacles, i.e. the ones which are in the passive state out of human control. These are most often physical obstacles related to the operating conditions, such as a late bus, which results in being late for work.
2. Active external obstacles are the ones which are outside the human control, but have an active impact on the human being. These are usually other people who obstruct or limit the ability to act, e.g. a demanding examiner is an obstacle to passing the exam.
3. Passive internal obstacles are rooted in the human being itself, as permanent constitutional features or permanent mental deficiencies, e.g. lack of organizational competence eliminating from applying for a managerial position.
4. Active internal obstacles that occur while there are two or more conflicting objectives meeting one or more simultaneous conflicting needs, e.g. difficulties in taking a decision in a decision-making situation.

The latter category of obstacles in the theory of frustration was particularly exposed and became the basis for the so-called motivational conflict (conflict between the aspirations of one person) (Yates, ed., 1965), the typology of which can be presented with the help of K. Lewin (1936) as follows:

1. The "aspiration - aspiration" conflict consists in the fact that we have to choose two goals (objects) with the same degree of attractiveness, while getting one excludes getting the other (e.g. "The donkey was given hay in one manger, and oat in the other").
2. The "avoidance-avoidance" conflict occurs when an individual is forced to choose between two equally undesirable ones, i.e. the so-called choosing the lesser evil.
3. The "aspiration-avoidance" conflict consists in the fact that one goal, satisfying a specific need, simultaneously has two different values: positive and negative, which evokes an ambivalent attitude (e.g. when we want to pet a dog, but are afraid of him at the same time). The correlation between the relative strength of aspiration (propulsive) and avoidance (repulsive) tendencies and the closeness of goal and intensity of urge is known in the literature as Miller's model of conflict.

The latter conflict is particularly interesting for doctors and clinical psychologists, because since the times of experimental research conducted on dogs for many years by Iwan Pawlow (1952), it is known that it leads to neuroses.

Dealing with frustration can take two patterns - task-oriented and emotional-defensive - characterized by different attitudes towards obstacles. The first one is characterized by the fact that the emerging obstacle does not change the basic direction of the goal, but only modifies the tactics of achieving it, despite the negative emotions that appear, while the second one is characterized by the emergence of strong negative emotions, as well as a change in the original direction of action (goal) and an attempt to reduce unpleasant emotional tension. These two coping patterns also appear in contemporary stress theories, such as those of R. Lazarus and S. Folkman (1984).

Concluding the discussion of the psychological model of frustration, taking into account its relation to aggressive behaviors, it is important to stress the unquestionable merit of the theoreticians at Yale University, consisting among others in the fact that they empirically verified the hypothesis that aggression is always the result of frustration, and frustration always leads to aggression, although it is true only in the first part. Moreover, the Authors also recognize other ways of reacting to frustration, such as those aimed at defending the ego against letting the information causing anxiety into consciousness (e.g. defense mechanisms in the form of: regression, projection, rationalization, transfer, identification, fantasy, imaginary reaction, substitution, dissociation, etc.).

1.3.2 Phenomenological concepts of stress

The term *psychological stress* was created by Irving L. Janis, who defines it as "a change in an environment that typically, i.e. in the case of an average person, causes a high degree of emotional tension that interferes with the normal way of reacting". (Janis, 1958, p. 7).

1.3.2.1 Irving L. Janis' clinical stress concept

The above definition, apart from the stressful situation itself, draws attention to the increase in emotional tension, caused by stress stimuli, responsible for behavioral disorders *(disruptive stimuli).* According to the author, emotional tension, caused by a threat, occurs in three phases: (1) the threat phase (perception of danger that causes fear, anxiety); (2) the operational phase of the threat (awareness of the threat and assessment of the likelihood of avoiding it on the basis of one's own or other person's defensive actions); (3) the phase of effects of stress (more or less prolonged negative emotional tension). Janis verified the emotional tension in a situation of threat through systematic observations of hospitalized patients waiting for surgery. Apart from clinical description of various emotional reactions in stressful situations occurring during the expectation for surgery, he attempted to explain them in terms of psychodynamic processes. Although Janis is one of the first to recognize the distinction between stressful situations and stress response, which other authors of psychological stress theories refer to, including *Reversal Theory* author Michael J. Apter.

1.3.2.2 Michael J. Apter's Reversal Theory

Michael J. Apter's *Reversal of Theory* is based on the assumption that there is a specific relationship between emotional tension and remedial effort (*tension-stress vs effort-stress*) in a threatening situation. The first part of the relationship, i.e. *tension-stress*, is described as a discrepancy between the preferred and current level of motivation for effort, while *effort-stress* is related to actions aimed at reducing *tension-stress* after coping with stress. It should be noted that these descriptions refer to the mental state of a person rather than to specific remedial actions taken. Generally speaking, *tension-stress* is associated with the experience of a threat situation, and *effort-stress* reflects attempts to deal with this situation (Apter, Svebak, 1984).

It should be remembered that the term *tension* is used in psychological, psychiatric and medical literature in various meanings. Apter uses it in a special sense, as a feeling accompanying the distinction between the current and preferred level of complexity of a threat situation. It is similar to feeling of *unease* when we don't know what to do with the encountered threat. The ideal state is the relative balance between tension-stress and effort-stress efficiency.

Both tension-stress as well as effort-stress are defined by Apter in terms of *arousal.* Effort-stress can be a response to a certain level of stimulation, which is not preferred by the given person. The tension-stress is directly proportional to the currently perceived level of stimulation.

Apart from the complex interactions between individual factors modifying the stress reduction effort and the level of task completion, it should be stressed that although the discussed Apter's phenomenological concept of stress is convenient for the operationalization of clinical stress indicators, from the theoretical point of view it does not have much explanatory value. He refers to the notions to which he gives his own, inconsistent with the literature of the subject, interpretation. In a new version of his stress concept, Apter seeks to broaden its theoretical basis by referring to the theory of motivation and the optimal stimulation level theory. He believes that both aspects of stress (tension-stress and effort-stress) can be experienced as a metamotivating telic and paratelic state. The telic state is characterized by a preferred high level of excitement experienced as anxiety, and in chronic stress - as fear, phobias, etc. Paratelic state causes boredom, and in chronic stress leads to alcoholism, drug addiction, prescription drug addiction, and so on. This is consistent with the theory of telic vs. paratelic motivation, according to which telic motivation is characterized by avoidance of stimulation, seriousness and goal oriented thinking, while paratelic motivation is characterized by search for stimulation, cheerful attitude to reality and spontaneity (Apter, Svebak, 1984). Both types of motivational states in relation to Apter's tension-stress and effort-stress concepts provide a system of four types of stress - telic tension-stress, paratelic tension-stress, telic effort-stress, paratelic effort-stress - which are characterized by various symptoms of stress:

1. High effort-stress intensity and low tension-stress (boredom) levels in telic states (avoiding stimulation) lead to classic symptoms of migraine, the risk of coronary heart disease, as well as neurasthenic symptoms.
2. High effort-stress intensity and low tension-stress levels in paratelic states (search for stimulation) lead to excitement in social life, and in extreme states - to hooliganism and crime.
3. Low effort-stress and high tension-stress (anxiety) levels in telic states lead to classical psychoneurosis and various psychosomatic symptoms.
4. Low effort-stress and high tension-stress levels in paratelic states lead to abuse of various drugs (e.g. alcohol, drugs, prescription drugs).

In this way Apter, enriching his theory of stress with an additional concept from the field of motivation and optimal stimulation theory, proposed an explanation of the psychological effects of tension-stress and effort-stress, especially in chronic form. Apter's theory of stress is general enough to describe two types of stress, but it does not specify its essence, except for the statement that it is the state of discrepancy between the current and the preferred variable level of motivation (Martin et al., 1987). The psychological mechanism of evaluation of this discrepancy indicates its cognitive character, which is emphasized by the interactive stress model prepared by R.S. Lazarus.

1.3.3 Cognitive risk assessment model of Richard S. Lazarus and Susan Folkman

Richard S. Lazarus and Susan Folkman drew attention to the important species characteristic, which is *a differentia specifica* of psychological stress, of a human, who – in contrast to the stress response characteristic for other mammals – is characterized by the ability to anticipate, i.e. plan and predict the consequences of stress resulting from future events. Together they developed a cognitive risk assessment model, known in the literature of the subject as Transactional Stress Theory. They defined psychological stress as "relationship between the person and the environment that is appraised by the person as taxing or exceeding his or her resources and endangering his or her well-being". (Lazarus, Folkman, 1984, p. 19).

It should be noted that Lazarus was primarily interested in individual differences in *coping with stress* and the variety of threats. Therefore, the basic psychological mechanism responsible for these individual differences was the *appraisal* of the threat, understood as a mechanism for evaluating, making aware and interpreting events. Applying the typical assumption of cognitive psychology that emotions are the result of cognitive activity, he distinguished two types of cognitive assessment – primary and secondary assessment – the model of which is illustrated in Fig. 1.8.

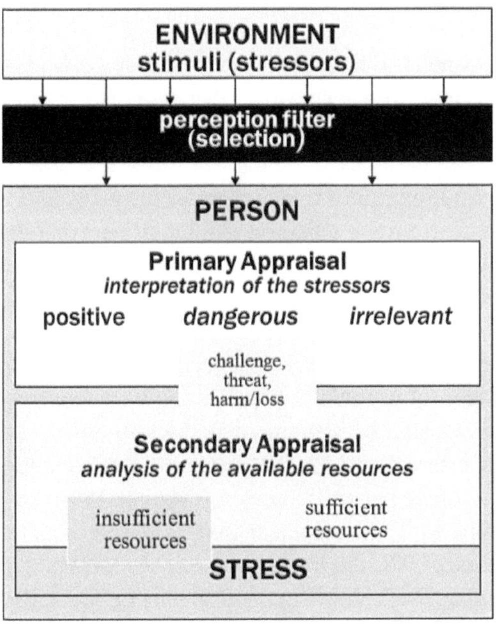

Fig. 1.8: Cognitive Risk Assessment Mechanism. (Source: own elaboration based on: Lazarus and Folkman, 1984)

Primary appraisal is a process which assesses whether the stimuli reaching the brain are *favorably-positive, dangerous or irrelevant*. The probability of a threat causes a state of tension, triggering certain negative emotions.

Three categories of stressors can be distinguished: (a) *harm*, (b) *threat*, and (c) *challenge*. *Harm* refers to damage or injury that has already occurred (such as death of a loved one, loss of sense of life); *threat* refers to the same damages or injuries that are currently occurring; *challenge* refers to future damages or losses that are anticipated with a certain probability and the possibility of coping with them. It is precisely by taking into account the cognitive assessment of the subject that makes the Lazarus' stress definition a definition of psychological stress, the essence of which is the conscious or unconscious sense of a person, that he or she is in danger and is trying to deal with it. Primary cognitive assessment alone does not provide a basis for defining a situation as stressful. A specific re-evaluation, called *reappraisal*, of one's own remedial abilities and access to support from others (individuals or institutions) is needed for this purpose. Primary and secondary cognitive assessment processes are complementary. The difference between them concerns the content to which they refer. For example, if someone takes action that gives them a high probability of success in the event of a threat, their primary risk assessment is in fact changed. The very awareness of controlling the threat reduces psychological stress. Such an assessment in favorably-positive categories leads to a positive emotional response (e.g. joy, love, satisfaction, relief). Predicting failure in a situation of threat causes negative emotions (e.g. anxiety, anger, jealousy, guilt). Thus, Lazarus clearly places emotions both before coping with stress (cf. Lazarus, 1991, p. 210), as well as attaches great importance to emotions in the process of coping with stress itself, which is reflected, among others, in emotional remedial strategies (Folkman, Lazarus, 1988). The primary assessment may also be influenced (on the basis of the feedback principle) either by changes in the relationship between man and the environment, or by personal reflection. However, if, despite the efforts to address it, the threat still exists, then the threat subjectively increases significantly and so does the re-evaluation of possible ways of coping with stress, which Lazarus and Folkman define as: "constantly changing (dynamic) cognitive and behavioral efforts to manage specific external and internal demands that are appraised as taxing or exceeding resources of the person" (Lazarus, Folkman, 1984, p. 141).

The ability to cope with stress can take two forms: measures to overcome stress and defensive measures. The common feature of the former is their effectiveness, i.e. that they are capable of achieving the previous or equivalent goals in spite of the stress. The common feature of defensive measures is their low effectiveness, as they usually lead to failure to achieve goals under the influence of stress, at the cost of escaping from stressful situations or symbolic actions.

Summarizing the Lazarus' Transactional Theory of Stress, it should be stated that its unquestionable advantage is exposing the subjective thread of threat assessment and emphasizing that this assessment is an active cognitive process. However, it is debatable to identify stress as a threat and to reduce the psychological mechanism of cognitive assessment to anticipation, and especially underestimating the impact of motivation and emotions (activation) on this assessment. This last postulate was included in the revised theory of stress of Folkman (2001) and Lazarus (2006).

It is worth stressing, however, that Lazarus' and Folkman's theory of stress focuses mainly on the mechanisms of coping with stress, its antecedents and consequences, which will be the subject of detailed reflection on the last part of the book, devoted to *coping*.

The model of Lazarus' and Folkman's Transactional Theory of Stress itself has been subject to many modifications consisting mainly in explaining the sense that a person gives to specific stress events, which are connected not only with negative emotions and often suffering, but also with searching for and discovering the positive meaning of emotions. This attempt to transform "primary distress into eustress", to put it in the language of late Selye, requires a person to include positive motivation for effort in the fight against stress (situational search for meaning) as well as to refer to the value system and often seek existential meaning, also of transcendental character.

Although Folkman's revised variant of the stress model (2006) significantly extends the understanding not only of the stress transaction itself, but above all of the process and strategy of coping with stress, it does not fully exhaust the issue of negative and positive emotions in the process of cognitive evaluation of stress (Małkiewicz, Terelak, 2016).

1.3.4 Aaron Antonovsky's stress salutogenic model

Aaron Antonovsky (1993), as a part of his salutogenic concept based on the new homeodynamic paradigm (as opposed to homeostatic concepts based on the adaptive model), developed a psychologically explanatory mechanism for coping with life stress, known as *Sense of Coherence* – SOC. It is understood as a global orientation of man in perceiving the world as: structured, predictable and understandable. It is dynamic and relatively stable with age and allows to meet the requirements imposed by stressful situations.

The larger the *generalized resistance resources*, the more consistent and beneficial the life experiences are, the stronger the sense of coherence. Thus, strong SOC is an important predictor of health and susceptibility to stress. The elements of the sense of coherence can be described as follows:

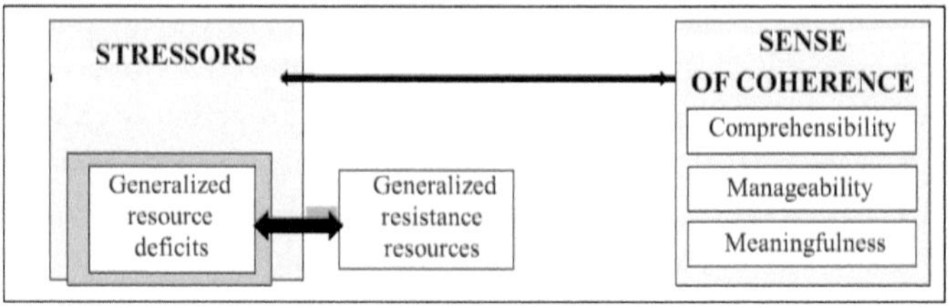

Fig. 1.9: Model of the relationship between stress and sense of coherence. (Source: own elaboration based on: Antonovsky, 1979).

1. *Comprehensibility* - refers to the degree of perception of the surrounding external and internal stimuli (information). They should be cognitively reasonable, organized, coherent and structured, as opposed to those that are chaotic, disordered, accidental, unclear, etc. It makes no difference whether or not a given stimulus is desired. A person can find sense even in an extremely painful experience.
2. *Manageability* - refers to the degree of perception of available resources as sufficient to cope with current stressful situations. Accessibility refers to both personal resources as well as various types of social support. It allows for coping with the adversities of fate.
3. *Meaningfulness* - refers to the degree of perception of the sense of life realized at different levels: emotional, moral, professional, philosophical, etc. Antonovsky considers the last dimension of the sense of coherence to be the most important one, because without sense of reasonableness the other two components would not be permanent.

The author draws attention to personal differences in the sense of coherence, which are relevant for coping with stress. On the basis of the collected empirical material concerning people with a strong sense of coherence, he made a distinction between a strong and rigid sense of coherence. People with a rigid sense of coherence block access to new information in order to have their knowledge well-ordered and consistent. People with a strong sense of coherence try to balance rules and strategies, possessed and potential information. They believe that new information can be used in a sensible way. They do not perceive the challenging, surrounding reality and openness to feedback as a subjective threat.

It is interesting that Antonovsky (1979) understands stress as a factor which, in the absence of appropriate life experience, causes cohesion disorders, under- or overload and limitation of involvement in decision making. The definition of stressor shows that apart from the content aspects (e.g. life experiences, decisions taken) there is also a formal aspect related to the burden, whose ends of the continuum are underload (boredom, monotony) and overload (physical, informational, emotional). This quantitative aspect of stressor refers to the aforementioned models of optimal stimulation vs. activation, characteristic for the physiological and temperamental concepts of stress of Leuba or Hebb. Stressors defined in this way can be divided into chronic and incidental stressors (stressful life events). Their positive or negative impact on a person's health depends on whether his or her sense of coherence is strong or weak. An important element of Antonovsky's concept of stress is the statement that there are no predefined or automated adaptation responses to the requirements posed by the stressors that appear in life. The role of the sense of coherence in coping with stress consists, among others, in the fact that, despite high emotional tension, a high sense of coherence makes the received stimuli - even if they are perceived as stressors - lead to the mobilization of the overall immune resources available to the individual. This in turn may prevent stress or significantly reduce its effects. There are many studies documenting the relationship between the sense of coherence with stress management styles by using the *Scale of Coherence* questionnaire.

1.3.5 Janusz Reykowski's stress information model

As part of the regulatory personality theory, Janusz Reykowski (1966) draws attention to the role of information reaching a person from the environment, which is stored in a hierarchically organized system of cognitive structures (the so-called cognitive network, standards and idealizations), remaining in a variety of attitudes towards the aspirations and expectations of the person. This cognitive mechanism is classified as a level of higher mechanisms (next to the basic ones, based on emotional experiences in the first years of an individual's life). The factors responsible for the essence of psychological stress are the pieces of information "burdening the regulatory system" reaching the subject, such as: task, difficulty, failure, which remain in a specific relation with the structure of aspirations and expectations. The types of information received can be divided into: task-type information (information generating the pursuit of a specific activity), facilitative information (information about the state of affairs, the appearance of which reduces the amount of time or effort needed to achieve the goal), neutral information (information which does not affect the structure of goals, but only indicates an equivalent option of action), success-type information (information about achieving the goal), difficulty-type information (information about an obstacle in the pursuit of a specific goal), failure-type

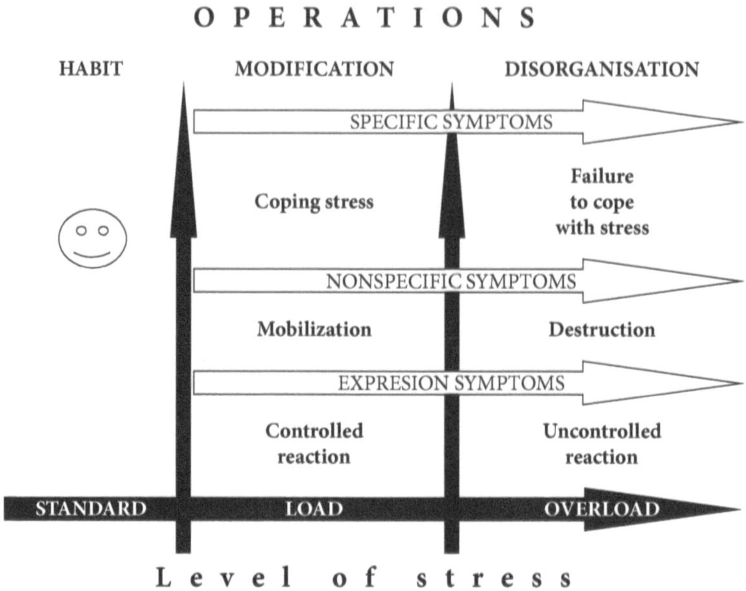

Fig. 1.10: Regulatory-informational model of stress. (Source: own elaboration based on: Reykowski, 1966)

information (stating that the goal is impossible to achieve). The latter two types of information are related to the essence of psychological stress, as difficulty-type information correlates with the definition of stress as a "burden of the regulatory system" of a motivational nature (cf. eustress), while failure-type information correlates with the definition of stress in the "overload of the regulatory system" category, which leads to destruction (cf. distress). This model is shown in Fig. 1.10.

More specifically, it should be added that the task-, difficulty- and failure-type information burden the regulatory system as "threatening and disruptive factors", burdening the regulatory system in three ways: 1) by forcing it to additional activity; 2) by forcing it to reorganize the already established order, anticipating and coordinating processes (expectations and aspirations); 3) by forecasting the possibility of deprivation or loss, which in itself disorganizes the more or less established structures (e.g. needs, values, self-image). Disruption and threat, which are the essence of psychological stress, may occur together or may be the dominant factor. Although Reykowski characterizes stress as existing objectively outside of man, a condition that must be fulfilled in order for a given stimulus to be considered as psychological stress is the relation that takes place between the stimulus and the current aspirations and expectations of a person. This is illustrated in Fig. 1.10, where the ratio is considered on a continuum load vs. overload of the regulation system, separated on the basis of an objective criterion, namely the undisturbed vs. disturbed level of functioning. The limits of the stress intensity continuum are difficult to determine unequivocally - whether it is a point on a scale or rather a band, because it depends on the size of the burden. The minimal value of the burden, which causes functional changes known as the state of stress, is called by Reykowski the "stress intensity threshold", which is distinctive for a given person at a given moment and for the type of stress factor. These changes have their characteristic path of specific changes (the area of coping with stress vs. defensive reactions against stress) and the path of non-specific changes (mobilization, disarmament, destruction). These changes are also accompanied by changes in expression (controlled vs. uncontrolled reactions). Thus, in his stress model Reykowski describes psychological mechanisms explaining three types of reactions: Thus, in his stress model Reykowski describes psychological mechanisms explaining three types of reactions: (a) adaptation processes (general mobilization, specific reaction to combat stress, release of tension in controlled forms); (b) defensive reactions (escape, attack, changes in perception and interpretation); (c) destructive reactions (disruption of cognitive processes, disorder of activity, uncontrolled emotional release reactions).

1.3.6 Resource distribution models

In resource distribution models, stress is defined as the cause or symptom of exhaustion of human or material resources or lack of (temporary or permanent) access to them.

1.3.6.1 Conservation of Resources Theory Stevan E. Hobfoll

The model of conservation of resources by S. E. Hobfoll – known in the literature as the Conservation of Resources Theory – assumes that psychological stress is the reaction to the environment in which there is either the threat of a pure loss of power, or the actual loss of power or, often caused by the exploitation of resources. This reaction results from the desire to obtain and protect the resources. The Hobfoll's model distinguishes four types of resources that are associated with satisfaction, while the lack or limitation thereof leads to stress: 1) material resources, which are objects, the possession or lack of which determines the socio-economic status of a person (e.g. home, car, gold); 2) personal resources, characterized by possessed skills (professional, social competences) and a suitable personality structure (self-esteem, optimism, hope, efficiency, temperament); 3) state resources - circumstances allowing access to or acquisition of other resources, which are very desirable and valued (e.g. health, permanent job, successful marriage, professional advancement, inheritance); 4) energy resources, deriving not only from one's own energy, but also from the other three types of resources (e.g. knowledge, money, time) that can be used to multiply other resources. Stress causes both the occurrence of real or anticipated loss, as well as the very fact of the absence of (real or perceived) increase in power. Thus, power resources, in the Hobfoll's model, are a theoretical category that explains the essence of psychological stress. They include such attributes as: objects, personal characteristics, conditions or powers appreciated by an individual or helping to accomplish these objects, characteristics, conditions or acquiring these powers (e.g. physical conditions of the environment, self-esteem, social position, economic state).

The author of this classification himself is aware of the arbitrary nature of this classification, as it has not, in fact, been derived from any theory. The model also contains arguments that the loss of resources does not necessarily lead to stress, as the actual loss can be compensated by replacing one resource with another. However, if such compensation is not sufficient, the very substitution of resources to deal with challenges is already stressful. An important element of the Hobfoll's model (2002) is to draw attention to the differences between individuals, which manifest themselves in the efficiency of the use of their resources. People are not endowed with resources or access to them equally, for both biological and socio-economic reasons - hence the differences in coping with the stress of everyday life. The model also takes into account the rationale for enriching life experience as a method of protection against future losses. Investing in resources is an inherent feature of a competitive capitalist culture.

It should be noted that there are several classifications of resources in the Hobfoll's concept, which are inseparable and arbitrary in terms of the criteria applied, e.g.: external vs. internal resources, primary (security) and secondary (access to other resources) and a quartet of resources: material, personal, state and energy. This is due to the fact that the author is sometimes a philosopher of culture and sociologist, and at other times - a psychologist with an evolutionary approach to stress. This evolutionary approach to stress, slightly different from the views of Lazarus, suggests that only part of the stress results from a conscious cognitive (especially secondary) assessment, because thanks to primary (atavistic) emotions a person can respond to the threat the fastest. A significant limitation of this concept is Hobfoll's omission of the interaction between man and the environment. On the other hand, it's definite advantage is to draw attention to the fact that resources have a variable and developmental character, both in the individual and socio-cultural dimension, as the latter has been developed by the author in the latest version of his theory of resources, considering resources from a broad not only psychological, but also philosophical, cultural and civilizational perspective, burdened with an American (USA) and partially European (Israel) viewpoints. This applies in particular to the characteristics of access to the resources of contemporary man in a world that is diverse in terms of culture and civilization.

1.3.6.2 Self-regulation of Resources Theory Roy F. Baumeister

R.F. Baumeister and K.D. Vohs (2004), also referring to the role of resources in human life, drew attention to "ego resources" or "control resources". The authors distinguished two types of resources: energetic (e.g. body capacity) and cognitive (level of performance of mental tasks, ability to control one's emotions, etc.). The essence of this concept is an a priori assumption concerning the exhaustion of ego resources (self-control) in the situation of coping with stress, sometimes up to their total deficit (e.g. extreme stress). However, the loss of resources is not irreversible and can be restored. And so, in case of energy resources, e.g. fatigue passes after rest, coffee, medicines, etc., while in case of cognitive resources deficit, a specific remedy is e.g. knowledge or social support. Furthermore, resources can be multiplied, e.g. energy resources through physical exercise, while cognitive resources can be multiplied through self-control, biofeedback or yoga. In this concept, stress is treated as a state requiring redistribution of the pool of resources remaining after their consumption or in a situation where it is impossible to supplement them or where there is no access to social support.

The presented concepts of resources by Hobfoll and Baumeister are not psychological concepts of stress, as the sources of stress and their effects are grouped in the same category, which disregards interactions between the subject and the environment. However, they have phenomenological value, useful in analyses of e.g. acculturative stress.

1.4 Psychosocial models of stress

So far, the stress models presented above all took into account human relations with the broadly understood natural environment of existence. Referring to the famous statement of the ancient philosopher Aristotle, "man is a social animal" (ζῷον πολιτικόν - zoon politikon) - psychosocial models of stress, which take into account the interactions between people which, according to social psychology and sociology, result from belonging to a social community, cannot be ignored. A social community is generally defined as a collection of at least three people, whose members interact with each other on a separative basis in order to meet their own needs, with a permanent structure and a permanent system of norms and values. All these components of the sociological definition of a social community can constitute potential sources of stress, among which organization and time management are at the forefront.

1.4.1 Jan F. Terelak's Chronohabilistic Stress Model

Psychological stress has a temporal and sometimes cyclic dimension, as bioperiodic phenomena occur in all living organisms, from single-celled organisms to humans. Biological rhythms are stored in the genetic code, and environmental conditions, apart from the alternation of night and day, have little influence on them. Phenomena of human biological rhythmicity on the behavioral level manifest themselves in ability (motor, mental). Although biological cycles depend on repetitive photo-ecological factors (daily rhythm, quarters of the Moon, seasons), in the case of humans their ability is strongly moderated by the psycho-social factor (type of job, way of spending free time, lifestyle of household members, neighbors, shops and offices opening hours). The discrepancy between photo-ecological and social factors is a source of stress that affects human ability. The relations between the "biological clock" and human ability are depicted in Fig. 1.11.

The chronohabilistic model of stress refers to the oldest paradigm in the human sciences: anthropology, biology, philosophy, comparative psychology, relations between human activity (physical, biological and psychological) and its natural determinants, which primarily include photo-ecological conditions in the place of existence - recorded by the biological clock regulating the daily rhythm of activity and rest of both humans and animals. An example of cyclical daily activity, of which body temperature is an important indicator, is shown in Fig. 1.12.

By reversing the sinusoid in Fig. 1.12 it can be adapted to the periods of human activity and sleep as follows: 4:00–5:00: The organism slowly enters the awakening phase; 5:00–6:00: Gradual increase in the level of the energy hormone cortisol (80 % of the daily dose) and loss of melatonin; 7:00–9:00: Stimulation of metabolic processes, increase in blood pressure, the organism demands food; 10:00–12:00: The organism works at full capacity, we are mentally and motorically efficient; 13:00–15:00: It is recommended to eat

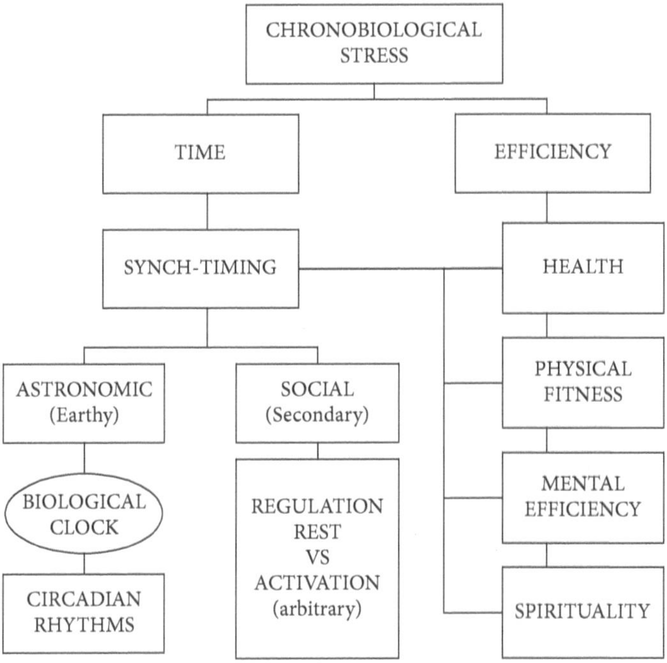

Fig. 1.11: Chronohabilistic stress model by J.F. Terelak (Source: own elaboration)

a meal at this time because the nutrients are absorbed better; Approximately 15:00: A siesta, i.e. a short nap (post lunch phenomenon). During this time, the body supplements 30 % of the energy hormone cortisol, which is supposed to be enough until natural dusk; 15:00–17:00: We are the most resistant to pain, motorically efficient (muscles and joints work efficiently); 17:00–19:00: We are efficient in absorbing information, because the brain works at full capacity. Around 19:00 you should eat the last meal because later the metabolic processes will be slower; 21:00–22:00: Increase in the level of sleep hormone – melatonin, and we start to feel the first signs of sleepiness; 2:00–3.00: Deep sleep – the most beneficial for the body.

In addition, each day in our bodies there are cyclical changes in the circulatory system (e.g. fluctuations in blood pressure levels) and the hormonal system (e.g. differences in the secretion of hormones: cortisol, stress and thyroid, etc.), which is the basis of our fitness, wellbeing and health. This ideal state of daily fluctuations of activity and sleep periods, together with the development of

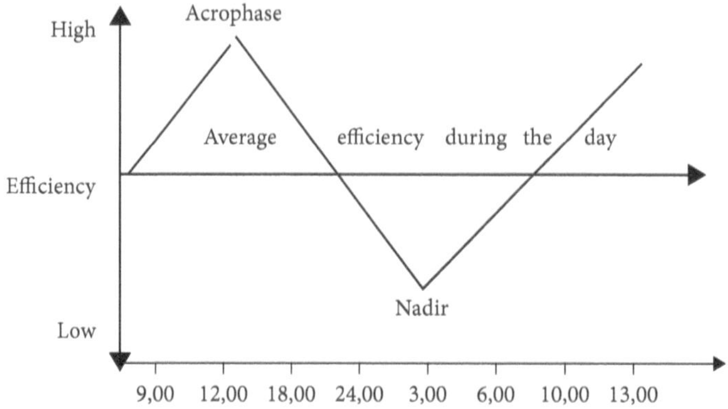

Fig. 1.12: Daily temperature cycle distribution of a man (Source: own elaboration based on: Szmigielski, 1974). Note: (Legend: frequency - number of cycles per time unit; period - duration of one cycle; amplitude - half of the span between acrophase and nadir; acrophase - duration of the occurrence of the maximum of the assessed feature in the cycle; nadir - duration of the occurrence of the minimum of the assessed feature; mesor - mean daily value; T(C) - temperature in degrees Celsius).

human civilization and the invention of artificial lighting (torches, kerosene, electricity) makes man, due to psychosocial reasons, change the natural day-night cycle, according to his own needs and preferences, remaining in conflict with natural adaptation mechanisms at the biological level (Kwarecki et al., 1982). These psychosocial needs (hours of work, entertainment and sleep), disrupting the everlasting order of things, are on one hand a source of stress, and on the other hand they entitle us to include this model of stress in the group of psychosocial concepts, as the second component of the concept presented in the Fig. 1.12 refers to efficiency as an important adaptation function, evolving from *homo habilis* to contemporary *homo sapiens*.

Homo habilis, i.e. a handy man, skillfully using tools, preceded *homo sapiens* in phylogenetic development. Therefore, ability is treated in philosophical anthropology and human biology as one of the most important values in the overall hierarchy, as it often determines survival in a threat situation.

Ability as a value is atavistically reflected in ancient and modern civilizations. This has both a subjective and objective dimension. In a subjective sense, people who deviate from the current civilizational model in terms of ability feel handicapped and, consequently, worse than others. In an objective sense, especially in societies with a high level of humanistic culture, ability, not only physical, but also mental, is a determinant of human value.

Within the Mediterranean humanistic civilization, the understanding of ability comes from Aristotle's definition: "ability is defined as a disposition which is well or ill disposed of in regard to itself or something else" (as in: Andrzejuk, 2006, pp. 50–51). Nowadays, the Polish philosopher Stefan Swieżawski (1956, p. 278) defines ability as follows: "Habitus is the possession of something, permanent equipment, or more strictly a permanent improvement of something in some aspect". It proposes to divide ability into two groups, namely: ability in existence (lat. *habitus entitativi*) and the ability enjoyed by the authorities of the entity (Latin *habitus operativi*). The fullest division of all human abilities can be found not in psychological works, but in Summa Theologiae (cf. Summa theologica) by Tomas Aquinas, who divides abilities into intellectual (knowledge, wisdom, conscience, prudence, art) and moral, in other words impulse-sensory (temperance, bravery). Intellectual abilities can be theoretical (e.g. intelligence, knowledge, wisdom), practical (e.g. fine and technical arts), mentally virtuous (prudence), morally virtuous (justice, courage, temperance) as well as of bodily character (agility, health, beauty). Within particular classes of abilities, the Philosopher lists several dozen more detailed ones, such as "prudence", which is characterized by such abilities as: personal prudence (memory, perceptiveness, sharpness of mind), family or educational prudence (instructiveness, common sense, prevention) and social prudence (forethoughtfulness, relativity, carefulness, diligence) (as in: Andrzejuk, 2006). Deviance from these performance patterns causes stress.

In psychology, ability is also associated with activity (actions), which, included in the categories of mental or impulse-sensory abilities, are highly correlated with the effectiveness of functioning. These categories, included in certain standards of professional requirements, are used as selection criteria, as for example in the case of candidates for pilots and astronauts, they concern both health (Cowings, 2013), as well as physical (Stelęgowski, Gaździńska, Kłossowski, 2014), and mental standards (Terelak, Szewczyk, 2013). Factors responsible for modifying the efficiency of actions are the domain of both medicine and psychology of motivation (e.g. two Yerkes-Dodson laws), as well as the psychology of learning and chronopsychology[3].

3 In Polish psychology the term *chronopsychology* was introduced by J.F. Terelak, who defines it as a discipline of psychology, remaining in the chronobiological research stream and being one of its components. It examines the psychological (behavioral, emotional and social) consequences of biological rhythms (ultradial, circadial and infradial) and social synchronizers of human activity. The Author has in mind to create

The second important paradigm to which the chronohabilistic stress model refers is the concept of time. It has its objective (astronomical and biological) and subjective (psychological and social) aspect. This is pointed out by R.H. Rahe (2007b), who in his "Coping and Stress: A Lens and Filter Model", describing coping as a process encompassing all the activities undertaken by an individual in a specific stress situation, takes into account ability (coping skills), which has its dynamics that is dependent on its temporal characteristics, such as astronomical time (photoecological factors), biological time (meal times) and psychological time (working and rest periods). In the process of coping one can therefore distinguish individual stages of coping efficiency spread over time, which is an important element of the chronohabilistic concept of stress and coping, whose author primarily takes into account the dynamics of astronomical time, determining the cyclicity of human biological processes, which are the basis of his ability, and social time, associated with work organization and rest (Nelson, Martin, Ii, 2007). The model refers to chronobiology explaining the mechanisms of cyclic variability of biological functioning of animals and humans (systems, organs, cells) and its activity, as well as being the basis for individual differences in preferences of different periods of the day. The basic synchronizers of functional rhythms in biology are all cyclical changes occurring in the natural environment, e.g. alternation of day and night, ambient temperature, seasons (Szmigielski, 1974).

From the point of view of the duration of biorhythms, the following rhythms are distinguished: *ultradial* - i.e. shorter than 20 hours (e.g. peristaltic rhythms, heart rate, respiration, electroencephalographic rhythms); ci*rcadial* - i.e. around the clock rhythms, lasting from 20 to 28 hours (e.g. sleep - alertness, metabolic processes); *infradial* - i.e. lasting over 28 hours (e.g. several days, monthly, seasonal, yearly, several years; menstrual cycle, hormonal cycles, etc.). Rhythms can be determined:

- endogenously, when they are conditioned by biological oscillations within the organism (e.g. rhythmic activity of nerve cells, organs, physiological processes) and reflect the natural frequency of spontaneously functioning biooscillators;

---

a methodology for scientific evaluation of chronotype (morning vs. evening) and its personality correlates, as well as the cost of psychological adaptation to the conditions of discrepancies between photo-ecological and social factors (e.g. multi-shift work, sudden change of time zones in transcontinental aviation and disruption of the circadian rhythm during space flights).

- exogenously, when they are conditioned by the variability of external phenomena that do not manifest themselves under constant environmental conditions.

The most important in the adaptation of living organisms to the conditions of the external world is the daily rhythm, which in the literature of the subject is called *circadian,* because it does not exactly coincide with the astronomical day[4]. For example, research was carried out by K.E. Klein, Wehmann H.M., Hunt B.I. (1980) on military pilots was found that during the daytime period some kind of *plateau* occurred between 12.00 and 21.00 and the level of performance dropped maximally between 3.00 and 5.00 at night. It should be added that the authors applied the curves of mental abilities and daily course of some physiological parameters (temperature, 17-OHCS, adrenaline, noradrenaline) to themselves, obtaining the same sinusoidal course of both examined ability levels. Many studies on people crossing time zones in parallel flights have shown that they are experiencing a shift in the rhythm phase while maintaining the same amplitude. When the phase shift reaches the maximum value of 180 degrees (half a period), we are talking about a reversal of the rhythm. Physiological rhythms of people adapted to night work are a typical example (Torbjörn, Göran, Mats, 2007). The phylogenetic adaptation of living organisms to the environment took place with the participation of biophysical factors, which have a cyclic character, such as photo-ecological, thermo-ecological factors, etc. Because they significantly influence the course of biorhythms, they are called synchronizers, which can be imagined as a "servo-mechanism", operating on the principle of negative feedback and bringing two or more phenomena, physical courses (e.g. some periodic courses) and processes to the state of temporal compatibility, e.g. the compatibility of periods and phases of a given physical course. In the case of living organisms, it is a biological system for bringing two or more phenomena, processes, etc. to a state of relative temporal compatibility (e.g., compatibility of periods, phases, etc.). Thus, the circadian rhythm is synchronized not only with daylight, but also with many other influences of the social environment. Thanks to the latter feature and function, synchronizers are "time givers". The role of the individual synchronizers is not equal.

---

4 One of the hypotheses explaining the source of circadian rather than daily rhythm is the assumption that apart from sunlight, the light emitted by the Moon influences our biological clock as a primary synchronizer, as well as the fact that the lunar day is 50 minutes longer than the solar day (as in: *Current Biology*: http://dx.doi.org/10.1016/j.cub.2016.07.079).

The development of physiological, and, in particular, biochemical research, have revealed, inter alia, the existence of multiple 'secondary' rhythms, conditioned by the superior ones, which have led to the concept of several interdependent 'clocks' existing in living organisms and the search for a hypothetical 'clock' that regulates the secondary clocks while being able to react representatively to changes in environmental conditions. Searching for the anatomical location of the biological clock, the so-called ESSO (*Endogenous Self-Sustaining Oscillatory Clock*) already has a history. This biological clock was placed in adrenals and pituitary glands, and now it's being indicated that the superior biological clock (circadian rhythm starter) is located in the central nervous system. Precise location indicates one of the nuclei of the hypothalamus - the suprachiasmatic nucleus (*nucleus suprachiasmaticus*). This nucleus contains nerve cells characterized by a constant impulse along the axon axis. Appearance of these impulses is consistent with a circadian periodicity. This property is passed on through the nerve cell genome. These elementary neurons can be known as counting neurons. The second part of the starter is a collective neuron, called a discriminant, which collects all the nerve impulses coming from individual elementary neurons. It eventually leads to an increase in potential and exceeding the threshold of sensitivity of the collective neuron - discriminator. Exceeding this threshold results in an electrical discharge along the axon. This, in turn, provides information for the entire organism about the need to change the circadian rhythm phase. Assigning the role of the "biological clock" to some brain structures should be treated as general, constantly verified hypotheses. Nowadays it is rather assumed that synchronization of circadian rhythms is a resultant of the activity of many structures and several neurotransmitting and neuroregulatory systems (Watterhouse, Minores, Waterhouse, 1993).

The secondary synchronizer is a social factor related to the usual meal and working hours.

1.4.1.1 Exogenous model of the circadian rhythm phase regulatory system

As already mentioned, the change in the circadian rhythm phase may be related, inter alia, to the environmental synchronizer (e.g. when changing the time zone during parallel flights) and to the social synchronizer (e.g. when changing the working hours in the case of multi-shift operation). Let's draw attention to a relatively young problem, which is related to easy and fast traveling in space (earth and cosmic). For example, intercontinental journeys that used to last for years (land caravans, sailing ships) or months (combustion ships, cars) have now been reduced to a dozen or so hours. Not everyone is aware of the fact that this benefit has some biological and psychological consequences in a situation where a jet flight travels along parallels (every 15 degrees of longitude there is one-hour difference in astronomical time between adjacent geographical zones). In the literature of the subject the biological and psychological effects of rapid crossing of time zones are called *"jet-pilot syndrome"*[5] and are associated, as in the case of circadian rhythm disturbances, with the deterioration of human ability and general wellbeing (Van Cauter, 2007). This means that, for example, both passengers and flight attendants, when crossing consecutive time zones, still maintain a local (point of departure) biological rhythm which is incompatible with photo-ecological conditions and social synchronizers at the point of arrival. Lack of compatibility between the biological time calculated by our organism (brain, organs and cells) and the local astronomical time causes a number of adverse health and well-being symptoms, which are considered to be markers of chronobiological stress.

When external synchronizers are switched off (e.g. in the isolation chamber), *free-running rhythms* occur in humans, where on one hand there is a lack of compatibility between biological time (calculated by ESSO) and local astronomical time, which leads to an imbalance in the internal consistency between the basic rhythms of body functions. The occurrence of *free-running circadian rhythms* may indicate endogenous determinants of biological rhythms. The organism's reaction to the change of the environmental synchronizer phase is adaptation to new conditions, called the resynchronization process. The mechanism of resynchronization can be explained by the activity of the circadian rhythm phase regulator, shown schematically in Fig. 1.13.

In the stationary state, there is an evenness between the phase of external synchronizers (a "set" signal) and the circadian rhythm phase ϕw (a "measured" signal). The frequency of external synchronizers fz determines the frequency of the circadian (internal) fw rhythm in this model. In case of fast ϕz phase change of external synchronizers at the beginning of the circadian rhythm phase regulator there will appear a Δϕ difference of incompatible phases of the set Δϕ and measured ϕw signals. After comparing the signals, the system changes the initial ϕw value in such a way as to reduce the valuc of the "error signal" Δϕ = ϕz

5 "Jet-pilot syndrome" - a name derived from American jet pilots, who often flew between the U.S. occupation zone from Berlin Tempelhof Airport to the U.S. and complained to their physicians about drowsiness, deterioration of attention and psychomotor processes, lack of appetite, etc., which were called by them: *jet-lag desynchronosis* or *transmeridian desynchronism.*

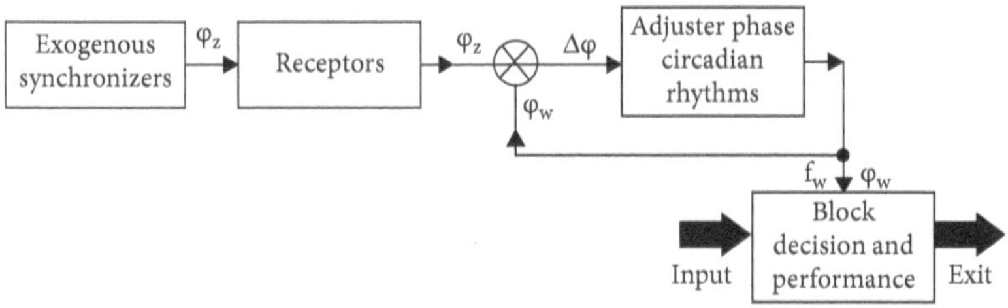

Fig. 1.13: Negative feedback loop in the circadian rhythm phase regulation system (Source: own elaboration)

- ϕw. In order to characterize such a system, the theory of regulation introduces, among other things, the concepts of speed and the nature of the response. The results of research on the resynchronization process, carried out with changes in time zones, allow us to state that the system of regulation of the circadian rhythm phase is similar to the integral regulator, while the response speed is about 1 hour per day. In the first approximation it is therefore possible to present the resynchronization process as a function of time t using the following equation:

$$\Delta\phi = \phi z - \phi w = \Delta\phi o - r\,(t - to)$$

where r is the resynchronization speed, and Δϕo is the size of the change of external synchronizers phase at the moment to. The resynchronization process ends when the error signal Δϕ reaches zero. Individual aspects of the resynchronization process are presented in Fig. 1.14.

The simple exogenous phase regulation system model shown in Fig. 1.14 is sufficient to explain the phase dependencies in the resynchronization process. However, the exogenous model does not allow to explain human functioning in an environment devoid of natural external synchronizers.

1.4.1.2 Mixed model of mutual regulation

Chronobiologists finally rejected the concept of the exogenous character of the circadian rhythm. Research, e.g. of speleologists accidentally imprisoned in caves, shows that the elimination of alternation of day (light) - night (darkness) phases did not interrupt the human organism's timekeeping, although it did disturb it slightly. The duration of a day under these conditions varies by 1 hour in comparison to a 24-hour astronomical day. Another proof of the endogenousness of circadian rhythms is the occurrence of these rhythms among cells transferred outside the organism (in tissue cultures), in which the 24-hour

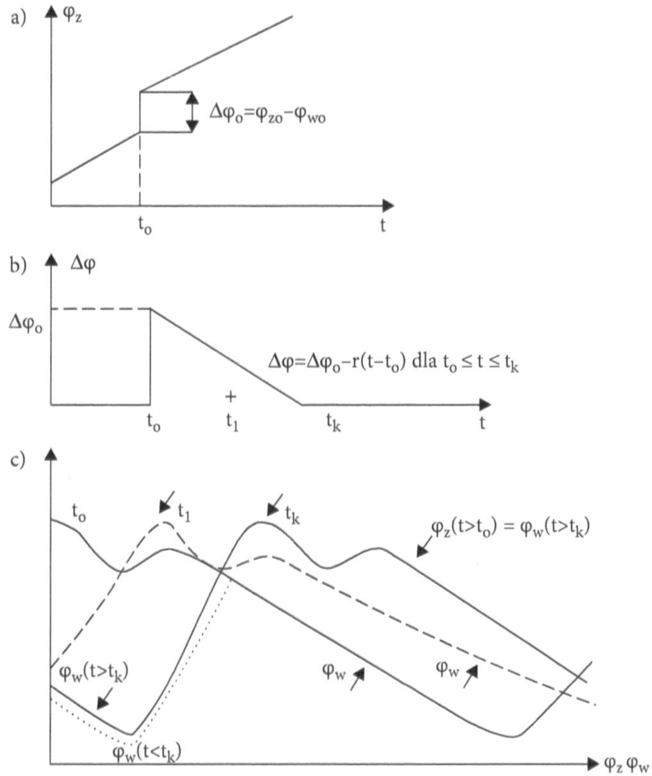

Fig. 1.14: The course of the resynchronization process: a) change of phase of the external synchronizer; b) change of phase differences as a function of time (effect of regulator activity); c) circadian rhythm in subsequent stages of resynchronization. (Source: own elaboration). Note: (Legend: to - the moment of external synchronizers phase change; tk - the moment of completion of the resynchronization process; $\Delta\phi o = \phi zo - \phi wo$ - the initial value of the phase difference (equal to the size of the external synchronizer phase change); $\Delta\phi(t) = \phi jz - \phi jw$ - the value of layer difference at the moment t (source: own elaboration)

rhythm of cell division still occurs (Kwarecki, 1985). Although chronobiology states that most rhythms are of endogenous character, i.e. they are not a passive reflection of external light conditions, but are deeply encoded in individual cells of the organism, which have their own “biological clock” which controls the rhythm of human life functions and only adjusts its course to environmental conditions, it can be seen, however, that the circadian rhythm is not perfectly adapted to the astronomical rhythms of the Earth (24-hour rotation around its axis), because the endogenous rhythm of physiological functions is influenced by various factors adjusting the "biological clock" to current environmental conditions, as confirmed by empirical studies (cf. Kerkhof, 1987). For the molecular level research on fruit flies (Drosophila melanogaster) explaining the mechanism of the biological clock, controlled by genes of biochemical processes in cells and tissues, which is responsible for daily regulation of the most important biological processes and body functions. The Nobel Prize in 2017 went to three American chronobiologists: Jeffrey C. Hall, Michael Rosbash and Michael W. Young. Scientists have confirmed that biological clock indeed adapts the physiology of each body to the specific phases of day and night, being responsible for changes in hormone secretion, body temperature, sleep, arterial pressure, metabolic processes.

In order to explain human behavior in the absence of natural external synchronizers, a model of human functioning in environments with different frequencies of daily rhythm, presented in the Fig. 1.15 can be proposed.

The above model treats the circadian rhythm as a natural endogenous rhythm, which, however, can be regulated by external synchronizers, which in turn can be regulated by deliberate human actions. The proposed model, in addition to the negative feedback loop described above, entwining the block of the

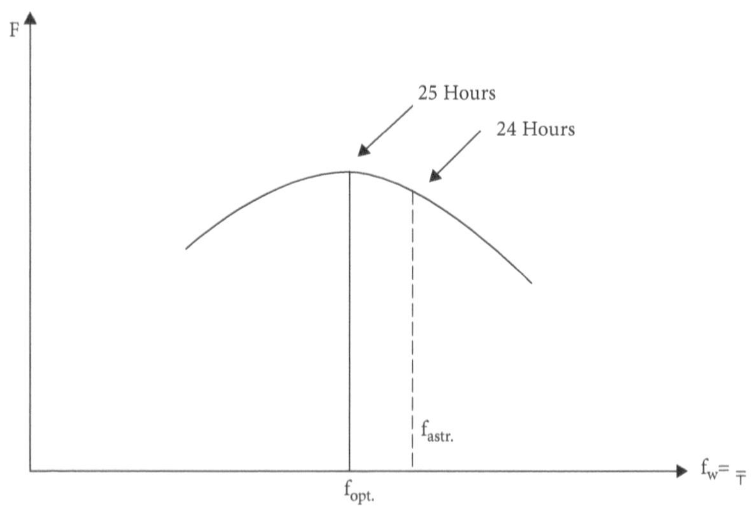

Fig. 1.15: The model of human functioning in the situation of elimination of the photo-ecological synchronizer (Source: own elaboration)

circadian phase regulator (the block is marked in Fig. 1.14a), contains two feedback loops embracing the entire control system. They are unnoticeable in natural conditions, but play a decisive role in conditions of isolation from the natural environment (caves, polar stations, space flights), when man has a significant influence on external synchronizers. Their existence makes it possible to transform the system of circadian rhythm phase regulator, the "adjuster" of which is the rhythm of external synchronizers, into a system of mutual regulation: the rhythm of man by the environment and the rhythm of the environment by man. The functioning of this system will be presented on the basis of a thought experiment. Imagine that a person is isolated from natural external synchronizers and at the same time has no influence on any artificial (external) synchronizers of his or her rhythm. Adaptation to the new conditions would mean that the frequency of the circadian fw rhythm would, after a certain period of time, be fixed at the size of fopt that is optimal for human functioning under certain conditions. The sensor of conditions (temperature, electromagnetic field, etc.) on which the circadian fopt rhythm of the person under experiment is dependent should be a hypothetical superior endogenous ESSO clock, which can be compared to the clock, which is part of the digital machine processor. If a person adapted to such conditions would be transferred to an environment where the synchronizers (natural or artificial) are in phase compliant with the current circadian fopt rhythm, an error message $\Delta\phi$ (Fig. 1.14b) would still be equal to zero. Therefore, it would only be possible to change the acrophase and nadir, without changing the frequency and phase of the circadian fopt rhythm. This thought experiment has much in common with the experiments carried out in caves, bunkers and laboratories, during which the examined people were deprived of natural external synchronizers, allowing for individual rhythm adjustment by means of artificial synchronizers. In these experiments, changes in the frequency of circadian rhythm of individual people were observed. In most cases a decrease in fopt frequency in relation to astronomical frequency was observed (extension of Topt day > 24 hours). The authors of individual experiments observed Topt circadian periods falling within the range: 24.5–27.2 hours. A shortening of the day was also observed.

In such experiments, it is of course difficult to control the factors that through ESSO can influence the fopt frequency. It would also be difficult to carry out an experiment aimed at investigating the quantitative relationship between the frequency of the fw rhythm and the functioning of F, understood as the entirety of human activity, but on the basis of the results of the cited experiments it can be assumed that the dependence of the functioning of F on the frequency of the circadian fw rhythm will be similar to the one presented in the figure above.

Moreover, the already quoted results of research on resynchronization speed in transcontinental flights prove that the average fopt frequency shifted towards decreasing frequency. Although the exact reasons for the asymmetry effect between flights in the west and east direction are not yet known, the difference between resynchronization speeds can probably be explained by the asymmetry of the F curve in relation to the fastr astronomical frequency among others.

With the prolongation of the day, the organism functions better than with shortening, so resynchronization should be faster in conditions of better functioning of the organism (west flight) than in conditions of worse functioning (east flight - to the right from fastr). This knowledge is extremely necessary for contemporary people in many professional (e.g. businessmen, politicians, sportsmen, artists, conductors, etc.) and personal (e.g. tourism) situations. We can easily see how synchronizers work by observing our sleep, rest and activity on weekdays and weekends. On days off, when we don't have to follow the schedule so strictly, our rhythm often slows down, we get up later, eat longer, watch TV longer in the evenings, lead a social life, etc. We can have problems with falling asleep at the usual hour, and on Monday morning we would like to sleep longer. A slightly different situation occurs in the case of forced multi-shift work, because regardless of our preference in terms of time of day, we are all subject to deterioration of our bio-psychical ability between 3 and 5 o'clock in the morning. Statistics of road accidents during these hours are confirmed by laboratory data (Akerstedt, Lindbeck, 2007).

Man has created many of his own rhythms, according to which he "manages" his own time and to some extent became independent from the natural environment and created a civilization that pulsates with its own rhythm. Apart from the natural rhythm of light and darkness, we are also influenced by silence and noise related to the intensity of traffic, our neighbors' lifestyle, hours of broadcasting radio and television broadcasts of our choice, the need to eat meals after returning from work and not during its duration. The degree of importance of synchronizers varies from person to person, e.g. blind people cannot be guided by changes in lighting, the sleep-wake rhythm, the rhythm of duties, or silence and noise are more useful for them.

Summarizing the chrono-habilistic concept of stress, it should be said that it has been applied both in occupational medicine (health effects of multi-shift work and sudden change of time zone), occupational psychology (evaluation of performance in multi-shift work and sudden change of time zone) and clinical psychology and psychiatry (circadian mood variability, depression) (Ledwoch, 2006). The fact that the desynchronization of endogenous and exogenous biological rhythms is a source of stress is underlined by the current extended definition of health proposed by the World Health Organization (WHO), which, apart from good physical, mental and spiritual condition, also takes into account the mutual synchronization of the important for life biorhythms. This psychophysical wellbeing, manifested in good general fitness and well-being, called quality of life, is referred to by many of the concepts of stress presented so far, which indicate that the stress zone is a departure from this pattern, and the indicator of stress, both in objective and subjective terms, is the deterioration of the quality of life (Skevington, 2007).

1.4.2 Robert A. Karasek's Model of Job Strain

According to occupational psychologists, various occupations have their psychological characteristics from the perspective of stress origins (e.g. Terelak, ed., 2007). In addition to the descriptive approach, it is worth noting the psychological mechanisms explaining the relationship between workload and mental discomfort caused by the discrepancy between the requirements placed on the employee and his or her ability to meet them. In the literature of the subject it is worth to refer to Robert A. Karasek's Model of Job Strain (1979), presented in Fig. 1.16.

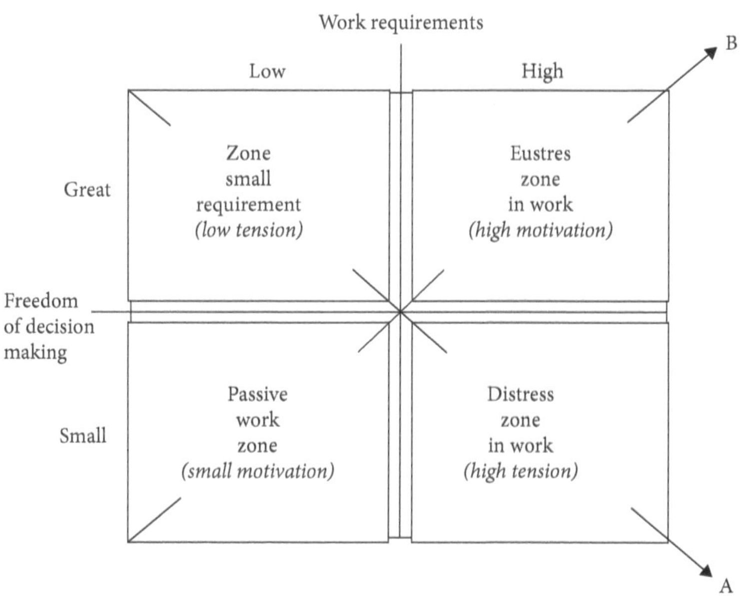

Fig. 1.16: Karasek's Model of Job Strain (source: Karasek (1997) - own elaboration)

As the above model shows, Robert A. Karasek drew attention to the fact that the interaction of high requirements and low control range generates specific psychosocial stress in the work environment. Focusing on the balance of occupational requirements and employee autonomy, the model illustrates psychological stressful situations in the workplace, such as: workers with high requirements and low control feel more stress than others. Symptoms of stress should also occur in a situation characterized by low requirements for the worker and high control level. The relationship of requirements level to control intensity is responsible for four mental states of the employee: passivity vs activity, tension vs relaxation reflects the zone: *A - stress and B - eustress at work*. The four stress categories of relations: human vs. work can be described as follows:

1. High requirements and low level of control create a stressful situation, resulting from the lack of impact on the task situation, and from the limitation of one's own creativity and forcing one to work passively.
2. High requirements with a high level of control promote active work and professional development.
3. Low requirements and small level of control generate passive work, because such situation has a low motivation value, e.g. for ambitious employees such a situation is stressful.
4. Low requirements and a high level of control create the conditions for a relaxing atmosphere (low tension) in the workplace. A high level of control allows for adequate response to the requirements. Karasek's model is useful for the operationalization and estimation of health costs as an indicator of psycho-social stress, as well as a theoretical basis for selection for the so-called stress professions.

The review of selected concepts of stress shows, among other things, that stress disturbs the relative balance between the body and the environment and that not only environmental stress factors (stressors) but also the state caused by these factors (emotional stress) should be described. The most characteristic for modern psychology is the interactive (transactional) stress model. The authors of transactional stress concepts emphasize the fact that both the assessment of the stress situation and the process of coping with stress always takes place through the prism of the ability and efficiency of the individual. Efficiency is determined by the biological resources an individual has at his or her disposal, and ability largely depends also on the capability to learn new ways of coping with changing environmental and social requirements. The process of coping with stressful situations has a loop character and is repeated cyclically. This interactive model of stress characterization is usually expressed by the formula: *person (feature) x situation → behavior.* The stress cycle analysis model is explained in detail by Joseph E. McGrath (1976), emphasizing how external stress situations transform into subjective cognitive representation, which is the basis for deciding whether or not this external situation is psychological stress for me, and in what form stress reactions, conditioning the choice of appropriate strategies for coping with stress, are manifested. This last element of the stress cycle analysis is particularly interesting, as stress responses, as a feedback, can start a qualitatively new cycle by reinterpreting a previous source of stress (e.g. a change in the assessment of remedial options for coping with or failing to cope with existing stress), or they can definitively end the stress cycle when a problem is solved.

At the end of the first chapter, it should be stressed that the chronologically presented stress models did not exhaust all the important issues discussed in the literature of the subject, although they certainly outlined the common aspects of the concept of stress.

2 Identification of stressors

Psychological stressors can be of various nature. The most commonly talked about are ecological threats to man and the Earth, shared by contemporary people, supporters of post modernity and global capitalism. It is difficult to accept any common classification of sources of stress, as they significantly exceed the list of environmental risks and, moreover, there are no applicable distribution criteria. The criterion adopted should cover both the type of stress stimulus, its strength (intensity), as well as the duration or frequency of its occurrence. In the latter case, we are dealing with a distinction between incidental and chronic stress, which is important because their effects can vary. The criterion of the strength of a stress stimulus is also not very convenient despite its quantitative characteristics, as it is not only the physical component of the force itself that is important, but the psychological significance of the stimulus, which significantly modifies the response to stress.

When contemplating the organism as a multidimensional unit, attention is drawn to the fact that environmental and personal factors are transactional because, by influencing each other, they cause stress responses to reflect the new systemic quality of the organism. This infinite number of transactions has prompted some psychologists to seek a correlation between a single environmental factor and an individual reaction of the organism, and others to take the approach that the environment is such a compact entity that it should not be dissected into individual factors at all. The first of these approaches led to many controversial results, while the second one led to completely unscientific discussions. In psychology of stress, similar extreme views can be found, but the situation is even more complicated if one takes into account the social characteristics of the environment and one's own deliberate activity.

In the absence of a convenient criterion for distributing sources of stress, the nature of the stress factor (stressor) seems to be useful. By stressor we shall mean such an element of stimulus or situation, which violates the relative balance between the subject and the environment and activates not only adaptation mechanisms (mental regulation) of human behavior, but also creative management of stress. Due to the nature of the stressor understood in this way, it is possible to assume a classification into environmental (natural and artificial environment), chronobiological, psychological and social stressors. The classification adopted is only of an organizational nature.

2.1 Physical environment as a source of stress

By human ecology we mean a specific system of mutual relations between man and the natural or artificial environment *(artificial satellites)*, in which they exist and act deliberately. Four branches of human ecology can be distinguished: 1) philosophical problems of relations between man and the environment; 2) natural and socio-economic problems of the human environment; 3) environmental problems of human biology; 4) cultural adaptation behaviors. The second and third sections will be particularly useful for our purposes.

Ecological stress factors have two features. Firstly, they are suitable for describing the external environment of human life. Secondly, they can easily be included in quantitative categories. The second feature, the measurability of physical stressor, makes it relatively easy to empirically determine both the stress threshold, i.e. the moment when a neutral stimulus triggers the action of adaptation mechanisms to meet new, increased requirements, and the stress tolerance threshold, i.e. the moment when the organism incurs losses because adaptation mechanisms are inadequate to a new, changed situation or when the organism refuses to act (e.g. illness, death). A convenient theoretical model to illustrate the described correlations can be the so-called model of optimal environmental conditions, described in Chapter 1.1 which assumes that stress factors on a continuum of performance requirements or operating conditions manifest themselves clearly in extremely averse conditions, understood in two ways: (a) as conditions requiring maximum resistance of the organism; (b) as a sudden change in living conditions or an action that requires adaptation in a very short period of time. The basic group of environmental sources of stress, which each person deals with, are natural environment factors, such as: climate and its components (temperature, humidity, wind power, atmospheric pressure), noise, ionizing radiation, etc.

2.1.1 Climate and its components

The stressful nature of climatic factors is not revealed until the change of seasons or a sudden change of geographical conditions, during a journey connected with the change of climatic zones, which trigger adaptation processes called acclimatization. Three stages are usually listed in the acclimatization process: (1) initial, where exposure to new environmental conditions may cause various discomfort; 2) gradual adaptation, the progress of which depends not only on climatic conditions (humidity, air temperature, visible radiation, wind speed), but also on the constitutional properties of man.

During this period numerous disadaptive nerve syndromes (so-called meteoneuroses) often occur, which may prevent further stay in a given climate; 3) proper acclimatization, i.e. relatively constant adaptation to specific climatic conditions.

The reverse process is also gradual and consists of two stages: deacclimatization, which occurs when returning to the previous climatic environment, and reactlimatization, which occurs when returning after a longer break to the harsh climatic conditions (e.g. the polar expedition members, who experience a so-called permanent acclimatization). There are well known symptoms of "meteotropic disease", which are associated, among other things, with sudden changes in atmospheric pressure. This disease is associated with symptoms of pressure, tinnitus, headaches or dizziness, drowsiness, weakness, fainting tendencies, etc. Although all these ailments are reversible, they are always felt to be uncomfortable.

As has been discussed so far, adaptation to climatic conditions, understood as the process of active adaptation changes, is possible. The acclimatization process itself, understood as a change in metabolic regulation leading to a new level of homeostasis, is, however, highly complex. This claim can be illustrated by the stressful nature of the interaction between high ambient temperature and high air humidity and the organism's reaction. The influence of air temperature on the psychophysical state at a relative humidity of 50 % is as follows: full ability to work is achieved at a temperature of thermal comfort which is about +20 degrees Celsius. Slight difficulties at work (annoyance, irritation, difficulty concentrating, reduced mental performance efficiency, etc.) can be observed in the temperature range of +21–26 degrees Celsius. A further increase in temperature to 27–30 degrees Celsius leads to significant discomfort at work (increase in the number of errors, decrease in efficiency of manual work, increase in the number of accidents, etc.). In the range of +32–35 degrees Celsius there appear physiological disorders (disturbances of water-salt metabolism in the organism, significant strain on the cardiovascular system, strong fatigue, the threat of emaciation), accompanied by a decrease in heavy work efficiency. The highest bearable limit temperature, accompanied by large physiological disturbances, is about +40 degrees Celsius. The analysis of the impact of thermal stress on the human organism is usually preceded by the assessment of the so-called thermal comfort, determined on the basis of a subjective assessment of the microclimate conditions of the surrounding environment. Such conditions should not cause any intensified reactions, such as sweating or shivers, in the organism. Disorders of subjective thermal comfort are accompanied by changes in physiological functions of the system, associated with the functioning of the thermoregulatory mechanism. The operation of this mechanism depends primarily on the internal temperature of the system and changes in ambient temperature (Taylor, 2007).

The condition for the operation of the thermoregulatory mechanism to function is a specific temperature level, maintained by the controlling system, the so-called *set point* of the system The most effective mechanism of reducing heat at high ambient temperatures is evaporation, the activity of which depends on three climatic factors: ambient temperature, air movement and relative air humidity. The improper configuration of these factors creates additional stress, causing the so-called heat stroke, which is characterized by the limited ability of the organism to release the generated heat to the environment. It is also accompanied by disturbances of water-electrolyte (dehydration) and acid–base homeostasis (loss of sodium). Heat exhaustion caused by dehydration manifests itself in strong thirst, general weakness and exhaustion of the organism. There may also be fever and symptoms of thermal shock. The heat exhaustion caused by sodium loss is characterized by headaches, apathy, nausea and vomiting, general weakness, lack of appetite, calf muscle cramps and even circulatory collapse. The above symptoms as a reaction to thermal stress may occur within a few days in a hot environment. In addition, the stressful nature of the impact of high temperature on the body is modified by the level of air humidity. There are many studies estimating the impact of the jungle climate (high temperature and high humidity) and desert climate (high temperature and dry air) on the human organism (Fig. 2.1).

Human functioning in high temperature and high humidity conditions is so stressful that some authors believe that physiological adaptation to these

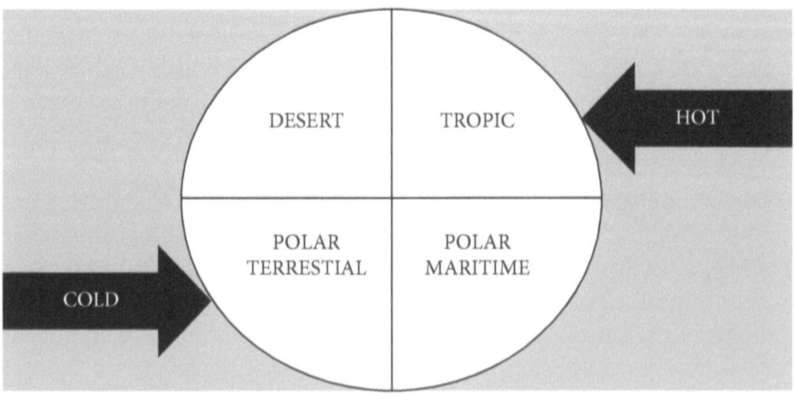

Fig. 2.1: Four extreme climates on Earth (Source: own elaboration)

conditions has a limited range and consists primarily in increasing the tolerance of increased body temperature. Medical data and occupational psychology show, among other things, that in the case of working steelworkers, miners, etc., who have adapted to the described climatic conditions, we are dealing with biological selection, not adaptation to these conditions (Blatteis, 2007).

The stressful character of low temperature (hypothermia) will be illustrated by research conducted in the Antarctic. The study of human adaptation to a stay in the cold climate of Antarctica provides empirical data supporting the thesis that human stay in extreme conditions, characterized by low temperature and high air humidity, causes the development of psycho-physiological reactions, leading to the development of relative adaptation to these conditions or disadaptation. The disadaptation indicator is decreased ability to work, and in the case of prolonged body cooling - symptoms of so called shivering thermogenesis with all its consequences, i.e. disturbance of mental functions, inability to sleep and rest. It was found that members of the Antarctic expedition of the Polish Academy of Sciences to the H. Arctowski Station during their stay in Antarctica are exposed to the cold sufficient to induce symptoms of acclimatization to cold, as evidenced by the fact that as the time passes by, the amount of clothing worn decreases despite the prolonged stay outside the living quarters and severe climate conditions. In experimental studies, consisting in a 90-minute stay of the examined naked person at room temperature of +10 degrees Celsius, the existence of human body adaptation to cold of hypothermic reaction character, characterized by lowering the resting rectal temperature and lowering the temperature curve during thermal load, lowering the thermal threshold of trembling and decreasing cardiovascular functions, has been found. Similar studies carried out one year after the return of polar explorers to Poland (at the end of winter) indicate a completely different course of physiological adaptive reactions to cold, excluding the hypothermal type of adaption (Kowalski, 1982).

This direction of interpretation of the results corresponds to the known fact that exposing the naked body to cold is currently only found among some primitive tribes of Australia (Aborigines) and South America (Indians). These people are fully adapted to cold, which is characterized by lowering of the threshold for triggering metabolic reaction (shivers) and lowering of the core body temperature. Other people on Earth, thanks to the constant wearing of clothing, maintain the temperature under clothes at the level of thermal comfort, corresponding to the temperature of the subtropical climate zone. The need to stay in a cold climate (e.g. fishermen fishing in subpolar zones, high mountain and polar expeditions, etc.) justifies conducting experimental research on the process of acclimatization to these conditions.

Presented arguments about the stressful nature of extreme climatic conditions, i.e. cold, heat, humidity and wind power, point to complex mechanisms of adaptation to these conditions and the relative adaptability to them. However, this does not happen without a certain cost, the first symptom of which is usually subjective discomfort.

2.1.2 Excessive noise

The ear, next to the visual system, is the second most important stimulus receptor, which provides important information about changes in the external environment. However, if sound stimuli, bringing about sound in the organ of hearing, are not desired, they are referred to as noise. Usually noise can be described by two physical parameters: frequency and intensity. Frequency is the number of total acoustic waves reaching the ear within a unit of time and is measured in cycles per second or in Hertz. The intensity, which is the power transferred per unit area, is defined in a conventional logarithmic unit, i.e. in decibels (dB). In practice, the sound pressure level (A) is measured. Let us recall that the human ear is adapted to the perception of sounds at frequencies of 16–20,000 Hz and, compared to the hearing organs of animals, it is severely handicapped. Distinguishing between harmless and harmful (stress) noises is difficult because the stressfulness of noise depends not only on the intensity of the sound, but also on the frequency characteristics and duration of the noise. Taking into account only the noise level in decibels, it is possible to construct an approximate psychological scale of noise, which is as follows. Noise above 120 dB (e.g. take-off of a large jet plane) can be harmful and dangerous to the organ of hearing (e.g. ruptured eardrum). A sound stimulus in the range of 100–120 dB (e.g. an ambulance siren) can give painful sensations located in the ear. Noise in the range of 80–100 dB (e.g. heavy construction or agricultural equipment) is deafening. Noise in the range of 60–80 dB (e.g. loud conversations) is perceived as high by other people. The average traffic corresponds to a high noise level of 40–60 dB. Moderate noise (e.g. conversation) has a scale of 20–40 dB. Finally, the lowest range of 1–20 dB (e.g. rustling leaves) is referred to as quiet noise. It is not possible to clearly identify the stressful nature of noise for several reasons. Noise, on the one hand, can damage the organ of hearing, and on the other hand, contributes to the fatigue of the nervous system and causes general discomfort, making verbal communication difficult. It was found that resistance to noise varies between different people and between the same people during different working hours. This depends on the physical characteristics of the noise itself, as well as on the state of the organ of hearing, health, fatigue, a person's well-being, and the combined effect of noise with other environmental stress factors, such as vibration, low and high temperatures, etc.

Above all, noise, as a stress stimulus, reduces work efficiency. This is mainly related to difficult verbal communication and distraction. Deteriorated audibility hinders the perception of acoustic warning signals, as evidenced, among other things, by the increase in accidents at work. The annoyance of noise also has its subjective dimension, expressed by general mental discomfort. Moreover, noise causes various vegetative changes in the human organism. These include changes in cardiovascular function (peripheral stenosis, small blood vessels and reduction of stroke and minute volume).

It is worth paying attention to the structure of the ear, which does not have a natural protection against noise, which means that we are permanently exposed to all sound stimuli. Therefore, the only defense against noise is to reduce it by: reducing the source of noise; creating a barrier preventing the spread of noise; introducing individual hearing protection (e.g. earmuffs, earplugs).

2.1.3 Lighting inadequate for the performed tasks

Turning to stress factors related to the ubiquitous existence of electromagnetic radiation of different structures in the environment, it is worth noting that light seen by man is only a small fragment of the spectrum of electromagnetic waves, for which there are no specialized receptors in the eye (e.g. ultraviolet). Focusing on lighting as a stress factor, we assume that it is an obstacle only if it makes it difficult or impossible to perceive the visual information needed to perform the task. The amount of stress depends, on the one hand, on the condition of the vision organ and, on the other hand, on the photo-ecological conditions of the environment and the physical parameters of lighting itself, as well as the type of visual task. For these reasons, the lighting required for a specific job is specified in the Polish Norm PN-71/B-02380.

The human eye only reacts to a very limited range of electromagnetic radiation frequencies with a wavelength of about 76 to about 38 hundred thousandths of a millimeter. This part of the electromagnetic spectrum is called visible radiation or simply light. Taking into account only the length of electromagnetic waves, it should be remembered that the eye is most sensitive to radiation of the wavelength located in the middle of the interval mentioned above and that it deteriorates in both directions of this interval, e.g. the wavelength extremes of the visible radiation spectrum correspond to the colors: dark red (76×10^{-5} mm) and violet (40–38 $\times 10^{-5}$ mm), while the colors yellow and green are associated with the middle wavelength. Moreover, the human eye has three systems of vision, taking into account the photo-ecological factors of the environment: night vision (rod vision), twilight vision (mesopic vision) and day vision (photopic vision).

The quality of lighting that determines the comfort of vision is also determined by its physical characteristics: *luminous flux* - this is a parameter defining the ability of radiant power to produce the impression of light (the unit of luminous flux is lumen - lm); *light intensity* - this is the surface density of the luminous flux falling on a given surface element (the unit of light intensity is lux - lx); *luminous intensity of a light source* - it is the angular density of the luminous flux emitted by this light in a given direction (the unit of luminous intensity is candela - cd); *luminance* - it is the ratio of the luminous intensity of a given element of the illuminating surface in a given direction to the projected area of this element on a surface that is perpendicular to a given direction. The subjective equivalents of luminance are the perceptions of brightness or luminosity (the unit of luminance is the Nit, i.e. the candela per square meter - cd/m^2).

Practically speaking, the eye reacts directly to luminance, therefore the limit of the stress nature of lighting is defined in the literature of the subject by the recommended minimum levels of illumination. Thus, the minimum luminance in the candelas per square meter (cd/m^2) various for different visual tasks takes into account: 1) extremely difficult task including the smallest details – 1000–600 (e.g. watchmaker's work); 2) very long task requiring concentration - 600–400 (e.g. fixing stocking); 3) difficult and long task with small details - 300 (e.g. drawing offices); 4) medium difficult task with small details - 200 (e.g. machining); 4) medium difficult task with small details - 200 (e.g. drawing offices); 5) normal task with medium size details - 100 (e.g. work in common offices); 6) roughing tasks with large details - 60 (e.g. assembly of heavy machines); 7) momentary gazing - 30 (e.g. crossing the corridor).

The state that causes visual discomfort and drastically reduces the ability to recognize objects is glare. It is the result of unfavorable distribution of luminance or its wide or excessive in space and/or time range. The phenomenon of glare (blinding) and its uncomfortable character are known to drivers, who know that an oncoming car, located more or less opposite, reduces the ability of visual perception. The mechanism of glare consists in the fact that the light that is its source causes reflection on the retina of the eye. The source of intense glare creates a cone of diffused light inside the eye, which we see as dashed lines. A car approaching at night, located opposite us and blinding with the long lights of its reflectors, reduces the visibility of the observed image (road, clocks on the car's instrument panel), because the reflection of this light gets into the cone of the diffused light. While maximum glare levels causing subjective discomfort, as well as differences in individual glare stress tolerance (e.g. for professional drivers) have been empirically determined, the establishment of optimal ranges of good visibility does not always coincide with the subjective perception of visual comfort.

The same is true of the stressful character of the flickering light. Although the light should switch on and off with a frequency below 10 Hz in order to bring about noticeable changes in the functioning of the average person, there are many technical devices generating flickering of a higher frequency, which is subjectively perceived as uncomfortable, e.g.: (a) malfunctioning fluorescent lamps flicker at 100 Hz, causing eye fatigue and a general feeling of exhaustion; (b) a flickering TV screen with a harmful frequency between 15 and 20 Hz, when sitting close to it, causes rapid eye fatigue (so-called burning eyes); (c) flickering light with a frequency between 3 and 100 Hz causes epilepsy symptoms in one person per 5–10 000 people.

For these reasons, preventive measures take into account, on the one hand, the production standards of various light sources and, on the other hand, the definition of the tolerance for light flickering in people exposed to this type of stress due to the nature of their work (e.g. exclusion of epileptics). Another type of electromagnetic radiation in addition to those already discussed (e.g. light, sound, temperature) is the so-called ionizing radiation.

2.1.4 Natural and artificial sources of ionizing radiation

Ionizing radiation is defined as molecules or electromagnetic waves, of natural or artificial origin, which have the ability to ionize matter, because they are supplied with energy emitted from an atomic nucleus or accelerated in an electromagnetic field. It includes all types of radiation that cause ionization of a material medium, i.e. the separation of at least one electron from an atom or molecule, or its removal from a crystal structure. Ionizing electromagnetic radiation is considered to be radiation in which the photons have a higher energy than that of visible light photons.

For many centuries man has not been aware of the stressful nature of ionizing radiation, the natural sources of which are space radiation and radioactive isotopes. Space radiation - has a corpuscular and electromagnetic structure. The corpuscular part of the radiation consists mainly of protons (90 % of particles), alpha particles (9 %), electrons (about 1 %) and a few heavier nuclei. Space radiation, the so-called primary radiation, reaches the Earth directly from space through the atmospheric protective layer, which minimizes its deadly impact on living organisms. Radioisotopes (radioisotopes) are variants of elements whose nuclei of atoms are unstable and spontaneously undergo radioactive transformation. As a result of this transformation other atomic nuclei are formed, elementary particles are emitted, energy is released in the form of kinetic energy of transformation products and gamma radiation is usually emitted. Radioisotopes are characterized by a half-life after which half of the nuclei of a given isotope undergo a transformation. These natural isotopes are natural sources of stress, while artificial sources of stress are: reactors, accelerators, X-ray apparatus and artificially produced isotopes. The latter is obtained from nuclear reactions in nuclear reactors and accelerators. Although they are more and more widely used in industry, medicine, agriculture, etc., since the first nuclear explosion and the contemporary repeating nuclear power plant accidents like Chernobyl or Three Mile Island, knowledge about the stress effects of ionizing radiation is not only common, but also a source of existential anxiety for entire societies.

The best known types of ionizing radiation are: alpha, beta, gamma and X radiation. Apart from discussing the nature of the types of radiation and the description of the mechanisms of their effect on the human body and individual tissues, it should be said that there is an International Commission for Radiological Protection as well as National Commissions, which on the basis of permanent research (including the condition of the atmosphere) determine minimum doses, so-called the so called threshold doses of irradiation of the organism, as well as individual groups of tissues and organs.

In the absence of sufficient knowledge of the stress effects of ionizing radiation, the mere determination of the body's irradiation threshold doses is of rather psychological significance, as this does not exclude the occurrence of injury even at these threshold doses of irradiation.

Although we are aware that any irradiation of an organism poses a risk of negative effects, certain artificial sources of radiation (e.g. isotopes used in medicine or X-rays) cannot be excluded as they have certain diagnostic or therapeutic benefits for humans. Thus, the so-called acceptable radiation doses take into account both the risks and benefits for the individual and the entire population. This strategy is widely accepted, especially in the battle against cancer cells in the organism, although ionizing radiation contributes also to the development of cancer. The choice of the lesser evil in this case, however, is of great therapeutic importance, as illustrated by Fig. 2.2.

Another problem is to protect against the harmful effects of ionizing radiation in industry. And so, for example, penetrating gamma rays or deep X-rays are used in the detection of errors during welding of metals or in other types of industrial defectoscopy. They are also applicable in the sterilization of medical instruments and food. In these cases, in addition to determining the so-called

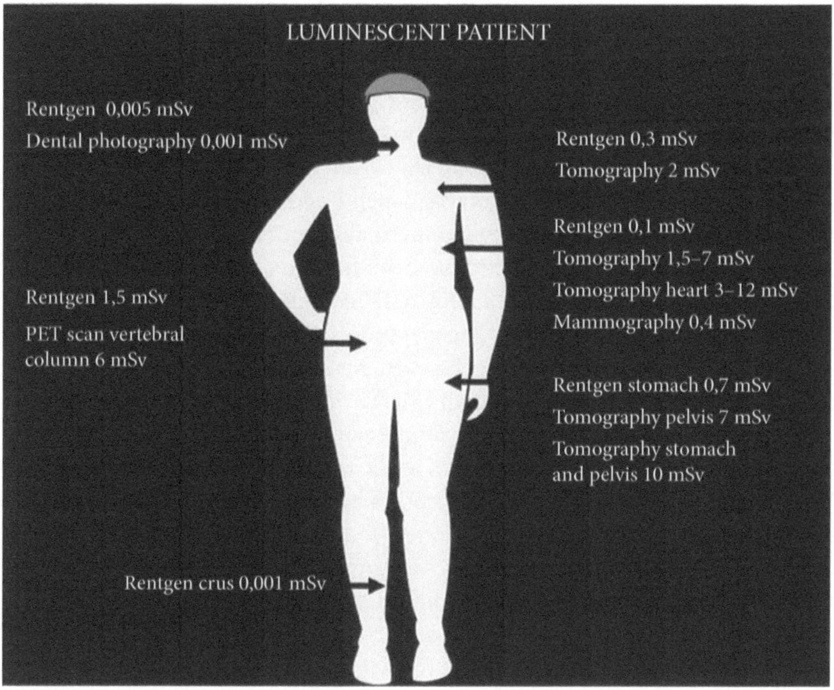

Fig. 2.2: "Glowing" patient as a result of therapeutic doses of ionizing radiation. (Source: own elaborations)

acceptable dose, special room protection (e.g. concrete, lead, iron) or worker protection (protective clothing, glasses) are developed. People working within the range of ionizing radiation using individual dosimeters determine the daily, monthly and annual dose. This is the basis for a special allowance for the so-called harmful factors at work or inclusion in the so-called occupational disease risk group.

Shortening the exposure time and, above all, automation of radiation sources is of great importance for protection. If the latter is not yet possible due to a delay in technical progress, the distance between radiation sources should at least be increased, as the radiation intensity (and thus its harmfulness) decreases in proportion to the square of the distance from the source.

A separate problem, more and more relevant in the 21st century in connection with the planned interplanetary flights, is cosmic radiation, the effects of which on the human body are fatal.

2.1.5 Microwave electromagnetic fields

Despite widespread contact with sources of electromagnetic fields of all frequencies (e.g. The 10^{-4}–$10^{-5\,m}$ range) used e.g. for radio and telecommunication, radiolocation or military purposes (e.g. microwave bomb), their biological, and in particular health and psychological effects are not yet fully investigated.

The biological effects of microwaves depend on both frequency band, intensity and exposure time. The so-called thermal effect resulting from the conversion of energy generated by electromagnetic fields into thermal energy, used in microwave ovens, is relatively well known. Direct influence of microwaves on the organism entails, among others, degeneration in the cells of parenchymal and myocardial organs, dystrophic processes in synapses and in the cells of various sections of the central nervous system (Marx, Hornowski, 1968). The Regulation of the Council of Ministers on occupational safety and health when using equipment generating electromagnetic fields in the microwave range (Journal of Laws No. 21, item 153 of 25 May 1972) which has been in force in Poland since 1972, establishes the so-called protection zones (indirect, hazardous and dangerous), defining the boundaries of individual zones on the basis of measurements of the average energy flux density expressed in watts per square meter (W/m^2).

Technical protection measures are divided into three groups of shielding: the radiation source, the workstation and the worker himself (protective clothing).

2.1.6 Vibration as mechanical vibration transmitted to the body

Mechanical vibrations transmitted from the external environment, mainly from various technical devices (e.g. tools, machines, vehicles, ships and aircrafts) on the basis of resonance to the human organism, called vibrations, are of a stressful nature.

In connection with the development of technical civilization and the emergence of a new type of human activity, the so-called operative, associated with the maintenance of technical devices, man is exposed to various types of mechanical vibrations transmitted to his organism from these devices. These vibrations with a frequency of 1–1000 Hz are harmful to humans, because they cause the so-called phenomenon of resonance, which occurs at very low frequencies (1–30 Hz), and absorb the mechanical energy of vibrations in tissues. The criterion for assessing physiological changes in the body under the influence of vibration is primarily the amount of transmitted energy, which can be determined by the following formula: $Q = ISt$; where: Q - amount of energy transferred, I - intensity of vibrations (N/s), S - area of contact (m^2), t - time of exposure (Turski, 2002).

The classification of human body reactions to vibration includes: subjective reactions, psychosomatic reactions and functional disorders of the organism.

They reduce to some extent the mental comfort and ability to work. And so, subjective reactions include, for example, headache, abdominal pain, chest pain, gluteal area, pressure on feces and urine, as well as reduced concentration, fatigue, drowsiness and general weakness. The intensity of the reaction depends, among other things, on the duration and magnitude of the vibration stimulus.

The effect of vibration, both local (mainly on hands) and general, causes in the organism disorders of system functions with sometimes very extensive effects. They have a negative effect on both the osteoarticular system and vegetative system (ischaemic changes associated with vascular contractions, anxiety); the effect of vibrations, especially vertical ones, on visual perception - so-called blurred vision, precision of movements in the vibration plane (so-called tremors of legs and hands) was also observed.

The long-term effects of vibration shall also be mentioned. For example, people working for years with pneumatic hammers, electric (combustion) saws are exposed to hand injuries. A characteristic symptom is, for example, greater sensitivity of hands to cold (Raynaud's disease). An industry worker can be exposed to two types of vibration: *general vibrations* - transmitted to the body and head via legs, pelvis, back or sides from a vibrating surface or seat; *local vibrations* - transmitted from a vibrating tool to the human body via the upper limbs.

The effect of vibrations depends not only on the frequency and amplitude of vibrations, but also remains dependent on the mutual movements of tissues or organs. At different frequencies, the most severe symptoms are caused by the resonance of certain organs. Knowing the resonance value of individual organs (e.g. digestive system, respiratory system, spine), so-called tolerance curves can be established, which take into account both the frequency and amplitude of vibrations, as well as their direction in relation to the body axis and duration of action. In recent years, occupational medicine has divided the vibration syndrome into the following seven syndromes: vascular dystonia syndrome, vasoconstriction syndrome, vegetative polyneuritis syndrome, vegetative myositis and fasciitis syndrome, neuritis syndrome, diencephalic syndrome with circulatory disorders, vestibular syndrome (Turski, op. cit.). The only protection against vibrations is their elimination through early detection and treatment of lesions and, above all, through ergonomic improvement of work stations and tools, which are a source of mechanical vibrations.

2.1.7 Hypoxia

In order for the human body to function properly, oxygen, which is part of the atmospheric air is required, along with other gases: nitrogen (78.09 %), oxygen

(20.95 %), argon (0.93 %), carbon dioxide (0.03 %), neon, helium, krypton and hydrogen. To be more precise, it is not just about oxygen alone, but rather about maintaining an optimal partial oxygen pressure, which at the sea level is at 159 mmHg (212 hPa). Thanks to homeostatic mechanisms that appeared in phylogenetic development, changes in atmospheric pressure within the range of 800–660 mmHg (1060–880 hPa), characteristic for barric pressure fluctuations on Earth, do not significantly change the partial oxygen pressure in the organism. However, the problem appears when ascending above sea level (mountaineering, aviation) with the subsequent reduction in atmospheric pressure and when descending below sea level (diving). Although, thanks to the existence of compensation mechanisms, man can maintain a certain balance within the system, despite changes in the external environment, the scope of changes in which people can function normally, however, is limited. For example, pressure below sea level, i.e. below 1013.3 hPa after reaching the depth of 10 m, increases to 2027 hPa and does not hamper the ability to work yet. At a depth of 20 m below sea level, the pressure of 3040 hPa already significantly reduces the ability to work, while at 30 meters, the pressure of 4053 hPa causes ear pain and rapid fatigue. These symptoms intensify at a depth of 40 meters below sea level at 5067 hPa. Below 50 m. if the pressure exceeds 6080 hPa, there is a so-called critical zone, in which acute sensory disturbances, nausea, vomiting, pulmonary oedema, respiratory paralysis, death, which are symptoms of "decompression sickness", whose treatment involves breathing pure oxygen to reduce other gases in the tissue, because the oxygen used by tissues in energetic processes is not released as bubbles damaging the tissues. This danger occurs in a situation of nitrogen accumulation in the blood of divers rapidly ascending to the surface, after staying at a considerable depth for too long, without "decompression stops" making readaptation easier. Moreover, the accumulation of nitrogen in the blood causes the so-called nitrogen narcosis, which reduces the situational awareness of the threat.

In turn, staying at altitudes above sea level, accompanied by a decrease in atmospheric pressure, is also of stressful character. And so, up to 2 thousand meters above sea level, the atmospheric pressure is equal to 750 hPa, which means that the pressure changes are within the limits of the system's adaptability (the so-called zone of working ability). Up to 5,500 meters the atmospheric pressure drops to 549 hPa, causing breathing difficulties (the so-called zone of poor working ability). At an altitude of 7.5 thousand atmospheric pressure is lowered to 439 hPa, resulting in a minimum ability to work, which is also evidenced by the fact that this altitude is not permanently inhabited by people. Finally, over 8,000 meters, the atmospheric pressure drops drastically to 338 hPa, which is the so-called critical zone, where staying requires the use of an oxygen device (Vaernes, 2007).

In the case of aviation, for example, the extent of these changes is determined by two factors: the magnitude and/or duration of changes in the partial oxygen pressure. Significant drop in the partial pressure of oxygen (e.g. in the case of sudden loss of cabin pressure in a passenger aircraft) leads to a shortage of oxygen in the system, which in turn causes functional disorders: physiological, behavioral. Different terms are used in the literature of the subject to describe the state of insufficient oxygen supply to the organism. The most commonly used term is *hypoxia* [gr. *hypó* – " under", *oxýs* – "acute", "sour"], which in medicine means lack of oxygen in relation to the organism's current needs. In the medical literature, in order to identify the same phenomenon, synonyms such as: "oxygen hunger" or "anoxia" are often encountered. Anoxia means a state of complete lack of oxygen, so it is not helpful in describing phenomena occurring under conditions of reduced oxygen content in the air. The terms "hypoxia" and "high altitude hypoxia" will be used interchangeably in this study to describe conditions where there is insufficient oxygen content in the inhaled air.

From the psychological point of view, it is important that the definition of high altitude hypoxia highlights the phenomenon of functional disorders of a physiological and performance nature. The tasks of the psychologist should focus on determining the level of performance and explaining the psychological and physiological mechanisms leading to the adaptation of the organism.

Generally speaking, the results of the studies conducted so far indicate high plasticity of human adaptation mechanisms to conditions of hypoxia in terms of cognitive processes and physiological reactions. An example of such adaptation are generations of people living at high altitudes, such as Peruvians or Tibetans. Such adaptation requires a number of adaptation processes which in the long run lead to the formation of wider blood vessels and a faster breathing rhythm. The lack of such long-term adaptation to functioning above 3048 m above sea level adversely affects human well-being and the achievement of the set objectives (e.g. mountaineering or piloting an aircraft).

From an information processing point of view, the findings on neuronal conduction disruption of the cerebral cortex due to hypoxia seem important. The conclusion from the previous studies is that the central nervous system is extremely sensitive to hypoxia. Taking into account the degree and duration of oxygen deficiency, we can distinguish between acute and chronic forms of hypoxia. Acute hypoxia is characteristic for a stay at high altitude in conditions of reduced atmospheric pressure (e.g. among mountaineers). Its symptoms include: increased heart rate, headaches, nausea, vomiting, muscle weakness, visual and hearing impairments and mental disorders (Sies, Joness, 2007). Chronic hypoxia is associated with long-term effects of oxygen deficiency. The symptoms are of psychasthenic nature: rapid physical fatigue and a sense of mental fatigue. Knowledge of the physiological and psychological effects of hypoxia is particularly important in situations where a person is staying in a changed or artificial environment, such as in the case of pilots or astronauts, and mainly when technical devices maintaining the optimal range of conditions fail (e.g. in the case of sudden loss of cabin pressure in an aircraft or damage to oxygen equipment). Since nerve cells are characterized by low resistance to "oxygen hunger", hypoxia disrupts the function of the nervous system, especially the central nervous system, which is known as a decompression illness. Decompression disease is a set of symptoms caused by the secretion of gas bubbles in tissues and body fluids as a result of a decrease in atmospheric pressure. Symptoms of decompression illness include: pain in the vicinity of large joints, muscles, chest, abdomen; weakness and numbness of limbs; severe dizziness; nystagmus; motor coordination disorders; dyspnoea; nausea and vomiting; bone necrosis; itching; urticaria; skin oedema. The risk of experiencing these symptoms and their intensity by air passengers during sudden decompression depends on its duration. The cerebral cortex hypoxia in the first place disturbs human mental functions. Researchers dealing with the influence of hypoxia on the mental state and efficiency suggest that the smallest height disturbing the sensomotor response time is about 5500 m, while the largest disorders occur above 7.5 thousand meters in the so-called death zone. For these reasons, pilots and mountaineers (Himalayan climbers) are obliged to stay in oxygen masks at these heights.

Studies on psychological effects of hypoxia can be divided into the ones conducted in natural (mountains) or laboratory conditions. Observations carried out in natural conditions (mainly of mountaineers) provide data on the occurrence of subjective symptoms of hypoxia depending on its degree and duration of action. It is also interesting to investigate psychological mechanisms underlying irrational decisions (despite possessed knowledge about the danger of death), resembling the "Russian roulette in the tsarist army", concerning the beating of specific world records of climbing the eight-thousanders without the oxygen apparatus. Meanwhile, acute hypoxia almost always causes functional disorders of physiological systems, and as a consequence leads to death. And so, e.g. in the initial states of hypoxia, there is a high emotional expression during conversations (gestures, raised voice, etc.), an increase in mood (cheerfulness), striving for active activity (often at the expense of quality). At the same time, as in the case of alcohol poisoning, this is accompanied by a reduction in self-criticism. This way of reacting to hypoxia is sometimes referred to in the literature of the subject as the state of *high-altitude euphoria*. At the same time, another behavior, characterized by contradictory symptoms, can be observed: depressive states, mood deprivation, decrease in activity, feeling of fatigue, sleepiness, etc. Both of these ways of reacting to hypoxia can occur alternately. Particularly dangerous (e.g. in aviation) is the situation of transition from high-altitude euphoria to unconsciousness without any intermediate states. Because mental disorders precede sometimes life-threatening organic disorders, psychological examinations in the hypoxia conditions have an important preventive significance. Although the lack of standard psychological tests for early detection of stressful psychological effects of hypoxia is the cause of controversial research results, literature analysis shows that the authors agree that the results of psychological tests requiring so-called selective attention (attention sharing) worsen under acute hypoxia conditions (altitude above 4000 m). An example of this type of test most commonly used in simulated pressure cabin conditions (diving chambers) is the arithmetic test of " subtracting from 1000", shown in Fig. 2.3.

As you can see, the longer the time spent at an altitude of 7.5 thousand meters, the worse the graphic structure of handwriting and mental fitness, which is reflected in the logical errors appearing in a simple arithmetical test. In other own research carried out in the diving chamber, adapted to create conditions of hypoxia occurring in aviation, after 20 minutes of pilots staying at an altitude of 5500 m above sea level, times of simple reaction with choice was recorded and a chase tracking test with motor compensation was given as a task. The follow-up group also stayed in the diving chamber, but without hypoxia (placebo). It was found that high altitude hypoxia at an altitude of 5500 m above sea level negatively affects human cognitive processes and psychomotoric functioning (Terelak, Truszczyński, 1999). This means, among other things, that altitude hypoxia primarily impairs active information processing processes, and to a lesser extent - automatic actions. Another little-known factor associated with working in unusual conditions is overload due to the occurrence of accelerations that are related to the speed variation in time, e.g. of an aircraft or spacecraft (during take-off and landing).

2.1.8 Accelerations exceeding the Earth's gravitational values

Accelerations, which are a consequence of a sudden change in speed and direction of movement, result in disorders of the system's function caused by the action of the force of inertia. Let us recall that the unit of acceleration is cm/s^2 or m/s^2. More often, however, the value of acceleration is defined in g units, assuming that 1 g is the gravitational acceleration of the Earth equal to 9.81 m/s^2. Using this unit, acceleration can be defined as a multiple of gravitational acceleration. According to Newton's second law of motion, it is also possible to calculate the

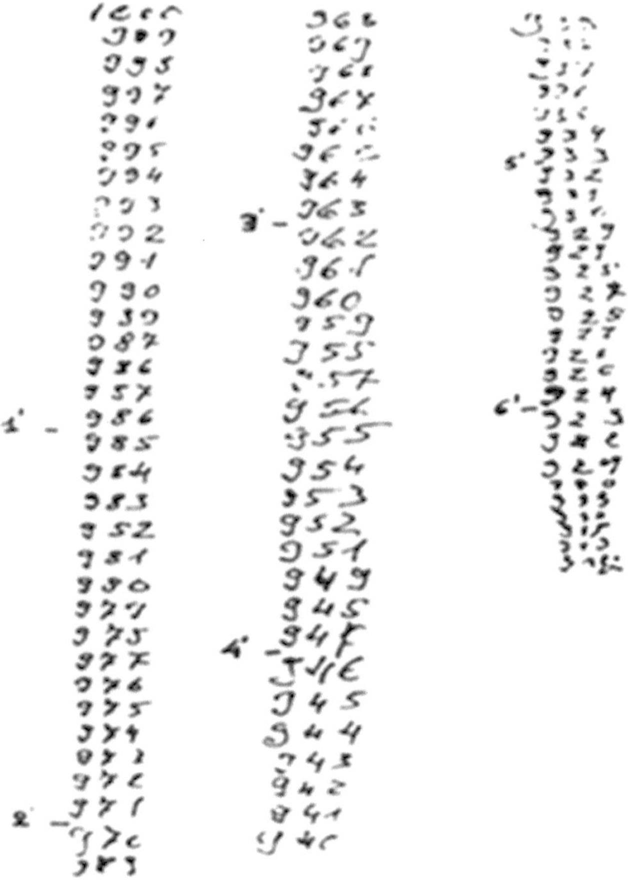

Fig. 2.3: Results of an arithmetic test of " subtracting from 1000" in the diving chamber at a simulated height of 7500 m. (Source: Terelak, Truszczyński, 1999, own research)

value of the force applied to the body if its weight and acceleration are known. According to Newton's third law of motion, this force releases a centrifugal force of equal value, but with the opposite direction, associated with the inertia of the body. The vector of this force is at the same time the direction of changes taking place in the system. The influence of mechanical forces acting under these conditions on the pilot's organism is referred to as *overload* in aviation medicine This is an isolated value indicating the ratio between the weight of the body at the moment of acceleration and its actual weight. In other words, it is a number indicating how many times the force with which the accelerating body acts exceeds the weight of the accelerated body. So for example, during curvilinear flight, a pilot weighing 80 kg, at the acceleration of 50 m/s^2 (i.e. 5g) will be subjected to a centripetal force of 400 kg, i.e. he will weigh this much.

From the physics point of view, we divide acceleration as occurring: 1) in rectilinear motion due to the change of speed of motion; 2) in curvilinear motion, otherwise known as centripetal motion, in which the direction of motion changes; 3) during the change of angular speed of motion, called angular accelerations; 4) as a result of the summation of different types of accelerations and defined as complex. When the speed increases, positive acceleration occurs, whereas when the speed decreases, negative acceleration, otherwise known as deceleration or braking, occurs. Positive accelerations occur during take-offs of airplanes with the use of afterburner, launch missiles or with the use of catapults, launches of rocket sledges, space vehicles, as well as during the evacuation of aircraft by catapulting. Negative linear accelerations occur during an emergency landing of an airplane, rocket sledge braking, parachute opening and landing in airplanes or other devices shortening the length of an airplane's run-down. They reach high values when the stopping distance is short. If the plane travels with a constant speed but still changes direction of flight, its acceleration is curvilinear. Such accelerations are most often found in such pilotage figures as: diving, turns, loops, half loops, Immelmann turns, spins, aileron rolls and others. When an airplane changes both velocity and direction of flight, angular accelerations occur.

When discussing acceleration from a biological and psychological point of view, the direction of acceleration in relation to the axis of the body should be taken into account. Overload of the organism is distinguished in aviation medicine as a result of different directions of acceleration: directions with (-) are corresponding to negative acceleration, and with (+) - positive acceleration. The direction of acceleration in the three main axes x, y, z, as shown in Fig. 2.4 is determined by the rotation of the human body in space.

The division of accelerations adopted in aviation medicine is based on the direction of blood movement as a result of its action and, unlike earth acceleration (g), it is marked with a capital letter G. The directions of acceleration are marked as follows: 1) in the sagittal axis: from sternum to back +Gx, from back to sternum -Gx; 2) in the longitudinal axis of the body: from head to feet, from feet to head -Gz; 3) in the transverse axis: from right to left+Gy and from left to right -Gy (as in: Mikuliszyn, Żebrowski, 2002). However, attention should be paid to the method of determining the limit of biological and physiological tolerance of accelerations, which is determined by this value of accelerations, beyond which disturbances of system functions leading to

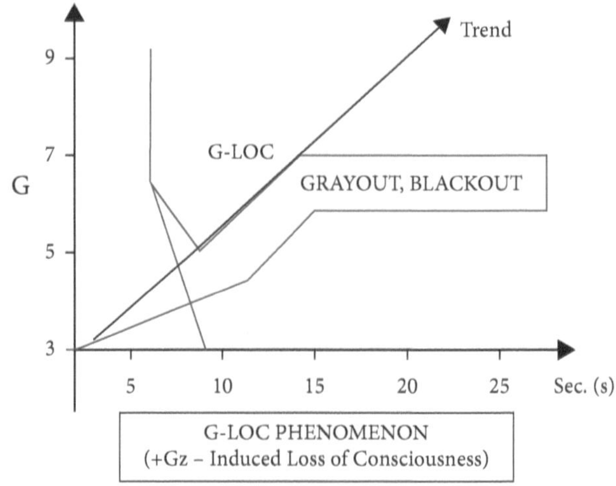

Fig. 2.4: Increasing impact accelerations lead to loss of consciousness of the pilot (Source: own elaboration based on Barański, ed. 1977).

impairment of human psychophysical fitness occur, while maintaining, however, full organism efficiency and lack of pathological changes. The limit of biological tolerance is at the same time the line between life and death. These limits are assessed in detail during the rotation in the centrifuge (overload centrifuge). During the flight, the most common acceleration is the centripetal acceleration, during which the centrifugal force acts parallel to the long axis of the body in the direction from head to legs. Under these conditions there is a strong effect of acceleration on blood in blood vessels. Changes in the distribution of blood and body fluids occur. The blood begins to move to the lower parts of the body. Thus, there is a drop in blood pressure in the upper areas and their ischemia, while in the area of hips and lower extremities there is an increase in blood pressure, congestion and stagnation. During this time, pilots often complain about unpleasant feelings of swelling, tingling, pain in the lower legs (Terelak, Jasiński, 1999).

Even during the accumulation of low acceleration values, significant differences in hydrostatic pressure in the vascular system occur. The changes mainly concern pressure values, e.g. femoral vein pressure increases due to accumulated blood in blood vessels of lower limbs. However, in the case of e.g. +5 Gz, the hydrostatic pressure can be as high as +370 mmHg in the lower limbs, 220 mmHg at the thigh level, 120 mmHg at shoulder level, and 0 mmHg at the head level. The effect of accelerations on the organism is multilateral. They very rarely affect only one of its functions, e.g. manual dexterity, body movements or speech or vision (Terelak, Jasiński,1999). The behavioral and psychological effects of acceleration fall into three categories:

2.1.8.1 Restrictions on arbitrary movements

As we know, the reference point for the magnitude of accelerations is the value of earth acceleration 1 Gz, which is practically not perceived by humans. In the case of +Gz accelerations, the first sensation experienced by the pilot during the flight is that the body is pressed into the base of the seat. As the acceleration increases, the weight of the entire body increases. Keeping the head upright is becoming more and more difficult, and movements of the limbs are only possible up to certain limits, which significantly hinders motor coordination due to acceleration of +Gz. Changing from sitting to standing position becomes practically impossible in these conditions.

As shown in Fig. 2.5 although in a well-balanced sitting position the pilot can withstand even +12 Gz, negative accelerations -Gz, occurring when the inertia force acts in the direction from leg to head and its vector is parallel to the long axis of the body, characteristic for pilotage figures in the inverted position (aileron roll, inverted loop, back spin, etc.) and for catapulting during the flight may result in spatial orientation disorders and loss of consciousness. Man can relatively best tolerate the so-called transverse accelerations in the direction of +Gx and -Gx as well as +Gy and -Gy. Can also endure a transverse acceleration three times stronger than the longitudinal -Gz.

2.1.8.2 Loss of consciousness caused by acceleration +Gz

In recent years, many researchers have drawn attention to the phenomenon of consciousness disorder and loss of consciousness during exposure to +Gz, abbreviated as *G-LOC phenomenon (+Gz Induced Loss of Consciouness)* .

Haemodynamic disorders occurring at the head level as a result of acceleration in the +Gz direction are symptoms of central nervous system hypoxia. The indication of this type of disturbances is initially the loss of peripheral vision (*grey out*), and a moment later also of central vision (*black out*) (Terelak, 2002), which is preceded by tunnel vision. Visual disorders precede loss of consciousness in psychological and biological sense, which can lead to clinical death in a short period of time. Aviation doctors point to the difficulties of investigating the *G-LOC phenomenon* consisting mainly in the fact that it is accompanied by temporary amnesia or a known psychological defensive mechanism of suppression.

In addition, the phenomenon also has a subjective dimension, which can be most generally characterized as psychological reactions, described by pilots: embarrassment, disorientation, loss of sense of reality, confusion, difficulties in assessing the situation, split personality (dissociation), euphoria, anxiety, fear, contradictory feeling, desire to reduce height, etc. The impact on flight safety is not precisely known for the reasons given above. The impact of the *G-LOC phenomenon* on flight safety is not known in detail for the reasons given above. The most serious symptom, however, is the 15 second long disturbance of orientation in the surroundings, which may lead to an air crash (Wojtkowiak, 2002).

2.1.8.3 Aviation illusions, the so-called somatogravic illusion

Aviation illusions are a separate important aspect of pilot's work and are associated with the perception of movement, body rotation and accelerations. The basis for somatogravic illusions are false sensations resulting from stimulation of otolith organs by linear accelerations. These are, therefore, feelings of spatial disorientation, in which a person subjected to linear acceleration in terms of gravity, feels the direction of force resulting from acceleration as if it was caused by gravity attraction (Kaczorowski, 2002). An example of spatial disorientation as a somatogravic illusion is shown in Fig. 2.5.

As shown in Fig. 2.5, the illusion of linear motion occurs when the resultant of gravitational force and centrifugal force coincide with the vertical axis in relation to the pilot. As a consequence, the pilot does not feel the turn as he does

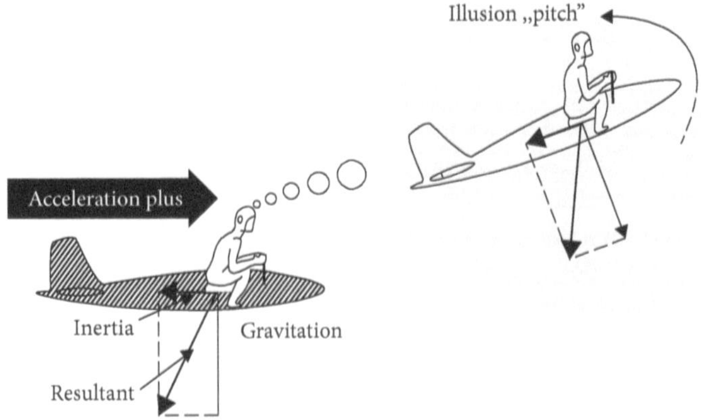

Fig. 2.5: Example of somatogravic illusion of a "nose up" sensation during positive acceleration (Source: own elaboration based on: Barański, ed. 1977)

not obtain information about angular accelerations and identifies the centrifugal force as the force of gravity.

The classification of aviation illusions includes:

1. *Vestibular illusions* - resulting from disturbances in the integration of impulses coming from three systems: visual organ, proprioreceptors and osseous labyrinth. They are characterized by an abnormality in transmitting stimuli from the vestibular organ to the central nervous system, which causes typical symptoms in the form of dizziness, nystagmus, imbalance.
   (a) *Tilt illusion in the direction of motion or vice versa* - typically occurring during instrument flight when an plane suddenly makes a quick lean to the left or right and then returns to its initial position. The pilot then feels that the aircraft is still tilted despite the fact that the flight is horizontal and straight ahead. The pilot will not notice the return of the plane to its initial position (if he does not observe the instruments), because this movement has a certain perception threshold.
   (b) *Inclination illusions* - resulting from the same mechanisms as tilt illusions, except that the pilot feels that the airplane ascends ("nose up") or descends ("nose down"), although it is flying horizontally and straight ahead, as illustrated in Fig. 2.5.
2. *Mixed illusions* (visual, vestibular, somatic) - causing spatial disorientation, being disturbances of integration and interpretation of stimuli coming from three systems: vision, proprioreceptors and osseous labyrinth. Types of these illusions depend on the action of angular or linear accelerations and concern false sensations of the spatial position of the body (and plane). These include:

   (a) *Optical-rotational illusions* - sometimes referred to by pilots as 'visual dizziness'. They are caused by the uncontrolled eyeballs movement (nystagmus) due to the excitation of the semicircular canals by angular acceleration and consist in the pilot feeling that objects in his field of vision rotate in the opposite direction to the rotation. This type of illusion can be observed in unrealistic movements of an object, in the cabin during rotation, in the Coriolis acceleration, in spins, etc.
   (b) *Optical-gravitational illusions* - based on false sensations due to stimulation of otolith organs by linear accelerations. Thus, these are feelings of spatial disorientation in which a person subjected to linear acceleration in terms of the force of gravity, perceives the direction of the force resulting from acceleration as if it was caused by gravity. The result is the illusion of moving an object, i.e. the apparent movement of a visual target, resembling moving from side to side or forward, backward, up and down.

The most common optical-gravitational illusions occurring during various types of manoeuvres can be classified as follows: (a) impression of ascending when tilting when turning; (b) impression of diving when exiting a turn; (c) impression of diving when exiting a diving flight; (d) impression of tilting in the opposite direction when turning with sliding outwards. A more detailed description of aviation illusions can be found in the works on aviation physiology and physiology (Kowalski, ed. 2002).

Finishing the characteristics of acceleration as a source of stress, one should pay attention to the fact that it is possible to increase the tolerance of overloads by only 1–2 g, using such projects as: a special overload suit, the so-called "intelligent seat" (automatically regulating its position), automatic pilot (piloting after a loss of consciousness of the pilot), special bodybuilding training (increasing muscle mass as a "barrier" against overloads), breathing training in hypertension under hypertension (consisting in reversing the order of expiration of air from the lungs from passive to active phase during overload). In addition, it should be mentioned that aviation illusions caused by accelerations will not be eliminated even by duplication of pilot instruments in the airplane or by the selection of pilots, because the only effective way is to lead (through work with a flight instructor) to a loss of faith in the "truthfulness" of one's senses (balance system, vision, proprioception) and restore faith in the indication of instruments. The falsity of sensory impressions and insights is the result of incorrect information sent to the brain under different types of accelerations. That is why the wrong analysis is the basis for all kinds of aviation illusions with so much suggestive power that pilots are willing to believe their senses and not the objective indications of navigation devices (which is often the cause of disasters in military aviation). Getting rid of confidence in one's own senses is a difficult process and involves long term aviation experience.

A completely unique stress factor for living beings, in both ontogenetic and phylogenetic development, since the middle of the 20th century is the situation of lack of gravity, i.e. the state of weightlessness. The construction of an international space station placed in orbit around the Earth and the dynamic development of astronautics for scientific and commercial purposes make the interest in this unique experience in the entire history of mankind grow in the 21st century, not only for purely cognitive reasons.

2.1.9 Zero gravity as a contradiction to the law of gravitation of the Earth

At the beginning it should be noted that the experiences with weightlessness are for the human species the newest in the entire phylogenetic development, because it is hindered by the vestibular system (balance organ), located in the middle ear, which provides the brain with important information about the spatial position of a person in relation to the vector of the gravity of the Earth. Recalibrating this organ to the lack of gravity is very difficult and has health and psychological consequences. It also requires many exercises, first in conditions of microgravity (e.g. underwater) and then completely without gravity (e.g. obtaining a short-term weightless state for a period of several dozen seconds inside an airplane performing a parabolic flight along the Kepler curve). Calibration of the vestibular system works in both directions, both in the case of transition from the state of gravity to weightlessness, and in the case of return from the Cosmos to the Earth or another planet. The level of difficulty in the transition from microgravity conditions to gravity can be illustrated by experiences from early childhood. On the one hand, while staying in microgravity conditions for the entire period of pregnancy in the immersion in fetal waters, our brain does not receive adequate impulses informing about the gravitational requirements of the external world. Therefore, the process of adaptation to full gravity is difficult and long-lasting, as evidenced by the different phases of the child's upright standing and visual-motor coordination, such as: rolling, creeping, crawling, unstable first independent steps, running, avoiding obstacles on the road, difficulties in maintaining balance while riding a bike, etc. The spatial coordination habits remain for life, but the described situation during early childhood is repeated after the astronaut's return from a long space flight or landing on other planets.

Weightlessness, as a state in which the body is not affected by gravity force, in the first phase causes in a person a cognitive dissonance at the level of sensation of weight loss while maintaining weight. This results in the so-called acute state of adaptation, which, according to the relations of novice astronauts, can be described in two phases. In the first phase, involuntary movement reactions appear, accompanied by fear and an impression of falling (waving hands, grabbing objects in the vicinity and the sensation of falling down). In the second phase, there is an increased emotional and motor activity with a predominance of positive emotions (joy and euphoria). Movements in this phase are already under partial control and the impression of falling down ceases. Along with gaining experience with the state of weightlessness, the so-called passive pattern of emotional adaptation appears, which is accompanied by even more difficulties in performing deliberate movements and the illusion of spatial orientation of overturn or upward ascent, and sometimes there are more or less clear symptoms of motion sickness. A characteristic feature of short-term stress of weightlessness is the phenomenon of "emotion dissociation" of either anxiety (e.g. fear of falling as evidenced by uncoordinated grabbing movements and rapid search for support) or alternately euphoric nature (Hermaszewski, 2017). Together with gaining experience with the state of weightlessness, there is rather a phenomenon of negation of emotions, consisting in the fact that the same emotional factor, originally focused on one's own experiences (dissociation of emotions), has a mobilizing effect on task-oriented motivational processes, which has been called an "active adaptation" to the state of weightlessness. This does not mean full adaptation, because e.g. in the case of some cosmonauts, in conditions of weightlessness, the time of processing digital signals is still increasing, the visual-motor coordination is worsening, caused by probably insufficient balance of antagonistic muscles effort in weightlessness, especially horizontal or loop movements (fast and rhythmic movements). There has also been a decline in the sense of hand location during the writing test. Details of significant localization errors can be found in the upward or downward tilting of the hand. Localization errors were also observed within the visual system. For example, in the initial contact with weightlessness, a person does not see the ambiguity of the figures (e.g. drawing of the weight vs. head profiles), which disappears after the adaptation period. The medical effects of weightlessness can be described as follows: blood flows in excess into the head and chest, tears do not want to flow, often flashes of light appear in front of the eyes (which hypothetically is associated with the penetration of cosmic radiation particles through the cover of the space habitat and the brains of astronauts), shrinking heart muscle (which causes a decrease in cardiovascular capacity), frequent dizziness and nausea (so-called "motor disease"), breathing difficulties, bone decalcification and slowed bone growth and brittleness (cosmic osteoporosis), muscle relaxation, loss of sense of body weight (which makes motor coordination difficult) (Kwarecki, Terelak, 1980).

The presented results of observation of astronauts in real conditions of long-term weightlessness indicate first of all medical consequences caused by such factors as: lack of stimuli registration by appropriate gravitation receptors located in the inner ear, lack of static and dynamic loads affecting the musculoskeletal system, elimination of hydrostatic pressure of blood and tissue fluids.

Since the state of weightlessness is not experienced under normal gravity conditions (1 g), man does not have innate adaptation mechanisms to such extreme living conditions in the space. Numerous observations of cosmonauts or astronauts as well as biological and medical research convince us about it. The basic medical effects of staying in weightlessness concern disorders of blood redistribution accompanying long-term weightlessness. Lack of gravity (1 g) causes the blood to remain in the upper half of the astronaut's body, and most of it at the head level (180 mmHg), which leads to increased intracranial pressure and acute headache, as well as to vision disorders (e.g. eye burning) caused by the pressure of body fluids on the visual nerve (the so-called moon face of astronauts). On the other hand, there is drastic hypoxia of the lower half of the body, which together with the lack of muscle load leads to a leaching of calcium in the bones, resulting in symptoms of acute osteoporosis and susceptibility to fracture after returning to Earth. In addition, leaching calcium from the bone results in its accumulation in the kidneys and bladder, which often results in kidney stones (e.g. renal colic attacks). Finally, an initial comparative study carried out on astronaut Scott Kelly, who stayed on the International Space Station for 340 days, and his twin brother who at the same time stayed on Earth, shows, among other things, that under conditions of weightlessness at the cellular level, we age slower and that our immune system works worse (for example, wounds heal longer). The mechanisms of these symptoms are the subject of analysis in space medicine. Not without significance is the information that astronauts deprived of gravity for a longer period of time are several centimeters higher, compared to the measurement taken on Earth before the space flight.

Apart from the state of weightlessness, which in the period of adaptation is the cause of disruption of position in space, reduced ability to work, reduced motor activity (hypokinesia), discomfort, etc., other sources of stress are mentioned, such as: s small living area, diet specification (lack of fresh and natural products, water recovered from metabolic products, lack of a clear daily cycle - 16 days and nights, specific microclimate (regeneration of the same air), the need to work in the same team, limited possibility of rest and relaxation, lack of intimacy, work overload, necessity of constant vigilance (watches), penetration of life-threatening cosmic radiation into the spacecraft, threat from small meteorites while being outside of the spacecraft to repair its external surfaces, etc. These factors were the subject of own research at the space station Salut-6, carried out under the international programme "Intercosmos - PAN" under the code names "Space Questionnaire" and "Relax" (Terelak, 1989). This questionnaire, containing 100 questions, concerned the evaluation (on a 10-stage scale) of the impact of 9 categories of space flight factors and living conditions on the self-assessment of the mental state of astronauts (cognitive processes such as perceptiveness, attention, memory, visual and motor coordination, sleep method, comfort, forms of rest, interpersonal contacts and preferences for the organization of leisure time).

These studies show, among other things, that two groups of difficulties caused by weightlessness are important for astronomers: limitation of work ability and discomfort connected with small size of a space station. For example, the inability of adequate gravitational receptors to register stimuli leads to sensory illusions, spatial disorientation and response from the vestibular ear (so-called motor disease). The lack of customary load on the musculoskeletal system leads on the one hand to atrophy of the musculoskeletal system, and on the other hand to a significant disorder of visual and motor coordination. The situation of weightlessness, as a completely new one, causes psychological stress, connected with the necessity to change not only movement habits, but also existing behaviors and preferences (e.g. sleeping "on a hanger in a wardrobe") (Kozerenko, Terelak, Miksik, 1991). Depending on the length of time a person is in a state of weightlessness, there are two phases: stress and so called acute adaptation. In a stress phase that usually lasts several hours, symptoms of discomfort, anxiety, spatial orientation disorders (relativity of the terms "up - down" or "left - right") appear. This is also confirmed by the cosmonauts in colloquial comments, such as the Polish cosmonaut Mirosław Hermaszewski (2017): *"Initially, I had the strange feeling that blood was flowing into my head with each beat of my heart, that my head is becoming heavier and heavier. After 20 minutes I had the impression that regardless of my position, I was still hanging with my head upside down. But after two hours the osseous labyrinth stopped fooling and everything returned to normal… However, careful movement remained."* Within a few days the cosmonaut achieves a state of relative adaptation, although it is not a goal in itself, as it is a transition state for re-adaptation to earthly conditions or to reduced gravitation on another planet (Terelak, Truszczyński, 1992).

From a psychological point of view, the transfer of movement habits and visual-motor coordination necessary to perform manual-type work is a difficult problem. The problem of the transfer of working habits will be illustrated by the experience of the first astronauts who landed on the Moon, who in conditions of reduced gravity on the Moon were performing activities practiced on Earth almost 30 % of the time longer than predicted in precisely designed graphics. It should be added that the extension of motion duration and disrupted visual-motor coordination are not only the result of reduced gravity (in the case of the Moon) or weightlessness (in open space), but are also caused by a rather uncomfortable suit. The presence of astronauts in open space and on the Moon proves that human activity in altered gravity (and total weightlessness) is possible, as evidenced by technical and research operations outside the spacecraft. However, the problem of changing the structure of action in conditions of changed gravitation remains unresolved. The literature draws attention to the wide variety of reactions in conditions of weightlessness: sensory, motor, emotional and vegetative. There are four approaches to their description (as in: Christensen, Talbot, 1986).

1. The pragmatic approach - describing the degree of deterioration of general wellbeing and reduced ability to work. The supporters of this approach dichotomize reactions in conditions of weightlessness, distinguishing reactions that increase or decrease the ability to work, and scale the intensity (strength) of these reactions.
2. The functional and physiological approach - describes the extent and degree of physiological changes accompanying the deterioration of general wellbeing and work ability. It is sometimes referred to as the so-called physiological cost accompanying the adaptation to the state of weightlessness.
3. The self-observer approach - this is creating a so-called internal viewpoint based on data from self-observation, visions and spatial illusions. These data, although very interesting, because they concern internal experiences of a human being in conditions of weightlessness, as inaccessible to an external observer, are of little scientific importance.
4. The external observer approach - focuses on data from observations of behavioral reactions and emotional and motor behaviors in a state of weightlessness.

It is also worth noting the visual illusions created in conditions of short-term stress of weightlessness. Among experienced cosmonauts, possible changes in visual perception took the form of distortion of perception of depth. The best known visual illusion in the state of weightlessness is the so-called autokinetic phenomenon, consisting in the apparent movement of orientation points. There were also illusions of an apparent growing distance from the objects or their enlargement, belonging to the same category of illusions. This apparent periodic shift of the visual orientation point is a nystagmus-like manifestation of an autokinetic phenomenon, caused, among other things, by the temporary domination of cumulative vestibular tonic interactions that cause the eyeball to move upwards, blocking compensation signals that induce the eye to lower the eyeball. Such disturbances in the visual assessment of distance reduce the reliability of action in situations when it is necessary to switch to the so-called manual control of a spaceship (Kitajew, 1989). An example could be a significant event during the landing of astronauts on the surface of the Moon. It is worth remembering that Neil Armstrong, an astronaut from the Apollo-11 program, had great difficulties with visual assessment of the altitude during the landing using the manual control system (automatic control of the lander was pushing it to the slope of the crater, which was about 180 m deep). Not without significance in the formation of spatial orientation disturbances in conditions of weightlessness is the lack of gravitational data essential for maintaining the vertical position (the Earth's gravity stabilizing the vertical posture of the body). Learning weightlessness orientation requires a rather complex brain process. New mental programs of spatial orientation together with the experience of astronauts stabilize to such an extent that manual work is becoming less and less difficult (Kwarecki, Terelak, 1980).

We have omitted to discuss some of the difficulties in everyday life at the space station caused by weightlessness, such as eating, bathing, physiological needs, sleeping, etc., because there is a plethora of literature based on the self-observation of cosmonauts. For example, Polish cosmonaut Mirosław Hermaszewski (2017) recalls it like that: *"I had a problem at night. I decided to sleep unattached, drifting freely inside the cabin. I just wanted to feel what it was like to sleep, floating in the air. But it wasn't so easy… During my sleep this saving air movement carried me around the entire cabin, hit the ceiling, woke me up. I had no choice, I had to fasten myself to the wall. […] The Russians solved the problem of bathing in conditions of weightlessness very amusingly. A transparent film sleeve was installed at the station, which was fixed on one side to the ceiling and on the other side to the floor. The water was sucked out at the bottom and its forced movement gave a perfect illusion of the shower on the Earth. Despite the weightlessness, it seemed as if a stream of water was pouring onto the head. The bathing cosmonaut breathed through a pipe led out to the outside of the shower, just like a diver. But there was still one problem with bathing. In the conditions of weightlessness the water wasn't running down the skin. It was sticking to it and forming a glassy shell on the body. Once I was tempted to wash my face with water. When I looked into the mirror later on, I looked as if I had been covered with chilled icing".*

Based on the results of experimental research and previous experience from orbital flights, it should be noted that the psychological analysis of human behavior in a spaceship or space station cannot only be related to the lack of gravity. This is especially relevant for interplanetary flights, in which, in addition to the survival of the human species in a state of weightlessness, the still unknown effects of long-term isolation from the cultural and social realities of the Earth are the main problem. We will return to these issues when discussing psychological stress factors. However, it is worth mentioning at this point that in many different laboratory tests or in real conditions, attempts are being made to create different types of Martian analogues in the form of habitats in which the behavior of individuals or small task groups in a situation of long-term social isolation is observed or the ability to cope with various unexpected life-threatening tasks in extreme conditions is being assessed. An example could be a Martian project under the code name *Hawaii Space Exploration Analog and Simulation (HI-SEAS)*, carried out in an isolated habitat (similar to Mars on the Mauna Loa side) in the "saddle" area of the Island of Hawai'i at an altitude of about 8200 feet above sea level. The HI-SEAS crew is deliberately selected for specific research tasks (as opposed to unexpected analogs such as Antarctic stations). The crew selection criteria are not controlled by scientists, and living conditions (residence, mission, communication, etc.) are clearly designed to meet the requirements of a future planetary mission, such as geological field work carried out by human explorers and/or robots. The ability to select crew members for specific mission profiles makes HI-SEAS the ideal tool for detailed research on behavioral dynamics, roles and crew effectiveness in space, especially in the case of long-term missions. Three HI-SEAS missions have been completed so far, two of them lasting 4 months each, one - 8 months and one lasting 12 months (Binsted, et al., 2016) www.hi-seas.org). Extrapolation of conclusions from such research for future Martian missions raises a lot of controversy, among others because of their low level of predictive accuracy. This is confirmed by modern space research of a logistic nature, focused on the development of the orbiting space station (its weight is about 500 tons), which on the one hand will be a scientific and industrial laboratory, and on the other - an intermediate stage during the flight to Mars or other planets. The problem to be solved is the standardization of connections with an international space station, enabling the berthing of about 30 space modules (laboratories). It is expected that in the future a hotel base for astronauts (researchers and tourists) and an overload centrifuge will be created, which would reduce the effects of weightlessness on the human body. A separate stress problem of astronauts are the so-called space debris and the effects of collisions with them, damaging ships and space stations, which need to be permanently repaired from the outside in open space. The damage caused by space debris is not only of an economic nature, but above all it threatens the survival in spaceships staying in space for a long time. Therefore, specialized space "vacuum cleaners" were developed and implemented, in the form of automatically controlled space shuttles, which can remain in orbit for about 270 days.

We have omitted another important source of stress associated with space flight, namely a significant acceleration at the launch of a space rocket and during the approach to Earth (landing or water-landing) after a completed space mission, the astronaut's organism is again exposed to sudden changes in gravitational conditions. They require multiple adaptations within the extreme limits of overload and weightlessness. And so for example in the case of the mission to the Moon, the adaptation cycle included: gravity acceleration of the Earth 9.806g - acceleration of the rocket during the launch into comic space several times greater than the acceleration of the earth - weightlessness 0g - acceleration during the landing on the Moon - gravitational acceleration of the Moon 1.622g (six times smaller than the Earth's) - acceleration associated with the launch from the Moon into space - weightlessness 0g - acceleration associated with the atmospheric entry 2–7g - gravitational acceleration of the Earth - 9.806g. The above mentioned stages of adaptive dynamics of the organism result not only in comfort vs. discomfort, but also in the efficiency of action (e.g. the fact that the astronauts on the Moon used only 30 % of their habits learned on the Earth in the field of psychomotor coordination, caused that they did not perform all the tasks planned on the Earth on the Moon despite the high motivation). On the other hand, significant accelerations at the launch of a space rocket and during the approach to Earth and launching after a completed space mission pose a great threat to astronauts. In addition, the high temperatures on the shells of a spaceship of up to 1,200 degrees Celsius associated with the friction of a ship passing through dense layers of the Earth's atmosphere are also a major stress.

2.1.10 Other environmental stress factors

At the end of the review of environmental stress sources, it should be emphasized that we focused only on those physical stress factors that are specific to extreme working conditions. We have omitted many others that are of a stressful character in the working environment and the surrounding nature, such as parasites, bacteria, viruses, molds, fungi, industrial and combat gases, carbon monoxide, lead, organic solvents (e.g. BTX), infrared radiation, acids, phosphorus, dust, mercury, mineral oils, tar, soot, eternit, aniline, etc. Consider, for example, the destructive effect of carbon dioxide in the form of smog. As it was explicitly formulated in 1922 by Alexei Pavlov, a Russian geologist of the author of the name of "Anthropocene epoch", in which man, considering himself to be the "navel of the world", became its greatest threat. Today we can say that this epoch is still valid, as highlighted by the latest book by Naomi Klein (2016), which presents in a comprehensive and accessible way the dangers of global warming and other climate change, placing them in a broad political, economic and social context. It is predicted that in 2037 such concentration of environmental pollution means an increase in global temperatures by two degrees Celsius, which is considered by experts to be relatively safe limit, beyond which there will be an increase in temperatures that may cause unpredictable consequences, related to the so-called greenhouse effect.

Dynamic industrialization processes have resulted in the highest level of carbon dioxide in the world's atmosphere in more than 400,000 years and have led to a systematic rise in the Earth's average temperature, which has risen by about 0.7°C on average over the last 100 years (data from the Intergovernmental Panel on Climate Change, (IPCC). The consequences of this seemingly small change of the Earth's temperature are so large, that we observe the growth of the so-called ozone hole above the geographical poles (the lack of atmosphere leads to the penetration of cosmic rays that are deadly for living creatures). It also causes the melting of huge areas of glacial cover not only in Antarctica and the Arctic, but also in high parts of the mountains (which results in rising sea levels and consequently endangers the flooding of many river deltas and coasts). The Kyoto Protocol, which has already been signed by more than 140 countries and which is committed to reducing carbon dioxide emissions, is a symbol of public awareness of the threat of this gas. Maintaining a dynamic balance between nature and man in counteracting the greenhouse effect is not only man's responsibility, as more and more often the primary role in global warming of various solar disturbances is emphasized.

The attempt to explain precisely the mechanism of the threat posed by the greenhouse effect in comparison to other threats in the methodology of modern ecology is not yet precise and still give rise to discussions. However, the threat is of a global character, with significant consequences not only for the present one, but also for future generations. It is also the most important challenge for scientific research and environmental education, as it requires, on the one hand, recreation of the history of our planet and, on the other hand, continuous observation of the dynamics of the Sun's activity, orbital changes in our solar system and the impact on the Earth of Jupiter and Saturn. On the other hand, changes in solar energy supply are the effect of changes in reflection or absorption of radiation, limiting the so-called cooling effect at the poles due to the rapid melting of glaciers in the last half-century. A significant percentage of the presented process of climate change is caused by pollution of the environment by man and interference with nature, which has been pointed out earlier.

2.2 Chronobiological environment as a source of stress

One can agree with the well-known Canadian neuropsychologist D.O. Hebb (1965), who once said that the basic question faced by a physiologist or psychologist is not "Why does a person take action in different periods of his life?", but "why in some periods of time a person's activity and effectiveness changes and is disturbed, while in others it is not?".

Answers to these questions are difficult due to the perspective of time - past, present and future - which includes the relationship between physical time (objective) and psychological time (subjective), from which it results that some physical dimensions of time (e.g. the age of the Earth or humanity in relation to individual life or a given moment) exceed the imagination of man. The problems of psychological time, although extremely interesting, go beyond the scope of this study. We refer to the category of physical time to draw attention to the continuity of life processes and their relativity. The fact that everything happens in space-time makes us realize that the essence of time is its linearity, continuity characterized by movement. In physiological and psychological processes, movement is characterized by repetitiveness and regularity, i.e. a specific rhythm. Definitions of rhythms highlight the periodic change, oscillations and fluctuations of a parameter between extreme values.

In living organisms, rhythmic changes in almost all vital functions are observed. The analysis and description of recurring life phenomena is of interest to a separate discipline - chronobiology. Although chronobiology states that most rhythms are endogenous in nature, i.e. they are not a passive reflection of external light conditions, but are deeply encoded in individual cells of the body, which have their own "biological clock" and only adjust its course to the environmental conditions, it can be noticed that the circadian rhythm is not perfectly adapted to astronomical rhythms of the Earth (24-hour rotation around its axis). Although under natural conditions all "clocks" of the organism function in accordance with the astronomical rhythms of the Earth, the endogenous rhythm of physiological activities is overlaid with various factors that adjust the biological clock to the current social conditions of the environment.

Where, then, should the genesis of the stressful character of circadian rhythms be sought? Undoubtedly, the primary source is the development of civilization and the introduction of the so-called civil twilight, which is defined as the moment of turning on artificial lighting after the natural (astronomical) twilight. It freely prolongs our daily activity, exposing us to health consequences resulting, among other things, from disturbances in the secretion of antagonistic hormones - cortisol (an energizing hormone responsible for activity) and melatonin (a sleep hormone responsible for rest) - which are atavistically subordinated to the biological clock. And so, about 80 % of cortisol is secreted into the circulatory system an hour before the usual wake-up time. It is enough until 2 p.m. called siesta *(post-lunch phenomenon)*, which is accompanied by sleepiness, decreased mental fitness, etc. It is recommended to take a short nap (Colquhoun, ed., 1971). The next 20 % of cortisol supplied to the body is supposed to suffice until natural dusk, which is an stimulus to secretion of melatonin (sleep hormone), which prepares the body for sleep. The disturbance of this cycle through the so-called civilization synchronizers (artificial lighting, professional duties, social obligations, meal times, etc.) causes at the end of the working day the necessity of functioning on the so-called energy reserves and leads to the shortening of sleep necessary for rest. Symptoms of these phenomena are known as excessive fatigue, which after some time can lead to exhaustion and various so-called stress diseases.

Interesting in this respect are the studies presented by H.M. Wegmann et al. (1983), who have made social variables modifying the shape of the circadian curve the subject of their research. They took into account such modifiers as: current psychophysical condition, professional experience, level of motivation, temperament, rest, work shifts (day and night). In general, they stated that none of the modifiers mentioned above affects the sinusoidal course of the circadian curve, but only modify the amplitude and its range. However, one of the most important factors modifying the ability to work in multi-shift mode is night sleep and sleepiness during the day (Torbjörn, Goran, Mats, 2007). All these factors are responsible for both the intra-individual differences (e.g. rest, motivation) and, above all, for the inter-individual (work experience, temperament) ability to work.

The factor responsible for inter-individual differences in masking circadian rhythms recorded at the level of ability to work is, among others, temperament. Although individual differences in the daily body temperature rhythm were the first basis for dividing people into morning and evening types, Colquhoun (1971) tried to explain the genesis of these differences on the basis of daily body temperature fluctuations. The characteristics of morning and evening types are as follows: The morning types reach their peak of body temperature in the afternoon (12.00–14.00) and the minimum temperature - just after midnight. These people show high efficiency in the morning and its noticeable decrease in the evening. Evening types are characterized by reaching their peak in body temperature later (16.00–18.00) and by their higher efficiency in the evening hours. M.J. Blake (1967) compared the body temperature charts of extroverts and introverts and found that introverts reach a higher body temperature in the morning and reach its maximum earlier in comparison to the temperature course in extroverts. He also observed that a general increase in the level of stimulation in both types occurs during the daytime and that the level of activation increases more during the day in extroverts than in introverts.

The stressful effects of sudden time zone crossings are experienced by an average passenger on a jet plane, which crosses subsequent astronomical time zones every 15 degrees of longitude. Inconsistency between rhythm phases and synchronizers leads to "external" resynchronization, while staying in such a situation (such as while staying in a new time zone) leads to "internal" resynchronization. The organism's reaction to the change of the environmental synchronizer phase is adaptation to new conditions, called

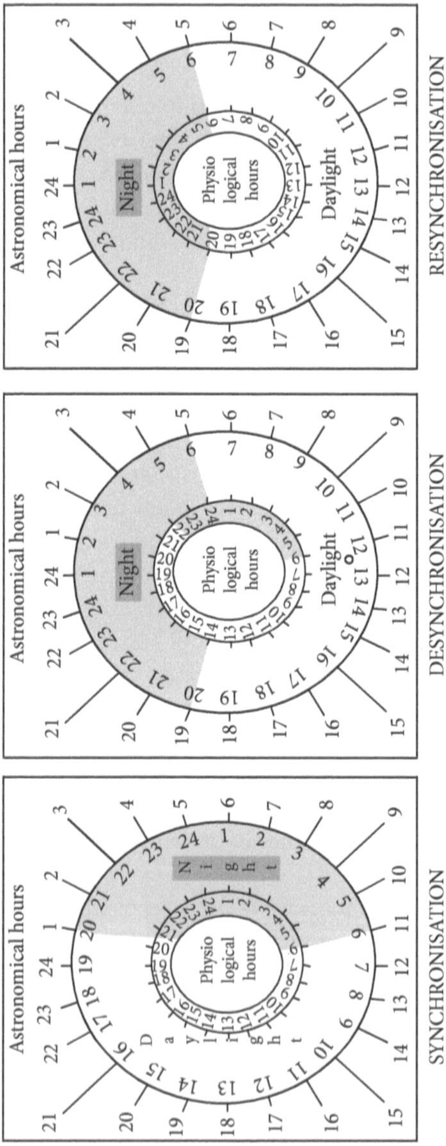

Fig. 2.6: The change of circadian rhythms after crossing time zones. (Source: own elaboration based on: Kłossowski, 2002)

the resynchronization process. The mechanism of resynchronization can be explained by the activity of the circadian rhythm phase regulator, shown schematically in Fig. 2.6.

As shown in Fig. 2.6, the source of chronobiological stress is the discrepancy between the astronomical synchronizers, which function according to the ESSO biological clock, and the social synchronizer, which is customarily controlled by meal times and hours of work and rest. This is confirmed by research in aviation medicine and psychology (Kłossowski, 2002).

Summarizing the current reflections on the chrono-habilistic concept of stress, it should be stressed that the compatibility of endogenous and exogenous rhythms is taken into account in the current expanded health formula proposed by the WHO.

Psychoprevention of chronobiological stress consists mainly in organizational actions, limiting the impact of civilization synchronizers on our around-the-clock efficiency in the form of e.g.: resignation from multi-shift work; resignation from work (especially car driving), resignation from nighttime bus excursions between 3–5 a.m.; compliance with the regulations in transcontinental aviation regarding the stay of flight crews for the duration of resynchronization at the place of arrival; adaptation of our own chronotype (if we have such a choice) to the around-the-clock distribution of our own professional activity; use (if possible) of daily nap in early afternoon hours (so called *post-lunch phenomenon*), not extending the so-called civil twilight (artificial lighting) to late night hours; using so-called *chronobiotics*, including melatonin, which affect our biological clock, facilitating the resynchronization of biological rhythms; use of light therapy (Borland et al. 1986).

A model of the synchronization process for to the east- and westward flights along parallels presented in the Fig. 2.7 can be useful for the prevention of stress associated with time zones crossing.

In order to facilitate the use of the nomogram, a mental training can be included. Knowing the time shifts between the airports of departure and arrival as well as the direction of flight (data on the y axis), one can - following the course of the appropriate curve - read the number of days necessary for re-synchronization, e.g. in the flight Warsaw-Seul, 8 hours of difference, in an eastward direction - 7 days minimum resynchronization time.

We have devoted a lot of attention to chronobiological stress factors modifying the effectiveness of human activity, because in today's world, characterized by high intercontinental and space mobility, it is extremely necessary and generally overlooked in medical and psychological literature on stress.

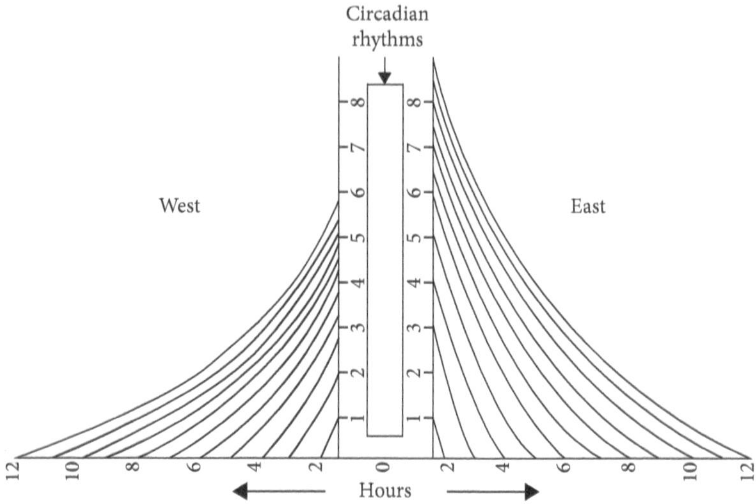

Fig. 2.7: A nomogram for calculating the resynchronization time of the human circadian biological rhythms after a sudden change of the time zone after transcontinental flights to the east and west (Source: own elaboration).

2.3 Psychological environment as a source of stress

Psychological stress factors are most often characterized in relation to the sources of stress or their symptoms defined as excessive emotional tension. Describing the possible impact of various negative sources of psychological stress, we will refer to the classification of difficult situations by T. Tomaszewski (1984), which includes: disturbances (obstacle, delay, lack, surprise, disappointment, requirements), threats (physical, to social position, to values), deprivation (underload, monotony, isolation, imprisonment) and overloads (physical, mental effort). All of them require adjusting the previous structure of activities to new situation requirements or lead to its complete disorder, which often makes it impossible to act without incurring certain psychological costs or completely prevents it.

It is also possible to accept the second temporal criterion for the classification of psychological stress factors, proposed by R.S.

Lazarus and S. Folkman (1984), namely: retrospective (harm), present (threat) and prospective (challenge). We will remain committed to the division of psychological stress factors proposed by Tomaszewski, due to the rather clear psychological mechanism of their explanation.

2.3.1 Performance-distorting factors

– **Disturbances** (barriers, obstacles) are situations in which there are some specific circumstances that force a person to make an increased effort. These may be, for example, physical deficiencies related to the shortcomings of a work tool, which reduce its quality, or subjective deficiencies resulting from limitations of the senses or of the human mind, which are inadequate to the set requirements.

A theoretical model useful for explaining the role of disturbances, e.g. in the work process, is the so-called human reliability, understood as the ability to maintain efficiency in work at a certain level and over a certain time. The model of human reliability coincides with the Gaussian curve, on which the optimal operating conditions are determined. All disturbances are supposed to push people towards hyper-optimal and suboptimal areas, characterized by impairment of performance, which is indicated by emerging errors (Terelak, 2011).

Among the factors that impede (hinder) a normal level of existence or productivity of human work, three groups can be distinguished. The first category includes factors related to the natural environment of existence and work, such as climate, landscape, nature (Rhoads, Pearman, Rick, 2007), or to the design and technology of the workshop, such as noise, vibrations, ergonomics of work tools, etc. (Lambert, Lambert, Yamase, 2002; Hsieh, 2004). The second group comprises factors related to the level of human preparation for a particular work and leading to mistakes and/or failures, such as education, training, organizational climate, workaholism, etc. (e.g. Johnstone, Johnston, 2005; Dougall, Baum, 2007). The third group includes constitutional and personality factors, including on the one hand age and gender (e.g. Avis, 2007; Suri, Aaltshuler, 2007) and genotype (heart efficiency, respiratory system efficiency, cancer, etc.) (e.g. Holahan, et al., 2005; Moskowitz, Wrubel, 2005), and on the other hand, a specific personality structure (features of intelligence, character of needs and motivation) (Enns, Cox, Clara, 2005; Koolhaas, 2007; Nash, 2007). This group of factors constitutes an important psychophysiological and psychological basis for individual differences in stress tolerance, which will be discussed in detail in the following parts of the book on the occasion of characterizing the so-called resistance to psychological stress.

It is not the purpose of us to discuss all factors that disturb life and work. We shall only pay attention to four classes of impediment situations (disturbances).

– **Conflict situations** - a human being is faced with the task of making a choice between two opposing, but subjectively equally possible and important decisions. The choice is made without any clear indication that in the case of implementation of this or another decision, what was intended will happen. The specificity of a conflict situation as a source of frustration is that man has to make a decision without a deeper analysis of the situation (Bolino, Turnley, 2005). An example of such frustration can be the situation of the so-called motivational conflict (a conflict between the aspirations of one person). In the past, Kurt Levin (1936) described it as: "aspiration vs. aspiration", "avoidance vs. avoidance" and "aspiration vs. avoidance". The latter conflict, the essence of which is a goal that simultaneously evokes tendencies of aspiration and avoidance as one approaches the goal, was the subject of empirical research by W.D. Fenz and G.B. Jones (1972), conducted on skydivers awaiting their parachute jump. Among other things, research has shown that the distant goal, which is a parachute jump, loses its attractiveness for beginner skydivers as the moment of the jump approaches, which is reflected in an increase in the level of anxiety. The motivational conflict before the parachute jump distinguishes between the beginners (n=14) and the experienced skydivers (n=16). The examination of heart rate as a physiological indicator of motivation (i.e. task-oriented emotion) was conducted telemetrically in the following situations: shortly after arriving at the airport (1), after putting on a parachute (2), after meeting with the aircraft crew (3), during the launch of the Cessna 180 engine (4), at the height of 100 feet (5), at the height of 2000 feet (6), at the moment of jump (7) and the last measurement after landing (8). It was found that regardless of the professional experience, the level of psychological stress increased until the moment of jumping (of course, relatively less in the case of experienced skydivers), as evidenced by the persistently high heart rate: over 130/min in case of the beginners and 105/min in the experienced skydivers. It is characteristic that in the situation of waiting for the plane to take off (the so-called stress of anticipation) these differences become blurred and stress increases evenly in both groups (Terelak, Przychodzka, 2015).

– **Unplanned result of action** - these are situations in which, when choosing the direction of action, we expect a specific result, but meet with the opposite effect. The situation becomes dramatic especially when a person who is not sufficiently prepared to do something has to take the risk of consequences. An example can be an unusual surgical team at the Henryk Arctowski Polish Antarctic Station, which included, apart from a surgeon, a psychologist, ichthyologist and a biochemist, who successfully performed an operation on the appendix of a deep-sea fisherman living in a nearby Antarctic fishing ground (Terelak, 1982a).

Fig. 2.8: An unusual team of the first historical appendix surgery at the H. Arctowski Polish Antarctic Station of the Polish Academy of Sciences, 22 December 1978. (Source: own photo archive). Note: (Legend: from the left in the upper row: dr. Józef Domaszuk (surgeon), dr. Jan Terelak (psychologist - as an "anesthesiologist"), dr. Maciej Rembiszewski (head of the Antarctic Station of the Polish Academy of Sciences). In the bottom row: Marian Bieńko (patient - fisherman from the fishing boat "Jowisz"), Dr. Anna Jakubiec-Puka (biologist - as a "scrub nurse")

– **Situations of lack of time and information** - this class refers to situations in which, regardless of the lack of information, we should make a clear and correct decision within a certain time limit (e.g. the situation of a pilot during catapulting, whose life depends on performing specific activities in a short time). In a situation when a person is not very aware of the situation, he/she does not know what the real consequences of the action will be, because there is no feedback about its effects. There are a number of experimental studies, describing e.g. the behavior of the driver in a road collision situation during the inflow of information of unspecified and high cognitive complexity (Terelak, 2015).

– ***Uncertainty situation*** - occurs when opposing signals from the environment are incorrectly assessed and this assessment is applied in one's actions. This situation differs from the previous class in terms of the duration of events and the speed at which an error is detected.

– **Threats** are situations where there occurs a violation of a certain value appreciated by a person through increased probability of accident, bodily injury, material or moral damage. These can be physical threats (threat of loss of life, disability, illness) as well as social threats (responsibility for the life of others, embarrassment in front of colleagues, etc.). For example, in the first years of the introduction of the catapult, the lack of knowledge about the reliability of this technical device caused fear of life threat or disability. The stress was so severe that many pilots did not use this device even in the ultimate situation, at the cost of losing their lives. This was a psychological problem which was solved by psychological means, by improving confidence in the reliability of the new technical device through the propaganda of successful catapulting and rewarding its users. The stress of a threat is so complex that it does not have to reflect the states of real, but rather of anticipated, predicted threat.

Disasters and forces (hurricanes, lightnings, volcanic eruptions, tsunamis and various types of floods, earthquakes) are governed by the laws of nature, over which man generally has no influence, therefore in the literature they are described in categories of extreme stress (e.g. Assanangkornchal et al., 2007; Bergiannaki et al., 2003; Chou et al., 2007). Terrorist threats exceed the moral sensitivity of the average person and are difficult to understand. Political or religious fundamentalism is the result of brainwashing, it completely changes the structure of terrorist values, legitimizing terrorist crimes against others and giving them the status of heroes of local communities (Smolicz, Terelak, 2002; North et al., 2004).

Other sources of physical threats have been presented earlier when discussing physical stress factors. Such threats are dealt with by occupational medicine and psychology. The extensive literature on the subject exempts from detailed listing of all sources. The subjective dimension of the threat complicates the psychoprevention of this type of stress. An example could be the technique of manipulating people, often used in advertising or politics, called "emotion management", as in the past when there was a threat of alien invasion, or the current threat of nuclear war, terrorists and/or immigrants or threats posed by modern technical civilization (e.g. cyborgs vs. people) (Thompson, 2007). A new discipline drawing attention to the distant psychological consequences of civilizational threats is called sozology, which is an interdisciplinary science on environmental protection, dealing with threats to life and health in the situation of contemporary ecological crisis (Dołęga, 2004). This discipline, due to the close link between risks from both the natural and industrial environment, should be closely connected with environmental and industrial (occupational) psychology. It is worth referring here to the research by A. Biela (1984), concerning anxiety reactions people living in rural areas threatened ecologically by (Copper Smelter) or Zakłady Azotowe (Nitrogen Plant), which shows, among other things, that the psychological threat increases (irrespective of the objectively existing one) with the increase of awareness of harmful environmental factors. A good example is the widespread fear of the threat from nuclear power plants in Poland, especially after the Chernobyl nuclear reactor explosion, which is still holding back the construction of Poland's first nuclear power plant in Żarnowiec, despite the huge financial losses associated with the abandonment of the significantly advanced construction works. It is interesting for social psychology that the identified fears of threat simultaneously narrow down other fields of consciousness.

An important mechanism of stress anticipation as a modifier of the strength of psychological stress is confirmed by numerous data from the literature on the subject. For example, the psychological observations of American military pilots, who during World War II performed combat tasks in the European Theater of warfare, show, among other things, that the anticipated threat based on information about the planes shot down caused so much psychological stress (the indicator was the number of anxiety reactions) that many pilots gave up service at the front without any flight, and were withdrawn to the USA (Grinker, Spiegel, 1945). Similar data on the role of stress-anxiety anticipation mechanisms were provided by our own research on Polish polar explorers, which shows that clinical symptoms of anxiety were the most intense during a cruise to Antarctica, compared to the results of anxiety surveys conducted at the H. Arctowski Polish Antarctic Station of the Polish Academy of Sciences, which means that the predicted threat was greater than the actual one. (Terelak, 1982b).

An attempt to precisely locate threats in a multidimensional space with the methodology of modern ecology is not precise. However, a rough attempt can be made to classify ecological factors threatening humans in the two-factorial space according to the following criteria: observed vs. impossible to observe threats and controlled vs. uncontrolled ones. In this situation, four types of threats can be distinguished:

(a) threats observed and controlled: skateboarding, smoking, lawn mowers, snow ploughs, trampolines, tractors, chainsaws, lifts, backyard swimming pools, downhill skiing, yachting, cycling, fireworks, drunk driving accidents and so on;
(b) threats observed and uncontrolled: carbon monoxide (exhaust fumes), paralyzing gases, transport and storage of liquefied gases, large water dams, fires in skyscrapers, underwater structures, mining accidents, parachuting, air accidents, motor racing, car accidents, handguns, dynamite, etc;
(c) threats controlled but impossible to observe: microwave ovens, water fluoridation, saccharin, nitrogen compounds, water chlorination, polyvinyl

chloride, oral contraceptives, X-rays, antibiotics, lead compounds (in exhaust gases), aspirin, lead compounds in coatings, vaccines, etc;
(d) threats impossible to observe and uncontrolled: risks not observable and uncontrolled: technological DNA, electric fields, nitrogen fertilizers, radioactive waste, nuclear reactor failures, pesticides, asbestos isolations, satellite collapse, mercury, coal combustion, etc.

Particularly the last group of threats is generally catastrophic, sometimes on a global scale, with significant consequences not only for the present generation, but also for future generations, leading to the existential fears of entire societies.

In addition to the so-called physical threat (to life and health), a major role in psychological stress is played by the social threat resulting from the many social roles, from the role of a student to the important functions of the state. The necessity of competition (the so-called rat race), being constantly assessed by others (exams, opinions) is a source of many stresses, causing a threat not only to one's own self, but also a violation of the values of people close to us. Many psychological studies have shown that the threat, especially chronic, to many values or value systems causes psychosomatic diseases, psychoneurosis and even psychosis in humans (Kościuch, 1984).

2.3.2 Excessive or action-limiting situations

Excess of stimuli - is usually an extreme situation, resulting from performing certain activities at the limit of one's physical or mental capabilities. In psychology, this type of stress situation is distinguished from the strain, i.e. the stress intensity that does not yet lead to disturbances in the organization of human activities. Overload (or excessive strain) refers to the intensity of stress that causes significant negative changes in a person's deliberate action (e.g. decrease in psychomotor, mental fitness, etc.). A good illustration is, for example, the situation of physical overload resulting from the acceleration of an airplane, which worsens the psychomotor skills of the pilot and/or his or her spatial orientation as a result of the blood movement into the lower half of the body, causing cerebral hypoxia.

While short-term overload situations lead to fatigue or exhaustion, long-term overloads ("chronic stress") lead to many psychosomatic disorders. The mildest form of overload is discomfort, forcing people to work in suboptimal conditions. The degree of mental overload depends not only on the conditions themselves, but also on certain aesthetic, cultural and civilizational standards (needs).

The omnipresence of various types of burdens is reflected in the concepts of negative life events, discussed in the first part of the book, based on the assumption that stressful strains of everyday life can accumulate, leading to overload, which in turn can cause worse functioning, as well as morbidity of the so-called civilization illnesses (Surtees, Winwright, 2007). Particularly strong stress or chronic stimuli are often described in the literature of the subject as derivatives of the progress of technical civilization. It is only an apparent paradox, not interfering with everyday knowledge about overloads, understood as exposure to factors harmful to the living and working environment exceeding conventional norms. After joining the European Union, the reality of Poland provides many examples of approaching world standards in terms of reducing almost all harmful environmental factors (Czartoszewski, 2004). The source of pre-scientific knowledge about the extreme values of overload stress in every aspect, both physically and psychologically, are observations of human behavior in Nazi concentration and prisoner-of-war camps. A broad review of literature on the subject was carried out, among others, by Kazimierz Godorowski, a former prisoner of Nazi concentration camps and clinical psychologist, who defines extreme overload as follows: "The conditions of living in the Nazi concentration camps cannot be compared to anything They were a terrible and unprecedented in modern history natural psychological and sociological experiment." (Godorowski, 1985, p. 10). The overload stress affecting many millions of people in all its forms - physical, mental and social - on a scale of decades of totalitarian systems of the 20th century and modern migration on a mass scale as an attempt to escape from overload stress, is still awaiting a reliable scientific study from an existential perspective.

Restrictions - these are total or partial difficulties in the inflow of informational, emotional or social stimuli. Just like in overload conditions, a worsening of performance and mental discomfort should be expected in a situation of deprivation. This is confirmed by numerous empirical, pre-scientific and scientific data.

2.3.2.1 Sources of data on the psychological effects of the restriction

The first experiences with perceptual deprivation come from 19th century balloonists, who described anxiety discomfort at the altitudes of balloon flight as brake off phenomenon, i.e. detachment from reality. Similar experiences are described by Alpine and Himalayan mountaineers at high altitudes (Lester, 1965). Other sources of data on deprivation, restriction or imprisonment, can be found in both fiction and scientific literature. An example of the first one can be legends, as for example about the founders of Rome, or about so-called "wolf children". An interesting popular-scientific description of the stress of deprivation can be found in the diaries of American Antarctic researcher Admiral R.E.

Byrd (1938), who in 1934 spent several months in solitude in a room carved in the glacier, named *Bolling station* in honor of his little daughter. In the diary he described his mental states after several weeks of loneliness and perceptual deprivation as: depersonalization, characterized by "separation of a conversation partner from himself". Before we move on to discussing sources of data on the stress of deprivation, we shall characterize its essence.

In the psychophysiological concepts, attention is drawn to the fundamental fact that each stimulation affects a person in two ways: non-specific (general activation) and specific (meaning of the stimulus). Thus, both the restriction of stimulus inflow, as well as a rapid change in the meaning of the stimulus (e.g. restrictions on freedom of speech) are of a stressful character, because they somehow disturb basic human needs. On the basis of the literature analysis, four categories of limitations can be proposed: perceptual deprivation, sensory deprivation, social isolation and imprisonment.

– **Perceptual limitations** - are situations in which the level of stimulation at the beginning does not differ much from normal, while the structuralization and meaning of stimuli are more or less strictly limited. The experimental model for the study of perceptual deprivation was developed by Canadian psychologists from McGill University - W.H. Bexton, W. Heron, T.H. Scott, (1954). Its stress-generating attributes were: a soundproof chamber (limiting the recognition of the structure of auditory stimuli), semipermeable goggles (limiting the perception of the structure of visual stimuli) and cotton padded cylinders put on hands (minimizing tactile sensations) as well as a specially constructed bed (lined with cotton pad to limit tactile sensations). Thus, the stimulus load is maintained at a relatively equal level, which effectively hinders the ability to differentiate stimuli, disrupting orientation in the environment. After only a few hours of staying in such conditions of the experiment, the examined persons (financially motivated) reported the state of discomfort, and after a dozen or so hours - expressed their willingness to resign from the experiment. Some of the participants experienced hypnagogic conditions similar to various types of drug hallucinations (Zuckerman et al., 1962).

– **Sensory limitations** - are situations in which access to all stimuli is limited to the maximum. For this purpose, among others in J.T. Shurley's experimental studies (1960), immersion tests were carried out using large glass cylinders filled with liquid of appropriate density were used, ensuring that the examined person floats in a constant temperature, which minimizes the gradient of the difference between the body and liquid temperature. Eyes of the participant were covered with a light impermeable headband. A breathing air mask was placed on person's head. The communication between the participant and the examiner was reduced to emergency situations only. In this way, the examined person was deprived of any environmental stimuli. It was found that the situation of sensory deprivation is more stressful than that of perceptual deprivation. This is evidenced by the fact that after just a few hours the participants declared their willingness to end the experiment or reported the appearance of hypnagogic hallucinations (Sutherland, 2007).

– **Social limitations** - a situation of separation from the social environment to which man had previously been adapted, characterized, among other things, by the lack of many important sources of emotional or social gratification, separation from normal sources of information and interpersonal communication (Jones et al., 1985). Investigating the stressfulness of social isolation exceeds the possibilities of a laboratory experiment, which is why a natural experiment is used for this purpose. An example of such an experiment is the research by J. Terelak (1982b), who used more than a year of antarctic isolation at the Henryk Arctowski Polish Antarctic Station of the Polish Academy of Sciences. The participants (n=20) for several months were gathered in a building consisting of single rooms for the so-called winterers, as well as a kitchen and a common dining room. A power plant, warehouses and laboratories were located in the closest vicinity. During the so-called Antarctic winter, lasting several months, the scientific station was cut off from the world, which created additional sources of isolation stress. The main sources of stress were: loss of professional and social position in favor of a standardized position of a member of the expedition, lack of significant sources of emotional and social gratification, monotony of activities and surroundings, etc.

Imprisonment - unlike the previous categories of sources of deprivation stress, it is not related to the task-oriented nature of the action. Its essence since the dawn of human history has been to use mainly the effects of social isolation in the form of discomfort, distress and humiliation, as a punitive method of social education (Whitehead, Steptoe, 2007).

As can be seen from the above characteristics of various types of limitations, the common feature of sensory deprivation and social isolation is the relative limitation of external stimulation, covering both its formal (strength, intensity of stimuli) and content (structure of stimuli, information, habits, needs, etc.) aspects. This is also the basis for stating that they are sources of stress not only for individuals, as in the case of autism (Barna, 2017) and the mentally ill (Lucksted, Treichler, 2017), but also for entire social groups, as in the case of cultural and social isolation and imprisonment of entire communities, such as in Cuba and

North Korea or in various ethnic reserves in Australia (Aborigines) or in both Americas (Indians) (Pieterse, Carter, 2007). It is therefore worth noting the data documenting the sources of deprivation/isolation stress. For example, a *break-off phenomenon* has been identified in aviation and cosmonautics, which occurs at the so-called ceiling altitude or in space flights. It is described as discomfort and anxiety associated with the loss of contact with reality and an intrusive desire to break out of this situation. The issue of psychological effects of sensory deprivation and social isolation has gained new significance especially in space psychology, which is interested in long-term manned space flights (orbital, interplanetary, and perhaps in the future outside the solar system). (Convertino, 2007; Terelak, 2016). In practice, the stress of sensory deprivation, social isolation and imprisonment can be encountered in places and situations such as: submarines, polar expeditions, deep-sea ships, anti-nuclear shelters, radar bunkers, prisoner-of-war camps, sports teams taking part in events abroad, psychiatric hospitals, isolated professional groups (working in other countries), maritime disasters (survivors) and mining accidents, single people (e.g. singles, divorcees, orphans, etc.). Due to the lack of an unambiguous criterion for the theoretical classification of sources of data on deprivation stress, I propose a practical criterion for the division into deprivation: experimental, natural, accidental, coercive and task-related isolation.

An example of stressfulness of deprivation and task isolation can be deep-sea ships, as shown, for example, by statistics indicating the occurrence of murders or physical violence, especially at the end of a long-term cruise (about 90 days). The emergence of aggressive behaviors at the end of the cruise is interpreted by psychologists as a symptom of monotony stress and an attempt to provide oneself with an appropriate dose of stimulation through increased aggression, as spontaneous aggression is a good stimulator in a situation of social isolation (Reykowski, 1977; Terelak, 1982b). Similar recommendations apply to the emergence of submarines after a 60-day submersion and the replacement of crews or at least the arrival at the port for relaxing purposes in order to counteract the "8 week submersion syndrome" (Earls, 1969).

The existing studies of cosmonauts or astronauts in real long-term space flights show, among other things, that sensory deprivation (weightlessness) and social isolation is such an important source of stress that it can threaten long-term space missions. The prospect of interplanetary flights means that the current record holder Valery Polakov, who stayed at the Mir space station continuously for 437.7 days, does not exhaust the demand for knowledge on human behavior in long-lasting space flights, resulting at least from the close perspective of the Martian expedition (Terelak, 2016).

Summarizing the current description of stimulation limitations as sources of stress, it is worth paying attention to the human brain's mechanism of adaptation to both monotonous and excessive situations.

2.3.2.2 Model of mutual regulation of stimulation levels by Jan F. Terelak

In reference to Hebb's theory of "optimum activation" and Leuba's "optimum stimulation", which were discussed in the Chapter 1 above, it should be remembered that for the efficient course of cortical processes determining human activity, a certain level of activation, resulting from an adequate dose of stimulation, is necessary. Cortical processes run smoothly only when the level of stimulation (activation) increases from sub-optimal to optimal value and decreases from super-optimal to optimal value. Considering this in the categories describing the external situation and observable behavior, we can state that the body tends to learn reactions that increase stimulation when its overall level is low and decrease stimulation when it is high. However, D.W. Fiske and S.R. Maddi (1967), introduced a distinction between "normal" and "optimal" level of activation and stimulation. The criterion for this distinction is "task". Thus, the "optimum" level is situationally determined by the task and the "normal" level occurs when there are no specific tasks. We seem entitled to assume that taking into account both specific and non-specific aspects of the activation or stimulation level presumes the existence of a general level of activation or stimulation consistent on the one hand with circadian (seasonal) biorhythm, and on the other hand with ad hoc corrective actions, determined by the task situation.

The above observations make it possible to look at the stimulation mechanism of human functioning in a situation of lack of stimuli as a regulatory mechanism in the psychological sense. A model of mutual adjustment of stimulation levels is presented in Fig. 2.9.

The above scheme assumes that physical stimuli flow from the environment (1) to individual receptors (2), where they are converted into signals[6], modified by a block of analysis of the meaning value of the stimulus (3). The amplification or weakening of the signal passing through this block is influenced by the emotional attitude, experience, etc. The signal coming out of the block (3) together with the signal coming out of the internal stimulation block (8) form the signal of the current stimulation level S, which in turn enters the stimulation level comparison block (4). In this block, the stimulation level signal S is averaged and

6 By "signals" we mean stimuli of various modality, which are characterized by a certain intensity (strength), as well as a carrier of information.

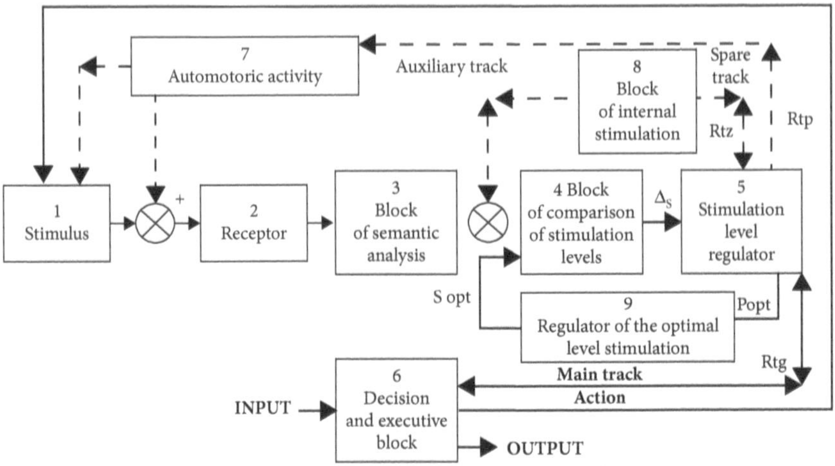

Fig. 2.9: Model of psychological mechanism of mutual regulation of stimulation levels of J.F. Terelak (Source: Terelak, Ruta, 1982 - own elaboration). Note: (Legend: S - current stimulation level signal; Sopt - optimal stimulation level signal; ΔS - error signal; Sp - stimulation level signal; Rtz - regulation of the signal by a back-up route; Rtp - regulation of the signal by an auxiliary route; Rtg - regulation of the signal by the main route).

stored, and the transformed Sp signal is compared to the optimal stimulation level signal Sopt. The averaging time is relatively short (e.g. individual auditory stimuli after averaging constitute music with a certain stimulus value), while the time of stimulus extension is proportional to its strength (e.g. blinking of the control lamp signaling engine failure is for the car driver a stimulus of high stimulus force, i.e. long prolongation time). The error signal, i.e. the difference between the transformed stimulation level signal Sp and the optimal stimulation level signal Sopt, equal to ΔS ($\Delta S = Sp - Sopt$), is transmitted to the stimulation level regulator block (5).

There are three feedback loops in the system which enable to change the adjustable S signal. The main loop is used to both reduce and increase the S stimulus level (depending on the value of ΔS). The other two routes, marked in the figure with dotted lines, are auxiliary routes, used only with a low level of stimulation.

The signal from the regulator (5) is transmitted via the main route to the decision-execution block (6). The block's (6) affects external stimulators (1) which causes a decrease or increase of the level of external stimulation (e.g. switching on or off the tape recorder causes a change in the level of sound stimulation). The magnitude of the signal flowing from the regulator (5) to the decision-execution block (6) simultaneously influences functioning of a person. If it is not possible to increase the stimulation level via the main route, the auxiliary route is engaged. The signal then runs from the controller (5) to the automotoric activity block (7), then it runs either through external stimulators (1) to receptors (2) (e.g. whistling, loud talking to each other, etc.), or directly from the block (7) to receptors (2) (e.g. scratching the head, tapping fingers on the table, etc.). In the case of the first one, not only the regulated subject but also the people in the immediate vicinity are stimulated. If the auxiliary route is not sufficient to achieve the optimum level of stimulation, or if the use of this route is not possible (as in the experiment in the laboratory), a back-up route for the internal stimulation block (8) is activated.

The signals emerging of the internal stimulation block are summed up with the signals received by the receptors and transmitted to the block (4). The internal stimulus block is responsible for phenomena such as hallucinations and, more specifically, for all kinds of hallucinatory-like phenomena. The Sopt signal, led to the block (4), is generated by the optimum stimulation level regulator (9). It is an integral-inertial regulator. The regulator averages (integrates) the input signal P for quite a long time period and simultaneously delays the signal, the delay time (inertia) is also relatively long. For example, due to the inertial and integrative nature of the regulator, after several days of perceptual deprivation, the individual optimal stimulation level of the subject should not change, as evidenced, i.a., by data on the so-called deprivation effects available in the literature. However, changes in the optimal stimulation level can be expected after a relatively long period of time, which requires empirical confirmation. The limitations of the magnitude of the signal of the optimal level of Sopt stimulation are: minimum and maximum stimulation levels, characteristic and relatively constant for a given individual (endogenous quantities) (Strelau, 1995).

Summarizing the considerations concerning the system of mutual regulation of stimulation levels, it should be stated that it consists in adapting the environment (external stimulators) to human needs (main and auxiliary routes), adapting to the state of the environment (the loop connecting blocks 4, 5, 9) and adapting the human being to the needs resulting from the previous state of the environment (the back-up route and the part of the auxiliary route, avoiding the environment).

A review of empirical studies on the so-called psychological effects of sensory and perceptual deprivation, which illustrate the legitimacy of the proposed model, was presented in other works (cf. Terelak, 1982b; Terelak, Ruta, 1982).

Although the analysis of human functioning presented in this paper concerns mainly the situation characterized by limited stimulation, it seems that based on the proposed own theoretical model, the phrase "mutual regulation of stimulation levels" can be used, and the stimulation mechanism be treated as one of the important regulatory mechanisms of human adaptive behavior to conditions deviating from the optimum stimulation range. This is confirmed by our own experimental research conducted at the Polish Antarctic Station of the Polish Academy of Sciences on the psychological cost of adaptation to long-lasting conditions of perceptual deprivation and social isolation, which is an important cognitive and pragmatic issue for the organization of future long-term space[7] missions.

2.3.2.3 Stress of social isolation in cyberspace[8]

Despite the fact of an excess of technical means of communication currently available, the sense of social isolation and loneliness has decreased. Many people have a lot of friends on social networking sites but not have in their close surroundings. Therefore, it is worth noting that the notion of social isolation is understood as a barrier separating from society and its influence. Common access to the Internet, and thus to social media, at first gave the impression of integration of individuals with society. However, many studies indicate that the lack of social interaction or communication with other people is becoming more and more common. Among the many reasons the socially isolated of a person are not only physical limitations related to e.g. disability, but also, to a large extent, emotional disorders such as anxiety or depression (Raut, et al., 2014). People who are socially isolated feel lonely, disconnected from the world, have low self-esteem, are often prone to depression, avoid the risks and professional

7 The uniqueness of the Polish natural experiment aroused the interest of NASA, expressing itself in the request to send a book entitled "Człowiek w sytuacjach ekstremalnych – izolacja antarktyczna" (*A man in extreme situations - Antarctic isolation*), just a few days after its release, to the U.S. Library of Congress, and the book "Introspekcje antarktyczne" (*Antarctic Introspections*) became the basis for a cinema and television film directed by Piotr Jaworski from Krakow.

8 The the issue of social isolation in cyberspace was co-authored by Łukasz Subramanian, a student of the 4th year of psychology, whom I would like to thank, for supplementing my modest knowledge on this matter, because as a representative of the post-modern generation, he has a more open attitude towards the virtual world than the author of this book.

activities that require contact with others. The feeling of loneliness seems to go hand in hand with social isolation, but it is worth remembering that there are differences between them.

Previous studies on loneliness did not focus on distinguishing loneliness from social isolation. It has been highlighted by J.T. Cacioppo, S. Cacioppo, D.I. Boomsma (2014) who consider the new research interesting because it focuses on a wider context than clinical research, e.g. differences in susceptibility to culturally determined solitude syndrome. As an example, he mentions the British culture, a characteristic feature of which is the "deadpan" of "poker face", which means that these people will be less likely to admit to feeling loneliness than, for example, the people living in the USA. Other researchers try to answer the question: Is social isolation possible in a virtual world so characteristic of social media? Some researchers suggest that the virtual world can become as significant for us as the real world, while others suggest that virtual reality cannot replace real social contacts - face to face interaction, for which we simply have less and less time, becoming addicted to modern media and exposing ourselves to social ostracism (Schneider et al, 2017).

Social isolation leading to dependence on electronic media can take many forms of development. A benign form begins with a slow withdrawal from social life. If a person who regularly visited websites, met with friends or talked to others on the phone suddenly becomes unavailable for an extended period of time, it may mean that they have entered the initial stage of isolation. Less social engagement in itself is not a cause for concern, but requires close monitoring. The next stage concerns the behaviors that increasingly cause people to become increasingly isolated from others, which very well may be a cause for concern. A severe isolation stage occurs when a person terminates all or most relationships with other people. Such behavior may indicate paranoia or even suicidal tendencies, as well as depression. At this stage, finding help for such a person is crucial, although this may be difficult as they often avoid contact with others. The effects of social isolation of a mainly emotional nature are the subject of research conducted by L.C. Hawkley and J.T. Cacioppo (2010). One of the authors' conclusions is that with long-term abuse of social media, middle-aged people suffer from chronic stress, insomnia and are helpless in the face of basic challenges of everyday life, and at the same time are less inclined to seek help. Long-term loneliness can cause people to drop out, abandon further education because they are unable to adapt to social requirements. Furthermore, such people have problems with expressing emotions and are less sensitive to feelings of others. The consequence of which is loneliness, which often leads to depression and alcohol addiction, and often even to suicide.

B. Primack et al. (2017) conducted a study in which they indicated that the negative impact of social isolation can be reduced by using social media, however, in the case of excessive use (the highest results) people feel more isolated. Social media platforms, commonly used by young Americans in the U.S., were used in the research. The test subjects constituted a representative sample on a national scale (n=1787) of American adults aged 19–32. Media usage was evaluated by time and frequency of use of 11 platforms: Facebook, Twitter, Google+, YouTube, LinkedIn, Instagram, Pinterest, Tumblr, Vine, Snapchat and Reddit. Psychological responses were measured using the PSI scale questionnaire. The respondents were divided into groups of users on extremes in terms of time commitment to playing games. The conclusions of these studies suggest that young adults who use social media more often are more socially isolated than those with a lower level of use.

In turn, the assumption that social media may also have a positive impact on social contacts, despite their high involvement in the media, was verified by H.M. Rus, and J. Tiemensma, (2018). Their research has shown that Facebook, still the most popular social networking platform, can both strengthen and weaken real social ties and also disturb well-being. However, little is currently known about the symptoms of stress reactivity, what is the influence of Facebook on stress reactivity in the case of acute social stressor, e.g. assessment, dispute, conflict, etc. Facebook users (n=104), men (mean age - 19.5) were randomly assigned to use their own Facebook account or read electronic magazines before they experienced severe social stress. All participants demonstrated significant changes in the subjective (self-esteem) and physiological (physiological) stress markers in response to stress. However, Facebook users experienced a lower level of psychosocial stress ($p < 0.05$). This study is one of the first to include both objective and subjective stress reactivity indicators in the study of the relationship between Facebook use and well-being.

The research presented emphasizes a serious problem of the "vicious circle" among the users of social media, which is that the more people isolate themselves socially, the lower their perception of the negative effects of stress is, leading to a greater intensity of use of social media, which then leads some people to an increasing social isolation and, consequently, to becoming "addicted" to social media. Examples of such people include those who play computer games excessively, described by H.D. Madran and E.F. Cakilci (2018). The authors investigated the relationship between aggression and the results of online gamers for game addicts. The study involved 205 participants who played online multiplayer games for more than 12 months. The age of the participants was 18–40. Data was collected using a personal data form consisting of questions about participants, a Turkish version of the Buss-Perry aggression scale and the Internet addiction scale. Statistical analyses have shown that there is a significantly high correlation between the results of aggression and the results of addiction to video games. Moreover, it was found that men have much higher levels of psychological aggression than women and that age was negatively correlated with the results of aggression and addiction to video games levels. It can be considered that this type of games can cause a lot of stressful situations, where the level of aggression increases as a defense response. Perhaps in the case of video game addiction the source of stress is overload (extensively long gameplay times) or an unfavorable result. It was also found that people who are addicted to video games characterized by on the one hand high social isolation and on the other hand financial benefits (rewards), have the personality of a gambler (Marczak, Terelak, 2014).

In turn the study by B.K. Wiederhold (2016) shows how addiction to social media leads to the worsening of communication with others in the real world. Based on the opinion of 100 students, it has been found that people are becoming increasingly dependent on communicating with family and friends via technology, neglecting personal communication, and communicating over phones and other devices, even in their presence. In another study 128 students admitted to use social network services to gather information and for scientific work, which also had a negative impact on social interaction, emotional health and completion of work. Text messages are the most obvious example of the destructive technologies that change the way people communicate, but whether these changes are bad is a good question. The general conclusion of the study is that wherever communication is at a purely verbal level without the elements of non-verbal communication (e.g. emotional expression), it cannot be treated as a normal social communication because its effects are typical for social isolation. This in turn leads to the deterioration of the relationship with family and friends.

Although virtual communities do not have many attributes of real social interaction and contribute to greater social isolation, some researchers believe that they cannot be denied having significant influence on people, also in the social context. Virtual communities exist and gather large numbers of people on numerous forums, such as guilds in MMORPGs and closed groups on Facebook. Virtual communities have become a new form of social life that often intertwines with real communities. For example, people who are in the same class can both actively participate in social life at school and in school groups on the Internet (e.g. Facebook, Instagram), are under the constant influence of both communities. Therefore, it is worth noting the important fact that the exclusion from the virtual community may become social isolation in the form of ostracism. This is emphasized by researchers of the "cyberspace isolation" phenomenon.

For example, W. Wolf et al. (2015) highlight the concept of "cyberostracism", a sense of being ignored or excluded over the Internet that poses a serious threat to basic human needs: belonging, self-esteem, control and a meaningful existence. According to the adopted model, responses to ostracism lead to immediate and common experience of negative emotions, as well as to satisfying a need. In two experiments (N_1=105; N_2 = 85) researchers examined these effects using the new computerized tool called *Ostracism Online*. In both studies, the researchers found that ostracism had a negative impact on emotional states, sense of belonging, self-esteem and the meaningfulness of existence. Moreover, the use of Facebook as a post-exclusion coping strategy did not have a significant impact on the need for re-inclusion.

Another study on the susceptibility to cyberspace isolation was conducted by R. Smith, J. Morgan, C. Monks (2017). The aim of the study was to assess the social perception of ostracism in social media among students of schools and universities. In both studies, participants were randomly assigned to read a vignette describing their inclusion or exclusion from a group on Facebook, asked to imagine that they were the target of that inclusion or exclusion, and evaluated how they would feel. In the first study (N=61; mean age=16.8) the "excluded" participants estimated a much higher threat to their sense of belonging in comparison to their self-esteem, control and significance. The second study (N=172; mean age=18.8) replicated and expanded these results by comparing the views of school and university students on ostracism in social media, while verifying their knowledge on Facebook. Both school and university students have "detected" ostracism in social media and the expected impact on their mood and mental needs. The authors of the study suggest that although both school and university students perceive ostracism in social media as psychologically painful, students during their first year at the University are particularly dependent on online social media and more sensitive to the potential effects of ostracism on this platform. Instead of commenting, it is worth to refer to experimental research, in which the answer to the following question was sought: Does real exclusion have any impact on our mental states? Such research, conducted by A.P.G. Donate et al. (2017), indicated that ostracism is characterized by social pain, provoked by being excluded and ignored in virtual space. To address the effects of social ostracism in virtual interactions, researchers developed a more realistic model and assessed its impact on the participant's expression of basic social needs, emotional experiences and painful feelings. Controlled interactions in a social dialog between the participants and two other (confederates) interlocutors appeared during an online "chat". The exclusion was manipulated by changing the number of messages received by the participant (15 % and 33 % respectively in the case of exclusion and inclusion). The analysis of the participants' answers (N=54) showed that the exclusion still connected with experiencing negative emotional states and increased anger, in comparison to the "included" participants. These results suggest that this manipulative procedure effectively induces social ostracism in a realistic experimental situation, which may mean that the mechanisms of "exclusion" and "inclusion" in the virtual community are very similar to those of the real community.

Summing up this part of the considerations on social isolation in the virtual world, the concept of cyberspace isolation should not be treated as interchangeable with loneliness and the interactions taking place in the virtual world should not be taken into account as the Internet and other cyber-media, which are more and more common in the real world, become an indispensable part of our lives. After all, "community" is not limited to sensual relationships and interactions, as evidenced by various internal states of our consciousness when meeting different people or simply remembering them (nostalgia, longing vs hostility, symbolic aggression, etc.). Sometimes, even if we are surrounded by people, we feel the need to isolate ourselves from them (e.g. monastic orders). However, the psychological problem begins when a new kind of isolation in cyberspace provides us with constant gratification and, at the same time, we feel no need to contact another person in real life (Thelwall, 2017). This mechanism leading to an "addiction", called the "vicious circle", is based on the fact that we are often unable to notice when isolation from the real world begins and even if we feel bad about it, we seek help in the virtual world (social media, games with virtual friends). As the studies described above indicate, the use of games or media "in small doses" can be very rewarding and stress-reducing, but excessive use often leads to depression or aggression. Real and virtual communities intertwine and interact actively. However, the effects of these transactions are still *in statu nascendi*, and require a lot of detailed research.

2.4 The social environment as a source of stress

The fact that humans are social beings has been indisputable since the times of Aristotle's social philosophy and his famous statement that humans are "political animals" (*ζῷον πολιτικόν*) (as in: Kraut, 2002). However, understanding of the scope of what is individual and what is social in a person as well as the occurring relations arises discussion. Assuming that a person is part of a social system, the extent of this system should be determined in terms of the requirements set for its members and group objectives, which can sometimes be a source of a lot of stress resulting from the working environment in which a person spends most of

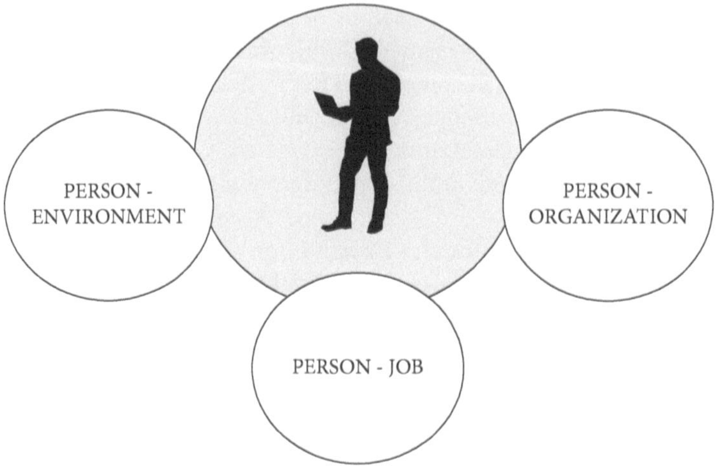

Fig. 2.10: Three aspects of transaction: man vs work (Source: own elaboration)

their adult life. One of the basic mechanisms of the relationship: person - professional work is the ability to adapt to the working environment, which the three aspects includes presented in the Fig. 2.10: *person-environment, person job* and *person-organization* as potential sources of stress.

These three aspects of adaptation manifest themselves, inter alia, in attitudes towards work, which, according to psychologists of ideas, have been very diverse throughout history. The following attitudes towards working on a continuum of a source of satisfaction vs. a source of stress can be deduced from the reflections on the role of work in the life of each person: punitive, instrumental and autotelic attitude. A punitive attitude manifests itself, inter alia, in perception of work as a physical constraint (slavery), economic constraint (early capitalism), moral constraint (enlightened capitalism). An instrumental attitude treats work as a way of satisfying basic life needs (physiological, security). An autotelic attitude is expressed in the conviction that work is a value in itself, an inalienable right of every human being and a source of personal development (Terelak, 2011). These attitudes towards work are therefore co-responsible both for dealing with stressful work factors and for generating new sources of occupational stress themselves. According to work psychologists, performing various occupations involves many sources of stress specific to them, which is generally defined in terms of mental discomfort, caused by the discrepancy between the conditions and requirements placed on an employee, and the possibilities of meeting them. (Levi, 1972; Terelak, ed., 2007).

The third aspect of transaction, *person-organization,* is worth presenting in more detail. Generally speaking, five groups of stress sources can be identified within the concept of organizational stress: 1) the structure of a group, both formal (occupying a place in a group of a specific social status) and informal (reflecting emotional relationships within a group); 2) tasks performed of varied levels of difficulty; 3) the development of technical civilization; 4) the organizational culture, sometimes remaining its own national culture; 5) people with different temperaments and characters.

Models of organizational stress have a rich history throughout the 20th and early 20th centuries, reflecting the complex cultural and civilizational mechanism of this social phenomenon (Dunnette, Hough, Eds., 1990). Chronologically speaking, we can distinguish the following stages of evolution of attitudes towards work stress:

- the British model of scientific management by Frederick W. Taylor (1919), which favors the economic man concept, places stress sources in inadequate pay for piecework;
- the inter-war model characterized by treating the employee impersonally, instrumentally as: "tools", "work force" etc. which is an insult to their human dignity and is a source of existential stress;
- the 60s Personnel Management (PM) model, which placed emphasis on teams of employees (staff) and interpersonal relationships *(Human Relations, Personnel Psychology*), which, if poorly managed, become sources of stress;
- the Human Resource Management (HRM) model treats people as one of the resources of an organization (human resources), partially ennobling employees, which is still associated with treating them instrumentally, on an equal footing with other resources, which also does not satisfy the employees, resulting in stress;
- the Human Capital Management (HCM) model, which increases the value of employees, treating them as a capital value (human capital), which means that although they are an important element of the organization, they are exposed to the stress of discrimination on the grounds of psychological selection and the necessity to upgrade professional skills;
- the Intellectual Capital Management (ICM) model refers to the essence of the human species, namely intelligence, indicating that this aspect of the employee is most valued in the organization (intellectual capital), but the same time it is a stressor, due to great differences between people in terms of the required creativity, which has become the most recognizable symbol of this model.

Organizational stress models often refer to negative attitudes and behaviors of employees, the consequences of which in the form of low work efficiency are extremely costly economically. Robert L. Kahn and Philippe Byosiere (1992). define work-related stress as a process that can be described at five levels:

1. Pre-organizational stress events: stress signals, characteristics of an organization (size, structure).
2. Organizational stress: physical environment (noise, light, temperature, etc.), psychosocial environment (ambiguity of roles, etc.).
3. Recognition and cognitive assessment of stress (assessment of hazard, loss or damage and assessment of one's own ability to cope with stress).
4. Direct consequences of organizational stress: somatic (cardiovascular, biochemical, gastric, musculoskeletal), psychological (depression, anxiety, job dissatisfaction, etc.), behavioral (failure to adapt to organizational requirements, absence, resignation from work).
5. Long-term consequences of organizational stress: health (psychosomatic diseases), psychological (worse functioning, bad mood, neurosis, loss of meaning of work, depression, and sometimes suicide, etc.), social (worse functioning in the role, change of job, etc.). The process of stress in the workplace can be modified, at each of the specified levels, by two types of modifiers: a) *personal modifiers*, related to inter-individual, genetic, personality and demographic differences; b) *situational modifiers*, related to unpredictable events, the distribution of which is random, such as the composition of informal organizational structure, lack of social - collegial or institutional support.

2.4.1 Certain organizational stress factors

Summarizing the sources of organizational stress according to R.L. Kahn and Ph. Byosiere, it should be emphasized that it is particularly important from a cognitive point of view to identify the sources of organizational stress at two levels:

1. *Intraorganizational level*, which includes: physical attributes of the working environment; personal aspects (e.g. workload for the organization, conflict of social roles, career constraints, responsibility for people); group aspects (related to characteristics of the attributes of the task force, such as: level of group cohesion, internalization of group standards, management style, types of communication networks, etc.); internal aspects (related to the technological level, organizational culture, organizational model, etc.).
2. *Extra-organizational level* - which takes into account the external conditions which affect the functioning of a particular organization, such as: economic problems of a country, race, district of residence, relationships within family.

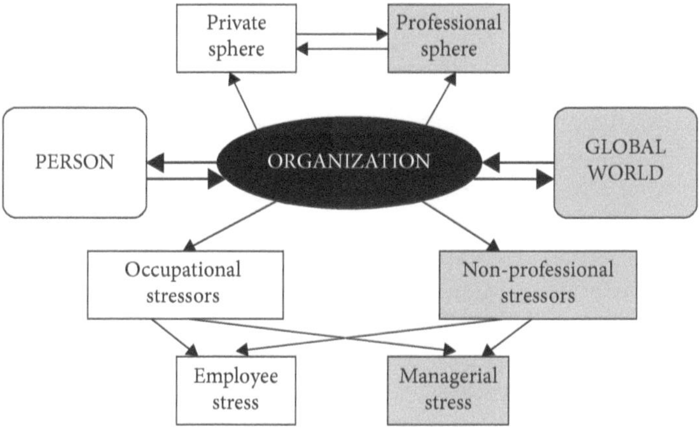

Fig. 2.11: A transactional model of sources of organizational stress. (Source: Terelak, 2005 - own elaboration)

There are many models of work stress in the literature, differing in the level of specificity and emphasis of particular groups of stress factors, in which attention is paid to incidental effects of organizational stress, translating to efficient professional functioning or to health-related sources of chronic stress at the workplace.

As Fig. 2.11 shows, the presented model of work stress includes transactions between the employee and the global world, which are moderated on the personal side by such components as: the employee's private life, the character of the profession and the social position held in the organizational structure, while the moderators of transactions on the global side are: the professional life and the non-professional environment, and the specificity of management in a given organization. This model is multivariate and can be useful in empirical studies.

The analysis of the sources of organizational stress in an informal group on the example of a crowd will be omitted, because it does not have an organizational structure and is characterized by the so-called collective personality. Therefore, for example the consequences of spontaneous and often irrational herding behavior can be a source of stress (Le Bon, 1986).

The primarily focus is placed on the participation of an individual in a task force in which abandoning one's individuality is in force, in favor of an organization that broadens the horizons of the individual by wide relationships with the global world. The community nature of the organization ensures, on the one hand, occupying an adequate place in the organizational structure and, on the other hand - that human resources are managed professionally. Thus, positive transactions between the private, professional and work life, on the one hand, and the social position in the organization, managerial stress and extra-professional stressors on the other, which are the basis for the good functioning of an organization, in a situation of negative transactions may become various sources of organizational stress, as they may manifest e.g. in such areas as: power authority (charismatic, formal and legal), management styles (autocratic, democratic, liberal), human resources policy, restructuring. The latter aspect in particular is a source of stress, which affects all members of the organization variably and therefore causes oppositional attitudes. The reasons for resistance to restructuring may include: habits, feeling of security, fear of the unknown, selective information about changes, structural inertia, threat to the system of power elites, poor education and social communication, badly conducted negotiations, deliberate misinformation, etc. Restructuring is related to many realistic fears of losing the current social position in a group. The stress sources that correlate with the core attributes of the organization itself shall be taken into account.

2.4.2.1 Group structure

The group structure is an important attribute of a task force and potentially a source of organizational stress (Terelak, 2005a). In addition to *the formal structure* (based on the hierarchy of its members) and the informal *structure* (based on liking and/or interests criteria), other attributes of the task force can also cause stress, such as: *group task* (resulting from the organizational distribution of work, aimed at achieving a group objective), *group interest* (determined by specific objectives, the implementation of which is subject to the action of all members of the group), (the end result of the group's activity, to which the actions of all group members are subject), *group norm* (regulations or customary duties of all members of the group, determining detailed rights and duties), *style of management* (autocratic, liberal, democratic). The structure of the group is extremely dynamic at different stages of its existence, because no group is a closed "monad" in which the structure can be kept unchanged (Terelak, 2005b). Because each group operates in a specific social space where clients, competitors, politicians, lawyers, etc. appear, it needs to adapt (and even anticipate) the structure to meet the new demands of the global world. Moreover, *the group's structures*, apart from having their own specific character resulting from the group's objective, which grades them into, for example, international unions, the state, ethnic groups, corporations, interest groups, religious groups, the army, hospitals, schools, families, etc., are also characterized by the non-specificity as pointed out by Henry Mintzberg (1983), proposing "a perfect model of the group's structure". This model assumes that each structure of an average company's organization consists of at least five basic attributes, which can be visualized by an area of an isosceles triangle, where one can distinguish: (1) *operational basis (*base of the triangle) - personal corpus, (2) *strategic top* (vertex of the triangle) - supreme management, (3) *middle management,* (4) *technostructure (*bureaucracy), (5) *support staff* (enterprise unions). These last two elements are situated outside the triangle. Each of these components of an organization's structure can generate different stressful situations. For example, the dominance of the "operational basis" entails conflicts of competence and requires decentralization and, above all, professional bureaucracy. The dominance of the "strategic top" leads to centralization and a simplified organizational structure, which often creates stress typical for an autocratic management. The dominance of "middle management" requires an autonomous departmental structure, otherwise there may come to constant conflicts of competence. The excessive amount of "bureaucracy", which is responsible for standardizing organizational procedures, leads to excessive control of the bureaucratic machine, which inhibits initiative and innovation. The dominance of "enterprise unions" leads to demanding attitudes, which can be a source of social conflicts in the workplace. Thus, exceeding one's own remit by specialized elements of the organizational structure can be a source of a lot of stress.

2.4.2.2 Social communication

Social communication defined as the transfer of information between people and its understanding often generates interpersonal stress of mutual misunderstanding. A particular form of interpersonal communication related to the performance of specific social roles is the circulation of information in the relations between: supervisor - subordinate and subordinate - subordinate. Types of interpersonal communication in the working environment are formal in nature (normal and pathological communication) and informal (gossip in real life from an identified source or virtual from an anonymous source).

An interesting model of stressful interpersonal communication in a specific group of government administration is the so-called *syndrome of group thinking,* described as a case study of American administration by Irving L. Janis (1982). It is worth remembering that the source of psychological analysis carried out by a team of psychologists led by Janis were the memoirs of members of the "Pentagon" decision making unit and the officially published documents concerning four cases of failure of American politics: Japan's attack on Pearl Harbor, the invasion of North Korea, the conflict in the Bay of Pigs and the escalation of the Vietnam War. These decisions were made in small groups of advisers and members of the government. For comparative purposes, examples of correct decisions made by groups with similar profiles were analyzed. In this case, it was the administration of president John F. Kennedy, and the actions taken were aimed at clarifying erroneous political decisions concerning: the Marshall Plan of 1948 and the so-called Cuban Missile Crisis of 1962. It was stated, among other things, that excessive trust in one's own competences leads to many defects of the information circulation process in the group, which may result in an erroneous decision. The syndrome of group thinking indicates a high dynamics of organizational stress, even in a well-organized task force structure. Eight different sources have been identified, such as (1) The illusion of omnipotence of the group shared by the majority; (2) Collective defensive rationalization of action leading to disregard for warnings; (3) Absolute confidence of the inborn morality of the group; (4) Stereotypical images of the enemy leaders as too malignant to make any arrangements with; (5) Authoritarian group leader, emphasizing the loyalty of each group member; (6) Group self-censorship; (7) The illusion of unanimity, referring to conformist judgments; (8) The emergence of "guardians of correct thinking" from the group, protecting against the influx of unfavorable information that could destroy the group members' self-satisfaction with the actions they have taken. The identified sources of incorrect communication flow in the group are extremely difficult to eliminate, mainly because they contradict the stereotype functioning in many organizations (e.g. political parties, etc.), that the "cohesion" of the group is the basis for its proper functioning, which the analysis of communication processes of the government administration, carried out by the team of psychologists led by Janis "proved to be untrue".

Another example of pathological interpersonal communication can be the communication technique, commonly called "brainwashing", and more scientifically "Menticide", i.e. intentional destruction of old cultural cognitive structures and ideological "reprogramming" of the brain in order to accept new ideological contents. R.C. Spaulding and C.V. Ford (1972) called this ethically drastic manipulation of other people "mental torture", which was described by them on the basis of experiences of 83 American prisoners of war, soldiers from the USS "Pueblo" ship, who had been kept in political prison in North Korea for 11 months and subjected to total indoctrination and absolute informational and cultural isolation, combined with mental and physical torture.

Brainwashing is *de facto*, by definition, an educational system that consists of clearly isolated subsystems: *interrogation, indoctrination and exploitation*. The stressfulness of this situation is evidenced, inter alia, by the behavior of American soldiers who, after a period of captivity, as an effect of total cultural isolation and permanent persuasion, supported by torture (in the case of those who were extremely resistant), radically changed their previous democratic views to communistic (Schein, 1958).

Effective brainwashing techniques cause such changes in behavior as: 1) fundamental change of existing beliefs and values without thinking; 2) complete blockade of all sources of information and social contacts; 3) complete control of the behavior in imprisonment conditions; 4) permanent indoctrination by a designated "guardian"; 5) promise that the current unpleasant situation can only be remedied if the information being the subject of persuasion is accepted. Changes under the influence of persuasion are achieved in three steps: a) thawing - i.e. physical (e.g., a lack of sleep and food) and mental discomfort (generation of various information, shattering self-trust and causing strong sense of guilt for the supposed war crimes; b) transformation - i.e. providing particular role models and manipulating with elaborate punishments and/or rewards in order to achieve pro-communist changes in thinking and behavior; c) freezing - i.e. perpetuating and deepening behavioral changes and attitudes by encouraging increased involvement (e.g. public declarations of newly adopted views, pro-communist agitation). This leads to a permanent loss of identity and reprogramming the brain to new views, to a loss of inner peace and self-confidence.

The analysis of the literature shows that we are dealing with two culturally separate Brainwashing systems:

a) Eastern Europe (tsarist and Soviet) - aimed at the "education" of its own citizens, for whom, within the expiation for disobedience, a system of "Labor Camps," so-called "Gulags", was prepared in which, apart from indoctrination, those rightfully sentenced by court had to admit their "guilt" and perform hard work as part of the expiation until complete political rehabilitation and "ideological righteousness", in favor of building large communist projects (Solzhenitsyn, 2008). Sources of data on the Soviet system of "brainwashing" are unique (Beck, Godin, 1951).
b) East Asian (Sino-Korean) - aimed at prisoners of war from the capitalist world who, after being imprisoned without a legal process, were subjected to total ideological indoctrination, were prepared for the function of propagators of the "superiority of communism" over capitalism, after being released from prison and after return to their own countries (Schein, 1958). The mysterious "brainwashing" methods have been identified by the Pentagon as "secret psychological weapon" that can threaten US national security, as evidenced, inter alia, by the two US Congress meetings dedicated to hearing of two recovered members of the USS Pueblo crew imprisoned by the Koreans, Maj. William

E. Mayer (physician) and Maj. Marion R. Panell (artillerist). These hearings formed the basis for the "Investigation Committee Report" carried out before the US Senate, which included a reconstruction of psychological techniques used by the Chinese and the Koreans which fall within the scope of "brainwashing", as well as a description of psychological reactions and an assessment of the health cost of American repatriates. These costs, as assessed by an extreme stress expert Bruno Bettelheim (1979), are typical for people who went through dramatic, traumatic event in concentration camps during World War II, described as *Post Traumatic Stress Disorder* (PTSD).

2.4.2.3 Organizational culture

Organizational culture, especially in the age of globalization, is a relevant source of social stress. It results, inter alia, from the fact that the world has been structured in such a way that people accept more or less consciously defined value systems characteristic for particular national cultures. According to Geert Hofstede (1980), culture is a consequence of structuring the world into: superiors and subordinates, which programs the minds to create cultural codes (mental and emotional). It should be noted, however, that culture has a hierarchical nature, with a national culture at its top, including such value systems and emotional codes as: regional, ethnic, linguistic, religious, gender, generational, social (professional) class, and finally organizational culture. Cultural codes are very diverse and sometimes are conflicting in their acceptance, at the same time being a source of existential stress and causing methodological difficulties in intercultural research. The place of organizational culture in global culture is illustrated in Fig. 2.12.

Within the scope of national culture, subcultures may appear, using a specific system of values and customs, e.g. at universities one can clearly distinguish subcultures of professors, auxiliary academic staff (assistant professors, assistants), administration and students. Similarly, high, medium and low level management subcultures can also be distinguished within the managerial culture. This is accompanied by appropriate imagery, the manifestations of which are usually grouped into three categories: *physical* (company logo, brand, buildings, exterior decoration, company clothes and badges, material environment, etc.), *behavioral* (ceremonies and rituals, patterns of communication, traditions and customs, rewards and punishments, etc.), *verbal* (anecdotes and jokes, jargon, names, nicknames, myths, chronicles, metaphors, etc.). The stress for the organization is usually the defection to this symbolism by individual employees, who shape poor opinions about the company (uniform, cassock or clerical collar, burqa, turban, etc.).

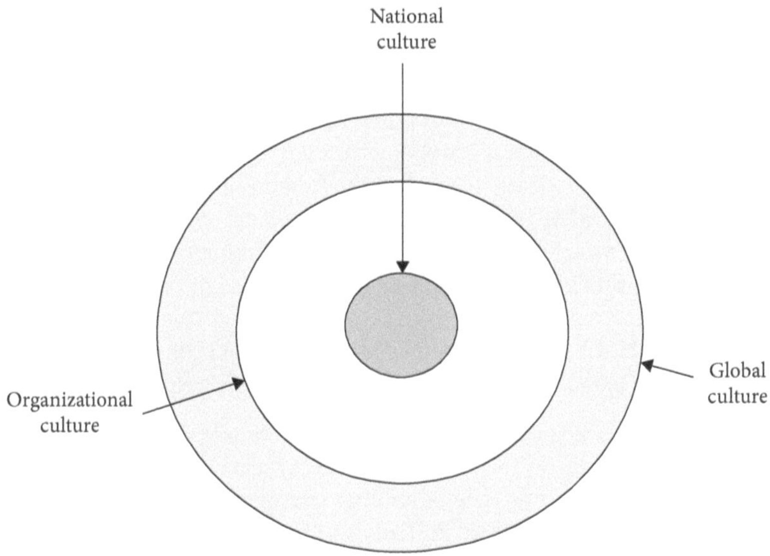

Fig. 2.12: Hierarchical structure of culture (Source: Terelak, 2005 - own elaboration)

A separate group of stress sources is connected with the socialization process itself, i.e. the adaptation of employees to the company's organizational culture. This process involves three stages: *initial* - covering the period of getting acquainted with new requirements of the organizational culture, *collisions* - covering the trial period of adjusting individual behaviors to the binding norms of the organizational culture, *metamorphosis* - the period in which the influence of the organizational culture (the value system and group norms) on the individual behaviors of an employee is noticeable. For each of these stages, different specific sources of stress can be identified, related to e.g. acceptance of traditions, rituals, symbols, professional language, etc. All the described attributes create different types of organizational culture (Terelak, 2005b).

Traditional cultures of companies, their global logo, language and value system related to the quality and promotions, also differ and are built up over generations of employers. Moreover, being in relation to the national culture or cultures of other nations (e.g. emigrants, immigrants), they cause many difficulties in the globalization of economic processes and social processes in particular, because there is a relationship between the organizational structure of the world and culturally shaped behaviors both on the rational (knowledge) and the emotional (feelings) levels. The most difficult, stress-inducing element is the so-called acculturative stress, resulting from difficulties in accepting new cultural codes, and the conflict between the tendency of culture to obtain a monopoly on social norms and values, which are the basis for the construction of social orders, and individual preferences, which manifest themselves in the so-called spontaneous, natural behavior (Berry, Ataca, 2007). Racist, xenophobic, 'brainwashing', indoctrinating attitudes, etc., clearly prove that the functioning of many cultures next to each other requires the application of the difficult art of mutual tolerance on a macrosocial scale, which in the initial phase of adaptation manifests itself by the so-called culture shock, not only of individuals, but also of entire communities.

2.4.2.4 Jeffrey H. Greenhaus and Nicholas J. Beutell's Theory of Sources of Conflict Between Work and Family Roles

The conflict of social roles as a source of stress results directly from Erving Goffman's theory of social roles (1981), which is based on the assumption that when a person is in the presence of another person (an observer, a spectator), their behavior changes radically, similarly to the way theatrical actors do it, so that the viewers perceive them through the assumed role. This is a reference to the views of Carl G. Jung (1951), who in his analytical concept of personality often referred to the original meaning of the concept of personality as a *dramatis personae* in ancient Greek theater, emphasizing that such a "mask" is used by person for social, cultural and professional purposes. Jung therefore believes that "persona" is not a component of an authentic personality, but of its facade. Goffman, on the other hand, draws attention to two ways of approaching the role of the "actor". The first one consists in identifying oneself with the role played, while the second one is characterized by maintaining a distance to one's own role and a lack of interest in the audience. In fact, Goffman is looking for an answer to the question: Who is an individual and what role do they play in society? And he assumes a thesis that an individual does not have a permanent personality and is characterized by the ability to put on many masks as an attribute of specific roles imposed by society. According to Goffman, the subject of the role is the actor's "ego". Their behaviors are directed by non-specific social norms, resulting from universal culture and civilization, or specific, concerning particular behaviors consistent with the culture of an individual organization. The conflict between them is described by psychologists as a source of stress.

All human organizations are characterized by a certain degree of conflictuality of roles. A conflict of roles occurs when two (or more) conflicting requirements arise simultaneously, and meeting one of them would make it difficult to meet the other. Taking into account the wider setting (going beyond one system), a conflict between roles, which occurs when expectations related to one role are contradictory and incompatible with the requirements of other roles performed by the same person, and a conflict between multiple roles can be identified. Each role imposes various obligations, fulfillment of which may force an individual to undertake conflicting actions; it may cause a conflict of time, place or resources or it may be inconsistent with the requirements of another role. In the case of a professional role, the behavior learned results from a standard of organizational behavior. In addition to our professional role, we perform a number of specific roles in our lives, periodically or permanently, such as: husband (wife), lover, parent, member of the local community, party, club, etc. Turning into a different role than that played here and now sometimes leads to a situational conflict that may disturb both professional activities (work efficiency) and private or family life (Peeters,et al., 2004).

The model of conflicting relationships: work vs family was described by Jeffrey H. Greenhaus and Nicholas J. Beutell (1985). The authors of the *work-family conflict* concept define it as a dissonance between the roles performed in a situation in which the requirements related to work and family life make it impossible or significantly difficult find balance between both areas. The authors identified three main causes of conflict between work and family: the time cause of the conflict (lack of time to perform well multiple roles simultaneously), the conflict resulting from stress (stress from one role is transferred to another) and the behavioral cause of the conflict (specific behaviors required in one role may be inconsistent with those expected in the other). The conditionings of this conflict are illustrated in Fig. 2.13.

Conflict increases when roles in the work and family area are important or central to the individual *(self-concept)* and when a failure to meet requirements is the cause of imposing high sanctions. An alternative in the form of theory of enriching work-family relationships, by J.H. Greenhaus and G.N. Powell (2006), emphasizes that engaging in the roles of worker and family member can bring positive results. The enriching of work-family relationships is of a bidirectional nature. These relationships are confirmed by the conclusions from the foregoing research, which can be formulated as follows: (1) experience in one role (employee or family member) improves quality of life in the other (employee or family member); (2) resources produced in one role promote a high level of performance and positive emotions in the other; (3) the acquisition of one resource can contribute to the development of another (e.g. a position that creates a conflict between work and family in connection with working after hours, can be a source of stress that an employee transfers home or otherwise, can at the same time bring mutual empowerment at work and in the family through financial

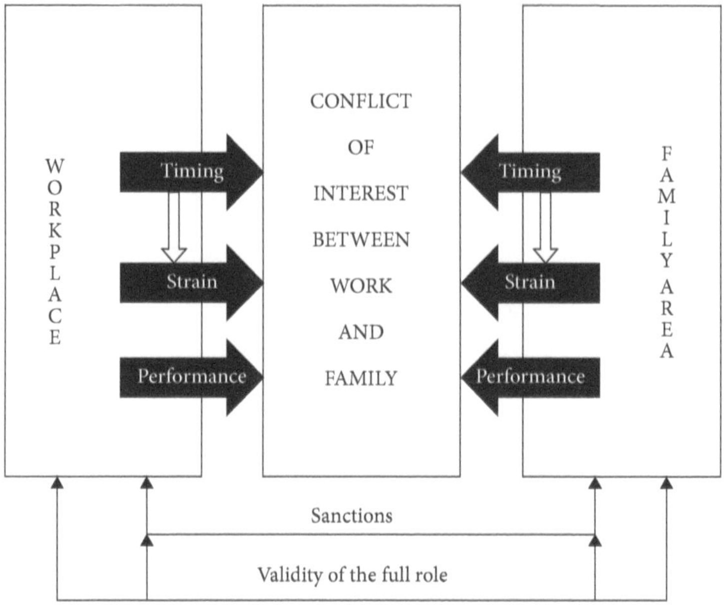

Fig. 2.13: Work-family conflict model. (Source: own elaboration based on: Greenhaus, Beutell, 1985)

stability or opportunities for professional and personal development). Greenhaus and Powell distinguish five types of resources that can be generated in a social role: skills and perspectives, psychological and physical resources, social resources (e.g. access to information), flexibility (e.g. freedom to set the pace, time and place of planning and performing tasks), material resources (e.g. money and gifts). Own research confirms the hypothesis of a parallel relationship between positive and negative expansion of the work-family relationship and that these are two theoretically distinct and empirically verifiable models (Terelak, Łozińska-Sheridan, 2011). Moreover, it was found that organizational factors are to a large extent responsible for shaping positive work-family relationships in case of both women and men, although they are more important for women (the relationship between the number of children and the type of marital partnership is interesting). The hypothesis of a positive relationship between the two types of conflict: conflict transferred from work to family and from family to work, was also confirmed. It is worth emphasizing that the factors such as high workload or low sense of control at work may increase the level of conflict transferred from family to work through interference of work with family life, which causes that family problems and/or responsibilities are not fulfilled. The research results also point to an important social fact - work of a woman is more likely to lead to work - family conflict situations than that of men, but this may be due to the fact that working women are still more responsible for household and family duties than men (cf. Ford, Heinen, Langkamer, 2007).

The results of research of the conflict between professional and family roles as sources of stress a little more have been presented in a little more detail, as the observed trends in the European Union and the United States, related to the dynamic economic development and growth in consumerism, cause more and more women and men to combine family life with work, which is related to a threat of straining family relations and health (Hammer et al., 2004), as well as new forms of help from the EU's institutional support (Zaleski, 2007).

2.4.2.5 Work as a source of stress

Work can be both a source of satisfaction and stress starting from the very definition of an employee, who was described by an outstanding Polish praxeologist - Tadeusz Kotarbiński (1986, p. 178) as a person "*...who is struggling in a way that is burdensome for his goals in various ways important to him, such as gaining means of subsistence for himself or his dependents*". The "burdensome struggle" at work emphasized in the definition is reflected in the rich psychological literature, from classical (e.g. Cooper, Payne, 1978) to post-modern (e.g. Terelak, 2011).

One of the main sources of stress at work, described by sociologists and social psychologists from the mid-20th century, are theories of "estimating the benefits and losses" of an employee. One of them is S. Adams's *Equity theory* (1965), which indicates the psychological mechanism related to salaries and rewards for employees. This mechanism consists in comparing one's own inputs to the outcomes obtained. Input, in the Author's understanding, is everything that the employee brings to the company (e.g. education, job seniority, effort, etc.), and outcomes are the received rewards and distinctions (e.g. salary, bonuses, but also promotions). The basis is the ratio of own input (Na) and outcome (Ka) in comparison to other employees (Nb/Kb) of a similar status in the company. An individual feels a sense of injustice not only when the ratio of other people's inputs and outcomes is greater than their own (Na/Ka<Nb/Kb), but surprisingly it concerns also the opposite situation (Na/Ka>Nb/Kb) when one's inputs are greater than those of others of the same social status. The author of the theory partially verified its validity in experiments concerning four salary situations: (1) overpayment at work per hour, (2) overpayment at piecework, (3) underpayment at work per hour, (4) underpayment at piecework.

A complementary theory of social justice/ injustice is M. Patchen's *Theory of Current and Potential Equity* (1961), which proposes a slightly more complex mechanism for feeling social injustice at work. The theory assumes that a salary is deemed adequate when one's salary (now and in the future) and the salary of others (now and in the future) are compliant. Thus, the adequateness of the sense of injustice regarding salary and currently held social position cannot be considered mechanically without taking into account the prospect of promotion in the company. However, the anticipated promotion prospect may be treated as a postponed reward, which will modify the sense of social injustice in the direction of job satisfaction. This theory, because of a rather complex mechanism, was never verified empirically.

In the 1970s many concepts were developed to explain the subjective estimation of inputs and outcomes of employees in a workplace, some of which are worth mentioning. *The theory of distributive justice* by G.C. Homans (1961), referring to the more general theory of learning, assumes that the employee is focused on profits, which are treated as a reward in the situation of favorable relations of own personal investments (e.g. education, competences) to received rewards and incurred costs in comparison to the same dimensions of other employees.

E. Walster, G. Walster and E. Berscheid (1978) go a little further in their *theory of profit maximization*, which considers expectation of profit increase to be a social norm. This subjective attitude leads to the conviction that the employer is an "explorer", which is a source of a lot of stress in the workplace. These stressors additionally result from the relative and subjective comparison of own gains with those of other people.

An outstanding Polish philosopher (ethicist), who later became pope John Paul II also observed other threats to welfare resulting from work, which he expressed in the *Laborem Exercens Ecyclic*, in chapters: (7) "A Threat to the Right Order of Values", (8) "Worker Solidarity", (11–15) "Conflict Between Labor and Capital in the Present Phase of History", (22) "The Disabled Person and Work" and (23) "Work and the Emigration Question". Multidimensional sources of stress at work are the subject of warning issued by a French psychiatrist and therapist - Henri Pull (2006), who quotes the results of research conducted in 459 enterprises in various European Union countries by Cubiks (Human Resources Department at PA Consulting), which show that about 25 % of employees of these companies live in conditions of high or very high stress. Due to this, some people (24 %) gave up their jobs (the so-called occupational disease), while others did not feel satisfied with their jobs, among the things blamed for this state of affairs were: workload (64 %), communication difficulties (58 %), employment security

(49 %), bad relations with their superiors (44 %), and the prospects of increase of stress at work (46 %). The author draws attention to the following threats which may result from work: reduced satisfaction or lack thereof caused by the mismatch of working conditions and the personality profile of the employee (e.g. fulfillment of mental needs, remuneration and secondary benefits, employment security); work organization (individual work, group work, stationary or mobile trade, seasonal worker, work rhythm and flexible working time, night shift work, three shift work, part-time work, work during weekends, work during any chosen time, telework, etc.); relationships with supervisors and colleagues (e.g., supervisors and co-workers opinions, customer opinions, rivalry, friendships and animosities, sexual harassment, mobbing); direct and indirect coercion at work (e.g., work time control, obligation to get results, challenges, excessive scope of duties, responsibility, competitions, transfer to the other position, promotion). Some of the above-mentioned sources of work-related stress will be discussed in more detail.

2.4.2.5.1 Workplace harassment

Among many aspects of a disrupted interpersonal relationship, mobbing is increasingly placed at the forefront in the subject literature (Nielsen, Einarsen, 2012). Focusing on the individual subjected to mobbing, H. Leymann (1990) draws attention to the most frequently described reactions: headaches (51 %), back pain (44 %), sleep disorders (41 %), symptoms of depression (41 %), excessive sensitivity (36 %), concentration problems (35 %) and other aggravation of mental symptoms: anxiety, depressive, including suicide attempts, and behavioral reactions, such as: excessive drinking and/or psychoactive substances abuse. Not without significance is the fact that apart from health problems, one should also take into account the fact that the job satisfaction and negative attitude towards work are to be expected. Source literature data suggests that strategies of dealing with the mobbing-related stress by victims of violence and difficulties in obtaining adequate social support are ineffective (Dewe, O'Driscoll, Cooper, 2010). This is confirmed by the studies carried out by N. Djurkovic, D. McCormack, G. Casimir (2005), pointing out that victims of violence prefer evasive tactics and perceive it as the only effective one and that they ignore institutional support. A number of other studies suggests that victims of mobbing have different strategies of dealing with it, depending on the situational context, although they do not indicate specific choices for particular remedial strategies (Karatuna, 2015). Victims of violence often blame themselves for the situation of mobbing, which is referred to in the source literature as the 'Stockholm syndrome' (Terelak, Kluczyńska, 2007).

2.4.2.5.2 Extreme work

Extreme work is a source of stress due to its burdensomeness. Since 1969, when cases of sudden death by overwork appeared for the first time in Japan, the phenomenon called *karōshi* has become synonymous with the negative effects of extreme work and at the same time a warning against taking up employment in many modern corporations. It has been confirmed by a survey carried out among the employees in the USA undertaking extreme work, commissioned by the private sector as part of the *Hidden Brain Drain Task Force* project (cf: Hewlett, Luck, 2007). The criteria for classifying a work as extreme are as follows: 60 working hours per week, excellent pay, unpredictable work rhythm, high work rates and short deadlines, very broad scope of responsibility for the company's profits and losses, being available for supervisors and customers, large number of business trips, physical presence at the workplace at least 10 hours per day, etc. The so-called "corporats" are a specific variety of employees, often forced by some corporations, which require maximum effort from their employees for the sake of the company. This means that employees often use alcohol to relax, energy drinks to stay awake, drugs to maintain their work rhythm or to "sharpen their minds", etc. This sometimes leads to exhaustion and addiction to pharmacological stimulants, which abused, over time become depressants.

Although the people taking up extreme work in the United States constitute a small social group, as they only constitute 21 % of the workforce (17 % - men and 4 % - women), in comparison with employees of global companies with the so-called culture of corporats, among which a group of as many as 45 % of employees chooses a well-paid extreme work (30 % - men and 15 % - women), however, this does affect the functioning of the family negatively in such areas as: household duties, developing strong relationships with children and/or with the spouse (partner), satisfying sexual life, etc. It is not without significance that extreme work has a negative impact on the upbringing of children due to poor parental supervision, which manifests itself, for example, in the consent to overly intensive use of TV, smartphones or computers, problems with children's discipline resulting from lack of attention, eating too much "junk food", poor educational results of children, etc.

These studies indicate, inter alia, that it is important for psychologists to become interested in this problem, as they not only identify sources of organizational stress more and more accurately, but also take psychoprophylactic measures, e.g. by promoting healthy ways of combining work and family responsibilities. For example, in 2004 the President of the American Psychological Association Diane F. Halpern set up a special team to develop ways of dealing with the requirements of being involved in work and family and raising awareness in the organization in this scope[9]. The main psychoprophylactic recommendations addressed to the government, organizations, schools and families are as follows:

1. employers should recognize that creating family-friendly policies is a good investment for the future - telework and flexible working hours reduce employee turnover, thus reducing the cost of hiring a new employee and training;
2. employers should train employees in the responsibilities of their colleagues, which not only allows a quick substitution of an absent employee, but also promotes flexible careers;
3. employers should counteract stress, that employees are often subjected to, as it influences their productivity and health negatively;
4. local governments should provide quality preschool programs and means of transport that would be accessible to the poorest;
5. schools and local communities should adapt the schedule of compulsory and extra-curricular activities to working hours.

Of course, these recommendations do not apply to specific professional groups, such as uniformed services, health care, etc., which are allowed to work unlimited hours due to higher public reasons.

Summarizing the benefits (e.g. earnings, development of professional competences, etc.) and negative effects of extreme work, J. McGowan, D., Gardner, R., Fletcher (2006) indicate excessive personal and family costs, which are borne by people who have a function professionally in extreme work. Therefore, such social projects as e.g. EPPR - Flexible Employee, Partner Family in Poland, operating under the European Social Fund as part of the social initiative EQUAL, which main task is to promote flexible working hours, telework and greater involvement of men in family responsibilities, are of great prophylaxic significance.

2.4.2.5.3 Telework

Telework, as a new form of employment, has been known in highly developed countries for many years and there are more than 40 million teleworking employees in the USA and the European Union. Due to the high dynamics of the development of telecommunication, telework will be an increasingly frequently used form of employment as it allows to function professionally in a flexible

9 Source: www.apa.org/monitor/oct04/balan-ce.html.

way. The experience gathered so far shows that both telework and its variant in the case of lifelong learning online, i.e. e-learning, have their advantages, but also are completely new sources of occupational stress. Comparative studies of teleworkers and groups working in a traditional form show, inter alia, that in case of the former, organizational stress is significantly lower and job satisfaction greater (Łodyga, 2007). Among the indisputable advantages of telework there are also: performing work in the place of residence (the most common form) or alternate working in several places, e.g. house, customer company, telecenter, employer (the mixed form) or work outside the place of residence (the experimental form). Another advantage is the further integration of the global information society, related to the interfusion of civilizational and cultural patterns (Konradt, Hertel, 2003).

Telework is the most convenient form of employment, especially for three groups of employees, due to the practically unlimited expansion of the communication space: the disabled (e.g. reducing architectural barriers), parents raising children (especially mothers), inhabitants of small towns and villages (e.g. access to work on the market in other regions of the country or the EU). The choice of a particular form of telework differs in the nature of work organization and may generate completely new sources of organizational stress (Kampa, Golda, 2007). The first source of stress is the failure to adapt to the requirements of telework, which in the absence of continuous personal control (supervisor, middle manager) favors employees with an appropriate personality structure, including character traits such as: self-discipline, task orientation, timeliness, regularity, responsibility, ability to organize working time, choice of optimal working hours, etc. The second group of stress sources is depersonalization of the work process. The lack of personal contact with the supervisors and staff of a teleenterprise leads to alienation, consumerist treatment of information, escape into the virtual world, dependence on computers, etc., and thus to the symptoms characteristic for the syndrome described in the source literature as the *Internet addiction syndrome* (Jakubik, 2003). These reservations also apply to students studying in the e-learning mode.

Workaholism is an extreme case of improper attitude towards work, the identification with one's professional role sacrificing other life roles.

2.4.2.5.4 Workaholism

Workaholism as a source of stress is characterized by excessive work, which ceases to be a source of satisfaction and pride (derivatives of the contemporary capitalistic stereotype of an achiever), and becomes a participant in the rat race.

This ruthless competition at work comes at a high health cost, which is why psychologists have attempted to describe the phenomenon of workaholism and explain its mechanisms (Spence, Robbins, 1992).

In the United States the term *work addiction* appeared as early as the 1970s, when Wayne E. Oates (1971), in his book *Confessions of a workaholic*, theorized that workaholics demonstrate similar compulsive behaviors towards work as alcoholics towards alcohol. Unfortunately, despite many publications on the subject, the term *workaholism* or *work addiction* is still controversial with regard to the psychological or psychiatric nomenclature referring to the disease entity. Obsessive commitment to work, manifesting itself mainly in extreme commitment to professional duties, lack of moderation, extreme perfectionism and dedication of private life to work, was initially described as a *work frenzy*. On the other hand, nervous behavior, somatic symptoms (headaches, nausea) were called *Sunday neuroses*. However, it soon became apparent that both were the result of a single syndrome, which was described as *work coercion* (McMillan et al., 2001).

Undoubtedly, at the end of the 20th century, workaholism became an important social problem, the source of which was the establishment of large corporations applying a specific organizational culture. For example, in America of the 1980s, during the era of the *yuppie* - young, talented, active go-getter employed in large companies, it was very fashionable to think about oneself in terms of workaholism. Extreme work, sometimes even double hours, has become the beginning of workaholism for many, and so a way of life and avoiding the privacy, the family. Even leisure time was to be spent with colleagues, talking of course about work. The empirical research conducted thus far has shown that workaholics are not really good workers. Although they dedicate themselves to their professional lives, they are only effective in the first phases of addiction, before their personality is destroyed. At a later stage, the very presence of a workaholic in a team causes many conflicts, suppresses spontaneity, creativity and leads to the disintegration of the team. This is due, inter alia, to the fact that, in their pursuit of perfectionism, these people are concentrating too much on their problems (Johnstone, Johnston, 2005).

Regardless of the lack of the status of a theoretical concept of workaholism, psychologists agree that we can speak of addiction when an individual is characterized by three or more of the following characteristics: 1) strong desire or sense of compulsion to take a dose; 2) difficulty with self-control in refraining from taking a dose, in its amount and in ceasing to take it; 3) physiological symptoms, occurring when the dose is not taken; 4) existence of tolerance, i.e. situations where, in order to achieve the intended effect, it is necessary to take higher doses than those which previously provided such an effect; 5) loss of interests which existed before the addiction, focusing on obtaining the measure; 6) taking a dose despite the existence of manifestly harmful effects (Burke, Matthiesen, 2004).

All of the mentioned features of workaholism make it possible to distinguish quite precisely between people who work hard (e.g. forced by their employers, as in the case of doctors or journalists) and workaholics. The latter can be described as people who allow work to take over all areas of their lives at the cost of family and friends. Moreover, they are people who are excessively excited about their work, do not feel fatigue during work (the so-called adrenaline fever) and treat their work as a sanctuary from other problems (e.g. family, social). They experience intrusive thoughts about work at every moment of their lives.

Individual differences occur among workaholics, which are the basis of many typologies. The best known classification was developed by Bryan R. Robbins (2000) and based on the so-called workaholic triad, covering the three components of workaholism: attachment to work, emotional involvement in the work process (feeling of internal pressure from work) and pleasure from working. The suggested classification makes it is possible, for example, to distinguish a job/work enthusiast from a workaholic and an enthusiastic workaholic. Thus, a job/work enthusiast is characterized by a high level of commitment to work and job satisfaction, as well as a low level of perceived internal pressure from work. Meanwhile, workaholic can be described as a person not satisfied with their job, including simultaneously a high level of internal pressure from work and a high level of involvement in work. Finally, an enthusiastic workaholic is characterized by a high level of commitment to work, a high level of internal work pressure and a high level of job satisfaction.

There are two groups of factors that determine the risk of addiction: the first is our internal beliefs, our value system, our temperament, and the second is our external environment. It is also worth adding that the distinction between workaholism and diligence is difficult, as there are many varieties of workaholism, namely: *compulsive-dependent workaholics,* who despite being aware of the fact of spending too much time at work, often at the cost of privacy, cannot restrain themselves; *success-oriented workaholics,* who feel strongly motivated to work due to a sense of need of rivalry and competition; who are perceived positively because they focus on the results of their work, which often is distant, and can postpone their gratifications; *perfectionist workaholics,* who are focused on details, places work above all other values, even private life. The authors also describe the notions of *an enthusiastic workaholic*, in whom the level of all three dimensions is high, and a person not engaged in work, for whom, on the contrary, this level is low. In addition, they mention the following types: *indefatigable workaholics* (works continuously and often performs many tasks simultaneously); *bulimic workaholics* (working frenzy, exhaustion and fear of failure, of not being perfect); *workaholic with attention deficits* (at work they seek stimulation, sensations and raising the level of adrenaline); *workaholics who enjoy their job* (slow, cautious, prudent and carefully planning his job). Another type of workaholic can be found in the literature on the subject, namely *caring workaholic* (fulfilling themselves by devoting to other people in need of help, thus strengthening their own self-esteem). A particularly difficult case, although quite common, is a workaholic as a head of a team. Which is a case of authoritarian style of management that generates organizational stress (Schaufeli, et al., 2009).

Summarizing the problem of workaholism as a source of stress, it should be emphasized that addiction to work has negative social and subjective effects, resulting from an inadequate attitude to work, which entails disorders of the emotional aspect and disorders of interpersonal relations at work and outside of it. That is why in May 2004, the *European Region of the World Health Organization* organized a conference in Copenhagen for associates from the Center of Occupational Health, during which the attention was drawn to the need to reduce the health strain of workers by systematically reducing weekly working hours and reducing extreme work (Cox et al., 2004).

As we have shown so far, work can be a source of stress, but due to the every adult person's inalienable natural and legislatively regulated right to work (e.g. by the Constitution of the Republic of Poland), unemployment can be a specific source of stress of anxiety-inducing nature, as it threatens the ability to meet a multitude of person's basic needs.

2.4.2.6 Unemployment

Unemployment, as Augustyn Bańka accurately describes it (1992, p. 509), "is not freedom, but the powerlessness of an independent and valuable existence". As such, it must be a source of multiple forms of stress. In the modern capitalism based on market economy, unemployment is one of the key problems, which most often results from the lack of contractual work for those able to work and looking for employment. Reasons behind the phenomena may range from individual decisions to macroeconomic conditionings, resulting from a particular economic situation at a given moment[10]. In economic literature we distinguish

10 Some data on unemployment were made available by Joanna Terelak-Subramanian (2002), whom I would like to thank here for her cooperation and permission to use this data.

frictional, structural, classic unemployment and unemployment resulting from a lack of demand. According to common contemporary terminology, the first three types of unemployment constitute voluntary unemployment, while the last type is compulsory unemployment.

Frictional unemployment is a natural phenomenon occurring in every dynamic society, the notion covers people with physical and mental disabilities, as well as people temporarily unemployed due to change of occupation, movement between regions of the country, etc. *Structural unemployment* is a type of unemployment that arises because of differences in human skills and the type of jobs available, in conditions of changing demand and production. *Classical unemployment* is a type of unemployment that occurs when salaries are above a level that guarantees a balance between supply of work and demand for work. It is considered that salaries should be subject to the same market rules as product prices, i.e. be flexible. If fixed salaries (trade union activities, national legislation regulating minimum wages) are maintained at too high level, i.e. above balance level, unemployment increases. *Unemployment resulting from a lack of demand* - cyclical, Keynesian - occurs when total demand for work is low, which is related to the decline in economic activity during the recession. In the business prosperity phases, demand expands and the unemployment level decreases even to the level of natural unemployment.

The basic features that differentiate people in terms of their susceptibility to unemployment stress are: age, gender, education. The following are listed as secondary: occupational structure, nationality, job seniority, race. The differentiating effect of some demographic characteristics decreases as the period of unemployment prolongs, and the differentiating features in terms of susceptibility to become unemployed do not necessarily have to be those that differentiate the susceptibility to emerge from unemployment.

Education and professional structure is an important unemployment generating factor. In general, highly skilled workers are less affected by unemployment, while less skilled workers are victims of mass layoffs during an economic downturn. Education provides good protection against unemployment, but if a person becomes unemployed, the chances of emerging from it depend only remotely on the level of education.

An effective way of emerging from unemployment is generally aiming at full employment through the growth of the level of the national economy. This is a long-term process, often the beneficiaries of which is the next generation, and therefore it is unsatisfactory for the currently unemployed. In a short amount of time, the government can help reduce unemployment by using fiscal and monetary policy measures to increase global demand. By reducing unemployment, the mood and expectations of enterprises concerning the level of future demand and profits are improving, it will result in an increase in investments and, consequently, in employment.

In addition to the economic aspects, psychological aspects should also be taken into account, as cyclical unemployment has a very high social cost and causes more human suffering and mental loss than voluntary unemployment. Forms of tackling the effects of unemployment can be divided into passive and active. Passive include: unemployment benefits, pre-retirement benefits, early retirement, single severance packages, etc. However, these are only forms that alleviate the effects of the stress of unemployment. Active forms of institutional dealing with unemployment include: training and retraining, intervention works and professional activation of graduates, public works, loans for starting up small enterprises, professional preparation of young people, etc. The experience of countries with developed market economy shows that there is no automatism between relatively high economic growth and a decrease in unemployment. High economic growth without increase in employment is possible - as so called *jobless growth*. This phenomenon, often referred to as the *hysteresis effect*, consists in the persistence of a high level of unemployment from the period of recession in the period of economic recovery and high growth. Its occurrence is undoubtedly favored by the development of a culture of unemployment, where remaining unemployed becomes a social norm and a way of life (Nowosiellska, 1995).

As emerging from unemployment is a continuous and long-term process, the psychological, health and social consequences of long-term unemployment are worth considering.

Psychological effects of job loss are connected with a multitude of disorders, such as: anxiety and depression, i.e. emotional disorders manifested by the feeling of sadness, affliction, discouragement, indifference, and suicide crises[11]. The most important symptoms of crises are somatic ailments, including headaches, feeling weak of an unknown etiology, insomnia, etc. Along with the prolongating period of unemployment, the focus on important life problems and the orientation in reality is deteriorating. Other symptoms include sense of guilt, shame, confusion, helplessness and hopelessness, lowered self-esteem, pessimism, shift towards feeling of external control, the feeling of social uselessness, disorganization of family life, inability to function in a group. Self-image of the unemployed as a

11 For example, in Poland, according to the Central Statistical Office (GUS), in 2016 8.3 % of suicides were unemployed (Central Statistical Office: Information note, Warsaw, 08.09.2017. Suicide attempts in 2016)

set of judgments and opinions which a person uses a point of self-reference for their physical features, abilities, ability to undertake and perform tasks, relations to the environment and the way of experiencing contacts with other people, is significantly deteriorating in comparison with those employed. Unemployment first and foremost affects the personal sense of dignity of a person, as it is a visible socially confirmed sign of their low value, insufficiency, being defendant from anonymous socio-economic mechanisms, and an expression of their social degradation. If it is followed by poverty and even misery, then the sense of humiliation and social harm becomes even more acute. Unemployment benefits do not solve this problem, because they do not economically equate the unemployed with those employed, they increase mental discomfort and often lead to psychosomatic health cost associated with an increase in the incidence of various diseases of this type (gastric or duodenal ulcer, arterial hypertension, cardiac infarction, coronary heart disease, etc.). Unemployment is also associated with reduced resistance to stress, which manifests itself in increasing hardship, social isolation (breaking social ties), difficulties in finding a new job, dependence on others. In particular, the lowering of self-esteem and the withdrawal from social life lead to the consolidation of the mechanism of self-fulfilling prophecy, which is responsible for the withdrawal from society. The unemployed subjectively interpret this as ostracism.

Social effects of unemployment are mainly related to negative consequences for society, which include: high costs of social benefits, non-utilization of the unemployed's ability to work, sense of risk of losing the job of the employed and the risk of increasing undesirable effects (e.g. alcoholism, divorces, thefts, growth of crime). The particularly acute consequences of the unemployment concern family stress, which causes emotional tension, destroys all prospects in family life, leads to destabilization of the family, deprives the father of authority, socially degrades the whole family, etc. Studies show a greater levels of stress among unemployed women, which according to G. Ruth and B Orly (2007) can be explained by, inter alia: (a) less attachment to work, and consequently being are treated as secondary workers and are therefore first to be dismissed; (b) greater susceptibility of women's occupations to recession; (c) high percentage of women in part-time work, which offers less protection against unemployment; (d) opinion that it is easier for them to become discouraged and to withdraw from the job market.

To conclude the analysis of the situation of unemployment as a source of stress, apart from the stressful factors of unemployment discussed, it should be added that a person needs work not only in order to earn money, but also in order to develop their skills and raise their ambitions and achieve life goals.

Unemployment limits the development of the personality of an unemployed person and the people closest to them. For this reason, at the very least, it is an existential stress associated with a loss of hope. This is emphasized above all by humanistic psychologists' concepts of unemployment stress, which draw attention to the dangers of alienation, resulting from a loss of job, which deprives people of autonomy, tends to transfer to all other areas of human life (Fromm, 1996).

As we have tried to demonstrate, different forms and conditions of work, especially unemployment, can generate stress. This problem is a significant one from the psychological point of view, because the economic migration observed nowadays, which often is caused by unemployment, is connected with the mixing of attitudes towards work, typical for different organizational (work) and national cultures (family), which is the essence of acute acculturative stress.

2.4.2.7 Acculturative stress

Emigration and acculturative stress are often associated with unemployment in one's own country or with the search for a better job, and are now a global phenomenon. Globalization trends emerging in the modern world intensify, in economic and political scope, migration in search of a better life. Different reasons for leaving one's own country form the basis for the typology of contemporary emigration, including, inter alia, political, creative, socio-cultural, ethnic, pathological, economic and consumption emigration. The last two types of emigration are the most typical for contemporary Poland. Thus, the theoretical aspect of the psychological consequences of an individual's emigration, both on a professional and private level, related to the external coercion to adapt to the new conditions of organizational or national culture in the new place of residence is interesting (Jamil, Nassar-McMillan, Lambert, 2007). The existing elements of local culture integrated with one's own value system are subject to a harsh review of opinions when it becomes necessary to work in new multicultural teams (the so-called multi-culti, e.g. branches of foreign companies in various countries) or in foreign countries (economic emigration or political immigration), which in turn is connected with acculturative stress, one of the manifestations of which is the so-called culture shock. The blending of regional and national cultures faces great psychological resistance, as evidenced by the permanently fought local wars, not over the seizure of territory, but over the value system (several decades of wars in Ireland between Catholics and Protestants, or the Palestinian-Israeli war, the war in Syria with the so-called Islamic State etc.). This is also confirmed by the weak ecumenical effects, which, apart from a few gestures, never entered the phase of substantive theological discussion. The emerging theoretical models concerning the universal key to the globalization of cultural processes are received with hope and great interest. For example, the model of Catholic contester Hans Küng (1997), known as "Weltethos", i.e. a global ethics based on religious studies and personal contacts with representatives of various religions. In this model, the common ethical essence consists of such universal values as: mercy, charity, equality and honesty. The author calls his vision of contemporary cultural globalization a realism of hope, especially since almost all great politicians and religious leaders have taken an interest in it. Studying these problems exceeds the competence of one field and generally has an interdisciplinary nature, including, alongside psychology, such scientific fields as: sociology, anthropology, philosophy, as well as theology.

Generally, the aim of empirical psychological research on the emigration stress is to examine the process of adaptation of people to changes in the new organizational culture with the so-called global companies as a new workplace, or in the event of migration - as an adopted "homeland" (Kinzie, 2007). There are three stages in the cultural adaptation process: stage of shock and disorientation, stage of struggle for mental well-being and a stage of acceptance of a new value system and its integration into identity. The first stage - culture shock, the most frequent indicators of which are: social functioning, identity changes, cognitive and emotional functioning, sense of well-being, as well as strategies and styles of dealing with culture shock, is the subject of psychological, sociological and anthropological research, in particular (Boski, 1994).

Let us recall that the concept of culture shock was introduced by anthropologist Karl Oberg (1960) in order to impress the psychological cost associated with the process of adaptation to a different, unknown or little-known culture.

Oberg has identified six phases of cultural adaptation: 1) tension connected with effort; 2) feeling of loss of current social status, loved ones and material goods; 3) feeling of rejection by the new community; 4) incoherence of current social roles with those performed before, with the new value systems, which may lead to disturbance of the sense of identity; 5) anxiety and aversion towards foreign morality; 6) feeling of helplessness caused by adaptation difficulties.

The theme of the culture shock was tackled again in the 1980s, by a Dutch engineer and social psychologist - Geert Hofstede (1980), who, while generalizing the results of research carried out on differences in productivity of multinational teams in transnational corporations (e.g. IBM), formulated a four-dimensional culture model (global culture - national culture - local culture - organizational culture). The results of his research led him to the concept of a culturally programmed mind of individuals, which was the result of group socialization related

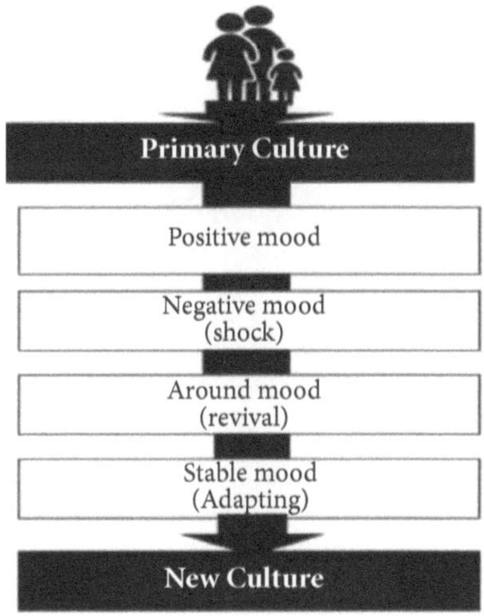

Fig. 2.14: Model of emotional cultural adaptation of K. Oberg (Source: own study based on: Oberg, 1960)

to the indoctrination of nation states. Therefore, adaptation to a new culture is associated with a culture shock. Hofstede compares it to a child's mental state, which has to be able to master the rules of functioning and the value system of its own environment. The state of mind of a little child must lead to such symptoms of culture shock as: sense of helplessness, hostility, tension, etc.

Elisabeth Marx's (2000) theory of the culture shock triangle refers to both mentioned concepts, diagram of which is presented in the Fig. 2.15.

As the Fig. 2.15 shows, it includes three levels of dealing with culture shock: thinking (from stereotypes to redefining cognitive patterns), feelings (from euphoria through depression to satisfaction), social skills and identity (from the social skills of a given culture to the acceptance of universal cultural codes). The course and pace of acculturation do not depend only on the interaction of these three levels, but can also be modified by factors such as: implanting in culture, distance between cultures, social context and personality.

The effects of cultural adaptation are manifested in the creation of new attitudes, from *colonial* attitude (reluctance to react to foreign culture in any way), through *imperialistic attitude* (forcing one's own value system and thinking about others), to *international* attitude (skillful adaptation to different cultures). Each of these preferences allows for different strategies of intercultural relations, identified by John W. Berry (1997), such as: *marginalization* (foregoing one's

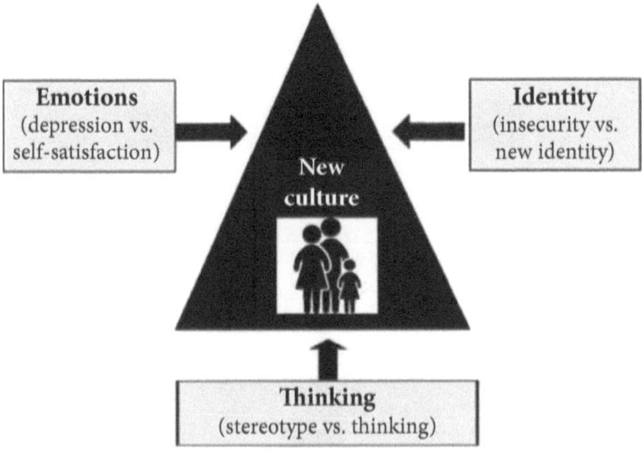

Fig. 2.15: Culture shock triangle. (Source: own study based on: Marx, 2000)

own traditions and lack of desire to establish contact with alternative culture), *separation* (focusing on maintaining own cultural identity and avoiding contact with alternative culture), *assimilation* (foregoing one's own cultural traditions and searching for contact with alternative culture), *integration* (desire to maintain own tradition and establish contact with representatives of other culture). Each of them is accompanied by stress of varying intensity and which requires a different style of dealing with it. J.F. Terelak's and A. Borkowska's (2007) research on the styles of dealing with the acculturative stress of the Polish employees who are members of a multicultural team in global companies in Canada and the Netherlands, showed, inter alia, that the most typical form for contemporary Poles is economic and consumption emigration. However, they differ considerably in terms of the sources of psychological stress. Thus, the motivational behind consumption emigration includes the following circumstances: good material situation before departure; expectation of a second chance; new challenges; leaving with the family; collecting reliable information about the destination country; work does not only about the income; the decision to leave permanently; quickly breaking ties with one's own country; avoiding contributing to national organizations at the place of destination. Meanwhile, economic emigration is based on a number of different motives, such as: poor material condition before departure; willingness to earn money quickly; fear of the unknown; incomplete information about the destination country; departure of only one person from the family; treating work only in terms of profit; the decision to leave for a short time with the intention of returning to the country with earned money; maintaining close ties with one's own country; contributing to community organizations in the destination country (religious, national), etc. According to the comparison of both types of emigration, unlike economic emigration, which is a typical "gainful" emigration, consumption emigration favors people who enjoyed a perfectly fine financial situation in Poland. Emigration was a new start for them to improve their financial situation in the conditions created in the most prosperous countries due to the industrial leap. Stress, characteristic for the consumption emigration of Poles, can be described as a process of striving to maintain well-being (happiness) in new culture conditions.

As shown by the theories of acculturative stress discussed so far, the emigrants[12] bear a specific health and psychological cost of the effort they make to achieve well-being, in the different stages of adaptation. A good exemplification of this process are various strategies and styles used to deal with cultural stress at different stages of the adaptation process. Thus, the style of dealing with stress manifested by the individual, connecting with the sense of mental well-being, concerns first of all the emotional, hedonistic dimension, general subjective well-being and partial satisfaction (Kofta, Szustrowa, 2001). Moreover, to achieve an individual's level of mental well-being, it is important to have a specific set of strategies that constitute their style of dealing with stress, and not just a spectrum of strategies. An active/a non-task style of dealing with stress is the least conducive to the mental well-being of individuals compared to other distinguished styles: active, passive and task/passive.

Summing up the research on acculturative stress presented as example, it is worth mentioning that it includes a large number of correlation indicators between the objective manifestations of stress (civilizational level, value system, job market, organizational culture of an enterprise, number of interpersonal conflicts, etc.) and how they are perceived. There is a clear asymmetry in disadvantage to subjective stress indicators, as acculturative stress is usually symbolic and difficult to define unambiguously. Moreover, spiritual factors, related to the value system within a specific religion, world view, are not without significance when attempting to fully describe the sources of stress. These factors not only

12 Immigration as a source of stress has been deliberately omitted, because refugees are primarily motivated to save themselves and their loved ones. The possibility of taking up work becomes a secondary goal and depends on the host country. The contemporary phenomenon of mass immigration from North Africa to the European Union encounters great logistical difficulties and is often discussed on a large level of generality of an existential nature. The refugees' responses are described by psychology as traumatic stress.

shape the attitude to duties resulting from the performed social and professional roles, but above all, they are responsible for shaping the value system based on the so-called central values, which give people a sense of happiness (well-being), to which we tried to draw attention earlier, and the meaning of life. All of these stress factors blend with each other, creating a global stress effect which is difficult to precisely separate into specific factors. These observations can also be made in relation to stress studies in general, while being aware that, from a methodological point of view, this holistic treatment of the effects of stress is undoubtedly a weakness. However, from a prophylactic and health promotion point of view, it is appropriate.

To conclude the discussion on the sources of stress, it is worth noting that the globalization of information at the beginning of the 21st century (satellite telephone communication, transcontinental flights by jet planes, scientific and commercial flights to the International Space Station, etc.) is generating new risks that have not yet been fully understood and researched. It also carries new forms of social support in various stressful situations of an institutional nature, not only for individuals, but also for national and transnational communities, which will be the subject of our debate in the fourth part of the book. However, it is already clear that stress at work, especially in some private sectors, is a major social and moral problem in many countries. This results, inter alia, in an EU directive limiting the working week to 48 hours.

3 Diagnosis of stress response

The experience of many generations concerning adaptive mechanisms of a person shows that stress responses are controlled by two adaptive systems: preventive or pathological. The preventive system is associated: 1) with the ability to learn new behaviors to prevent or minimize the adverse effects of stress by regulating the level of stimulation; 2) with the organization of a conceptual system in order to identify sources of stress and to plan strategies for dealing with it. The transition to a pathological system is associated with a lack of effectiveness of the preventive system in the long run, which is caused by the specific features of the individual or the features of stress (type, strength, duration). The pathological stress response system is characterized by such reactions as: 1) learning disorders which make it difficult to use previous experiences when dealing with stress; 2) failure to cope with extreme situations of sensory deprivation or excessive stimulation, specific to different types of neuroses; 3) disorders in the integration of the individual conceptual system specific to different types of psychoses (e.g. schizophrenia), causing withdrawal from the real world and closing oneself up in the subjective world. The latter pathological system of adaptation to stress is most often associated with extreme stress (e.g. catastrophes, cataclysms) or chronic stress (e.g. long-term imprisonment).

Before moving on to a detailed characteristics of the stress response, let's consider a general model that takes into account both stress adaptation systems.

3.1 Stress response model

Of the many models useful for describing stress responses in detail, the most interesting seems to be the one developed by J. Reykowski (1966), previously presented in Chapter 1 in the Fig. 1.11. This model takes into account both adaptive and disadaptive responses to stress, which is in accordance with the author's thesis that stress can be talked about only when the burden reaches the appropriate intensity threshold, the so-called stress threshold. A state of stress is a set of responses, functional changes, that can be observed or recorded at a physiological or behavioral level when a stressor exceeds a certain stress threshold that is specific to a given person at a given time. Stress responses have both non-specific (primal) and specific (individual) characteristics. These characteristics can be described in two areas: *control system burden* (responses within the adaptive system, although modified by the presence of stress); *control system overburden* (disadaptive responses, focused not on the task but on the effects of stress defense). Reykowski distinguishes three levels (routes) from the stress response process point of view:

1. *The route of non-specific changes*, mainly related to emotional reactions associated with stress. When the stress threshold is exceeded, the first phase - *mobilization* - can be distinguished, during which, due to an efficient compensation mechanism, such stress adaptation responses as: increase of activity and energy of behavior, acceleration of action pace, improvement of motor and intellectual efficiency, etc., can be observed. This phase in the adaptation system is motivational to the fight against stress. The second phase, which is associated with an increase in stress, is characterized as a *disintegration phase*, signaling a transition from an adaptive system to the disadaptive stress responses, as evidenced, i.a., by the transition to an activation of an overcompensation mechanism. It is characterized by an increase in emotional tension, deterioration of orientation processes (narrowing of the scope of attention, memory gaps, deterioration of problem solving, etc.), psychomotor processes (disorders of sensitivity to stimuli, disorders of visual and motor coordination, etc.). The third phase, which is associated with a further increase in stress, called *the destruction phase*, is pathological, as it involves exhaustion of the body and disorganization of the action. The destructive responses typical for this disadaptive phase may manifest themselves in the disorganization of orienting processes (e.g. decrease in perceptual abilities, repetition of irrational solutions), psychomotor processes (e.g. uncoordinated movements, delayed reactions to stimuli). Emotional tension reaches a very high level, which leads to the above described disorders of psychomotor responses and to a decrease in interest in the result (apathy, lack of motivation to act).
2. *The route of specific changes* includes responses, the content of which depends on the type of stress and concerns two forms of responses, depending on the stress tolerance threshold and of a mobilizing type: elimination of stress sources. These may include activities such as: removal of a source of stress (obstacles), repeating attempts to deal with stress, modifying the manner of action, passive submission to a stressful situation (e.g. ignoring a threat), research on the situation (endless combating stress, so-called art for art's sake), etc. When the stress[13] tolerance threshold is

13 It should be recalled that the stress tolerance threshold is not understood as a point on a scale, but as a band within which both specific stress combating and stress defense responses can co-exist.

exceeded, defensive responses occur, proving that the responses applied so far, are ineffective. Their nature can be either real (e.g. withdrawing from a stressful situation, avoiding it or attacking an obstacle) or symbolic (e.g. fantasizing, denial or other personality defense mechanisms known from the literature).

3. *Changes of expressive activities* are connected with discharging behaviors, because their essence is that they do not serve to achieve any specific external goals, but they signal the state of emotional tension caused by stress. Emotional responses can be: controlled, partly controlled and uncontrolled. Thus, expressive activities related to controlled emotional responses concern, for example, expressing disapproval, dissatisfaction, but in a socially acceptable way, in the form of a joke about one's problems, verbalizing unpleasant experiences, etc. Partially controlled emotional responses can generally be characterized as symptoms of discharge of anger, helplessness, and fear in a socially unacceptable form. A further increase in stress leads to uncontrolled emotional responses, characterized by a high degree of violence (despair, rage, panic, etc.), which completely disorganize a person's activity or lead to its abandonment.

When characterizing the generally presented model of the stages of responses to psychological stress, it should be stated that it is based on an abstract continuum of changes, characterizing a varying degree of deviation from the optimal level of functioning. Of course, this model is of a classificatory nature and does not exhaust all possible responses and does not exclude interactions between them and individual differences in stress tolerance, but it can certainly be very useful in designing a diagnosis of the effects of stress.

Treating the mechanisms responsible for certain stress reactions as a basis, one can follow Norman F. Dixon (1987) and adopt the following classification of stress responses types: physiological, emotional, behavioral (somatic) and cognitive. A distinction must be made between incidental stress responses and distant (cumulative) chronic stress responses.

3.2 Symptoms of response to incidental stress

When attempting to characterize the types of stress responses in terms of the mechanism responsible for their formation, it should be emphasized that these are only different aspects of the human response to the expectations of life. Their intensity increases the normal (usual) burden until the conventional moment (stress threshold), the exceeding of which is called stress state, manifested both by non-specific (typical for humankind) and specific (characteristic for a specific person) responses.

3.2.1 Physiological correlates of stress responses

The use of physiological stress indicators in psychological research arouse a lot of controversy about the alleged objectivization of psychology through the introduction of parameterization of physiological indicators recorded with the use of technical devices. The opinion of a well-known Viennese ethologist Konrad Z. Lorenz (1972) is worth mentioning here. Among other things, he claimed that one must speak out definitely against the epidemically spreading misconception that only what can be counted, measured, deserves to be called real. It must be convincingly explained that the process of our subjective experiencing has the same degree of reality as everything that can be expressed in the terminology of natural sciences. As far as physiological indicators of emotions are concerned, it should be emphasized that nobody generally doubted the close connection (correlations) between certain processes in our body and the form in which we experience them. However, the phenomenon of this isomorphism can be interpreted in three different ways, which are equal from the theoretical and cognitive point of view. The first way - is to rely on the confluence hypothesis. Proponents of this approach assume that physiological phenomena can be considered as the cause of appropriate experiences and assume that they in turn have a retroactive effect on physiological processes. According to Lorenz, this convincing, seemingly causal link is misleading and unacceptable in terms of logic. It is burdened by a fallacy of jumping between two parallel, but independent, chains of physiological and psychological events. The second hypothesis - about psychophysical parallelism - assumes such a parallel course of two chains of events, between which there is no logical connection. Nobody denies that all mental processes are accompanied by neurophysiological processes, but under no circumstances can this statement be reversed. Thus, the metaphor expressed as psychophysical parallelism is doubly incorrect, because there are subjective processes without physiological equivalents (or at least they cannot be proven) on the one hand, and neurophysiological processes without a noticeable mental correlate on the other. The third stance in this matter is based on the hypothesis of the identicalness of soma and psyche. It is claimed that physiological and emotional phenomena are simply the same "real in itself" and that we experience both (as in the case of matter and energy) through independent, irreducible to itself ways of cognition. This view is the most justified when considering the physiological aspects of stress responses. The most commonly used indicators

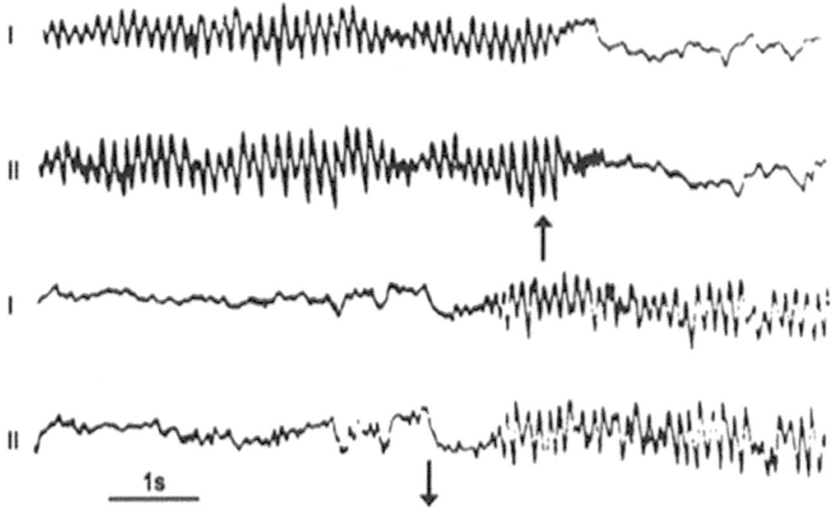

Fig. 3.1: The electroencephalogram changes from the occipital cortex area showing the transition from alpha to beta rhythm at the moment of eyes opening (upward arrow) and alpha rhythm forming at the moment of eyes closing (downward arrow) are a good example of the activation rate index in the EEG as the emotion correlate (Source: own study)

of physiological responses that characterize organism burden level or stress level are i.a. heart action (electrocardiogram - ECG), brain bioelectric activity (electroencephalogram - EEG - and many of its components, e.g.: the percentage drop of alpha rhythm in EEG, evoked cortical potential: visual or auditory), muscle activity and tone (electromyogram - EMG), galvanic skin response (GSR), blood pressure (systolic and diastolic), catecholamine level, metabolites level, lung ventilation, rectal temperature, vision dysfunction (electro-oculography - EOG) and various combinations of these indicators. Examples of such electrophysiological parameters of the activation level are[14] illustrated in Fig. 3.1.

Another interdisciplinary discipline is psychoneuroendocrinology, which is useful in explaining the very complex mechanisms of stress responses (catecholamines, adrenaline, norepinephrine, cortisol, etc.). Let us recall that the role of hormones in human life was pointed by ancient medics, such as Galen,

14 The discussion on the scientific status of "activation" and "arousal" constructs in psychological research was conducted by J. Strelau (1995).

the continuator of Hippocrates, who distinguished four temperaments and the medical criterion of their division on the basis of four basic bodily fluids - blood, bile, phlegm, black bile. The predominance of one of these hormones (humors) was to differentiate between four temperaments: sanguine (predominance of blood), choleric (predominance of bile), phlegmatic (predominance of phlegm), melancholic (predominance of black bile). His Latin maxim "*Humores regnant in nostro corpore*" seems to be adequate to this day. In everyday life, this maxim is translated into humor as the mood that regulates our social, including professional, behavior (Szymanik, Terelak, 2015).

Apart from the specific issues of psychophysiology, attention will be drawn only to examples of the use of physiological indicators, useful in psychological stress research, to assess formal aspects of stress, such as intensity and size. One of the most commonly used physiological stress indicators, especially by physicians and in laboratory tests, is the analysis of cardiovascular system activity at the following levels: pulse, blood pressure, amount of blood reaching a specific area of the body. The pulse indicates the heart rate, and a detailed analysis of this indicator is carried out using an electrocardiogram (ECG). Blood pressure (systolic and diastolic) reflects the magnitude of the force exerted by the blood flow on the blood vessels. The simplest measurement of this indicator in outpatient conditions is performed with a strain gauge. Laboratory tests, due to the need for continuous recording of changes in blood pressure, use complex technical procedures of automatic recording (monitoring), which since the 1950s have been associated with Norman J. Holter, who recorded brain waves and heart area waves using radio waves. The device, commonly known as the "Holter monitor", allows recording an electrocardiogram line of a patient, which is then used to diagnose various types of so-called diseases from stress overload (diseases of affluence). The use of a miniature computer for ECG recording analysis allowed a versatile quantitative and graphic analysis of selected parameters, an example of which is the assessment of the workload of passenger plane pilots during take-off, flight and landing, presented in Fig. 3.2.

As it appears from the above Fig. 3.2 the most strenuous for cardiovascular system is the moment of take-off and landing, which is in line with subjective assessments of the pilots who claim that the source of stress during these phases of the flight is not the physical factors of flight but the psychological factors associated with the personal responsibility for the safety of passengers.

Another parameter of the cardiovascular system activity is the amount of blood reaching a specific area of the body. As we know, changes in the rate of the blood flow are mainly related to the condition of the arteries. Therefore, in medical practice, the recorded with the use of a non-invasive ultrasound

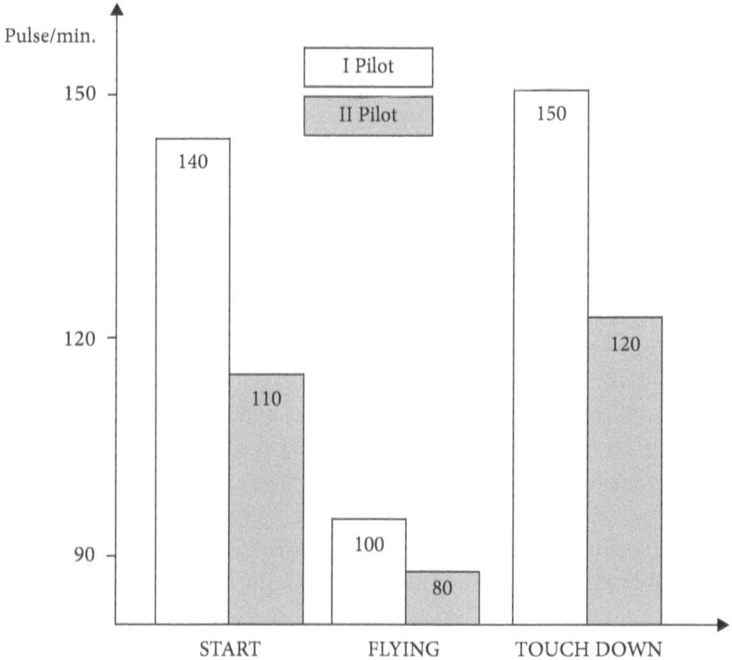

Fig. 3.2: Heart rate test as an indicator of stress in pilots in three phases of an aircraft cruise on the route Warsaw - Vienna Warsaw (source: own research

method based on the *Doppler Ultrasonic Photometry* phenomenon arteriogram curve, is used to diagnose arteries diseases. Psychophysiological studies use the classical plethysmographic method to determine changes in the amount of blood flowing through a given area of the body, the method is not easily accessible for an average stress researcher but used in psychophysiological laboratories. An example may be a very spectacular and unique in the source literature study of the assessment of the actual physiological cost of a pilot in the event of loss of geographical orientation and life-threatening danger after the failure of a plane engine at the low altitude, which was recorded using telemetric ECG. The *post factum* comparison of three ECG curves, performed during rest (baseline test), during flight at low altitudes and in a life-threatening situation, indicated a clear differentiation in mental load. This is evidenced, among other things, by early ventricular excitation symptoms characteristic of a pre-infarction life-threatening state (Sarol, Skibniewski, Śliwak, 1974).

Another example of the assessment of anxiety reaction at heart rate level is own research from the perspective of individual differences between beginner and experienced skydivers. It was found that regardless of the professional experience, the level of psychological stress increased until the moment of jumping (of course, relatively less in the case of experienced skydivers), as evidenced by the persistently high heart rate: over 130/min in case of the beginners and 105/min in the experienced skydivers. It is characteristic that in the situation of waiting for the plane to take off (the so-called stress anticipation) these differences become blurred and stress increases evenly in both groups (Terelak, Przychodzka, 2015).

In own studies on estimating the physiological cost of students of flight school for pilots, who were subjected to the effects of accelerations in a high-G training centrifuge, a significant increase in production of both adrenaline and noradrenaline has been found in the urine samples taken half an hour before the training and a quarter an hour after the training. What is more, during the centrifuge training sessions, the heart rate measured at the peak moment of the training reached its cut-off point (heart rate 164/min), compared to the baseline measurement (105/min), which also correlated with the level of anxiety measured with the Spilberger STAI questionnaire (Domaszuk, Terelak, 1982).

The most sensitive physiological stress response indicators that tell us how the human body prepares to manage stress come from the following systems: 1) *heart and circulatory system*: heartbeats rate increase, vessels in the abdominal cavity organs narrow and vessels around the circumference of the body, i.e. limbs, dilate; cardiac muscle vessels (coronary vessels) also dilate; blood pressure increases; 2) *digestive system*: tension of the digestive tract muscles decreases, digestive glands cease secretion; digestion and secretion are inhibited; 3) *adrenal glands*: intensify the secretory activity, as a result of which adrenaline is released into the blood, which has a very multilateral effect on the functioning of the system, similar to that of a sympathetic nerve. Adrenaline increases the heart rate, inhibits intestinal movements, increases secretion of sugar into the blood, accelerates blood coagulation; 4) *thermoregulatory system* activates sweat glands.

All the physiological indicators of stimulation must be regarded as an inseparable whole, but for research purposes they can be regarded separately, as relating to cortical, autonomous and behavioral activity, as they are generally correlated.

We shall omit the discussion of methods of measuring individual physiological indicators used to assess the so-called physiological cost in stress, which have become highly specialized in recent years with the use of microelectrodes (e.g. *single-unit and local field-potential recordings*), as in the case of hemodynamic (PET and fMRI) and/or electromagnetic (ERPs and ERMFs) measurements, as these are the subject of many detailed studies (cf. Zani, Proverbio, Eds., 2003; Luck, Ed., 2005).

It should only be emphasized that ways of recording physiological responses exist and are based on two general principles. The first method involves capturing, filtering and amplifying relatively strong electrical signals spontaneously generated by the body (e.g. EEG, EOG, ECG, EMG, GSR, EOK), while the second method refers to other physical values related to the functioning of the body without measurable electrical signals (e.g. breathing, blood pressure, blood flow through the body, eye pupil changes, critical flicker rate threshold, etc.). In many studies on physiological correlates of stress responses, polygraph tests are preferred.

The physiological responses mentioned, regardless of how they are measured, are of interest to psychology because they are based on the paradigm of correlates of emotions accompanying stress. They are used in stress psychology to quantify the amount (intensity) of stress.

3.2.2 Emotional and behavioral stress indicators

The emotional aspects of stress response are mainly related to the mechanism of adaptation to changes of the habitat. The adaptive meaning of emotions has been known for a long time. The fact that emotion mobilizes the body reserves necessary for a long exertion or for short yet intensive exertion is essential for adaptation (e.g. in animals: a violent attack or an exhaustive escape from an aggressor). The accompanying hormonal changes, caused by stimulation of the appropriate structures of the central nervous system, modify the functioning of this system, increasing the level of excitement *(arousal)*, increasing the effectiveness of the nervous processes underlying the extremely complex psychophysiological processes (Stein, Leventhal, Trabasso, Eds., 1990). The anticipative value of emotions is a particular property - it causes the body to prepare for the expected strain. Psychologically speaking, this particular anticipative significance of emotions is related to the ease with which they are triggered by non-specific (conditional) stimuli and to the ease of conditioning the vegetative changes, which accompany emotions (Scherer, 1993).

Apart from the anticipative meaning, emotions play another physiological role, namely motivational. For this reason, some personality psychologists define motivation as a task-oriented emotion (cf. Obuchowski, 1982). The motivational role of emotions is to strengthen the mechanisms of exertional adaptation, which allows to reach deeper into the so-called functional reserves, mostly the energy reserves of the body. In this sense, psychophysiology distinguished, for example, delaying physical fatigue by emotional stimulation. An example may be the case of Stanisław Skalski[15], an excellent Polish pilot of Royal Air Force fighter planes, who after a few hours of strenuous air fight lost consciousness just after leaving the plane due to exhaustion. Delayed or reduced pain sensations and pain responses in states of strong emotional excitement have been described multiple times (Bedard-Gilligan, et al., 2012).

The changes in the energy level of the body in the state of emotional stimulation in stressful situations, discussed so far, as well as other accompanying physiological reactions do have an impact on human health, especially in the context of the so-called chronic stress. Today's diseases of affluence, as a syndrome of long-term emotional stress, raise questions about the adaptive significance of emotions without specifying the concept of adaptation. This misunderstanding stems from the fact that we succumb to too many analogies of somatic and vegetative manifestations of emotional reactions in humans and animals. The first mistake is the similarity of the basic elements of situations in which the so-called simple emotions spelling an escape or an attack in a dangerous situation in animals occur. In this sense, these simple emotions are undoubtedly of an adaptive nature. Sometimes, these reactions are of an adaptive nature in case of contemporary people as well. But only sometimes, as generally in social situations, even though the conflict is analogous to the emotional stimulation (e.g. rage) in an animal that has been in contact with an individual of another species on its own territory, the anger caused by such a social conflict does not cause an identical reaction in a human being and an animal. Generally speaking, although physiological reactions may be analogous (release of catecholamines and adrenal cortex hormones into the blood, metabolic changes, acceleration of heart rate and increase in blood pressure, etc.), in case of animals these changes are justified as they are the basis for energy mobilization for the motor activity (attack or escape). In case of humans, there is generally no motor reaction. All the above-mentioned physiological changes are not only unused, but are an interacting factor in the pathogenesis of some diseases as well. In the latter sense, they are not of an adaptive nature. At the psychological level, the fear of a threat is indicated by an emotion of fear, which is extremely complicated in terms of its content, because in one situation it can play an adaptive role

15 Data obtained during a personal interview conducted during a psychological examination extending the air-health license at the Military Institute of Aviation Medicine in Warsaw in 1975 with Gen. pilot Stanisław Skalski, a legend in military aviation, known as "Fighter Ace of World War II", who since 1940 fought in the Battle of Britain as a member of no. 306 and no. 316 squadrons, as a commanding officer of no. 317 squadron, "Skalski's Circus" squadron in Tunisia, no. 601 squadron in Malta and no. 133 Polish Wing, and shot down 18 German planes.

when warning about a real threat, and in other cases a non-adaptive role, leading to an unreal threat (e.g. from the past, symbolic, moral) or even to pathology (e.g. phobia or computer addiction). A good example is the dilemma of the brain in the form of FOMO *(Fear Of Missing Out)* syndrome, which cannot be explained on the basis of the classical concept of W.B. Cannon's homeostasis, according to which a distinction should be made between short-term and long-term homeostasis. It is only from the point of view of long-term homeostasis that emotional reactions are of homeodynamic nature. The difference between homeostasis and homeodynamics is, i.a., that the former concerns the ability to maintain constant internal and external environmental conditions which favor the proper functions of the biological structure, while the latter concerns the ability to ensure proper functioning of the biological structure despite the dynamic variability of the environment. Such an extended understanding of classical homeostasis is primarily aimed at survival in an emergency situation, which is facilitated by emotions. This thesis can be illustrated with the Winter-Over Syndrome in Antarctica presented in Fig. 3.3 draw.

Fig. 3.3: Winter-Over Syndromes in Antarctica (source: Terelak, 1982b - own research)

As the Fig. 3.3 shows, the winter-over syndrome, characterized by insomnia, anxiety, mood changes including depression, irritation turning into aggressive behaviors (physical, verbal, latent). These symptoms intensify with the duration of antarctic isolation and disappear after return, which means that they are an adaptive response to a long-term stress situation of homeodynamic nature.

In the civilized life\, a direct threat to a person's existence is rather rare. On the other hand, emotional reactions, typical of a dangerous situation, still occur together with a set of accompanying vegetative changes which, as in the case of animals, cannot be consciously inhibited (kinetic reactions of an attack, defense or escape are subordinated to will).

However, it is worth stressing that emotion, as a category explaining the internal states of human behavior in descriptive and theoretical terms, raises some controversies about its usefulness (cf. Krzyżewski, 1986). Still, due to the common attribution of primary functions and specific features (beside the non-specific ones) to emotions, two currents can be distinguished among psychological concepts of emotions: cognitive and motivational. The relation between emotions and specific mental processes (e.g. orientation processes, value and usefulness assessment processes) is emphasized in the broader context of their relation to cognition or motivation, and their specificity, on the basis of which they are considered to be separate mental processes, is not questioned. This specificity, not fully known, manifests itself in the regulatory character of emotions, both on the lower (limbic system), reactive level of organization of mental processes (in relation to phylogenesis and ontogenesis), as well as on the higher level (cortical system), characterized by goal-oriented behavior. For the above reason, it is justified to distinguish between simple emotional processes (also called subcortical) with atavistic, natural responses of the body to specific situations (e.g. reaction of escape or fight) and complex emotions (called cortical ones), whose function is to select information coming from the environment and already contained in the human memory. This cortical aspect of emotion is a process composed of two elements: non-specific (emotional stimulation associated with brain activation) and specific (content aspect of capturing the relationship between the incoming information and conscious control of our behaviors). The specific content element determines both the intensity of emotional stimulation and the sign of emotion (positive or negative), and thus also the behavioral and cognitive aspects of behavior in a stressful situation. This type of reasoning can be illustrated by aggressiveness, one of the symptoms of the Winter-Over Syndrome in Antarctica, as shown in Fig. 3.4.

As shown in Fig. 3.4 above, the most commonly occurring form of aggression was verbal aggressiveness, i.e. largely controlled. Aggression turns out to

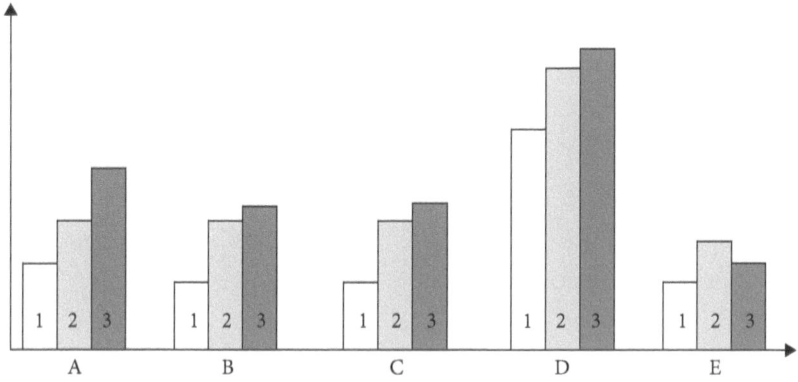

Fig. 3.4: Increase in manifestations of aggressiveness as uncontrolled emotions of polar explorers during a yearlong antarctic isolation (sources: own research)

Note: Legend: A - general aggression; B - physical aggression; C - transferred aggression; D - verbal aggression; E - irritability; 1 - pretest, 2 - halfway point of the wintering; 3 - after a year of isolation

be a good, learned form of stimulation and one of the ways of adapting to the conditions of long-term monotony, especially at the end of Antarctic wintering. This is also confirmed by a comparative own research carried out at a small polar station at Spitsbergen, where only 10 people winter, i.e. half as much as in the case of the Antarctic station (n=20 people). This research show that on average more aggressive behaviors occur at a small polar station than at medium and large stations in terms of the number of wintering polar explorers, which indicates, i.a., not so much a disturbance in the behavior of polar explorers as rather a specificity of adaptation to low stimulation living conditions (Terelak, Maciejczyk, 1989). For this reason, psychological literature sometimes mentions *an emotional stress component* that occurs alongside a cognitive stress component. L.A. Kitajew-Smyk (1989) characterizes the emotional-behavioral stress component model as comprising two patterns of response: an *active pattern of emotional-motor response*, which consists of two types of response, namely responses programmed for threat (fear, escape) and situational responses (euphoria, anger, embarrassment, triumph, aggression) and a *passive pattern of emotional-motivational response* (feelings of discomfort, anxiety, tone). The possibility of subjective experiencing and realizing emotions, on the one hand, and manifested responses to stress, on the other, make emotions as a whole elude research. Therefore, the different aspects of stress responses are usually highlighted. An example of this is research based on self-assessment under various stress conditions, such as

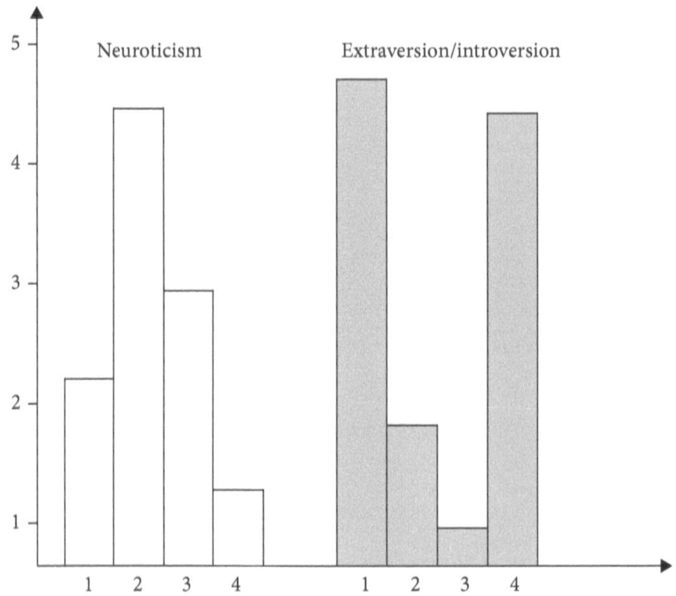

Fig. 3.5: Symptoms of introvertization as one of the Winter-Over Syndrome in Antarctica symptoms (sources: own research)

Note: (Legend: 1 - Pretest, 2. 3. 4 - beginning, middle and end of wintering)

long-term stress of social isolation, the results of which at the level of symptoms of the Winter-Over Syndrome, namely introvertization and the increase in neuroticism, are shown in Fig. 3.5.

Fig. 3.5 clearly shows the tendencies towards introvertization (closing up), which, in addition to increasing irritation, mood variability and aggressiveness, reflect the mechanism of adaptation to this type of extreme stress.

Clinical observations of various symptoms of stress responses are usually the source of such studies. Observations often form the basis for a number of detailed studies. However, the old Hippocratic dilemma of whether a person reacts actively or passively in a situation of mental stimulation is difficult to resolve unequivocally. Empirical research shows that activity/passiveness of behavior in stressful situations is determined both by the system of internal and external factors.

Many systematic experimental studies have been carried out in psychology in order to learn the psychological mechanisms explaining the highly complex interactions that occur between stressful situation, emotions and effectiveness of action. For example, from own experimental research on the influence of anxiety emotion on learning psychomotor tasks by young military pilots in situations of threat-related stress, which featured a punishment, in the form of an electric shock (500 mA; 0.01s) used when a mistake was made (not maintaining the light spot on the center of the coordinometer's screen), differences in learning outcomes of a simple psychomotor task to the disadvantage of people with a high level of anxiety were found. Thus, it can be said that people who usually react intensively with fear in various life situations, function worse in stressful situations.

Assuming that temperament also manifests itself at the emotional level, some psychologists mention behavioral syndromes consisting of so-called action styles that are more or less effective in stressful situations (cf. Matczak, 1982). For example, from the point of view of the style of an action, people differ in terms of: the number and duration of certain essential activities (i.e. those that directly lead to the achievement of a specific objective) in proportion to supplementary activities (i.e. those that secure, facilitate, correct the essential activities); their susceptibility to fatigue when performing homogeneous, monotonous activities (stress of sensory deprivation); their effectiveness when performing a range of different activities or in terms of time deficit (stress of overload and time deficit). The issue of action styles brings us closer to the cognitive level of organizing behavior in a stressful situation.

3.2.3 Cognitive stress indicators

The literature shows that cognitive aspects of stress responses can be considered in three groups of problems: activation of thinking, overactivation of cognitive processes, escape from stress-inducing problems. L.A. Kitajew-Smyk (1989), distinguishing *a cognitive stress component*, characterizes it as follows. The first type of reaction to stress, which manifests itself in *activation of thinking*, concerns mainly discursive-logical thinking, which consists either in intellectual integration of available information or in its disintegration (differentiation). This is the basis for a simplified, conceptual model of stress situation, based either on selective information, reduced (intellectual integration) or on comprehensive information (experience, knowledge of stress) associated with a specific stress situation (intellectual decomposition of the situation). Both types of activation of thinking are aimed at coping with stress. The optimal way to manage stress is, of course, to harmoniously associate the processes of integration and differentiation of information. In the cognitive component, there may also occur *overactivation of stress thinking* (e.g. intrusive thoughts, excessive fantasizing,

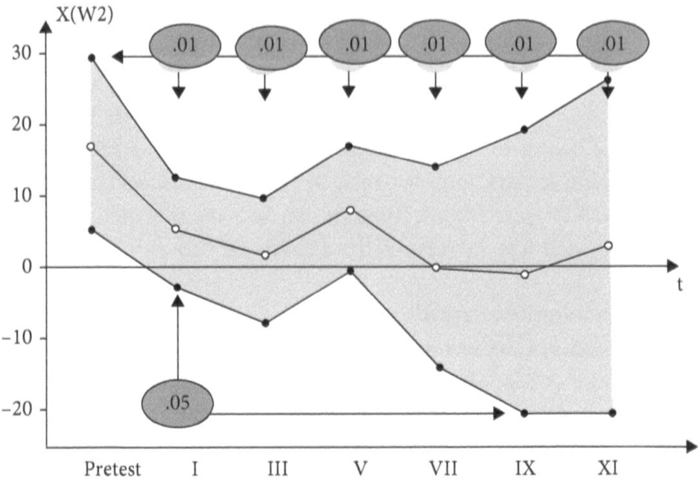

Fig. 3.6: Dynamics of mental capacity during social isolation (source: Terelak, 1982b - own research) (Legend: X (W) - percentage, average increase of pace of work; t - duration of antarctic isolation in months)

suspicion, increased vigilance) and *escape from the problem* (e.g. reduced mental activity, amnesic states, timidity, loss of interest in life, paroxysmal sleepiness, constant returning to the same problem, etc.). Within the cognitive stress component a decrease in mental activity under the influence of sudden, severe stress or under the influence of long-term stress can be distinguished as well. The latter case confirms another symptom of Winter-Over Syndrome in Antarctica, presented in Fig. 3.6, illustrating the decrease in the mental capacity of polar explorers under the influence of long-term antarctic isolation.

As the Fig. 3.6. shows, seven measurements of mental capacity were performed in longitudinal studies (every 2 months) using an hour version of the Kraepelin Test. The subjects were male polar explorers, average age of whom was 37. It was assumed that the deterioration of mental capacity would be a function of the duration of isolation and monotony. The results of the study confirmed the assumption made, which is reflected by the mental capacity index in Kraepelin Test X(W-2) concerning the percentage of the increase or decrease of the pace of mental work (determined as an index of the difference between the initial and the final segments of the test). A statistically significant deterioration of mental capacity was observed along with the duration of antarctic isolation (Terelak et al., 1985).

When discussing the cognitive aspects of stress responses, the impact of stress, especially extreme stress, on cognitive processes, studied at the level of self-assessment, cannot be ignored as well. This aspect of stress was the subject of own research during the yearlong isolation of a small task force in the conditions of the aforementioned Antarctic expedition of the Polish Academy of Sciences. We will pay attention to only three elements: self-assessment, assessment of other people, assessment of the current situation in research using Osgood's and Tannenbaum's semantic differential (SD) technique. In our case, the SD technique was used to measure attitudes towards personal and professional categories such as: "my wife", "my parents", "my children", "my supervisor", "my colleagues", "I as a father", "I as a man", "I as a husband", "I as a worker", "I as a colleague". The research was carried out every quarter, throughout the yearlong isolation period, with baseline tests conducted in Poland before leaving for Antarctica and final ones on board of a ship, on the way back to Poland. It was found, among other things, that attitudes towards the relatives left behind in the country change in the direction of idealizing their image with the during the course of the isolation-related stress. Such an idealization does not occur so clearly in the case of assessment of people, with whom the subjects had a looser emotional connection (e.g. "my superior", "my subordinate"). Similar tendencies occur in the area of idealizing oneself ("I as a father", "I as a man", "I as a husband"). The data presented above indicate an important cognitive aspect of stress response, which manifests itself, i.a., in a change in the perception of oneself and others, as well as in the perception of the stress situation itself (Terelak, 1982b). The latter problem was also the subject of own research. It has been assumed that the perception of a situation defined as a totality of subjective conditions on which it depends whether the surrounding reality is of significance to a person (stimulating, emotional) is a good indicator of the cognitive assessment of the degree of stressfulness of the situation.

To determine the degree of interpersonal attractiveness of the Antarctic polar explorers wintering together, a list of 20 adjectives was used, which were assigned a 5-point scale. The results obtained are shown in Fig. 3.7.

The data obtained show that the assessment of the social situation is increasingly negative with the duration of the stress of isolation, despite the lack of objective causes.

The cognitive aspects of the response to psychological stress discussed so far illustrate its essence, as the cognitive assessment of a situation determines both its classification: norm - stress, and the choice of stress management strategies.

This is also confirmed by the own laboratory studies on the influence of stress on such mental functions as decision making at the visual attention level (Terelak,

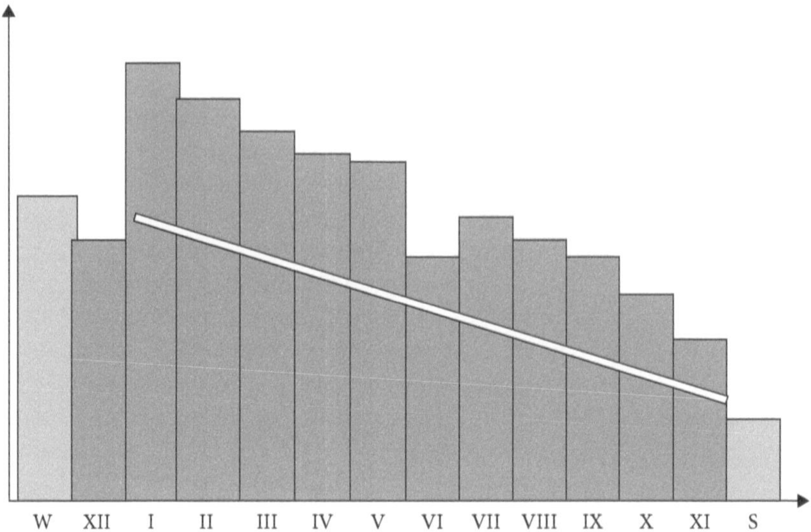

Fig. 3.7: Decrease in interpersonal attractiveness of members of the group together during the course of the antarctic isolation (source: Terelak, 1982b) - own research). Note: (Legend: W - initial examination on the ship on its way to the Antarctic Station of the Polish Academy of Sciences; I-XII - tests at the station; s - examination on the way back to the country).

Tarnowski, 1999). It has been assumed that a person's activity, even in a relatively simple man - machine relationship (task situation), is a resultant of many complex mental processes, including perception, inference and processing of information, making decisions about activity, and then coordinating movements. In this paper, the understanding of visual attention according to Michael I. Posner's (1994) concept was adopted, which distinguishes three mechanisms responsible for attention: (a) *orientating*, responsive to new stimuli; (b) *detecting*, allowing intentional search for information; (c) *supporting*, allowing attention to be kept continuously on one task or object. The detecting mechanism is therefore a function of the central attention mechanism, responsible for the overall control of the intentional action of a human being. In the presented own research the influence of a distractor on the functioning of the detecting attention mechanism was analyzed. The experimental task required two simultaneous actions (adjusting the position and size of the item on the screen). It was expected that the introduction of a distractor would change the priorities of activities related to the distribution of attention resources between competing tasks, especially that these were difficult tasks, requiring the involvement of a large amount of attention resources, and that at the same time the attention was deinvolved by the distractors. In an arranged experimental situation, the task required maintaining two parameters of the element's movement on the screen, and, at the same time, an adequate response to additional events. The main problem explored in the experiment was the allocation of attention resources within the main task - maintenance of movement parameters. It was examined to what extent the presence and complexity of the distractor, as a stress factor, changes the allocation of resources to maintain each of the parameters.

The survey involved 70 men, students of Warsaw Universities, aged 19–24. To assess psychomotor performance and attention resources, the Vienna Test System was used, consisting of a control computer and a set of peripherals: a panel with a monitor and a chronometer. Three-dimensional pursuit tracking was used, which involved keeping the tracking element (diagonal cross) on a square that changed its position and size, while adjusting the size with a lever controlled with the right hand and a knob controlled with the left hand. If an additional sign appeared on the screen, the participant had to press the right foot of a pedal. The difficulty of the main task was determined by the speed of the square's movement and the suddenness of changes in its speed and direction. The distractor was introduced on three levels of difficulty. In the first experimental situation, the task of the participant was to react to triangles appearing on the fringes of the screen by pressing the pedal, no other figures were shown. In the second, with higher level of difficulty, the task of the participant was to react to triangles appearing among other figures by using the pedal. In the third, the highest level of difficulty, the task was to press the right pedal when a triangle appeared, while the left pedal was to be pressed when a square appeared. The allocation of resources of the central attention mechanism between two activities comprising the main task: adjusting the position and size of the cross in accordance with the moving square was the depended variable. The results of the research confirmed the expectations concerning the changes in the allocation of attention influenced by the level of difficulty of the main task and the strength of the distractor. As the difficulty of the task increased, the level of performance of the main task decreased, while maintaining the size of the pursuing element was better performed, which is consistent with the theory referred to in the English-speaking literature as *dual/multi-task interference.* (cf. Wickens, 1991).

It is also worth discussing, on the example of aerial visual illusions, the disturbances of cognitive processes at the sensual and mental level, which occur under the influence of a distractor, i.e. information conflict. It is believed that visual illusions are the result of erroneous interpretation (at the stage of preliminary selection of information) of visual stimuli (information) reaching a human being. Some visual illusions experienced by pilots include: *autokinetic phenomenon* - (illusion of a luminous point moving on a uniform background, i.e. when there are no other visual reference points); *relative motion*; *false horizon* formed by a cloud heap; *mistaking or confusion of lights* - as landmarks during night flight; *poor assessment of depth* (e.g. flight altitude; confusion between earth lights and star lights, etc.).

Summarizing the presented aspects (physiological, emotional behavioral, cognitive) of stress responses, let us recall that such a division is very useful for the diagnosis of psychological stress response. The theoretical model of stress response and four aspects of stress response presented so far show, on the one hand, the complexity of the problem of diagnosing psychological stress, both in terms of research methods and psychoprophylaxis, and, on the other, people's incredible capability to adapt, triggered under the influence of the stressors discussed so far. Learning that capability to adapt to changed conditions of action mainly concerns the description and estimation of the so-called psychological cost, which undoubtedly arises when a person is forced to act in a situation of stress, especially the so-called chronic stress (Terelak, Maciejczyk,1989).

3.3 Symptoms of response to chronic stress

Chronic stress responses have been the subject of medical research since its inception. An example is the theoretical model of stress - H. Sely's disease (1956), known as GAS (General Adaptation Syndrome), which consists of three stages: alarm reaction stage - resistance stage - exhaustion stage. In the last stage, the symptoms of the disease occur when the normal level of stress resistance collapses. When capability to adapt is exhausted irreversibly, this means that, especially in the case of chronic stress, it is pathological adaptation to stress, which manifests itself in the specific symptoms of disease and often leads to death. Responses to chronic stress, which manifests itself in disease-related symptoms, are explained theoretically using psychosomatic and psychological stress concepts as well. For example, psychosomatic concepts assume that in case of stress of a high severity or long duration and when coping with stress is ineffective, it often leads to a disease that e.g. A. Antonovsky (1979) places on a continuum of health. Disease is therefore defined as a breakdown in human functioning, resulting from failures in the prevention of stress. This breakdown can affect both the somatic, mental and social levels, and may therefore be manifested by psychosomatic symptoms, mental disorders (e.g. neuroses, psychosis) and social deviations (alcoholism, drug abuse, crime, suicide, etc.).

This variety of consequences of chronic stress has led to a discussion about the foundations of the theory of *life events,* based on a hypothetical mechanism of additivity - *stressful life events.* The knowledge of the positive and negative role of difficult situations in human life is emphasized not only by contemporary psychology, pedagogy, sociology or medicine, but also reaches back with its roots to antiquity and the times of Hippocrates. Modern stress psychology, especially since the research of Roy R. Grinker and John P. Spiegel (1945) from the period of World War II on the influence of war stress on the well-being and health of a person, provides many arguments on the validity of the thesis that in human development the so-called crisis situations, which have a significant impact on human life should be reckoned with. These include the so called *combat stress* syndrome, which includes the following reactions: reduced resistance to frustration, frequent flu incidence, paranoid behavior, aggressiveness, tendency to isolate oneself, alcohol, drug and/or drug abuse, depressive tendencies, and sometimes suicidal thoughts (Figley, Nash, Eds., 2007). Sources of data on chronic stress come from research on concentration camp prisoners, combatants and war veterans, victims of the Holocaust, terminally ill people, prisoners with long sentences, residents of nursing homes, etc. (Solomon, Mikulincer, 2007). The chronic stress model is based on the assumption of synergy between the homeostatic level (metabolic reactions: excessive effort, malnutrition, excessive body dehydration, etc.) and the allostatic level (stress management reactions: excessive demands, unrealistic expectations, bad stress management strategies, responsible for the pathogenesis of chronic stress). This model is referenced by a well-known Polish psychiatrist - Antoni Kępiński (1972), who stated that not only extreme incidental stress, but also the long-term chronic character of such features of modern civilization as excessive haste (mental overload) or boredom (sensory deprivation) leads to the neurotization of technical civilization society and to the so-called psychosomatic diseases and neuroses. The chronic effects of stress always begin with uncompensated fatigue, which tends to turn into exhaustion.

3.3.1 Fatigue and exhaustion

Before we discuss the causes and symptoms of exhaustion as a reaction to chronic stress on the example of occupational burnout, it is worth straightening the basic theoretical concepts used by stress theorists. This applies in particular to the concepts used in psychology, physiology and ergonomics, such as: *stress, load, workload, fatigue.* There are many models in the literature that use these terms (Hancock, Desmond, Eds., 2001). Many researchers, such as M. Fąfrowicz and T. Marek (1999) in Polish occupational psychology, suggest the distinction between three similar concepts, i.e. mental stress, fatigue and mental strain. To this end, they distinguished two types of effort. The first type is *the mental effort* related to the level of difficulty of the task performed (mental strain), the second type is the *compensatory effort* related to the control of body states (mental stress and mental fatigue). The International Organization for Standardization (ISO 10075, 1991), referring to the transactional concept of stress from the perspective of the occupational psychology, on one hand points to the elements of the environment (in the broad sense) and, on the other hand, to the specific features of the individual. The transaction taking place here is important for the occurrence of chronic stress.

Other attempts to index the workload of operators of highly specialized technical objects, such as: high-maneuver airplanes, spacecraft, etc., can also be found in the literature. An example of which is the *NASA Task Load Index - NASA-TLX*, which covers six load aspects, namely: 1) mental demand (type and level of mental activity), 2) physical demand (type and level of effort), 3) temporal demand (required time and pace of work), 4) overall performance (success rate and level of satisfaction), 5) effort (consumption of physical and mental energy), 6) frustration level (stress symptoms). One of the more significant problems for the theory of chronic stress is the distinction between stress and mental fatigue. Stress occurs when there is a shortage of resources, i.e. when the demands of the situation exceed person's capabilities. Over time, fatigue begins to develop, which is a natural psychological and physiological state.

A convenient category allowing to differentiate the analyzed concepts of chronic stress and fatigue better is the category of effort that occurs both in case of stress and fatigue. However, *psychological effort* is associated with the amount of strain and mental capabilities of a person, while *compensation effort* is associated with deficits in mental functions (skills, abilities, etc.). Mental effort can be attributed to *workload on stress*, and compensation effort can be attributed to *fatigue*. This distinction is used in many empirical studies on the estimation of the so-called psychophysical cost. In the subject literature one can find a suggestion of three complementary methods of strain and fatigue testing, namely: 1) measurements of effectiveness (assuming that the difficulty of the task itself will reduce productivity, e.g. errors at work, prolonged time of action, etc.); 2) psychophysiological measurements (assuming the existence of physiological correlations of the level of stimulation and/or CNS activation, e.g. estimating psychophysiological costs using heart rate, ECG, EEG, etc. as a response to stress); 3) subjective measurements (assuming that the individual work-related effort can be subjectively estimated by means of specially constructed assessment scales). It is worth noting the subjective methods of measurement, as they are available to all psychologists, without the need for special equipment. An example is the *Subjective Workload Assesment Technique* - SWAT, which is known from the literature and by means of which three subjective aspects of workload can be defined: time load (often - rarely - never), mental effort load (small - medium - high), stress load (small - medium - high) and their reference to three levels of their incidence. This results in a combination of 27 subjective workload assessment grades, which in turn have to be ranked by the tested subject in ascending order. The proportions of the different load dimensions must also be assessed, which makes it possible to assess the subjective degree of load and its three types (cf. Biernacki, Bicka-Capała, Tarnowski, 2007).

Returning to fatigue itself, it is worth mentioning that there is no uniform theory of fatigue. We will therefore refer to an additive fatigue model: "Stress - workload – fatigue" (Hancock, Szalma, Eds., 2008). In the scope of this model, fatigue vs. exhaustion is defined as the body's response to prolonged stress, which results from the additive effect of various everyday stressors in an appropriate period of time (day, week, month, year). It is based on the distinction between incidental and chronic stress. If an assumption is made that incidental stress reflects the relationships that occur between the person and the environment, which are assessed in terms of the strain on the body to an extent that goes beyond its efficient functioning and reduces its well-being here and now, then in the case of chronic stress we are dealing with a long-term stress situation, reducing the body's capabilities to adapt, and with a deterioration in well-being. In the first case, fatigue is the sum of stress incidents in short periods of time, and exhaustion reflects the body's long-term workload and associated stress.

Thus, fatigue is the average human response to the combined effects of all stress factors: ecological (lighting, temperature, humidity, various types of radiation, vibrations, chemicals, etc.), social (working hours, workload, family status, economic status, unemployment, etc.) and personal (temperament, personality and character traits, illness, etc.). If the rest appropriate to the fatigue keeps people at a certain level of daily load, no negative changes in individual performance are observed. However, when the daily load exceeds the person-specific level (fatigue resistance) and accumulates over time, an overload phase occurs which manifests itself with relatively permanent negative consequences for the person's functioning. Fatigue processes, e.g. leading to occupational burnout, are often monitored using clinical methods, based on a retrospective record of stress events correlated with an electronic record of certain physiological parameters (e.g. 24-hour record of heart rate or pressure using a Holter).

Fatigue, and in particular physiological and psychological exhaustion, as a response to daily stress, is a warning signal against excessive body strain leading to significant functional disorders resulting from failures in terms of dealing with stress (e.g. too short or ineffective rest). The first symptom of these disorders is a constant feeling of fatigue, which is one of the main symptoms of occupational burnout, followed by psychosomatic diseases and various types of neuroses (e.g. neurasthenia). One of the reasons for the fatigue of contemporary people living in economically developed countries, apart from the exhaustion discussed earlier, is occupational burnout.

3.3.2 Occupational burnout[16]

In general, the burnout syndrome is defined as one of the possible responses of an individual to chronic emotional stress associated with working in occupations where continuous contact with people is a common feature, e.g. social workers, teachers of non-academic schools, academics, doctors, midwives, psychologists, nurses, clerics, telemarketers, journalists, officials, lawyers, police officers, managers, etc… This syndrome consists of three separate components, which constitute the basic dimensions of the burnout syndrome: emotional exhaustion, excessive depersonalization, personal dissatisfaction with the work results. The definition of the concept of occupational burnout syndrome varies among different researchers. The basic statements of the classic concept of occupational burnout developed by Ch. Maslach and M.P. Leiter (2007), colloquially called *the loss of concern for people*, refer to clinical descriptions of symptoms of dehumanization of interpersonal relationships at the workplace, forming a three-phase syndrome. The first component of burnout is *the emotional exhaustion phase*, in which psychosomatic symptoms dominate, e.g. headaches, fatigue, insomnia. The place of actual disorders is often taken by hypochondria, which intensifies attempts to physically escape from the difficulties that are impossible to cope with into illness. In general, it can be said that this is a stage of somatization of difficulties and physical escape. The second factor, described as *depersonalization*, is characterized by a loss of concern for people and the meaning of work in general (e.g. avoiding mental contact, demonstrating a lack of interest and compassion, blaming a subordinate or a client for having to take care of them). The third factor combines all of the previous symptoms, as it is characterized by *the*

16 "Burnout" is a neologism taken from physics, used to describe "processes connected with the movement of mass and energy", whereas in psychology it is used to describe reactions to specific conditions of the working environment.

loss of sense of personal achievement, i. e. reduced effectiveness of work, increased conflict-rate with co-workers, too frequent use of alcohol or drugs, accompanied by fear and a sense of grievance and guilt.

The causes of the occupational burnout syndrome can be traced back to three levels: personal, interpersonal and organizational. Among the features of an employee which are conducive to burnout are: passivity, uncertainty, low self-esteem, defensiveness, dependence, psychopathic personality traits, immaturity of personality, hysterical traits. Factors that reduce the risk of this phenomenon include management staff's awareness of burnout, knowledge of the vulnerable employees about the conditions and symptoms, drawing attention to developing interpersonal skills among the vulnerable employees, organizing greater opportunities for social support, etc.

It is worth emphasizing that various new concepts of occupational burnout, although have been extended to other occupations that do not require professional contact with people, are not in essence concepts of stress, although the attempt to combine the concept of occupational burnout with the theory of stress was made by a Polish psychologist - Helena Sęk et al. (1996), who suggested a cognitive-competence model, combining elements of Lazarus' cognitive theory of stress with the C. Maslach's concept of occupational burnout.

As we have tried to demonstrate, the relationship between stress theory and the clinical concept of occupational burnout has not been fully explained yet and remains controversial. Although the concept of occupational burnout does not have sufficient explanatory power, it has become popular, especially in occupational psychology, for estimating the so-called psychological cost of occupational stress (Dermerouti, Mostert, Bakker, 2010).

It should be added that psychiatrists extend the model of symptoms of occupational stress to all stressful events, not only those occurring at a workplace. They see neuroses and psychosomatic disorders as a health cost that modern civilization, entangled in constant wars, global information and migratory movements entails.

3.3.3 Psychosomatic disorders and neuroses

T.H. Holmes and R.H. Rahe (1967), who diagnose the effects of daily stress events using the *Social Readjustment Rating Scale*, predicts psychosomatic disorders, which first as so-called affective disorders, manifest themselves with mood variability during the day, and then with depressive symptoms. On the other hand, P.L. Miller and colleagues (1989) found that in addition to neurotic symptoms associated with chronic stress, such as anxiety, asthma, irritability, compulsiveness, somatization and insomnia, psychiatric disorders with a depressive component occur as well. The psychological mechanism explaining the severity of depressive symptoms is seen by the authors in the self-esteem, or more precisely in a lowered self-esteem.

A similar mechanism explaining the relationship between the severity of stress events and neurotic disorders is referred to by other clinical psychologists who conclude that there are correlations between chronic stress and neurotic symptoms such as low self-esteem, self-destructive behavior, elevated levels of anxiety and depression, sleep disorders, insomnia and depression (cf. Dyson, Renk, 2006).

Two types of responses were described in the correlation between chronic economic stress and types of mental reactions. The former is characterized by a depressive and passive behavioral pattern and the latter by an expansive behavioral pattern geared towards pushing through. However, a decrease in mood is observed as the primary symptom of a stress response in both types. This discomfort pattern of behavior, which manifests itself in mood swings, is also typical of chronic stress in Antarctic isolation (Terelak, 1982b). R.M. Ganley's observations (1989) are interesting as well. Ganley, who analyzed the results of experimental and clinical studies for 30 years, pointed to yet another neurotic pattern of behavior under the influence of chronic stress, namely a pattern based on the mechanism of reducing anxiety through pathological appetite (the so-called neurotic obesity).

The ever-increasing number of cases of various neuroses, threatening the mental health of contemporary people, has become the basis for the formulation of judgments, especially in journalism and popular science studies, that neuroses are a disease of the 20th and 21st centuries. As early as the beginning of the 20th century, after World War I, in 1919, Sigismund Freud recognized the clinical symptoms of the "post-traumatic neurosis", which could be considered as a precursor to the PTSD (Figley, Nash, Eds., 2007). It is stressed that modern civilization entails not only air pollution, water contamination and biological imbalance in nature, but also a rapid pace of life, haste, rivalry, a lot of information, and so on. The neuroses, which threaten people's mental health, have become a sign of our era. A lot of psychiatrist try to argue with this fatalistic view, they point to the confusion of facts and myths, as similar views existed in the 19th century (cf. Jarosz, 1975). Their reasoning is based on the following statements: civilization is not only a source of neurosis-inducing stressful situations, but also a means of protection against emotional factors; the weakness of human adaptation mechanisms is deceptive; the pursuit of detection and removal of neurosis-inducing factors should not go hand in hand with the dissemination of destructive myths, as they contribute to the hypochondria of societies and are an iatrogenic factor.

This view, which opposes certain stereotypes, cannot in any way diminish the relationship between chronic stress and the severity of symptoms of neurosis. It is up to epidemiologists to maintain the right balance in estimating the extent of the phenomenon, and it is their task to study the quantitative aspect of the neurosis phenomenon in the 21st century. The source of the difficulties in estimating neuroses may be twofold. Firstly, neuroses can occur in people without personality disorders as reactions to stressful situations, and these are then situational neuroses (so-called exogenous ones). Secondly, neuroses can occur in people with personality disorders, the so-called character neuroses, which are the result of chronic stress, often originating in childhood and covering specific personality areas with varying degrees of intensity. However, one more important factor in overestimating the relationship between neurosis and stress are the cultural and psychological implications. I am thinking here of the impact of psychoanalysis and so-called humanistic psychology on the contemporary culture. The exposition of existential threats, blind instincts, hostility of the environment, lack of love, loss of reason to live, etc., which generate fear, a neurotic need for love, competition, a sense of guilt (up to and including masochism), created the view that our times are characterized by a neurotic personality (Horney, 1976).

It is worth stressing that the relationship between psychoneurosis and traumatic stress, especially chronic stress, is obvious. This is evidenced, for example, by neuroses experimentally induced in dogs, the so-called experimental neuroses, the examination of which we owe to experiments conducted by Ivan P. Pavlov (1952), proving that, like in case of human neuroses, chronic stress (conflict) was the main cause of animal neuroses (functioning of the nervous system). This has also been confirmed by modern research. As an example, there are experiments conducted on mouse, which took into account sociological and situational factors, as described by Paul C. Henry (2005). Placing in a cage several mice previously "bred" in isolation causes an increase in their blood pressure to pathological values after 3 months. The author links this symptom with increased activity connected with fighting for social position within the group. After the following month, when the social hierarchy was established, pressure returned to normal values.

Slightly less controversial than in the case of neuroses are views on the relationship between stress (especially chronic stress) and psychosomatic diseases in humans. One reason for this is that empirical data are primarily based on clinical material. However, methodologists draw attention to the difficulties associated with the quantification of stressful life events (standardized interviews, questionnaires and scales for the assessment of stress events), as well as the elimination of so-called masking psychosomatic effects in the form of stress events that result from earlier diseases (e.g. neuroses discussed earlier) (Theorell, 2007).

3.4 Traumatic stress symptoms

There are two variations of response to traumatic stress known in the literature: *Combat Stress Reaction* – CSR (cf. Dobson, 2007) and *Post-Traumatic Stress Disorder* – PTSD (Holen, 2007). This division is in line with the "one-third phenomenon" known in clinical psychology, which results from the Platonic paradigm of individual differences. According to this phenomenon, one-third of people do not experience a severe and prolonged traumatic reaction to the same traumatic situation, one-third experience a severe trauma which they are able to extinguish and return to the *status quo ante* in the near future, as in the case of PTSD, and one-third - after experiencing a severe trauma only seemingly cope with it, but never return to normal functioning, and after some time experience it again through the eyes of their imagination and conscience, as in the case of *Delayed-Post-Traumatic Stress Disorder - DPSD.*

Diagnostic taxonomy of traumatic stress response in the literature distinguishes two groups: *chronic-without-acute-stress* and *chronic-with-acute-stress*. The latter response is generally intense and persistent, and sometimes deferred, and tends to recur cyclically.

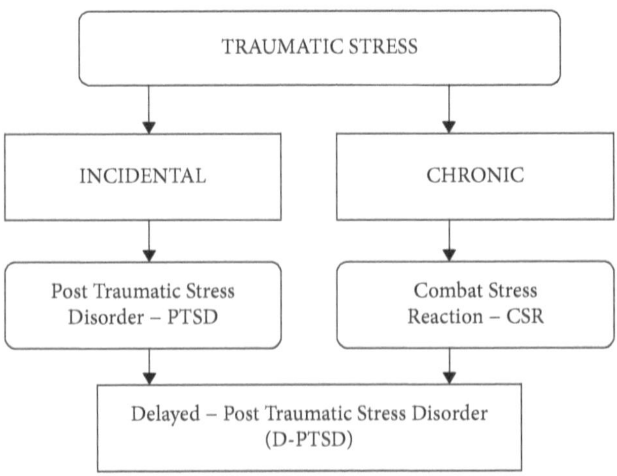

Fig. 3.8: Traumatic stress classification (own elaboration based on: Holen, 2007).

3.4.1 Shell shock syndrome

The early interest in acute stress and reactions stems primarily from military psychiatrists, participants in the World War I, as well as psychiatrists and psychologists conducting observations of American soldiers participating in activities at the European theater of war. It has been observed that in over 20 % of the studied cases the symptoms of *acute stress* were intensive psychological responses caused by the specific trauma resulting from participation in armed struggle, known in the literature as *Combat Stress Reaction (CSR)*. Its symptoms are: anxiety, depression, confusion, narrowing of the affect, susceptibility to irritation, somatic pain, withdrawal from the battlefield, apathy, paranoia, nausea, fear, increased activity of the sympathetic nervous system, etc.

There are primary and secondary causes of CSR. The primary cause is a cognitive assessment of the threat to life and inability to fight it, which leads to irritation and helplessness. The secondary cause is, above all, the lack of counter-measures of own and others' resources that can be counted on (the so-called common fate), which leads to limiting effective coping with the threatening situation or even making it impossible. Moreover, an axial symptom of shell shock is an existential fear of death and a cognitive dissonance between the need to kill fellow men and the moral norm found in the Ten Commandments, i.e. "Thou shalt not kill". The overwhelming fear is "extinguished" by various types of stimulants (drugs, spirits), which have been used by every army in the world since the dawn of the ages (Rahe, 2007a).

CSR is not a theoretical construct because it is purely phenomenological and poorly defined. The narrowest and oldest definition of CSR concerns only those soldiers evacuated from the battlefield among whom clinical signs described as "war neurosis" were observed. When attempting to explain the mechanism of traumatic stress occurring in the brain, a book titled: "*The Triune Brain in Evolution: Role in Paleocerebral Functions*" by Paul D. MacLean (1990) may prove to be useful, as a basis for explaining the mechanism of war neurosis, i.e. traumatic stress, including the division of the brain into three structures: the brainstem and the midbrain; the limbic system; and the neocortex. *The brainstem*, or the so-called reptilian brain - an archaic part of the brain located in midbrain, regulating the basic instincts related to biological survival, which are beyond our intellectual control - the world of reptiles. It is responsible for the concentration of all energy resources needed to fight and for sudden closure of the blood flow to organs less important when in a fight for survival, organs such as the digestive system, the neocortex; *the limbic system*, which appeared in early mammals 200 million years ago, is responsible for the emotional aspect and social behavior (mammalian world); *the neocortex*, also called the neopallium and isocortex, typical of thinking beings - the world of humans and primates - controlling their behavior.

War neurosis is defined narrowly at the level of the reptilian brain and the limbic system as increased and memorable affective activation. A more broad definition of CSR refers to all evacuated soldiers who present any symptoms of psychopathological disturbance. The broadest definition of CSR refers to all soldiers evacuated from a battlefield, injured by the enemy, injured in an explosion or injured in other way than a direct contact with the enemy, but showing behavioral and somatic symptoms. Lack of an applicable definition is an obstacle when comparing the results of the studies on the stress responses of combatants of different wars, such as World War I and World War II, the Vietnam War, wars in Israel, Kuwait, Bosnia, Uganda, Iraq and Afghanistan presented in the literature. Another problem with forming a definition is the so-called *secondary traumatic stress syndrome*, counted into CSR category. It usually occurs long after the battle is over (delayed stress response), when the direct source of stress ceases to affect soldiers. Most of them leave the battlefield not presenting any reactions to stress. Before the Vietnam War, the literature rarely mentioned the CSR indicators related to the period after leaving the battlefield. On the basis of longitudinal studies, sufficient evidence of delayed traumatic responses was obtained and included in the specific symptoms of the CSR (Schnurr, et al., 2006). At this stage, from a few months to a dozen or so after experiencing trauma, many symptoms are reduced, and the remaining symptoms form what is known in the subject literature as the post-traumatic process, which was initially characterized as a conflict between the need to respond to traumatic memories and the competitive need to suppress them (Bedard-Gilligan et al., 2012).

3.4.2 Post-traumatic stress disorder

The late, delayed traumatic stress responses during the Vietnam War period were called "numbness", which R.K. Pitman, B., Altman, M.L, MacKlin (1989), based on psychiatric studies of the Vietnam War veterans, described as the following behavioral disorders: alcohol addiction (67 %), drug addiction (30 %), depression (63 %), social phobias (26 %), generalized anxiety (22 %), obsessive-compulsive disorders (19 %). They are treated as the main symptoms of post-traumatic stress. As long as numbness was effective in inhibiting anxiety, soldiers did not seek therapeutic help and support. It was only when the emotional inhibition became intrusive that they reported health problems, often already entangled in withdrawal from society, as well as in the use of drugs, medications and alcohol.

Concluding the characteristics of shell shock, one must be aware of a yet to be mentioned important existential element, which results from the fact that soldiers are forced to kill the enemy, i.e. to commit unethical acts, which has an impact on their moral sensitivity and exceeds the capabilities of *debriefing* (cf. Robinson, Mitchell, Murdoch, 1995). This method is aimed at cognitive response, emotional trauma within the group and covers seven stages - introduction, fact, thought, reaction, symptom, teaching and re-entry, but it does not free from the sense of guilt, as the moral doubts remain (Wessley, Rose, Bisson, (1998)). While in this case interim effects can be achieved, restoring the proper functioning in the nearest future, it does not solve the delayed process of psychopatization of an individual or the existential crisis. Psychological techniques of moral desensitization are commonly known, they are aimed at increasing the killing predisposition of soldiers on the battlefield (MacDonald, 2003). They cover the following groups of measures: (1) brutalization of military life (shaving the head; uniformity of clothes, behavior and daily routine; omnipotence of the superior; subculture of violent hazing; deindividualization of moral responsibility in favor of a group; depriving the enemy of human dignity, etc.); (2) developing a conditioned response in killing the enemy (death penalty for not obeying the order to kill and rewarding its performance); (3) ideological indoctrination (assurance of being morally right, legendary symbols of courage, creating a sense of solidarity, creating a specific ethos of suicidal death for the cause, e.g. for kamikazes, terrorists, etc.).

The moral responsibility of an individual cannot be fully waived, as evidenced by the fact that, among the soldiers who were forced to kill directly on the frontline, more than 90 % presented symptoms of war neurosis after 30 days of experiencing this traumatic stress, while among soldiers who did not have the duty to kill the enemy (e.g. doctors, priests, cooks, etc.) - only about 10 %. We must also take into account the drastic effects that are remote in time, characterized by an escape from past traumatic events, either into drug addiction or suicide (Rose, Bisson, 1998). An example of which can be the fact of about 200 suicides committed in the British army after the victorious Falkland War in 1982 and 50,000 Russian soldiers committing suicide after returning home from the Chechen war front (cf. Hazboun, 2007). Post-traumatic stress disorder is well documented empirically, as evidenced by studies conducted by H. Klonoff et al. (1976), who evaluated the long-term health effects (physical, neuropsychological and psychiatric) over a period of 30 years after World War II. Two groups of people with different levels of stress were studied. The first group consisted of 45 people who were interned in Japan for a period of 3.67 years. Due to the cultural isolation factor, this group was classified as a "high stress group". The second group consisted of 42 people who were interned in German prisons for a period of 2.08 years. Due to the lack of significant cultural differences, this group was classified as "a group with a low level of stress". Representatives of both groups before the period of internment, as soldiers of the Canadian Armed Forces, were both physically and mentally fit (average age: 56). The results of the study confirmed the persistence of anxiety neurosis in both groups, the higher intensity of which was observed in the group classified as a high stress group, i.e. prisoners of war interned in Japan. Similar differences were noted in the ratio of 51:11 % neurological and general health disorders to the disadvantage of the high stress group.

Post-Traumatic Stress Disorder – PTSD is a new disease entity added into the American Diagnostic and Statistical Manual of Mental Disorders in 1980 (Fenny, Stines, Foa, 2007:). The American Psychiatric Association, adding the PTSD concept into the DSM (3rd edition published in 1980 and 4th edition of the *Diagnostic and Statistical Manual of Mental Disorders* in 1994) and to the *International Classification of Diseases (ICD-10)* recommended by the World Health Organization (WHO), first and foremost took into account the already classic observations of military clinical psychologists and the results of research conducted on the Vietnam War veterans and also Jews who survived the Holocaust (cf. O'Donnell, et al., 2007). The latest editions of both systems, i.e. DSM-IV and ICD-10 suggest a new disease entity, named: *Delayed-Post-Traumatic Stress Disorder – DPSD* (cf. Holen, 2007). Longitudinal studies conducted on the same war veterans over periods of several months, five and twenty years after the occurrence of traumatic stress show that the current criteria for diagnosis of PTSD occurring after 6 months are not adequate to diagnose the disorder. People who suffer from PTSD are not only fighting soldiers, but also e.g. journalists (frontline reporters), victims of terrorist attacks, families of victims of aircraft and road accidents. For example, the study conducted by R.A. Bryant and A.G. Harvey (2002) on the victims of 103 car accidents shows, i.a., that the symptoms of PTSD persisted in some people for a month, in others for 6 months, and in others for more than two years. This has been confirmed by, i.a., researchers studying the chronic symptoms of PTSD, which persisted up to three years in the victims of car accidents

(Buckley, Blanchard 2007) and the victims of a bombings in Oklahoma City (North et al. 2004). Therefore, regardless of the classification of the disease, the key to making a diagnosis is the occurrence of classical traumatic disaster-based stressor - *man-made disasters*, i.e. concentration camps, bombings, torture, acts of terrorism, *combat*, natural disasters (e.g. floods, earthquakes), transport and industrial accidents, as well as violence by others (DSM-III). According to

DSM-IV, a traumatic stressor is an event associated with a threat to life or physical integrity, during which a person experiences intense fear, feeling of helpless or terror. In addition to the occurrence of a traumatic stressor, diagnostic criteria in subsequent editions include 17 symptoms falling into three groups. The first group includes symptoms related to the constant reliving of the trauma (criterion B), e.g. repeated insistent memories, recurring dreams. The second group of symptoms is related to the persistent avoidance and reduction of overall responsiveness (criterion C), e.g. efforts to avoid thoughts, feelings and conversations about the trauma; reduced interest in and participation in daily activities (DSM-III). The third group (criterion D) covers symptoms associated with persistent psychophysiological stimulation, e.g. difficulty falling asleep or sleep disorders, irritability, anger outburst (DSM-IV).

Mardi J. Horowitz (1993), as a leading theoretician of traumatic stress from the perspective of cognitive psychology, points to the non-specific symptoms of PTSD resulting from a dissonance between the external situation and own cognitive patterns, which go beyond the scope of daily experience. Current experiences do not integrate with consciousness and remain active in memory in the form of five stages: outcry, denial, intrusion, working through and completion. The *outcry stage*, i.e. the emotional outburst of fear, sadness or anger, is a direct response to a threatening event. The next stages are: *denial* and *intrusion*. The stage intrusion includes unwanted thoughts, a rapid surge of feelings, or impulsive actions. Moreover, reactions of panic and excessive vigilance, as well as repeated thoughts, emotions and behaviors associated exclusively with a stressful event, and lack of focus on other events are all typical. While in a state of denial, a person ignores the implications of threats and losses, forgets about problems (partial or complete amnesia), and is not interested in life activities. An attempt to escape from reality into the world of fantasy occurs. Next a symptom of battle, escape or exhaustion caused by the permanent excitement occurs. Theoretically, the information on trauma pours into the consciousness until it is processed. After which the person experiences an information overload and the denial-numbness stage occurs again. The next stage of the traumatic response is *the working through stage*, during which the previously impaired functioning is improved. Emotions, thoughts, communication and relationships with other people take their proper shape. This is based on the new or revised information structure schemes produced during this stage. Both omissions and excessive focus on something or a falling back to denial and intrusion occur in this stage. The gradual restoration of the internal equilibrium transforms into a state of relative end of trauma. The working through stage is developmental in nature, it prepares for new commitments after experiencing a loss or injury and accepting a true image of oneself and the world depending on the new and current situation. Fantasy is separated from reality during this stage. After experiencing a stress event, people learn to be more flexible, cautious and skillful, despite the losses they have suffered. *The completion stage*, which frees a person from trauma, means the relative end of the most active stages of the processing of life events. The end is relative as trauma patterns will tend to persist for a long time and sometimes throughout lifetime. This cognitive model of response to traumatic stress is confirmed by various studies which suggest that both the intensity of symptoms and their dynamics and the disturbed aspects (behavior, memory, emotions, health) depend on the magnitude of the traumatic stimulus and the time passed from it taking effect, and also on the availability of social support, etc. (McFarlane, Yehuda, 1995).

We omitted a more detailed discussion of the symptoms of *Acute Stress Disorder* (ASD) of an incidental nature due to the availability of information on this issue in the literature. However, it is worth mentioning how the nosologic category of ASD differs from PTSD. These differences are mainly pointed out by clinical psychologists, who indicate above all the diagnostic criteria, which include: contact with violent stress, dissociative symptoms (e.g. numbness, lowering of awareness, depersonalization, derealization, amnesia), recurrent thoughts (images) of stress situation, avoiding thoughts of stress trauma (images), overstimulation (anxiety, insomnia, irritation, etc.), impairment of functioning. An important criterion is the duration of symptoms: from at least 2 days to less than a month after the trauma. The new nosologic disease entity - ASD, was previously known as shell shock, which the subject we have discussed earlier in the context of war-related acute stress disorder (ASD) (Bryant, Harvey, 2002).

Concluding the discussion of the model of response to traumatic stress, the validity of new directions in the development of this problem, such as the extension of the PTSD construct by a new D-PTSD model should be emphasized (Safir, Wallach, Skip, 2014). It is also justified in observing the real world. Since the terrorist attack on the World Trade Center in New York on September 11, 2001, public expectation of studying the extensive effects of traumatic stress, both on individuals and on communities, has become widespread. As we have tried to demonstrate, this is already reflected in the world psychology's growing interest in research. A large number of scientific publications on traumatic stress document practically all traumatic events in the modern world, such as: modern wars, peacekeeping missions, terrorism, earthquakes, hurricanes, industrial disasters, car accidents, floods, political emigration, mobbing, etc. (Balducci, Alfano, Fraccaroli, 2009). Research for ethical reasons is *post hoc*, including standardized interviews and psychometric tests, which in a way average acute response to traumatic stress. Therefore, it is worth noting that war reports of witnesses of traumatic events and subjects of dramatic experiences all the same. This method, although flawed by introspection, has an added value for stress psychology because of its authenticity and the ability to describe the dynamics of a stress response. `

Three types of studies on traumatic stress, and chronic stress in particular, have been mentioned so far, covering: (a) clinical observations and biographical data (lists of stress events); (b) sociodemographic studies; and (c) animal psychophysiological studies, all support the polyetiological concept of PTSD. While discussing the contemporary directions of research on factors broadening the PTSD concept in the direction of D-PTSD, we deliberately omitted such psychological factors as personality and temperament. Despite numerous studies on the subject conducted in last several decades, many basic questions about individual differences in response to traumatic stress still remain unanswered, as they require longitudinal studies, which are rare in psychology. One of the symptoms of PTSD is alcoholism and toxicomania, which are a result of ineffective coping with traumatic stress and the insufficient effectiveness of social support.

3.5 Alcoholism and toxicomania as stress responses

According to longitudinal clinical studies on the psychological consequences of traumatic stress, in addition to the symptoms discussed earlier, i.e. neuroses (especially with the depression component) and psychosomatic diseases, the third consequence is increased alcohol consumption, sometimes leading to alcoholism as a reaction to stress, especially chronic (Kaysen, et al., 2006). Modern civilized man often tries to reduce nervous tension and anxiety by using chemical substances, which are divided into three groups: medications, drugs and alcohol.

Analyzing the clear relationship between stress and alcoholism, experience shows that the first response to a negative emotional state is reaching for alcohol, which in small doses is a stimulant, although in large doses it becomes a depressant. This quite interesting mechanism of the vicious circle of stress - alcohol - stress is primarily the cause of neurasthenic drinking style, which often ends in addiction. A similar psychological mechanism can be observed in the case of other substances, such as medications, drugs, etc. Apart from the neurasthenic style, the literature describes other styles of alcohol drinking, such as contact (social), Dionysian (pleasurable), heroic (record-breaking) and suicidal (self-destructive). In addition to the listed styles, attention should be paid to the "front" style, which by military medicine is treated as a stimulant, increasing courage before the fight and allowing to reduce emotional tension after the fight and to forget for a while about the guilt or loss (Taft, Kaloupek, Schumm , et al., 2007).

As with alcohol consumption patterns, five patterns of consumption of drugs can be identified: (a) experimental use, (b) social and recreational use, (c) occasional and situational use, (d) intensive use, (e) compulsive use. The last two patterns are characteristic of addiction (Hayman et al., 2007). The mechanism of addiction to narcotics is extremely complex and is the result of two separate systems in the brain - the so-called reward (pleasure) system, which is a part of the limbic system and stress center. Researchers from *The Scripps Research Institute* (TSRI) located in La Jolla, California, have proven that these systems are interconnected. The cerebral cortex of the reward system contains specific neurons that are activated both when under the influence of a substance, e.g. nicotine, drugs, and when the effects disappear (the so-called vicious circle). So far, the area of the brain where these neurons were found, known as the ventral tegmental area (VTA), has been linked to the reward system and not to the feeling of hunger and stress. The neurons found in VTA were known to produce dopamine, a neurotransmitter associated with the feeling of pleasure. Scientists from a laboratory at the University of Toronto discovered the protein responsible for stress in the VTA. This peptide, known as the corticotropin-releasing factor (CRF), is associated with anxiety and depression (George, 2014).

Mechanisms, structures and transmitters responsible for developing addiction have not been fully explored. In addition to dopamine and the reward system, there are also different psychoactive substances with different mechanisms of action at the level of neurotransmitters. Moreover, an important aspect of the mechanisms controlling substance use is the situational context, which is difficult to research, but extremely important to explain the role of social stimuli, motivating people to reach for various types of substances. A thorough research is required in the scope of the mechanisms controlling the search for rewards not only in the form of substance use but also in the form of experiencing novelties (searching for new information), which related to the universal access to technological novelties in the social space, leads to new "quasi addictions" to television, Internet, smartphones, etc., and requires therapeutic aid. Addiction is a "disease of the brain" the treatment of which requires knowledge of complex mechanisms that involve many brain structures and systems.

The relationship between stress, alcoholism and drug addiction as a phenomenon associated with the use of different chemical substances for non-medical purposes (to become intoxicated), as presented so far, does not cover yet another issue, namely addiction to medications. This aspect of the remote consequence of chronic stress is widespread, especially in countries with a high level of civilization. It involves the self-application of medications and other substances for non-medical purposes (e.g. medication abuse) and is a more widespread phenomenon than drug addiction.

In view of the change in the model and structure of the use of narcotics, the World Health Organization has recommended the use of the term *addiction to medication* since 1969, which means: "a mental, and sometimes physical, state resulting from the interaction between the living organism and the medication. This state is characterized by behavioral changes, which always include the need to continuously or periodically take medications to experience their psychological effects or sometimes to avoid unpleasant symptoms resulting from their absence." However, in the scope of the provided definition the term *medication* does not only mean a chemical compound used in medicine, but also any substance which, after introduction into the body, may affect its functioning (cf. WHO, 1969, 1970). The above definition of addiction to medicines shows, on the one hand, the relationship between drug addiction and stress. In this case it is secondary because it concerns the purpose of taking medications, which is to "avoid unpleasant symptoms resulting from their absence" (so-called "medication craving"). On the other hand, it points out the connection with the learned way of dealing with stress, because the purpose of taking the drug is to "experience their psychological effects". The latter issue will discussed in Chapter 5.

The process of addiction after a trauma is progressive, with a paradoxical escape from stress into situations that in a short time give psychological relief (euphoria) and then themselves become stress-inducing, inevitably leading to mental deterioration and often self-destruction. At the behavioral level, alcoholism and drug addiction are linked to destructive behaviors: self-destructive (suicide) and anti-social.

3.6 Destructiveness: self-destructiveness and socio-destructiveness

When characterizing the psychological mechanism of traumatic stress, we pointed out the relationship between stress and negative emotions, which manifest themselves in various forms, such as: aggressive behavior, irritation, outbursts of rage and other seemingly unjustified strong destructive responses. We will present two types of such reactions to chronic stress: socio-destructive responses (crime) and self-destructive responses (self-mutilation or suicidal). The issue the socio-destructive reactions expressed in various types of anti-social behavior and crime has been mentioned earlier when we discussed addiction to medications, alcohol and drugs.

For example, the relationship between chronic stress, drug addiction and crime is indirect, but it is evident at least on three levels: (a) the direct link between the acquisition of the drug and its theft, forging prescriptions, blackmailing and coercing of third parties under threat of violence, etc.; (b) the increasing role of the drug in the motivation to commit a criminal act in order to satisfy the craving; (c) the supporting role of the drug in criminal activities. This group includes such acts as: active assault, murder, rape, disturbance of peace, causing transport accidents (Hołyst, 1984).

Longitudinal studies on the link between stress and crime in London's unemployed population show, inter alia, that crime increases with the duration of unemployment stress (Farrington et al., 1986). However, referring to economic theories or to the excess of free time at the hands of the unemployed carries no explanatory power and psychological theories, such as frustration and optimum stimulation theories, which indicate individual differences in dealing with stress, should be taken into account instead. I am thinking here of the suggestions made by J. Reykowski (1977), who, referring to the latter theory, suggests that the asociality or anti-social behavior of criminals should be treated as a source of strong and varied stimulation in the situation of its deficiency, in the conditions of environmental monotony.

Self-destruction in the form of suicide is another problem of the stress response, which is difficult to explain without reference to a hierarchy of values. The fundamental theorems of Victor E. Frankl's logo theory (1947) suggest that the loss of meaning in life leads to existential anxiety. The impossibility of overcoming this fear leads to the exceeding of a critical point, in which the self-preservation instinct, resulting from the primal principle of biological survival not only for the good of an individual, but also for the good of the species, is violated (Oquendo, Giner, Mann, 2007). Suicide attacks undermine this fundamental biological principle and indicate that people can give new meaning to suicide (e.g. kamikaze, religious martyrs, for their homeland) because suicide is not an isolated, temporary manifestation of individual behavior, although a direct cause can always be found at its root. Suicide attacks cover a wide range of contexts, including: suicide gestures, threats, demonstrations with low death threat; ambivalent suicide attempts when a tragic outcome is probable; 'potentially fatal' attempts where a chance to survive is unlikely. There are approximately one million deaths related to successful suicide attacks around the world every year, whereas there are 10–20 million suicide attempts that fail. Generally speaking, the causes for this are seen in two groups. The first group includes some predispositions of an individual manifested by depression (especially endogenous), neurosis or some psychopathic syndromes. The second group includes the cumulative effect of incidental traumatic stress (death of a loved one, loss of property, etc.) or chronic stress (monotony, boredom), which can be recognized before the suicide act as *a pre-suicidal syndrome*, characterized by three phases: (a) the phase of manifesting dissatisfaction outside, (b) the phase of aggressive behavior, (c) the phase of decreasing life activity. In addition to these two groups of causes of suicide acts, the wider social context also plays a modifying role, such as vogue for using alcohol, drugs, some depressant drugs, or imitating certain prominent figures from the world of literature, film, or show business (Lester, Walker, 2007). The relationship between suicide and traumatic as well as chronic stress (e.g. as a sum of stressful life events) is documented in the source literature. Military psychiatrists suggest that as many as 82.5 % of soldiers who committed suicide did so under the influence of factors unrelated to military service (arguments with a loved one, betrayal, etc.), and that only 17.5 % of suicides were directly related to the conditions of the military environment (Rydzyński, 1975). The latter information on suicides of young people confirms, on the one hand, that this dramatic way of copying is a serious social issue, on the other hand, it is a proof of the lack of remedial experience at a young age, which is confirmed by statistical data, which shows that in the years 2015 and 2016 11,093 people in Poland, including 1029 children and adolescents committed suicides[17].

Concluding the third part of the book, devoted to the description of responses to incidental and chronic stress, it should be emphasized that stress is a part of the outer and inner world of a human being. Therefore, with the exception of a few cases (suicides), people are adapted to this world better or worse, unless they completely lose their meaning of life.

Recapping the considerations presented thus far, it is worth noting that the variety of theoretical approaches to the analysis of stress proves, on the one hand, the complexity of the phenomenon and, on the other, the dynamic development of stress psychology. There are two ways of reporting on the state of knowledge on stress in the source literature. The first one consists in presenting individual theoretical stress models, the second one - in a meta-analysis grouping the results of stress research around more general hypotheses, with drawing conclusions for future research. In this book we are closer to the first method, because the second one is burdened with the arbitrariness of choosing a criterion determining a target perspective of the development of stress psychology.

17 Barbara Pietkiewicz (2018). Nikt nigdy się nie dowie (Nobody will ever know). „Polityka", 30(3170), 30–33.

The integrative (and even transactional) model of stress, preferred in contemporary literature, developed from the perspective of cognitive psychology, is increasingly criticized for omitting emotional and motivational elements. Their omission causes the appearance of some difficulties in understanding stress management strategies, which are not always rational. We will address these issues in the next chapter of this book.

4 Coping with stress

Resistance to stress is a theoretical construct that is not only controversial but also difficult to define unambiguously. To avoid misunderstandings, it is important to remember the terminological explanations and theoretical differences in identifying the essence of stress that have been detailed in the previous chapters of this book. The source literature features some motions to define this construct by connotational distinction between: stress resistance, the behavioral index of which can be e.g. relatively low emotional reactivity as an inborn feature of the subject, and stress resistance as a feature acquired in the course of life, the psychological index of which is e.g. the acquired ability of organized functioning despite emotional stimulation. Both connotations are complementary as they focus on the one hand on the sources of stress resistance (emotional reactivity), and on the other on the ways of coping with stress. We consider these aspects jointly as components of a broader concept of *stress resistance.* This term was popularized in psychological literature years ago as a carbon copy of the biological concept of *stress resistance.* It should be remembered, however, that in the field of psychology it functions as an analogy of the concept of immunology. Therefore, its original and proper meaning should be recalled. (O'Driscoll, 2013).

4.1 Theoretical status of the concept of stress resistance

The concept of resistance derived from immunology refers to the inability of an organism to be exposed to pathogenic microorganisms or their venom (toxins). In a broader sense, resistance is the state of an organism conditioned by a set of processes designed to restore the integrity of its internal environment, which has been compromised by antigenic factors. The concept of resistance has been derived from immunology and applied in stress psychology only on the basis of a semantic analogy, has a rather controversial scientific status. People have a relatively high tolerance for stress, which allowed us to dominate the entire globe and dream of exploring the cosmos. This natural mechanism of adaptability to changing environmental conditions is its dynamically developing intellect, due to which we have evolved from *homo habilis* (handy man), who have mastered the art of passive adaptation to environmental conditions, to *homo sapiens,* who creatively transform the environment, creating optimal living conditions of individual and institutional character, and because of this cope with stress more and more efficiently. In this respect, Pierre Teilhard de Chardin's theory of evolutionary anthropogenesis (1967) is an interesting anthropological concept. It refers to the following stages of evolution: cosmogenesis (gradual formation of the universe from cosmic matter), geogenesis (formation of the planet Earth), biogenesis (formation and development of organic life), psychogenesis (appearance of simple mental processes, especially among animals), anthropogenesis (evolution of humans as a species with a reflective consciousness), noogenesis (organization of the sphere of common human thought, i.e. the noosphere). Thus, by presenting the structure and evolution of the human species, this theory emphasizes that in terms of inborn, ready-to-use patterns of stress protection, humans are handicapped when compared to other animals. However, Chardin does not underestimate the important relationships between humans and their biology, as he emphasizes the constant socialization trend in the evolution of *homo sapiens,* leading to the development of a noosphere (the mind) through individualization, totalization and personalization. Aware of the limitations resulting from coping with stress independently and individually, humans evolve towards the search for a synthesis of social wisdom (totalization), through, i.a., ethnic coupling (creating social structures), economic and technical organizations, interdependent increase of awareness, knowledge and activity. In this synthesis, people search for their own creative place more frequently, creating a personalistic concept of life. In this way, philosophical and natural anthropology attempts to reconcile biological determinism with personalistic indeterminism. It is also reflected in psychologists' views on coping with stress, in which the evolutionary consequences of *homo sapiens*, i.e. a clear separation between *here and now* what is genre and what is individual in man cannot be ignored. This is constantly reminded by biological and psychosomatic concepts of stress, which expose the individual's inability to cope with atavistic (species-specific) physiological responses, increasing the body's energy level necessary for a supposed "attack" or "escape" from the species' enemy, on the one hand, and, on the other hand, cognitive concepts indicating an unlimited psychological mechanism for defining symbolic threats, past, present and future. This mechanism automatically (without biological justification) and generally in excess produces physiological responses, which, due to socialization, must be reinhibited.

Recalling the basic knowledge about biological immunity, we draw attention to the fact that the introduction of the term *stress resistance* into stress psychology is a distant analogy to the original biological meaning of the term. Assuming that such an analogy is permissible, it may, however, concern only some of its aspects. For example, it can be partially used for our purposes in its natural (non-specific) species-specific form, which manifests itself in partial innate species-specific stress response patterns (e.g. atavistic responses to escape or fight an enemy). Individual natural stress resistance may manifest itself in a special constitution and personality type, which is the basis for the classification of people to those resistant to stress and those not resistant, which is made on the basis of the so-called type of strong and weak nervous system or temperament division developed by I. Pavlov. This type of stress resistance is included in the so-called psychophysiological stress theories. Finally, acquired resistance can only be an analog for psychologists in the form of active acquired resistance. Thus, the acquired (specific) natural stress resistance can result from individual experience with a given type of stress situation (stressor). This type of resistance is taken into account in the so-called crisis stress theories (cf. Dąbrowski's theory of positive disintegration). Acquired artificial stress resistance can manifest itself in two forms: socially acceptable, including, but not limited to, "vaccines" such as Spartan education, physical training, survival training, and so on. This type of resistance is included in the so-called educational and psychotherapeutic stress theories, such as the *Stress Inoculation Training* (SIT) theory by M.E. Jaremko (1984). The socially unacceptable form of this type of stress resistance includes, i.a., the types of "vaccines" such as addiction to medications, self-destructive behaviors, social deviances, neuroses and mental illnesses. This type of stress resistance is included in medical and sociological concepts of stress.

On the basis of the presented motion of searching for analogies between the concept of resistance in the biological and psychological sense, one can propose some analogies of this term. In psychological literature several concepts, which are often used interchangeably, can be found namely: "frustration tolerance", "stress resistance", "mental resistance", "emotional resistance", "mental suppleness", etc. These concepts are most commonly found in clinical psychology and psychiatry. They are a consequence of defining mental stress as a state of increased emotional tension.

In our deliberations, we will use the concept of stress resistance, assigning it a theoretical status, derived from the theory of temperament (an innate type of nervous system) and the theory of intelligence (an innate potential in terms of the ability to learn). Thus, we define stress resistance, on the one hand, as a natural species-specific ability, i.e. a relatively constant feature of the body, and on the other, as an acquired individual ability to cope with stress, by maintaining the previous direction, efficiency and level of organization of behavior in spite of stress, while at the same time minimizing the physiological and psychological cost. Both of these aspects of stress resistance, which are complementary in nature, are illustrated in Fig. 4.1.

The above figure also takes into account the classical understanding of resistance to stress as an ability conditioned by certain natural features of the body

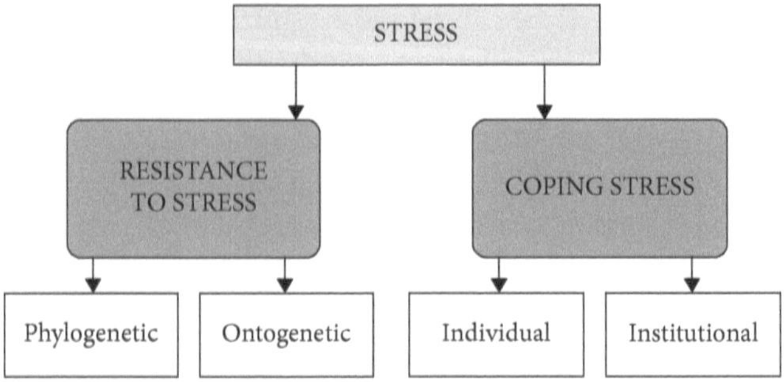

Fig. 4.1: Psychological model of stress resistance (own elaboration)

(e.g. type of nervous system). The second psychological aspect relates to the ability to cope with stress as an acquired way of dealing with it.

When considering stress resistance as a natural species-specific ability, we need to refer to a more general biological concept, namely adaptation to changing environmental conditions (homeostasis), which is a common feature of all living organisms. Currently, the term - adjustment seems to be more common in social science, the use of which emphasizes its dynamic and creative character (homeodynamics).

There are some analogies between the habitat of animals and humans. For example, the responses of animals, especially mammals, to environmental stimuli or injuries can be described as being composed of two components. On the one hand, each species exhibits a non-specific pattern of physiological responses and behavior determined by the nature and strength of the stimulus. On the other hand, all mammals, including humans, tend to respond to stress situations with a complex series of highly individualized phenomena, almost independent of the nature of the stimulus. However, humans are equipped with intelligence to creatively shape the environment and not just passively adjust to it, although some of the innate responses are still the same as those that evolved in his past to allow people to adapt to circumstances that were then of extreme significance, but now, are no longer relevant. An example of which can be the stimulative patterns of physiological responses to stress, described in physiology, which, from the psychological point of view, currently are often of an atavistic nature and largely inadequate to the present situation. In a normal person, as in animals, physiological and metabolic changes occurring before effort are foreseen by the body. The ability to mobilize the considerable amount of energy required to escape or fight in advance and immediately was undoubtedly a great evolutionary achievement in the past. Nowadays, this ability not only does not help people to fight stress, but often becomes an obstacle. The anticipatory mobilization of physiological processes occurs under the influence of emotional sensations (psychological stimuli), without any connection with the actual physical threat. Thus, it has nothing to do with the threat posed by the species enemy (each species has a different image of the enemy), which causes an automatic response by mobilization of the body. Despite the lack of a real threat, the human being perceives this symbolic experience similarly to the real effects of supposed physical threats. Although psychological (emotional) stress and even real threat rarely require greater physical effort in the conditions provided by modern civilization, the nature and strength of these anticipatory physiological and metabolic changes are almost the same in modern humans as in our palaeolithic ancestors. This is certainly an argument for the existence of innate forms of resistance to species-specific stress (at the level of characteristic physiological response patterns). A good example is the familiar to everyone goosebumps effect as a response to thermal stress from cold or to a threat. It is undoubtedly an atavistic form of stress protection, a remnant from the past, dating back to the prehistoric era, when our ancestors were covered in hair either completely or more than modern humans. Hair, that raised when a threat was sensed or when it was cold (raised hair is an insulating layer that reduces heat loss), was formerly used to protect against the cold or to scare off enemies of the species. Today, goosebumps, as a reflex caused by the nervous system (contraction of muscles at the base of hair follicles), is of no adaptational significance as protection from the cold or an enemy, because we use clothes as means of thermal protection and, what is more, we do not have an image of the enemy species programed in our brains.

Remaining in their residual form, old - from a phylogenetic perspective, inborn patterns of behavior in ordinary conditions of modern civilization may be a source of physiological (i.e. physiological responses inadequate to the threat) and psychological conflicts, negatively affecting the state of our well-being (e.g. excessive fatigue) or health (e.g. psychosomatic, cardiological diseases). Perhaps, humans have also preserved certain needs from their evolutionary past, which do not have to be satisfied in the conditions of modern life. Therefore, different patterns of human behavior, usually considered purely psychological, are in fact similar to animal behavior and are likely to have been developed during the evolution of mammals, such as the drive to hunt animals and to fight found in humans (numerous wars fought since the dawn time); the drive to play and have fun as an essential element of animal breeding in zoos; and the drive to play and have fun as a ritual element in many cultures (*homo ludens*), etc., which is one of the subjects tackled in detail by cultural philosophy and anthropology (Krąpiec, 2008).

The atavistic nature of innate patterns of physiological responses to stress may be demonstrated by research which as an indicator used blood pressure of pilots before, during and after flights. The flights took place in simulated conditions, without any real danger, but only with a symbolic one (social assessment). During a four-hour simulated flight, the pilot's systolic pressure increased to 220 mmHg, diastolic pressure to 150 mmHg; at rest, these values were 120 mmHg and 70 mmHg, respectively. The experiment can be illustrated by the familiar to everyone goosebumps effect as a response to thermal stress from cold or to a threat. It is undoubtedly an atavistic form of stress protection, a remnant from the past, dating back to the prehistoric era, when our ancestors were covered in hair either completely or more than modern humans. Hair, that raised when a threat was sensed or when it was cold (raised hair is an insulating layer that reduces heat loss), was formerly used to protect against the cold or to scare off enemies of the species. Today, goosebumps, as a reflex caused by the nervous system (contraction of muscles at the base of hair follicles), is of no adaptational significance as protection from the cold or an enemy, because we use clothes as means of thermal protection and, what is more, we do not have an image of the enemy species programed in our brains, as this enemy is defined individually by us. This reflex, having a purely symbolic character, remained unchanged in homo sapiens as an element of the emotional response to stress. As the experiment shows, from the point of view of physical effort, the preceding increase in cardiovascular function is inadequate (i.e. excessive). The increase in blood pressure alone is not good and almost certainly is dangerous when it occurs solely as an expression of psychological stress (i.e. a social threat as an expression of disapproval). This imperfection of innate stress protection mechanisms is compensated by other forms of resistance to acquired stress, which is primarily a function of intelligence. Therefore, not all pilots respond with a similar increase in blood pressure under simulated flight conditions. Significant individual differences were found to indicate that individual susceptibility to stress also plays a role in natural stress resistance. We will look at it in a little more detail, because this natural form of stress resistance is fundamental in relation to its various acquired forms.

Before we move on to the characterization of stress resistance as a natural individual ability, determined by the type of nervous system, temperament, we will point to some features of this resistance, allowing us to characterize it as an individual feature. It can be assumed that the characterization of individual resistance to psychological stress should include: (a) the degree and extent of universality of this personality trait, on a continuum of which those completely resistant and those not resistant to stress can be distinguished; (theoretically of course); (b) the specificity of resistance, mainly related to reduced tolerance to specific stress situations; (c) the variation of resistance over time, occurring in the same person, depending on the situation, e.g. on time of day, health, experience, etc.).

When analyzing stress resistance from the psychological perspective on individual differences for specific populations (interpersonal aspect) or individuals (intrapersonal aspect), we generally use statistical models based, for example, on the Gaussian curve. For example, on the basis of the so-called interquartile deviation we can distinguish two 25 % cohort, one resistant to stress and the other not, and the remaining 50 % that are moderately resistant.

According to the psychological literature, the natural determinant of stress resistance is the nervous system, and especially some of its functional features manifesting itself in a specific type of nervous system (Pavlov, 1952), which is correlated with some features of temperament or type of emotional excitability. The temperamental conditions of stress resistance were described in detail in Polish psychological literature by Jan Strelau (1995), who emphasized that temperament can be treated as a moderator of coping with stress.

The presented model of natural conditionings of resistance also takes into account some personality traits, such as introversion vs. extraversion and neuroticism, which in Anglo-Saxon psychology are treated as biologically conditioned (Eysenck, 1990), and new models of stress resistance, among which such theoretical constructs are recently exposed in the literature as *resilience*, which is

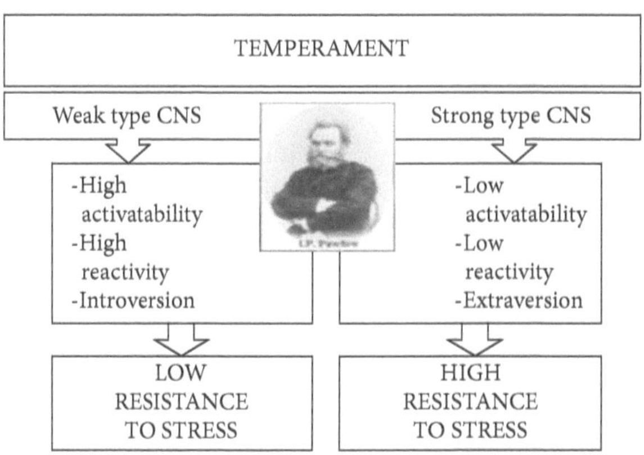

Fig. 4.2: Temperamental model of stress resistance (own elaboration).

characterized by such traits as: emotional stability, openness to new experiences, sense of coherence, effectiveness in action, optimism, emotional intelligence and high IQ, ability to learn effectively, speech fluency, planning ability, social competences related to self-regulation of emotions, positive self-image (Charney, 2004).

4.2 Ability of coping with stress

In addition to their natural abilities, which determine the specific range of stress resistance, attention should be paid to ability to learn which is of importance to humans. Although due to this ability humans are deprived of some ready-made stress management patterns, they can learn new methods to cope with stress throughout their entire lifetime.

The way the authors of the psychological stress concept call the activity of the subject in stress confrontation varies. For example, supporters of psychoanalysis distinguish between control and defense mechanisms, while representatives of the theory of frustration distinguish between responses focused on needs and on the defense of the ego. Theoretical problems in understanding the role of emotions in coping with stress should be reminded, as a result of which psychologists did not always combine cognitive activity with experienced emotions, describing them as two independent systems, between which different interactions take place. Some scientists, such as K. Krzyżewski (1986), voiced their opinions "about the uselessness of emotional categories" in explaining human behavior. Others, in turn, pointed only to differences in understanding the cognitive definition of emotions .

Appraisal theories, to the development of which R. Lazarus was one the biggest contributors, define emotions by combining different areas of human psychology: cognition, motivation, emotions and coping. Thus, they break with the traditional way of understanding these concepts, originating from the ancient Platonic philosophy, which separated thinking (reason, mind, Greek: *logos*) from emotion (Greek: *pathos*) and motivation (lust, passion, Greek: *dioksis*) (see Aristotle). The cognitive approach to emotions assumes that they are generated as a result of evaluation of events (not necessarily conscious and controlled). Individuals continually evaluate the relationship between themselves and their surroundings, referring to their personal well-being. Thus the key aspect for emotions is the interpretation, not the event itself. The content of a cognitive evaluation determines an individual's emotional response and behavior. Each emotion is generated according to a specific cognitive evaluation pattern, which is a specific set of evaluations. Furthermore, the identification of these cognitive evaluation patterns, allows us to answer the question, why various situations evoke the same feelings in various people, and why the same events may cause different emotions in various people (Carver, Scheier, 1994).

Another problem concerns the difficulty of explaining the relationship between cognitive assessment and emotions. Some theorists assume that assessments precede the emotions, while others treat them as components, i.e. parts that build emotions (Łosiak, 2007) .

Despite the common assumptions underlying the cognitive approach to emotions, there is no consensus between the authors of different theories within the same current in defining the components of the cognitive evaluation process that are important for evoking specific emotions, or in treating cognitive assessments as anticipatory to or components of emotions. The states that some authors consider to be emotions are not accepted by others. Additionally, not all theorists of the current define the mechanism of generating of emotions. Some limit themselves to defining the components, e.g. K.R. Scherer (1993) considers this fact to be a considerable theoretical problem, as it only allows for studying the structure or limiting to different semantic connotations within a given emotion. It does not explain the relation between emotions and events serving as their background, i.e. it does not explain the mechanism of evoking emotions.

According to R. Lazarus the mechanism of cognitive evaluation is important in coping with stress, as certain evaluations are accompanied by emotions specific to them. In addition to the classic dimensions of emotions: stimulation, expression, strength, Lazarus (1993) also mentions the content of emotion, which he calls *Core Relational Themes*. By this he emphasizes that emotions are directly related to the outcome of a stressful transaction. The author defined relational themes for 16 emotions: negative emotions (e.g. anger, jealousy, envy, anxiety, fear, guilt, shame, disgust, sadness), positive emotions (e.g. relief, joy, pride, love) and undefined emotions (e.g. hope, gratitude, compassion). And so the evaluation of an event in terms of harm/loss is usually accompanied by emotions such as anger, grief, sadness. The evaluation of a threat is accompanied by emotions such as anxiety, fear and worry. The evaluation of a challenge can trigger both negative and positive emotions, such as excitement, enthusiasm, joy and hope. The evaluation of three aspects is of significance in the process of initial cognitive evaluation: *goal relevance*, *goal congruence* and *type of ego involvement*. The different outcome of the cognitive evaluation in the above categories will trigger a different repertoire of emotions and remedial strategies. In case of anxiety responses, the stressor is evaluated as important but not conclusive with the expected objectives, needs or motives of the individual. What is more, fear is a prediction of a seemingly unfavorable future. An individual anticipates a lack of sufficient remedial capacity to meet requirements. With the experience of joy and fear we are dealing with two non-overlapping evaluation paths. Thus, it is worth noting that anxiety is part of the model of evaluation of stress transaction, and joy is part of the positive and supportive evaluation model. In terms of hope, it involves evaluating an event as relevant and noncongruent to an individual's well-being and evaluating the uncertainty of achieving the desired outcome, while at the same time being confident of the possibility. It can therefore be included into stress transaction, as opposed to joy. At this point it should be added that positive emotions (i.e. joy, pride, relief, happiness), although not related to the evaluation of the transaction as stressful, can be experienced in relation to the evaluation of the results of the undertaken coping, and thus at its very end. The basic relational theme, which is at the heart of the hope-arousing transaction, defines the difficulties an individual is facing, the desire to change unfavorable conditions, and the conviction, despite the uncertainty of the outcome, achieving it is possible. It is difficult to unambiguously indicate the behavior typical of hope and physiological correlates. Finally, it is assumed hope is connected with *action tendencies,* which encourage the individual to actively try to overcome the difficulties and to sustain the efforts already underway. Each emotion is connected with a different basic relational theme and a different model of cognitive evaluation. On the other hand, models of cognitive evaluation describing action tendencies point to a strongly motivating nature of hope and suggest possible links with the strategies taken as a result, indicating the mediating role of emotions between the characteristics of a person and the environment as well as the used strategies of coping with stress.

In our own research we referred to the basic statements of Lazarus's transactional theory of stress in the scope of *Core Relational Themes* (content) presented earlier and the role of antecedents in developing *coping* strategies, with particular emphasis on "hope", which favors undertaking active remedial strategies, focusing on the problem and controlling emotions. Our research shows, i.a., that the "hope", as in case of any other emotion, is a response to specific antecedents and therefore closely reflects the perception of the event by an individual, which allows us to predict 23 % of the preference for effective strategies of coping with stress. And so, high level of hope is positively associated with active coping, planning, positive reinterpretation and growth, and negatively with denial, behavioral and mental disengagement. Our findings indicated that hope determines active coping by motivating an individual to reinterpret a situation, to plan steps to overcome obstacles and to take actions to achieve goals (Folkman, 2010)..

Summarizing the place of emotions in Lazarus's model of coping with stress, it should be stressed that emotions, being secondary in relation to cognitive assessment, are at the same time an integral part of the process preceding the selection of a copying strategy, also have a feedback effect (e.g. by distorting the original choice of a copying strategy), thus regulate the whole process of copying.

As we know, R. Lazarus (1993) describes *coping* in two ways: problem-focused (instrumental) - when coping is oriented towards maintaining or improving relationships with the environment, and emotion-focused - when coping concerns reducing negative emotions that disorganize action or stimulating emotions in order to mobilize for action. In addition to the copying function, which is instrumental and regulates emotions, other contexts such as the level of analysis (physiological cost, intensity of emotional responses, social effects of stress) and the time span (past, present and future) should also be taken into account when assessing the effectiveness of coping.

Different definitions of copying can be found in the psychological literature. K.B. Matheny and his collaborators (1986) in their meta-analysis of definitions from the perspective of the so-called integrative stress model, based on taxonomy of 35 definition of coping with stress, found that the definition emphasizing a conscious or unconscious effort to prevent, eliminate or weaken stressors or to tolerate their effects in a way that is least harmful to the individual is the most universal definition.

It is worth specifying some structural aspects of copying. The first distinction to be made concerns coping in itself and automated adaptive behaviors. It is not very clear. One clear criterion could be the sense of novelty. For instance, the first few hours of driving lessons are stressful for the student driver, and we are certainly dealing with an example coping with stress. After a lot of practice, the same action of driving will become an automated behavior. This division presents itself very clearly in the so-called extreme stress situations (concentration camps, catastrophes, surgery, etc.). The second distinction concerns the separation of coping as a process from its result. In experimental (animal) and psychoanalytical models coping is used interchangeably with the concept of adaptive behavior effects. However, the definition of coping should take into account the effort involved in "fighting" stress, regardless of the results achieved. The psychological and physiological cost of this effort is a separate problem on its own. The third distinction concerns *coping* and *general adaptability*. Coping with stress is a particular case of this general problem with all the biological, psychological and social conditionings (Jacoby, Keinan, 2003).

R.H. Rahe (2007b), in his "*Coping and Stress: A Lens and Filter Model*", distinguishes six steps between stress and its objective effect: 1) perception of the stress situation - depends on past experience, social support, etc.; 2) psychological defense mechanisms - denial, transference, repression, isolation, etc.;

3) psycho-physiological responses - mood reduction, headaches, muscle tension, etc.; 4) preventive responses - relaxation, exercise, medication, situational adaptation; 5) stress-induced illness - symptom recognition, absence from work; 6) disease diagnosis - hypertension, etc. The author believes that the difference between *coping processes* and *coping styles* can be reduced to certain questions. In the case of the first - *process*, questions focus on the specific stress events and responses (so called psychological and physiological response patterns), and in the second - *style*, questions focus on ways of detecting stress and the coping strategies. So in its model, Rahe describes *coping* as a *process* that covers all the activities an individual undertakes in a particular stress situation. It is a complex process and runs dynamically within a defined period of time. The coping process affects the original stress situation, and by changing it, it changes the course of further steps of remedial action *-coping skills*. Therefore, individual steps (units) of remedial activity spread over time can be distinguished in the coping process.

The definition provided by R. Lazarus and S. Folkman (1984), referring to *copying* as a *strategy*, emphasizes the involvement of cognitive processes related to the estimation of own internal and/or external resources, which are the basis for planning remedial behaviors in relation to stressors assessed as burdening or exceeding human capabilities. *Coping*, in this sense, undoubtedly is a sequence of processes that emphasize three elements. The first is related to the non-specific aspect of a person, i.e. observation and assessment of what the person is currently thinking or doing in a stressful situation, as opposed to what they usually do in such a situation (stress resistance as a trait). The second element is related to the situational context, i.e. what a person is currently thinking or doing in a particular stress situation (e.g. illness, examination, economic crisis, parachute jump, unemployment, etc.). The third element is related to the anticipatory aspect, i.e. the planned selection of the coping strategy most beneficial for the individual and adequate to the stress events encountered. These three aspects are taken into account by R. Lazarus in his theory of stress, who sees coping as a function of the process of primary cognitive evaluation of a threat, which results in a person classifying a transaction as stressful, which is tantamount to beginning the process of *coping*. However, the very course of coping depends mainly on secondary evaluation of threat, in which people estimate their own ability to deal with a specific threat situation from two perspectives: (a) change the situation into a better one by changing one's own destructive action (focus on the "I") or by changing the environment that poses a threat; (b) control emotions (self-calming). These functions may come into conflict and there is a risk that coping strategies will be mismatched. For example, this is the case when the self-calming function prevents more effective action from being taken (denial, rationalization, avoidance of unpleasant thoughts, use of sedatives). Sometimes the calming function does not block remedial actions and can prove to be very helpful in certain situations (e.g. traumatic situations) (Lazarus, 1993).

In stress psychology, *coping* studies are considered from three perspectives: (1) process, (2) strategy, (3) personality disposition.

(1) ***Process*** - refers to the entirety of action taken by a person in a specific stress situation. *Coping,* in this sense, is dynamic and complex, sometimes taking a long time, when the standard situation changes radically. Remedial action, regardless of the specific form of coping, is non-specific, reflecting effective and ineffective *coping*. In the course of the *coping* process, attention was generally paid to the role of negative emotions, leading to the use of unfavorable remedial methods (*coping ugly*), and to the high effectiveness of positive emotions in coping with stress (Fredrickson, 2001). This reference to the paradigm of the so-called positive psychology (cf. Gable, Haidt, 2005) partially corresponds with *Revised Coping Theory* by S. Folkman (2001), in which the main emphasis is placed on the difficulty of getting away from negative emotions (*bounce back*) and turning to positive emotions through reevaluation, which can lead to more effective remedial strategies. One of such positive emotions, which are motivational in the search for better coping strategies, is hope (Małkiewicz, Terelak, 2016).

(2) ***Coping strategies*** - are an attempt to structure the remedial processes in their time course. It focuses on smaller units of remedial activities of relatively similar effectiveness, due to which people different within the scope of the same process. Each of these groups of strategies has a dual function: to solve the problem or to control emotions. They can also be oriented towards one's own "Ego" or the environment and it can take into account three perspectives: the past (pity – loss), present (novelty) or future (threat or challenge). Lazarus includes: searching for information, direct action, refraining from action and intra-psychological processes among these methods. For example, direct action can be determined by so-called antecedents (anticipators), specific features of situations and/or personality dispositions. On the other hand, intra-psychological processes aimed at reducing anxiety and emotional tension associated with stress activate mechanisms defending personality (e.g. denial, projection, avoidance of danger), which, although reduce the sense of failure, do not solve the problem. Nowadays, the psychology of stress emphasizes the effectiveness of *coping* strategies, based on the so-called balance between the rational and

the emotional (Clark, 2000), which is illustrated well by a fragment from one of Horace's songs: *Aequam memento rebus in arduis servare mentem*, which loosely translated means: "Remember to maintain balance in a difficult situation".

Apart from these four basic *coping* strategies, many other strategies have also been distinguished through empirical research, such as: confrontation, distancing oneself, seeking social support, self-control, planned problem solving, assuming responsibility, wishful thinking, escape/omission, positive revaluation, etc.

It is worth noting that contemporary coping researchers attach great importance to the role of antecedents in remedial strategies, pointing out that reducing negative emotions and revaluing them towards positive emotions (hopes) alone is not a simple reversal of the mechanisms of negative emotions (Scherer, 1993). Although it is worth pointing to the results of empirical research of, i.a., M. Małkiewicz and J.F. Terelak (2016) that the mediation role of hopes correlates with such psychological variables as optimism, extraversion, neuroticism, anxiety, and beliefs about the kindness and order of the world, the ability to create new goals and ways to achieve them, motivation to fight stress, sense of allocating control, predictability - the ambiguity of the situation and its *timing*, which can significantly affect the active choice of effective *coping* strategies. Among the main sources of the effect of active coping strategies are, on the one hand, positive revaluation - an attempt to change the understanding of stress situations emphasizing benefits, and focus on the problem, and, on the other hand, the moderating role of personal and situational antecedents, over whom man generally has no influence . Before we move on to discuss styles of coping with stress, let us focus on the common in literature integrated model of coping with stress by K.B. Matheny and his collaborators (1986), in which they singled out two main *coping* strategies: (a) *preventive* - adaptation to living conditions and the level of requirements, changing stress-generating behavioral patterns, developing ways of coping with stress by controlling the levels of stimulation, increasing own personal, social and economic assets; (b) *stress fighting* - registering stressors and symptoms, assessing their potential, fighting stressors through: problem solving, firmness, desensitization. The discrepancy between the level of requirements and the individual capacity of a human being leads to a shift from a preventive strategy to stress fighting strategy.

Different stress psychologists adopt different divisions of *coping* strategies, such as prevention, intervention, confrontation. An example would be I. Heszen-Nieodek (1989) - the author of the Polish adaptation of WCQ by R. Lazarus and S. Folkman (1984), who, on the basis of factor analysis, identified 9 factors partially different from those obtained by Lazarus and Folkman, which she classified into two groups of strategies: 1) problem-oriented strategies - confrontation, planned and systematic problem solving; 2) emotionally oriented strategies - distancing oneself, avoiding/escaping, self-blaming, self-control, seeking social support, positive revaluation.

(3) ***Stress coping styles as a personality disposition***. There are different concepts and types of stress coping styles in the literature, but there is no consensus, as in the case of coping strategies, on which of them are universal and relatively stable.

Among the most frequently used concepts of copying in empirical research, i.a., are *N.S. Endler and J.D.A. Parker's Coping Style for Stressful Situations*. According to the authors coping styles are typical for a given individual ways of coping with difficult and stressful situations. The authors distinguish three types: *task-focused style* - the individual usually struggles to solve a problem through cognitive transformation or changing a difficult situation due to stress; *emotion-focused style* - mainly concentrated the individual itself and their own emotional stress responses; *avoidance-focused style* - the individual does not think about the problem, does not focus on it. The latter style can take two forms: engaging in substitute activities or looking for social contacts (Endler, Parker, 1994).

When analyzing the types of coping styles, the attention needs to be paid to two stances, most often quoted in the source literature. The first one is inspired by psychoanalysis, the epigones of which include the mentioned Endler and Parker, referring to the psychoanalytical understanding of defensive tendencies: repression and sensitization, which are the basis for distinguishing their own two styles: 1) searching for information about the stress event; 2) omitting information that poses a threat (rejection, denial or denial). Although these styles are not defensive in nature, as they are described as being cognitive-behavioral, they include not only behavioral, but also intra-psychic processes. The second stance found in the literature, is correlative in nature, which is the basis for developing the *Miller Behavioral Style Scale* (MBSS). S.M. Miller (1987) describes eight possible ways of *coping*, four of which express a tendency to search for information about a threat, the other four a tendency to avoid information about a threat, which are negatively correlated with each other. This provides a basis for not so much recognizing the existence of the two opposing remedial styles, but rather allows to distinguish four styles: 1) high vigilance/strong avoidance - using information about the stressful situation and at the same time protection against it; 2) high vigilance vs. low avoidance - information processing; 3) low vigilance vs. high avoidance - avoiding information about the stressful situation; 4) low vigilance vs. low avoidance - low remedial activity. Such understanding of coping is referred to by *C.R. Snyder's Interactive Steps in the Stress and Coping Sequential Model*, which singles out two strategies: effectiveness of coping approach (e.g. using environment directed strategies, using self-directed strategies, selecting active approach strategies) and not adaptive avoidance coping (e.g. submitting to reactive avoidance strategies; paradoxical hyperattention to stressor, increased disruptive thoughts and emotions; intensified self-focus). Individual differences variables moderate the nature of the subsequent stress and coping activities. Snyder suggested that the personality variables may serve as potential moderators of stress: (a) positive moderators: emotional intelligence, hope, humor, optimism, locus of control, problem solving, self-efficacy, self-esteem' (b) negative moderators: depression, hopelessness, hostility; (c) positive and negative moderators: neuroticism, extroversion, openness to experience, agreeableness, and conscientiousness (Snyder, Pulvers, 2001, p. 6). From the perspective of empirically specified personality moderators, particular strategies may compose a general disposition called a style in the literature.

Summarizing the considerations on *coping* strategies and styles thus far, it may be concluded that the more strategies individuals have in their repertoire, the more flexible and effective they will be in applying stress coping styles. What is more, it should be noted that the search for the configurations of coping strategies and styles is a new subject for researchers, mainly psychometric in nature, which should encourage them to interpret carefully and continue searching for as well as analyze the configuration of stress coping styles, taking into account many demographic and personality variables. An example of such research is the concept of *The Proactive Coping Inventory* (PCI) by R. Schwarzer and S. Taubert (2002), which proposed four types of coping with stress, considered on two levels, the certainty of occurrence of a given stressor and the time of occurrence of a given event: (1) *Reactive coping* - referring to harm or loss in the past, performing the function of a classic type of coping focused on a problem, emotion or relationships, aimed at compensating for harm and/or loss; (2) *Anticipative coping* - referring to a threat that may occur with a certain probability in the near future; (3) *Preventive coping* - taking into account potential future threats that cannot be predicted with a certain probability; (4) *Proactive coping* - involving distant challenges that are perceived as an opportunity for self-improvement. The latter type of copying, i.e. *proactive*, is implemented by accumulation of the resources at one's disposal, but also by developing skills and strategies helpful in achieving one's own goals. This is in line with the valuation thread by R.S. Lazarus (2006), which he included in the following questions: “Effective coping - but for what purpose?” and “At what cost?”. The answers to the questions above are not fully known in the present state of stress psychology. Not much is known about the coping patterns used by most people and various social subgroups, as well as about individual and intercultural differences in efficiency of coping with stress. We do know, however, that the remedial activities differ from ordinary activities in that it takes place in a situation difficult for the subject, exceeding the previous experience and knowledge about action. The problem of assessing the good effects of remedial actions from the perspective of individual and social life is a separate issue that is beyond the scope of this book.

4.3 Types and forms of coping with stress

Coping with stress, i.e. the ability to use one’s own experience with specific stress situations or with the interim support of the closest people, it can be called an individual form of remedying a stress situation. On the other hand, seeking support from specialist governmental and non-governmental agencies appointed for this purpose is an institutional form of *coping*.

4.3.1 Individual methods of coping with stress

Individual forms of *coping* are a consequence of one’s own experiences at each stage of self-development and of superficial observations of how others cope with stressful situations. The two most common ways of responding to the threat through denial of reality, commonly known in fiction as: “sweet lemons” or “sour grapes”. The first pattern consists in telling oneself that unpleasant events are, in fact, pleasant. The second consists in autosuggestion that an impossible objective is not important or is less ambitious. More scientifically speaking, these behaviors can be categorized as defense mechanisms, apart from their effectiveness.

Another aspect of the effectiveness of one’s own experience as an individual acquired skill in the socialization process is highlighted by many researchers. Among them, the experimental research conducted by D. Gołuch (2018) is worth mentioning. It concerned the behavior of students in stressful situations related to social exposure in three situations of a varied level of stress: (a) high difficulty of the task - social exposure situation; (b) medium difficulty of the task - simulation of a written exam (it is a component of being evaluated, but the respondents were not the subject of many people’s attention); (c) low difficulty of the task - memory exercise (the respondents were not assessed and were not the subject of the attention of others). The authors found, i.a., that in each of the three experimental situations, the subjects used different stress coping strategies, assessed on the basis of a questionnaire by C.S. Carver, M.F. Scheier i J.K. Weintraub (1989): *The Coping Orientations to Problems Experienced* and COPE. Factor analysis also showed different combinations of emotions experienced in each of the three situations. Statistically significant intergroup differences in physiological correlations of emotions, measured at the Heart Rate (HR) level were also found. The highest level of stimulation was observed in the group tasked to speak in public, as compared to the group of people writing a test and performing a memory exercise. However, there is no statistically significant difference in HR between the two latter groups. Coping strategies included traditional counter measures: focusing on the task, emotions or avoidance. In addition, during the public speech, distancing from the situation or interruption of the activity were observed. In the case of the task with a medium level of difficulty, a factor was identified which included both a positive revaluation and distancing. In a situation with low levels of social stress, an additional strategy with a focus on planning has emerged. The factor analysis concerning *Core Relational Themes* of emotions indicated the general division of emotions into positive and negative in each experimental situation. However, during the public speaking - situation with the highest level of stress, an additional factor was obtained, identified as a negative attitude towards others. In the case of the written test, apart from positive and negative emotions, a feeling of compassion was also noted. On the other hand, in the social exposure situation with the lowest level of stress, only negative and positive emotions were noted.

Experimental studies have shown that depending on the different stress situations, different *coping* strategies and experiences of different emotions should be taken into account. Moreover, the authors indicated the moderating role of temperament in the choice of *coping* strategy, which was evident mainly in the most stressful situation, characterized by public speaking and exposing oneself to the audience's assessment.

Similar research on the behavior of school children in situations of stress related to social exposure (performance in front of the school audience) was conducted by M. Tyszkowa (1977), who concluded, i.a., that the behavior of children in difficult situations is subject to developmental changes, in order to cope with stress better as they acquire experience in this type of stress. This applies both to emotional responses caused by stressful situations (mood, anxiety) and to cognitive functioning (e.g. memory blocks). In terms of emotional responses, emotional control is increased. If extra-punitive response patterns dominate among younger children (blaming other persons or external objects for failure), then intra-punitive patterns dominate among older children (tendency to self-criticism and increased sense of guilt). In terms of instrumental responses, it was noted that task-based responses, i.e. those which, despite their difficulties, lead to increased effectiveness, increase with age. The results obtained by Tyszkowa are consistent with the concept of life cycle development by E.H. Erikson (1968), which describes non-specific stress sources and types of support in all human development cycles (infancy, early childhood, pre-school period, middle childhood, adolescence, early adulthood, middle adulthood, old age), in which the alternate role of biological, psychological and social factors contributing to coping with life crises is highlighted.

Analyzing the forms of "fighting" stress in one's life, the advice of H. Sely (1980a) can be used that in a situation of stress, first and foremost one can reach in for natural or acquired ways of coping with stress, to avoid illness. This means that one should concentrate on eliminating the sources of threat and/or minimizing its effects, which from the perspective of cognitive psychology is described primarily in terms of problem solving, which includes the following steps: 1) defining general needs, proposals and personal goals; 2) defining a detailed problem; 3) analyzing reality in terms of the current situation (what is?), possibilities (what could be?) and duties (what should be?); 4) drawing up a list of problems; 5) assessing one's own behavior (self-assessment); 6) generating alternative solutions; 7) analyzing alternatives; 8) choosing an alternative; 9) supplementing and controlling decision-making activities; 10) assessing the effectiveness of decisions.

This "decalogue" of steps in the process of solving problems in stressful situations is presented as a basis for assessing a threat (nuisance) and designing ways of coping with stress, which in the literature is often described as a strategy of *well-being* or *quality of life*. The criterion for assessing the effectiveness of coping with stress can vary. For example, N.B. Belloc and L. Breslow (1972), basing on a 5-year study of stress resistance in 11,000 young boys, pointed to the category of health (according to WHO, the resultant of physical, psychological, sociological and chronobiological factors) as the basis for quality of life and mental health, and distinguished a positive and destructive lifestyle, i.e. two opposing strategies to deal with everyday stress. Regular meals (3 times a day), 7–8 hours of sleep, drinking with moderation, non-smoking and maintaining a healthy body mass were included in the first one. The destructive lifestyle included, i.a.: using all kinds of substances, irrational eating, alcohol abuse, underweight or overweight, lack of physical exercise, lack of proper rest, lack of recreational activity, overworking or irrational behavior of the so-called preppers, who see threats everywhere.

From the psychological perspective, modern preppers are no different from their past historical incarnations, because all of them were or are filled with fears of incoming war, hurricane, flood, intensive snowfall, stock market crash, economic collapse, and so called visionaries also with a fear of nuclear explosion and the end of the world. The whole activity of preppers is focused on preparing a safe shelter for themselves and their families as well as gathering supplies of water, food, fuel, etc., which will allow them to survive a disaster, at least for thirty days, and perhaps even longer. They prepare themselves physically for a meeting with their "destiny", training in the so-called survival arts, which consist in practicing human skills and gathering knowledge useful for "survival" in extreme conditions. This art can take the form of fun or real tasks of overcoming many dangerous obstacles, which is often used by instructors for the natural selection of candidates for e.g. commandos.

4.3.2 Social patterns of coping with stress

Social experiences reinforce or correct individual *copying* methods. Commonly a dozen or so socially accepted coping patterns are mention, such as, i.a.: 1) physical exercise: from gymnastics, aerobics to sophisticated professional sports; 2) health care - rational nutrition (appropriate dosage of vitamins, sugar, salt and fats), proper sleep, lack of stimulants; 3) relaxation - avoiding muscle and mental tension and using: relaxation training, autogenic training, transcendental meditation, breathing yoga, etc.; 4) massage - classic, underwater, water jets, etc.5) communication skills (also non-verbal communication); 6) self-confidence; 7) ability to live together in a group; 8) conflict resolution; 9) lessening the effects of a crisis; 10) problem solving; 11) decreasing the fear of death through dignified dying conditions; 12) new mental health concepts based on integration of body, mind and spirit; 13) proper work organization; 14) removal of incompatibilities between requirements and own abilities; 15) care for the physical working environment (natural, artificial). These methods can be categorized into three groups: (A) physical training, (B) pedagogical training, (C) psychological training.

(A) ***Physical training*** - as a way of increasing stress resistance, it has been the subject of many studies by sport psychologists. For example S.E. Frazier (1989) tested 86 women aged 18–36 who had been doing aerobic exercises for 15 weeks to reduce the effects of stress. Out of six mood level indicators: tension, depression, anger, vigor, fatigue, confusion, a positive Pearson correlation coefficient ($r=0.60$) between pretest and posttest was obtained only in the case of vigor. Discussing the obtained results, the author refers to the literature, in which the results proving the positive influence of various types of physical exercises on the mood of a person as an important element of mental health are cited. P. Khatri and A.J. Blumenthal (2007) found improvements in a number of physiological parameters (heart rate, hypertension, catecholamine, etc.) and psychological parameters (anxiety, depression, self-esteem) in their research on the effect of aerobics combined with relaxation. In turn, the research conducted by S. Siek, J.T. Terelak and J. Bielecki (1986) indicate, i.a., that regular aerobics and especially Tai-chi gymnastic exercises aimed at reducing the effects of stress correlate positively with increased mood, reduction of mental tension and depression, better anger management, increased vigor, etc. Physical training, as an important form of reducing the effects of daily stress, is also connected with shortening working hours (e.g. 20-hour working week is a realistic demand in highly industrialized countries) as well as increasingly common unemployment and lowering the retirement age. Sociologists suggest that the time of the early-capitalist *homo faber* is slowly coming to an end, and that in the near future the excess of free time will create a new type of *homo ludens*. For this new people, physical exercise, games and fun, and thus active forms of spending free time, will be the main ways of defending against the stress of boredom and monotony. For this reason, psychologists became interested in recreation as an important form spending leisure time, largely culturally (subcultures, counter-cultures) and economically diverse. For this reason, there are a number of sociological, psychological and economic studies on the distribution of free time. They are used to forecast the stress resistance in the situation of excess of free time, as well to forecast the infrastructure of the recreational base, taking into account such variables as: the level of unemployment, retirement age, health, financial status, etc. In the 1990s, a famous American sociologist - T.M. Kando (1980), reviewed the world literature on the relationship between culture and free time in the early postmodern era. Taking into account two criteria of literary classification: idealistic perspective vs. realistic perspective, and the problem of free time vs. mass culture, he divided the literature of the subject into four sections: (1) An idealistic view of free time - the authors define free time idealistically like e.g. ancient Greeks or supporters of the contemporary idea of Olympism do; (2) A realistic view of free time - the authors define free time in terms of recreation, e.g. mass sports, tourism, clubs, etc.; (3) Idealistic approach to mass culture - the authors criticize mass culture and support the so-called higher elite culture, e.g. theater, classical music; (4) Realistic approach to mass culture - the authors emphasize the value of mass culture, also from the economic point of view, the so-called show business.

Free time in the modern world is not only a person's individual matter, but also a sociological and economic category. A 20-hour week of work in wealthy countries can lead to excess of free time which may be a cause of stress (e.g. weekend neurosis syndrome). The solution to the problem of free time is therefore a matter for the cultural development of a give country or region of the world (e.g. American culture, European culture, Far Eastern culture, African culture, etc.) and for the cultural policies of the government or its agendas. The differences in the approach to the definition of free time and mass culture can be reflected in a country's cultural systems. The second important factor shaping the level of consumption of "cultural goods" is the economic factor, both at the level of the state and at the level of economic status of individual citizens. Numerous sociological data confirm the thesis, especially in the case of the so-called *high culture,* which includes a network of such cultural institutions as: philharmonic halls, opera houses, theaters, cinemas, art galleries, libraries, etc., that they are used by smaller and smaller social groups. In the post-modern era, with the development of satellite TV and the Internet, mass sporting events and show business are becoming more and more global in scope.

Many years of own research into free time activities in conditions of long-term social isolation (e.g. astronauts, arctic explorers, prisoners) have shown that there is a high correlation between the preferences of certain forms of recreation (passive vs. active), habits of one's own cultural circle and coping with the stress of isolation. For example, people staying at polar stations for a period of several months, cope with the excess free time very differently. It was found that people who have a wide repertoire of ways to spend their free time (for example, extroverts), find it easier to cope with the stress of monotony than those who mostly prefer a narrow set of passive forms of spending free time (this applies mostly to introverts) (Terelak, 1982a). This problem is particularly acute in cases of mass unemployment and early retirement, especially in countries with a high level of automation of production lines and modern technologies which decrease the demand for human labor. As indicated by own research concerning the change of preferences regarding the forms and ways of spending free time by astronauts on spacecrafts, i.a., the accuracy of forecasting these preferences from the perspective of Earth-based research is very low (Kozerenko, Terelak, Miksik, 1991; Terelak, 2013). The changing preferences for free time activities and rational use of available resources are evidence of a low level of awareness of this issue before venturing on the space mission. This applies in particular to certain free time activities, as their choice largely depends on the preferences that can be categorized as following types: autonomous or organized; participant or supporter; active or passive; exciting or regenerating strength after work; creative or idle; to kill time or for pleasure; self-expression or instrumental; competitive or collaborative; single or community; self-integrating or divided into roles. As can be seen from the above list, these types are in many cases complementary and also result from individual differences in personality and socio-cultural affiliation.

(B) ***Pedagogical training*** - has been known as a way of spending free time since the dawn of the mankind. The example of the so-called ideal of Spartan upbringing, based on the principle of increasing physical fitness by applying strict rules from early childhood, is a good illustration of this acquired form of stress resistance.

Nowadays, the Anglo-Saxon literature presents pedagogical training under the term *graded stress inoculation - GSI* (Jaremko, 1984), based on an analogy with a vaccines used in medicine. This method has been used in astronautics since day one to prepare candidates for astronauts for a possible emergency landing of a space capsule in various regions of the world (such as: seas, forests, deserts, glaciers, mountains) and concerns many months of physical and mental training in real extreme conditions (Klukowski, Skibniewski, 2013).

Taking into account three systems of coping with stress - learning, stimulation control and concept organizing, S. Epstein (1983), in his research on skydivers, empirically stated that by making progress in aviation training (number of parachute jumps), they are also resistant to the stress related with the next jump. Getting used to stress was manifested in the suppression of anxiety responses, both at the subjective level and at the physiological level.

B.J. Blythe, B.J. and J.C. Erdahl (1986) used *graded stress inoculation* with patients waiting for a complicated cardiac surgery. Based on the notion that any dangerous event that mobilizes the body to defend itself against it can be categorized as stress, it has been assumed that the risk of surgery will trigger one of the two coping strategies: disadaptive or adaptive. Graded stress inoculation is designed to encourage the patient to choose an adaptive strategy. The entire training process includes three phases: - improving the ability to conceptualize and analyze stress events; - practical control of emotional states and application of various relaxation and activation techniques; - generalizing acquired skills of coping with specific stressful situations for the whole behavior (psychohygiene of everyday life). Favoring a disadaptive coping strategy leads to the emergence of specific thoughts and ideas which increase the level of anxiety about the pending surgical procedure. The consequences of a disadaptive coping strategy concern, on the one hand, "unproductive instrumental behavior" and, on the other hand, "health disorders" (e.g. headaches, hypertension, gastric and duodenal ulcers, etc.). In addition, such a state may reduce the effectiveness of rehabilitation after surgery and lead to the reinitiation of the stress process with more serious psychosomatic and psychological effects. As there is no universal coping strategy, as a part of the training the patient is encouraged to develop the widest possible range of ways of coping with stress. For example, a set of such measures is designed to control negative emotions and accompanying physiological response, and to increase overall physical fitness (e.g. relaxation training, diaphragm breathing, autogenic training, etc.). The second set of preventive measures focuses on the reevaluation of stress events, as the pending surgical procedure as a source of stress is treated as a problem to be solved and not only as a personal threat. In such situations, the individual is taught to develop cognitive procedures focused on the perception of stress, its confrontation with own remedial abilities and, finally, is taught to evaluate the effectiveness of coping. In this way, unproductive thoughts and ideas can be replaced with thoughts which are constructive from the coping standpoint. The proposed set of countermeasures is connected with training such skills as: interpersonal communication, problem solving, studying and working. Training in these skills is an important component of the graded stress inoculation system. GSI is designed for both individuals and groups. Most often, 12–14 hour sessions, covering three phases, are used. The first phase focuses on helping to properly assess the essence of stress and one's own stress responses, both psychological and physiological. During the second phase, the individual is taught specific countermeasures that result directly from the cognitive assessment of their own effectiveness in fighting stress. In fact, GSI is effective when a person can suggest certain techniques on their own and then improve them under the supervision of a therapist (coach). The third phase involves the ability to put into practice the coping measures that are appropriate to the threats involved. A critical moment in this phase is the training of early identification of one's own stress response in order to adjust the appropriate measures to counteract further development of these responses. Failed attempts at preventive actions is the basis for improving remedial techniques and discussing them with the coach during regular meetings (Snyder2000).

On the example of behavioral medicine. R.L. Wernick, M. E. Jaremko, P.W. Taylor (1981) demonstrated that GSI can help patients reduce the subjective sensitivity to pain associated with invasive medical procedures. On the other hand, I.L. Janis (1983) drew attention to the effectiveness of GSI in the rehabilitation treatment of people addicted to cigarettes and alcohol. This GSI has also been successfully used to fight occupational stress, the first symptom of which is the so-called chronic fatigue (Krebs, 2007).

Finally, it worth mentioning that GSI is not only used as a one-time solution to a specific stress situation (e.g. in hospitals, workplaces, schools, etc.), but also has further social consequences, especially when the coach consolidates the acquired coping skills and includes them in the repertoire of coping techniques. That is why GSI training we have classified as a pedagogical training, because its effects concern more than just an individual and are of great social importance, although it is undoubtedly highly correlated with psychological training, which aims not only at reducing anxiety in a stress situation, but also at developing one's own personality.

(C) ***Psychological training*** - as a way of increasing stress tolerance, similarly pedagogical training discussed earlier, dates back to ancient times and is undoubtedly connected with the influence of eastern cultures on our European civilization. Contrary to physical training, which was discussed earlier, which promotes the increase of stress resistance mainly through external physical activity, being in motion and active rest, psychological training is only seemingly associated with passive rest and being motionless, because it offers an effective accumulation of both physical and mental energy in a state of deep relaxation and concentration. Nowadays, the ability to consciously and willingly relax and focus is increasingly appreciated as an effective way of coping with stress in everyday and professional life. The term relaxation, from Latin relaxāre meaning to loosen, to open, to free, has become a synonym of passive leisure in our culture. Commonly speaking, it means a form of calming, loosing up muscles and reducing mental activity to a minimum. From the physiological perspective, the essence of relaxation is to reduce the amount of impulses to the CNS (central nervous system) in order to provide it with optimal rest conditions, which not only has psychological (symptoms of internal calming), but also physiological (so-called pulse patterns, EEG, GSR, breathing, etc.) correlations (Whitehouse, Orne, Orne, 2007).

Relaxation combined with breathing exercises and elements of autosuggestion has long been considered a valuable method of psychological training and has been of interest to physicians and psychologists, who have provided the scientific basis for the Hindu practices known for two millennia, derived from the Yoga system. Let us recall that the Hindu yogis know many methods of controlling their reactions and actions in order to get closer to perfection in the sense specific to their religious and cultural circles. The dominance of the spirit over the body is a goal known only to monks in our culture. Hence, some of the yoga methods were adapted to the modern western civilization.

The scientific literature covers the following varieties of psychological training techniques: (1) relaxation (Jacobson's progressive muscle relaxation, Schultz's and Luthe's autogenic training, emotional induction, Maltz's "visualization" technique; (2) transcendental meditation (yoga); (3) *biofeedback* - consisting in monitoring the physiological correlations of emotions and reduce their value through mental relaxation; (4) conditioned behavioral therapy: systematic desensitization - involving creating in vivo or imaginary anxiety situations, assertiveness training - involving placing an individual in anxiety situations related to social roles, implosive therapy involving evoking anxiety scenes in the imagination; (5) change of attitudes by changing the system of values; (6) Rogerian therapy - focused on the patient's problems in the form of individual (*client-centered therapy*) and group sessions (*encounter groups*) (Kristeller, 2007; Villani, Riva, Riva, 2007). Their purpose is to reduce muscle tension and physiological activation (reducing the overall mobilization of the body). People react with states of general mobilization of the body not only to an actual threat, but also to an imaginary one. Among the best known relaxation techniques are Jacobson's progressive muscle relaxation, Schultz's autogenic training and transcendental meditation.

- ***Jacobson's progressive muscle relaxation*** involves contracting and relaxing individual groups of muscles found in hands, legs, torso and face. A few weeks of training teaches us not only how to perceive the differences between "tension" and "relaxation", but also the habit of relaxing our own muscles as well. The benefits of mastering this technique not only can be applied to counteracting anxiety through a general reduction in emotional tension, but also as a way of counteracting fatigue through rapid mental regeneration. For example, A. Fujita (1975) in his experimental research on Japanese athletes stated that the use of Jacobson's ideomotor training has a beneficial effect on learning tasks requiring the use motor skills and maintaining high level of psychomotor fitness in stressful conditions of high-ranking sports competitions.
- ***Transcendental meditation (TM) methods*** are more difficult to master as they are based on oriental philosophies of life. They are not only aimed at achieving a state of relaxation, but also at relieving of old traumas and stress, and achieving a deeper state of consciousness. People who are able to master this technique gain a better insight into themselves, better control of their emotional states and self-acceptance. Because of this, they are included among the methods that intensify the development of human personality.

Since TM methods are difficult to master in their original form due to cultural and religious reasons, they are generally not available in their entirety and usually focus on the relaxation part. Psychological effects of yoga exercises at the separated level of relaxation include the ability to maintain a high level of concentration and reduced level of anxiety and aggressiveness, which significantly increases the likelihood of focusing on the task at hand, in case of a stress situation as well.

However, Anglo-Saxon psychology mentions a much more serious problem and it concerns the methodological plane of searching for "unity" in the scope of the components of a human being as such. From the very beginning, the psychological tradition, first speculative, and now empirical, has been entangled in two cognitive trends: philosophical (speculative psychology) and biological (psychophysiology). This led to endless discussions on the subject of psychophysical isomorphism, for example, as manifested in three concepts by Konrad Lorenz (1972):

(1) The concept of interaction between the *soma* and the *psyche* - assuming that somatic phenomena can be considered as the cause of adequate experience and that they in turn affect physiological processes. This concept, being based on a cause-and-effect relationship, is illogical.
(2) The concept of identicalness of the *soma* and the *psyche* - it assumes that somatic and psychological phenomena are simply the same "real in themselves" and that we experience one and the other (as in the case of matter and energy) through independent, diverging methods of cognition. The concept is most justified when using physiological phenomena in psychology and psychosomatics, only as *psyche* correlates.
(3) The concept of psychophysical parallelism – emphasizing the parallel course of two chains of events, between which there is no logical link, since nobody denies that all mental processes are accompanied by neurophysiological processes, but in no way can this statement be reversed. One of the best known forms of psychophysical parallelism is the Cartesian concept of psychophysical dualism, which contrasted *res extensa* (corporeal substance) with *res cogitans* (non-material, mental substance). He took the view that reality consisted of two, fundamentally different substances, functioning on different principles: the material world – on mechanical principles, and the spiritual world – on principles of freedom. Both types of substances, being divergent, meet in the human being. To this day, this antireductionistic approach poses many methodological problems for scientific psychology, referring to the study of the relationships between the human corporeality

and spirituality as the subject of both these phenomena, the descriptions of which we encounter in the course of the revision of traditional philosophical dualisms, such as: mind/body, nature/culture, fact/value, idealism/realism, subject/object, individual/community. J.T. Lamiel, (2010), asks the contemporary psychology an important question: Why was there no place for personalistic thinking in 20th century psychology?

Returning to meditation-based therapy, one of the best-known methods in psychology of anxiety treatment is desensitization, which involves reducing the intensity of anxiety response (e.g. to traumatic experiences) by proposing situations in which a person (in fact or imaginatively) can confront a less severe version of their anxiety. The desensitization technique involves three stages: (a) diagnosis of anxiety and its hierarchy; (b) learning relaxation-relief skills; (c) systematically imagining anxiety situations and substituting anxiety responses with relaxation-relief responses. A variant of this technique is the implosive technique of getting used to the danger within one's imagination.

In recent years, attention has been paid to mixed methods, e.g. increasing the ability to work as a pilot performing nearly day-long transcontinental flights based on psychosomatic self-regulation and designed to reduce emotional tension (autogenic relaxation variant), maintaining high ability to work despite being fatigued (autogenic stimulation variant) and improving the quality of work (relaxation-ideomotor training variant). These methods also improve the subjective mood. The mechanism of positive influence of psychosomatic self-regulation related to central nervous system stimulation under the influence of autogenic stimulation is confirmed by EEG data, which document the decrease of alpha and theta rhythm activity with simultaneous increase of beta rhythm frequency (Voge, Goldberg, 1986).

- **Schultz's *autogenic training method*** involves self-provoking relaxation and concentration responses with the use of simple formulas of autosuggestion. The author himself calls it "concentrative self-relaxation" (*Konzentrative selbstentspannung*) (Schultz, 1956). The exercises cover several groups of reactions of manipulating one's own body and mental states: (a) learning to adopt an appropriate posture to facilitate the relaxation of individual muscles, the relaxation of the body by evoking the feeling of "heaviness" and "warmth"; (b) learning to "focus" on the responses of one's own body; (c) learning to control the responses of one's own body and switching the rhythm of its functions (e.g. slowing down the heart rate and breathing); (d) acquiring the ability to transform one's own states of consciousness. Research on the influence of autogenic training on the level of anxiety shows that mastering this technique allows to reduce anxiety as a state, increase perceptual-motor fitness and improve the effects of memory learning.

Methods of active relaxation such as transcendental meditation (TM) and hypnosis are more difficult to control because they require professional medical and cultural preparation, because they are based on specific philosophical concepts of life, which are aimed not only at achieving a state of relaxation of the body, but also at relieving of "old trauma and stress" and achieving a deeper state of consciousness. Those who master this technique gain a better insight into themselves, improved self-control of their emotional states and regulation of certain physiological processes, which requires medical supervision. In addition, R.K. Wallace et al. (1983) point out that the evident effects require a few years of training (e.g. over 5 years it is possible to achieve a reduction of hypertension without the use of medication). Because of this, they are included among the methods that intensify the development of human personality and for maintaining good health.

In recent years, attention has been paid to mixed methods of increasing the ability to work (e.g. of a manager) based on biofeedback and designed to reduce emotional tension, maintain high level of ability to work despite the fatigue and increasing the quality of work (e.g. relaxation-ideomotor training variant) .

– ***Biofeedback*** involves providing feedback to an individual on the changes of their physiological condition, which is monitored online using devices designed for such purposes, such as: EEG (*Electroencephalography*) - recording brain waves; EMG (*Electromyography*) - measuring muscle tension in microvolts; GSR (*Galvanic Skin Response*) or EDR (*Electrodermal Response*) - measuring the electrical conductivity of the skin, dependent on the general stimulation of the sympathetic nervous system; HRV (*Heart Rate Variability*) - measures heart rate changes; RSA (*Sinus Arrhythmia Respirators*) - measures vegetative functions; BT (*Body Temperature*), etc.

The essence of biofeedback is that the information is communicated to the test subject either visually (e.g. on a monitor screen) or aurally (e.g. pleasant or unpleasant sound depending to success or error during the task). Biofeedback is also used during therapy as a complementary part of the diagnostic process (e.g. using EEG to record brain waves illustrating the state of relaxation, vigilance or concentration and neurofeedback as means of its assessment) or documenting the amount of psychophysiological cost (breathing, muscle tension, pulse and electrical conductivity of the skin) in stress situations. Its results are also useful for discussing the results of the diagnosis and the plan for the next stage of therapy with the patient or client. The methods of psychosomatic self-regulation can be used to rationally manage the body's reserves and reduce the fear of patients waiting for a surgical procedure, as R. J. Edelmann and S. Hardwick (1986) were trying to prove.

We have decided to omit the discussion of such fashionable methods as aromatherapy, music therapy, as well as other classic methods of individual and group psychotherapy, as they are a subject of concern for institutional forms of support in crisis situations (Hamaoka et al., 2007).

Summarizing the discussion of mental training as a way of coping with stress, basing the provided review of the literature it can be concluded that psychosomatic methods such as autogenic training, psychotronic therapy, desensitization methods, relaxation training, hypnosis, psychocorrective training and other psychotherapies are used and widely accepted (Villani, Riva, Riva, 2007). The impact of these methods on coping with stress is also the subject of a lot of controversy, which is discussed by P.M. Lehrer and R.L. Woolfolk (1984) basing on a comparative review of empirical literature, and concern such problems as: stress reduction techniques being equivalent in terms of their effectiveness or not and whether the results are a placebo or concern real changes in health. Answers to these issues, especially at the level of empirical research, are subject to difficulties related to the multidimensionality of the subject of research, which from the cognitive-behavioral perspective of J. S. Beck's (1995) therapy consists of three elements: body - soul relaxation. In this sense, Beck's concept of cognitive-behavioral coping includes: (a) Behavioral techniques (e.g. anxiety-related activity planning, bibliotherapy - knowledge on the stressor; familiarization), and competence training depending on the needs of the patient (e.g. assertiveness training, social skills training, planning training, etc.); (b) Relaxation techniques (breathing exercises, Jacobson's progressive muscle relaxation, progressive contracting and relaxation depending on the signals sent by the body); (c) Attention training (focus on the present moment and event; raising awareness). Due to the change of meanings associated with stimuli, the subjective interpretation of the relationship between the individual and their environment is modified in terms of mutual relations: thinking - emotion - physiological symptoms - behavior.

When discussing the coping mechanisms and techniques, we focused on one aspect only, namely the assumption that coping is an acquired ability of emotional control. We have omitted many specific psychological techniques, often of a magical nature, which are mastered by people in their individual lives (upbringing, culture) and whose subjective effectiveness is known from experience. An example of which is the presently fashionable shaping and improving of the so-called assertive behavior through specialist training, a characteristic feature of which is the ability to assert one's own reasons in interpersonal communication while simultaneously showing respect for others. The classic method of training assertiveness is e.g. the rational emotive therapy by Albert Ellis (1991).

Apart from individual ways of coping with stress, a person as a social being, has the so-called social support in a situation of personal or group crisis, which usually has an institutional character.

4.3.3 Three aspects of support in a stressful situation

Just reaching for one of many magazines available shows that in almost every one of them, in every issue features a column with various expert advice on coping with stress. The experts include psychiatrists and psychologists, and in situations of mass threats, the so-called crisis committees are established at various levels of the government, having experts in various fields and means of communication at their disposal. Such a form of support in a crisis situation not only is a reflection of what is currently in vogue, but also point to the need for social assistance in a situation of individual or mass crisis. Institutional help covering various social programs and social organizations aimed at fulfilling people's needs, especially those which are difficult or impossible to meet, has a common name - *Human Services.* The list of help programs and specialist social support institutions is long and very diverse, it includes such institutions as: centers aimed at battling alcoholism, drug addiction or the issue of unemployment, services for care of healthy and sick children, educational services, general hospitals, psychiatric hospitals, special education centers, charity institutions, mental hygiene centers, mass sports, recreation and tourism centers, physical rehabilitation institutions, etc. The list of institutions and the scope of national and international social assistance programs depend to a large extent on the civilizational level and economic condition of a given country.

The most general model of social support was developed by H. Selye (1980a), who defined it as a state of social awareness, translated into individual actions and institutions of social assistance, which are aimed at providing assistance to individuals and groups in crisis situations of both a developmental (childhood, youth, maturity, old age) and situational nature. Three basic aspects of support in stress situations: immune, personal, and social are universal and at the same time complementary, creating a system of coping based on three pillars of support: biological, psychological and social. These three systemic aspects of support for each individual and each situation of civilizational development of societies are each time responsible for a new quality of coping with stress, creating a quality of life.

4.3.3.1 *Immune coping*

The concept of resistance derived from immunology refers to the inability of an organism to be exposed to pathogenic microorganisms or their venom (toxins). It can be natural or acquired. Natural (innate) resistance is a type of resistance that is not acquired through prior contact with an infectious agent (or a related species) but is genetically determined. This kind of non-specific resistance can be considered as species-specific and individual. The natural resistance of a species means that a given pathogenic micro-organism is often able to cause disease in one animal species while it is not pathogenic for another. When there are clear racial and genetic differences in infection resistance within a species, we are talking about individual resistance (immunity). Among the factors affecting the individual natural resistance are: genetic defects of reactivity of the immune system, nutritional status, age, irradiation with ionizing rays, immunosuppressants, hormonal balance, etc. In other words, inborn immunity or resistance, i.e. genetically conditioned immunity, resulting from the structure and function of the entire body, will depend on the condition of the skin and mucous membranes, which are natural barriers protecting us against the ingress of germs into the body. Reflexes such as sneezing, coughing, tearing, bactericidal action of saliva, gastric juice, tears and the presence of lysosomes in bodily fluids are another type of protective barrier. The body is also capable to react with an inflammatory reaction to infectious agents. Innate immunity can be lost, as in the case of AIDS (*Acquired Immunodeficiency Syndrome*), caused by the *Human Immunodeficiency Virus* - HIV.

Acquired immunity (resistance) is the result of the body's individual experience in the fight against germs, e.g. in case of an infectious disease. The duration of this type of resistance may range from several weeks (e.g. in case of a flu) to many years after healing (e.g. typhoid fever, typhus, chickenpox). Resistance is also acquired artificially through protective vaccination (its duration varies). Acquired immunity may take a passive and active form. Passive resistance means a condition of relative temporary invulnerability to infectious agents, which has been induced by the administration of antibodies previously produced in the body of another host and not actively produced in a given host. As antibodies break down constantly and new ones do not form, passive protection lasts for a short time - usually only a few weeks. The antibodies can be transmitted naturally through the mother's placenta or with her milk while the baby is being breastfed (which protects the newborn against some common infections for 4–6 months) - in this case we are dealing with the naturally acquired passive immunity. There may also be antibodies transmitted artificially by administering an immune serum with the antibodies - then we are talking about artificially acquired passive immunity (Jawetz, Melnick, Adelberg, 1991).

Comparative studies in the field of zoopsychology (ethology) have shown that the lower the level of development of an animal, the more innate mechanisms (behavioral patterns) to defend itself against stress it has. One such mechanism is the ability to regenerate. For example, an earthworm can reconstruct the rest of its body from almost every fragment of it. In higher animals, however, the ability to regenerate is very low, which is reflected, for example, in the healing of tissue defects by the formation of substitute tissue (the so-called scars). In humans, the regenerative abilities vary from almost perfect (e.g. blood cells, epidermis, epithelial mucous membranes, gastric, intestinal, uterine and sebaceous glands, ovaries and testes) through limited (liver, kidneys, pancreas, lacrimal glands, connective tissues and smooth muscles) to lack of thereof (nervous tissue and striated transverse muscles). In general, it can be said that the regeneration of each substance in the body is determined by: the genetic pattern that determines the formation of a specific structure and the environment that affects the efficiency and often the possibility to regenerate. It is well known that the fight against life stress, i.e. the process of aging of the body, is a losing battle. Regeneration is only connected with a relative prolongation of life.

Living organisms, especially highly organized ones, have innate patterns of coping with stress, among which we will pay attention to the most spectacular ones. All of these patterns involve innate programmed ways to avoid or scare off an enemy. Avoiding an enemy is connected with such phenomena as: mimesis (imitation), i.e. the fact that some species of animals become similar to the ground in terms of their shape, color, pattern, etc. (chameleons). Mimicry is a variation of mimesis, which consists in the imitation of predatory (e.g. fish) or venomous (e.g. snakes) species by these that are not predatory; self-amputation in the close presence of an enemy (e.g., some lizard species shed their tails); behavior aimed at confusing the opponent, pretending to be more dangerous than the animal actually is (e.g. some snakes change their behavior to imitate venomous vipers or change their appearance - triangular head, thickness). The innate repertoire of behaviors aimed at deter the enemy (the source of threat) may include: size alone (e.g. great bustard has no enemies in the air, grizzly bear on the ground and orca in the water); deterrent body built (e.g. poisonous spines in some fish - sandy skate or stingers in scorpion); aggressive coloring (e.g. bright colors in some fish); deterrent odor (e.g. hoopoes fill their nest with excrements); attacking the enemy (e.g. venomous vipers); defense by forming an organized group (e.g. swarms of bees, schools of fish, etc.).

The latter mechanism of defense against stress can be traced on the basis of observations made by Stanley Schachter (1980) concerning the behavior of animals on the pasture in a situation of threat. When cows, horses and sheep were gathered on one pasture, they moved about freely around the entire area of the pasture in unity. In a stress situation, when a threat (e.g. a storm) appeared, they were grouped into "specialist" groups, within a single species in separate parts of the pasture. Another pattern of innate defensive behavior against the approaching enemy was discovered and experimentally confirmed by the German physiologist Erich von Holst (as in: Lorenz, 1962). He described rooster's "innate image of a sworn enemy of its species". The essence of the Holst experiment was the electrical irritation of the brain where the electrodes were planted. The intensity and curves of electrical impulses used in the experiment corresponded to the actual nerve impulses. By electrical irritation of the brain, Holst achieved an effect that he called "a pattern of defensive behavior against the approaching earthbound enemy." An animal's response always started a few seconds after being electrically stimulated. The rooster would stop suddenly, stiffen and straighten its body, and look around with an oscillatory head movement typical of its species. After a while, it would behave as if it had discovered something, staring at a specific point on an empty table top. As if an invisible "something" was approaching it. The rooster would start marching back and forth on the table in increasing tension. While flapping its wings, it was making movements as if trying to evade this approaching "something". At the same time, it would strike hard with its beak in the direction its attention was focused on. Holst, as a naturalist, drew the right conclusion from this experiment that the bird felt endangered. It behaved on the table as if being in danger and having to defend itself. After the power was turned off, the rooster would usually regain its composure and would often crow. This experiment could be repeated endlessly and it would provide the same results, which confirms that the described repertoire of defensive behaviors is an innate pattern, available in a ready-to-use form in the brain of the rooster. Zoopsychologists know more such ready-to-use patterns, not only defensive ones, e.g. courting mates, caring for the body, and searching for food.

4.3.3.2 Personal coping

The oldest forms of support in an emergency refer to myths found in our cognitive systems and are in opposition to the emotional aspect. A myth is a mental construction that connects elements of experience with a purpose of life by referring to categories of values such as truth, good, evil, to give meaning to existence, and is therefore suitable as a form of support in an emergency. Ancient mythology embodies the universal values of truth, good, evil, beauty, suffering, and so on. The famous Roman "Lares and Penates" supported various types of mythical deities in any case of threat and obstacle to purposeful action. There is an abundance of mythology in literature and iconography from every epoch, culture and religion. Their protective effectiveness is undisputed as it is of an intersubjective nature. Myths in the form of situational superstitions are well known, they are to protect us from an unknown misfortune, such as fear of the number 13, grabbing a button when seeing a chimney sweep, crossing fingers for good luck, knocking on wood to avoid bad luck, the number 666 as herald of misfortune, breaking a mirror as a sign of misfortune, carrying a rabbit's paw for good luck, a black cat crossing one's path bringing bad luck, etc. In these superstitions, we give thinking to a sense of purposeful warning against the real danger hidden in the real world. As it appears from the above, myths are associated with their specific rituals, some of which are archetypal, whether in the form of an absolute (truth, deities, ideologies, etc.) a political canon (political correctness, sovereignty, good and bad political systems, holy wars, etc.), a moral canon (good and bad, charisma, heroism, etc.), or an aesthetic canon (beauty, art, fashion, etc.).

Such forms of support have been handed down from generation to generation and, being part of culture, are not subject to empirical verification and are therefore effective and very simple to use. Mircea Eliade (1993) suggested a certain ways of ordering of myths found throughout history, in his concept called Hierophany (Greek: *hierós* – sacred i *phaínein* - to reveal or to bring to light), he presents sacredness as a manifestation of the *sacrum* aspect in the reality of the *profanum*. According to this concept of sacredness, myths have always been used to reduce the cognitive dissonance of the real world and the world of ideas, on two levels: the sacred and the profane. It is noted that even though these aspects are separate, sometimes they may overlap, because the sacrum aspect is generated by our minds. Eliade points to the purposefulness of referring both to myths connected with the profanum, which allow us to understand the passing history of humanity, and to myths of the sacrum, which for the passing profanum are a way of stabilizing the meaningfulness of the perception of the real world. "Myth is always a challenge to the passing of time", and as such it belongs to the inalienable qualities of human beings. It therefore provides support in situations of existential stress in particular. Eliade proposed a useful taxonomy of all kinds of myths, based on detailed areas of cognitive interest of a person searching for the meaning of existence in the universe. These include a "decalogue", which consists of such areas as: 1) Heaven (uranic deities, rites and symbols of heaven), 2) Sun (solar cults, e.g. Egyptian sun deity - Ra, etc.), 3) Moon (lunar mysticism, e.g. rituals of death, initiation, destiny), 4) Water (aquatic symbolism, e.g. water of life, symbolism associated with the biblical flood, christening by immersion in water, water deities etc.). 5) Holy stones (signs and forms, e.g. funereal megaliths, meteorites, insemination stones), 6) Earth (symbol of the woman and fertility, e.g.: Mother Earth, homo-humus, motherhood), 7) Plant life (rites and symbols of rebirth, e.g. sacred tree of wisdom, tree of rebirth, maik), 8) Agriculture (cult of fertility, e.g. harvest festivals, sacrifices made of agricultural products, Easter eggs, agricultural deities), 9) Holy space (temple, palace, "center of the world", e.g. various taboos), 10) Sacred time (the myth of everlasting renewal of things, e.g. celebrating the new year, New Year's Eve parties, Ramadan, spiritual retreat).

N. Hansell (1976) presented a biosocial model of seven basic categories of support on which an individual system of coping with stress depends and which are based on a criterion other than myths, namely the unfulfilled human needs as a source of stress. The essence of this system is the ability to fulfill needs. It includes the following categories: supply - in the broad sense: from food, oxygen, to new information about the living and working environments; identification - related to determining one's own identity; other persons - needed for the establishing permanent or incidental contacts, which are the basis of intimate life; groups - of which one is a member, the basis of social relations and norms of conduct; social roles - determining the scope and method of action for interim purposes; money - determining social status, standard of living and partial objectives; meaning of life - being an important existential category integrating all life activities of a human being. All these elements of this dynamic biosocial model interact with each other. Disruption of one of them becomes a cause of a crisis and requires intervention of an individual systems of coping with stress. An example of an individual way of dealing with everyday stress is to regulate the mood of a person the main attribute of which is humor (laughter) as a method to distance themselves from various types of stressors surrealistic in nature. People with a sense of humor have the ability to see the funny side of life in the form of verbal parody (e.g. jokes) or behavioral parody (e.g. skits, comedies). This self-distance (self-mockery) and distance to the environment, taken from the virtual situation of joke, helps to cope with the threats occurring in the real world more efficiently . Psychologists see therapeutic value in humor, as evidenced, for example, by the fact that satirical graphic art found on the Internet is called "meme therapy".

Research on the role of humor in coping with stress has shown, i.a., that in the natural conditions of the military environment, the so-called active humor, in opposition to the reactive one, helps in coping with occupational stress (cf. Szymanik, Terelak, 2015).

Clinical data are also important, such as a personal account by a clinical psychologist of a dramatic episode in the life story of a friend physician working in aviation medicine for the Polish army[18], who owes his life to humor, a life that was saved when being in a situation that would extremely difficult for every human being, namely waiting for the execution in a death cell in a concentration camp in Dachau. This physician was a master accordion player and being sentenced to death he had the right of last will. He asked for an accordion to be brought to his cell. Throughout the night, waiting for his death, he played cheerful Warsaw folk songs called - sztajerek, which echoed all over the camp and attracted the attention of German soldiers, including the camp commander. In the morning, instead of being executed, he was brought to the office of the commander, who pardoned him and hired him in the camp orchestra.

4.3.3.3 Social coping

There are situations in life that an individual cannot cope with and that require institutional support. Military psychologists[19] describe, for example, panic responses of residents of Israeli cities during SCUD ballistic missile strikes during the so-called Gulf War. The average citizen could not cope with the uncontrollable fear of the possible attack using gas warfare. The panic caused dozens of people to lose their lives by not leaving their homes for a few days, after they blocked all openings in fear of gas warfare, whereas nobody was actually killed by the approaching SCUD missiles, which were shot down by anti-aircraft artillery on time. Social support was needed in the form of permanent calming messages broadcast by radio by specially designated expert military psychologists, which significantly reduced panic and, indirectly, mortality of the inhabitants.

Thus, among the three aspects listed in Fig. 4.3. in addition to *immune coping* and *personal coping, social coping* plays an important role, it includes all the principles of supporting people in crisis situations, such as: individualization of a problem, planning of interventions, access to a professional advisor, counselor

---

18 The conversation took place in the office of psychologist Jan Terelak at the Military Institute of Aviation Medicine in Warsaw on October 28, 1967 and was a social, non-confidential conversation, a form of support given by person telling the story to a colleague who was at risk of being dismissed with an immediate effect for political reasons.

19 The data comes from a personal conversation between Jan Terelak and the Chief Psychologist of the Israeli Army during a meeting at the 28th International Applied Military Psychology Symposium in Berlin, Germany, June 1–5,1992.

or therapist, access to education on coping mechanisms, opportunities to benefit from institutional support and help of others, awareness of existential goals (e.g. life must go on despite the crisis, planning to return to health, etc.). These principles are taken into account to varying degrees depending on the main objectives pursued by social services: search for areas and crisis situations, prevention or rehabilitation, as well as on the level of crisis intervention and professionalism of the social services personnel. The latter can be divided into the following categories: professionals (physicians, psychologists, nurses, social workers, therapists) and paraprofessionals (friends, psychics, priests). Such a complex area of social support makes it difficult to measure its effectiveness, which has been emphasized by R.L. Payne and J.G. Jones (1987), who attempted to construct a methodological model for research of social support that would take into account its multidimensional character. These authors have reconstructed the "decision tree" for the researcher trying to measure social support, taking into account the following dimensions: *content* - e.g. emotional, instrumental, informational or evaluation support; *disposition* - e.g. support available or currently received; *evaluation* - the very description of support and its perception; *direction* - e.g. support received or provided. The dimensions presented are not obligatory, although in general the research concerns the support received. H. Sęk (1996) points to other features being researched namely: adequateness of the support provided, satisfaction with social support received, seeking support and, finally, positive or negative impact of support on the functioning of an individual.

The concept of social support appears quite often in stress research as a variable that mediates between stressful life events and ways of coping with them. Let us recall that the term *social support* entered the scientific jargon of psychology in the 1970s. In the 20th century, it became a synonym for help and care, and in the mid-1990s, a synonym for definiendum. Undoubtedly, the current trend of activities defined as social support is the result of the humanization of life in highly developed countries. The status of this concept is not theoretical, but rather pragmatic, descending from the therapeutic community, psychological help and the self-help group movement, as the purpose of functional support is the general maintaining remedial processes, reducing or overcoming stress, regaining the level of the sense of security and hope from before the stress situation and sometimes strengthening confidence in one's own remedial effectiveness.

Apart from specific problems with defining, we propose the following understanding of the concept of social support - as asymmetrical interpersonal relations in which one side expects help (*expressis verbis* or intentionally), and the other - is able to meet this expectation. These relations have a humanitarian and moral value when one of the parties is in a difficult life situation. The literature distinguishes between various forms of social support, such as emotional ("we love you, you are not alone", etc.), material (direct assistance in the form of donations, loans or services), information (crucial information, advice, etc.), prestigious (social ties with significant organizations), instrumental (providing help), motivational (incentives to persevere in the fight against stress).

In a more descriptive way, the essence of social support can be presented as a specific social interaction, including such components as: a) initiation of help in a difficult situation; b) exchange of information, emotions, instruments of action or material goods; c) interaction between the supporter and the supported; e) adequacy of support provided in relation to the needs of the recipients and their personal dignity; f) compatibility of support objectives with the expectations of the recipients (Van Kaam, 1969). The support understood in this way is influenced both by context factors (e.g. social network, reference groups), process variables (emotional, informational, instrumental and valuation processes), competences possessed (life, interpersonal, mental, moral), types of social contacts (support interactions: partner - non-partner, formal - informal, institutional - non-institutional, professional - non-professional and interpersonal trust level). This interactive approach to social support emphasizes its dynamic character, which on the one hand depends on: the support perceived, and on the other hand, the support received. Therefore, the attempt to construct a theoretical model cannot be reduced to the previously known theory of social behavior. It is important to take into account not only the characteristics of the subject (who provides or receives support), but also the real existing social networks and access to them, which exceeds the remit of psychologists and is the domain of sociology, pedagogy and social economy.

The issue of social support has been the subject of interest of stress researchers for many years. Unfortunately, despite intensive research, it has not been possible to develop an empirically proven and accepted theory to explain the role and mechanism of social support in the relationship between stress and well-being. One of the reasons for this is that researchers are striving to create an overly general theory that is unable to include the multidimensional nature of social support. In this case, any outcome of empirical research is important to complement the theoretical model of social support in relation to coping with stress. In the literature features such empirical indicators of social support as: satisfaction with the received social support; readiness to seek social support; adequacy between expectations and obtained support; perception of compatibility vs. discrepancies between ideal and current support (O'Donnell, Steptoe, 2007).

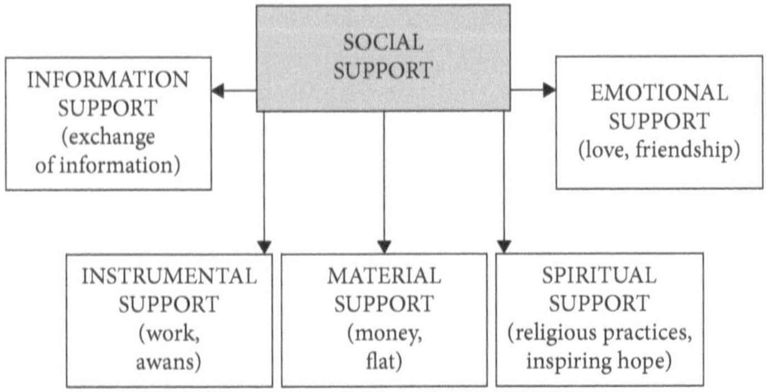

Fig. 4.3: Typical types and forms of social support (own elaboration).

The data on which sources of support play a positive role in preventing negative effects of stress do not provide unambiguous information, as they cover various dimensions, such as: *structural* (e.g. structure and geography of social networks on an area), *quantitative* (e. g. density of social networks and homogeneity in terms of age, gender, social class, religious class, etc.), *functional* (e.g. accessibility to support institutions) and *qualitative* (subjective sense of support, adequacy of forms and evaluation of help functions).

Summarizing the role of social support as a form of coping with stress, emphasis should be placed on its positive features, such as: reduction of stress level, giving a sense of togetherness with other people who are ready to help; reduction of subjectively negative effects of stress and evoking positive emotions, accompanying the overcoming of another obstacle on the life path, which is conducive to further development of personality and health in general. Nowadays, assistance activities are effectively supported by social networking sites, which not only speed up the support, but also complement or support government institutions, which in the event of disasters or dramatic accidents invite the support of the UN, governments of other countries or international charities (e.g. International Red Cross and Red Crescent Movement, Magen David Adom etc.). An example of the speed and effectiveness of such international relief efforts is the rescue operation of 12 boys and their 25-year-old sports instructor became trapped on VI. 2018 in a flooded cave in Northern Thailand and after 17 days of being stranded, were rescued by 90 divers, including 50 from abroad, another one is the international support from firefighters in extinguish forest fires in large areas of Sweden and Greece in July 2018.

In addition to positive, humanitarian values of social support, the disadvantages of this form of coping with stress are also emphasized. Negative effects of social support are often related to the fear of revealing one's problems and not being understood, to the threat to self-evaluation and to dependence on others. The biggest disadvantage of support is the probability of reducing the sense of one's own competence and ability to cope with stress on one's own in general. The concept of learned helplessness by M.E.P. Seligman (2006) alludes to the latter. The concept refers to the psychology of learning (rewards and punishments) and to the so-called training of helplessness, to which both animals and people are subjected, in situations that do not provide the possibility of escape or avoidance. As a result, in contact with new situations so-called deficits of learned helplessness occur, such as: cognitive (difficulties in detecting and learning the relationship between behavior and result), motivational (manifested in reduced motivation to produce new responses, in slower response time, general passivity, lack of spontaneous behavior), emotional (initially fear occurs, then mood reduction, hostility, sense of hopelessness and incompetence, feelings related to the state of depression). This leads to a decrease in self-esteem, which strengthens the training of learned helplessness, on the basis of a vicious circle. In her opinion, people tend to seek to function in predictable situations, i.e. situations where they feel in control and avoid becoming defendant on others. A situation of dependence on others, which in the first phase gives a sense of security and support in overcoming stress situations, after some time begins to threaten the person's autonomy. If we get used to counting on others more than ourselves in case of life's difficulties, we are dealing with *learned helplessness*. This incapacitation is often accompanied by: reduced motivation for effort, decline of new initiatives, reduced mood, emotional disorders, sense of inferiority, etc. This response may become permanent. Therefore, it can be said that learned helplessness is a set of symptoms of cognitive, motivational and emotional disorders caused by the belief of self-ineffectiveness in coping with stress. This self-ineffectiveness is usually related to past experiences, typical for uncontrolled events, such as (a) situations of long-term lack of achievements (e.g. unrequited love, financial problems); (b) sudden and unpredictable random events (e.g. death of a loved one, permanent disability or incurable illness).

4.3.4 Types and forms of coping with stress

Types and forms of social support are related to the expectations of people who cannot cope with stress on their own and often ask for help or require empathy-based help. If social support in a stress situation is understood as a specific systematic effort connected with introducing changes in the life of an individual, social system, population or the structure of a social system, which is aimed at better adjustment of elements of the people-environmental system, then a very diverse level of support understood in this way should be assumed, including e.g.: (a) individual intervention (upbringing, skills training, medicines, psychotherapy); (b) individual change of personal goals (e.g. change of occupation, divorce, change of environment); (c) population-based intervention (e.g. preparation of society for economic crisis, unemployment, cataclysm, war); (d) national system of social services (e.g. social education system, police system, etc.). (e) international aid system (e.g. in case of drug addiction, crime, acts of terrorism or natural disasters); (f) national and international social service networks (e.g. the activity of Ministry of Health, urbanization programs, the activity of Ministry of Environment).

A common feature of all employees of social services is, first of all: quantitative and qualitative evaluation of unfulfilled human needs; assistance (advocacy) in taking care of official matters; mobilization for effort; counseling and advising; rehabilitation; consulting (individual, institutional); collecting data on institutions and crisis support systems; gathering information on managing programs, crisis support systems; supervising programs, institutions and crisis support systems. There are seven levels of social service systems: 1. individual systems; 2. family and friends; 3. education systems; 4. work and economic systems; 5. housing and social care; 6. cultural and leisure management systems; 7. health and psychiatric care. We shall discuss individual social support systems briefly.

Another example is obesity as a source of stress and a way of coping with it by seeking social support in the health care system, so-called rehabilitation camps for the obese or bariatric surgery (Ganley, 1989). This problem was the subject of research on the relationship between self-esteem, body image (being overweight), sense of coherence and coping with stress. Among other things, it was found that obese people had a lower self-esteem in terms of their body image and a lower level of cohesion, which was a significant source of stress compared to those with a healthy body mass (Nieśpiałowski, Terelak, 2016).

Modern existential fears related to industrialization, the so-called ecological and geographical fears (e.g. related to nuclear power plant disasters in Bhopal, Three Miles Island and Chernobyl or the ozone depletion) (Speckhard, 2007) and to terrorism (Richman et al., 2004), are resistant to individual systems of coping with stress. That is why the so-called environmental movements (e.g. Greenpeace) aim to reduce fear of environmental stress by raising public awareness of environmental threats and, indirectly, to induce a self-calming effect by making people aware that they are coping with this type of threat to health and life as intelligent beings.

4.3.4.1 Family as a basic social coping

The family as a community is both natural and institutional (having not only its formal rights but also its legal obligations) form of support in stress situations. Experience provided us with examples of families (including extended family) being the main source of support for an individual, especially in so-called crisis situations (e.g. in adolescence or old age). In addition to formal statutory obligations (e.g. the obligation to financially support a family member until adulthood or to pay child support), positive family attributes include: emotional climate, economic status, being a multi-generational family, etc. There is an abundance of sociological, pedagogical and psychological literature on positive family ties, which documents how a family provides social support in times of crisis (e.g. war, unemployment), as well as points out the limitation or lack of such support from in case of a dysfunctional family (e.g. orphans, single mothers, separation from one or both parents due to economic emigration) (Bifulco, 2007). This is why some authors prefer the method of family therapy to increase the effectiveness of the family as a form of support in crisis situations and to make better use of it as institutional support in terms of stress. The process of family therapy usually includes: mapping out family problems, highlighting the point of view of each family member (including that of children), forming crisis hypotheses and a map of countermeasures. The family can be a means of support and help in solving both personal and professional problems, regardless of whether they are biological or foster families (Barnett, Hyde, 2001).

4.3.4.2 Educational systems as a form of support

Education is connected with the concept of harmonious development of the human health, based on a holistic rule formed by H. Selye (1980a) who based on the ethics of: “integration of body, mind and soul” which exposes the role of support provided by school, educational and religious systems. Psychotherapists, commonly known as “preachers of the twentieth century” in the USA, admit that in many extreme cases (victims of disasters, terminally ill patients, etc.) they are practically helpless without referring to their clients’ religious system of values (Ano, Vasconcelles, 2005). This direction of psychotherapeutic activity is successfully developed within the scope of logotherapy of V.E. Frankl (1947). In the literature, there is also an increased interest in research on the moderating role of religion in coping with stress and providing support, especially in situations of extreme threat to life, manifested, i.a., by the international humanitarian support movement with about 97 million volunteers worldwide, created to protect human health and life, under the banner of well-known symbols of: Red Cross, Red Crescent, Red Crystal, Magen David Adom, etc. The detailed discussion of these issues is beyond the scope of this study. In general, the concept of education systems is linked to national or international institutions (e.g. European Union, UNESCO). The problem of institutional support in a crisis situation is connected with educational programs which are to prepare citizens for the consumption of civilizational and cultural goods (the so-called comprehensive human development), as well as with special programs and a network of special schools designed for people who are exceptionally talented or physically and mentally disabled. Different religions and systems of beliefs play an important role in education systems, and in life crises situations can be a source of stress (e.g. conflicts of conscience, fear of sin and eternal punishment) on the one hand, and of institutional support (religious associations) and moral support (religion) on the other.

4.3.4.3 Religion as a support in the situation of existential stress

The literature on the topic of positive role of religion in the process of coping with stress emphasizes the psychotherapeutic significance of religious practices, especially in case of people with life-threatening diseases (e.g. waiting for heart or kidney transplants) and some mental health disorders (Emmons, (2005). . Psychiatry appreciates the role of religion in treatment of various mental disorders. For example, priests of various faiths have always been involved in "psychotherapeutic" activities, using techniques such as listening, encouragement, advice, referring to transcendental values (goodness, love, justice, mercy, etc.) (Medea, 1966). . People of faith find support in their spiritual counselors, especially in crisis or terminal[20]situations. This is evidenced by the increase in religious activity on the part of both the people of faith and priests of practically all the major denominations operating in the USA (Catholics, Protestants, Jews, Muslims and others), as well as various religious sects, following the terrorist attack and destruction of the World Trade Center on September 11, 2001 (Richman et al., 2004).

---

20 Even in the so-called communist times in Poland, the heads of some hospitals allowed priests to provide "spiritual services to patients" upon their request, especially in terminal situations.

The arguments for treating religion as a form of support in the event of existential stress are as follows: 1) religion reduces the level of depression; 2) religion reduces fear and anxiety; 3) religion strengthens the sense of value; 4) religion strengthens the needs of a higher order of a transcendental nature; 5) religion raises hopes in existential crisis situations; 6) religion increases tolerance of suffering; 7) religion determines the meaning of life for a person, both earthly and the afterlife (Burker et al., 2005). On the other hand, theses about the harmful impact of religion on mental health refer to the following arguments: sometimes it is a source of self-torment, emotional trauma, and weakens a person, and sometimes even it attracts the mentally ill (e.g. religious delusions and cases of self-injury) (Galanter, 2006; Gall et al., 2005).

Z. Chlewiński (1982) notes that religion integrates and directs the functioning of the personality of those of faith through: providing a meaning of life, sacralization of the system of values, safety and trust, auto-identification, identification with the group, autopsychotherapy. When reviewing the concepts of humanistic psychology, it can be seen that religiousness should be treated as one of the dimensions of the specific human way of existence, its highest and deepest potentials, which people use regardless of whether they treat religiousness subjectively or objectively. This is confirmed by empirical evidence, which describes the facts that in crisis situations the therapeutic nature of religion (in the psychological sense and not theological sense) is also used by people who are not religious. Thus, regardless of the emphasis being placed on the positive or negative role of religion in building coping strategies, it should be noted that the authority of religion as an institution provides moral support in stress situations , especially those of an existential nature (Van Kaam, 1969). Therefore, humanistic psychology, based on the existential-personalistic concept of personality, emphasizes that through religious behavior one achieves *self-transcendence*, which is essential for fortifying coping strategies with an element of the "I – world" system in all its dimensions, including the spiritual one (Paloutzian, Park, 2015).

Educational programs may also cover very specific issues, such as upbringing in sobriety, health education, sexual education, religious education, programs for overcoming drug addiction, AIDS awareness programs, interpersonal communication programs or programs aimed at helping to accept of one's disability (Terelak, 1973).

4.3.4.4 Social security systems and charities

Institutional support schemes cover different government agencies in a country, such as economic systems and work organization, social protection systems and charity institutions. Sociologists have calculated that people spend most of their active adult life in a working environment, where new requirements often arise and where sometimes the customary norms are exceeded. Thus, the system of protection standards is at the same time an institutional system for coping with stress. The protection of people from stress at a workplace is covered by government and international programs (e.g. the national institutes for occupational safety or the International Labor Organization in Geneva, or European Union directives concerning a 48-hour working week for physicians).

The safety of human beings in the working environment is primarily about protecting their health, defined by the WHO as physical and social well-being, and not just as the state of not being ill. Preserving such health requires maintaining a balance of the internal environment of the body, called homeostasis. Meanwhile, the working environment poses a significant threat to it through the impact of many of the stress factors on people which upset this balance. The homeostasis of a human body, for example, requires maintaining an internal temperature of about 37°C. Meanwhile, in the working environment, the temperature can range from -20°C to +70°C. This huge temperature difference must be balanced by the body, through wearing protective clothing, changing the blood flow from 0.2 to 100 ml/100 g of tissue/min and increasing sweat production from 0 to 4 l/h. Maintaining the homeostasis of the body in an unfavorable thermal environment is therefore connected with a huge physiological cost of work. To maintain homeostasis during intense physical effort, heart rate must be increased from 50 to 200 per minute; respiratory rate from 16 to 50 per minute; and oxygen consumption from 1.5 to 4.0 liters per minute. All other factors in the working environment, such as noise, mechanical vibration and radiation, also pose the risk of disturbing this fragile physiological balance and becoming pathological when they exceed a certain level. This justifies the need to design work processes appropriately to the limited psychophysical capabilities of a human being. The following are also derivative effects of occupational hazards: increased mortality of men and women in aged 35–44 and increased myocardial infarction .

The provisions of the International Labor Organization (ILO) conventions set out the following obligations for the state to provide institutional support in the field of people's safety in the working environment: 1) establishing the parameters of acceptable exposure of employees to dangerous, harmful and arduous factors of the working environment; 2) establishing uniform methods of control and assessment of occupational hazards at the national level; 3) establishing uniform principles of registration of causes and effects of occupational hazards at the national level; 4) establishing criteria, methods and requirements of safety and ergonomics for machines, equipment, technologies and production facilities; 5) establishing criteria, methods and requirements for personal and collective protection equipment of employees; 6) creating socio-economic mechanisms for shaping appropriate working conditions.

Psychologists and sociologists often study the state of awareness on the issue and the level of satisfaction with the changes that are taking place. This requires the cooperation of three support institutions in the field of occupational safety, which, in accordance with ILO Convention no. 155, are the state, employers and employees. Employers have at their disposal appropriate institutions, such as the National Institute of Public Health and specialized occupational health and safety services, which are primarily responsible for preventive functions and for informing employers, employees and their representatives in the enterprise about: the requirements for maintaining a safe and healthy working environment and for adapting work to the abilities of workers in terms of their physical and mental health.

Furthermore, Article 5 of the ILO Convention defines very precisely the functions of OHS services, in terms of support, including, i.a., not only the identification and assessment of health hazards at a workplace, but also forms of assistance such as: welfare measures, counseling on organizing work, health and safety training, access to individual and collective protective equipment; workers' health surveillance, provision of first aid and emergency management; prevention and treatment of occupational diseases.

A separate problem of support is counteracting the employee's mismatch with the social working environment, the model of which including supplementary and complementary mismatches was presented in the *Person-Organization Theory* (POT) by Amy L. Kristof (1996). This theory reveals the ineffectiveness of all institutional programs for managing stress at work, in which all people are treated equally, i.e. without taking into account the system of needs and values of each employee. Therefore, in many work environments, so-called social support groups are created spontaneously or at the suggestion of psychologists. An example of such a group are the *Pilot Advisory Groups* functioning inside of some international airlines (e.g. International Federation of Air Line Pilots' Associations) which aim to provide psychological support to pilots and other staff working directly with them (e.g. flight attendants, air traffic controllers, flight mechanics, navigators) who present the effects of occupational stress (e.g. anxiety, depression, neurosis, alcoholism, drug abuse, as well as family conflicts) (Tsang, Vidullch, 2003). Similar groups of social support often have a local character, in the form of various foundations and charity institutions offering social support.

The latter forms of institutional social support are often complemented by various types of state government and local government agencies, which are not always effective. This is confirmed, i.a., by the studies conducted by R.R. Weigel (1988), who analyzed 10 economic programs concerning methods of cope with stress in low-income families living in small towns. A positive correlation was found between effective coping with economic stress and a network of well-functioning social service institutions. The system of social support in a situation of economic stress may take the form of international (e.g. exchange of economists and advisors), national (determination of the economic and social system of the state, activities of e.g. ministries of labor and social protection), and also local programs (secular and religious charity institutions).

Social protection systems and charity institutions support the members of a community in the process of coping with stress in various areas: economic, health, rehabilitation, education, public safety, package holidays, etc. For example, homeless unemployed people are an important social problem resulting from the inability to meet basic needs concerning work and living, which is the cause of many existential crisis situations, condemning people to chronic discomfort. State support activity results from a formal and legal social contract with its citizens, while charity activity of various secular and religious institutions should be considered in terms of social sensitivity (level of social culture, ethos of economic elites, expatriation, etc.). One of the most interesting and oldest forms of charity support is *Rotary International* (RI), - an international organization founded by American lawyer Paul P. Harris in 1905, based in the suburbs of Chicago, in Evanston, Illinois, USA, with several dozen regional offices in Europe, Africa, South and North America, Asia, Australia and Oceania. This association adheres to a morally respectable creed: "Service Above Self", as it is a voluntary association of entrepreneurs and people of various professions, providing humanitarian aid to individuals and communities in need[21].

---

21 There are more than 520 districts of Rotary worldwide, grouped in six regions, one of which is CEEMA (Continental Europe, eastern coast of the Mediterranean and Africa). The organization is headed by a president who is chosen every year and a board of directors, chosen every two years. All Rotary managers at international and local level carry out their duties as volunteers and do not receive any remuneration. Currently, there are 1.2 million rotarians in more than 200 countries, associated in more than 32,000 clubs. One of the most spectacular actions taken by Rotary International was the famous mission, initiated in 1985, to vaccinate all the children of the world against polio.

This movement is intensifying today as a result of the collapse of many political and systemic structures as well as emigration movements on a national scale. International (e.g. UN, EU) and government programs can only partially address the situation of economic and consumption emigrants or people forced to migrate around the world in search of a place to live due to political persecution or war. Gastarbeiters and migrants are a reproach of international organizations dealing with social support in this type of crisis and an economic and political problem, but on the other hand they are a support improving their well-being and at the same time a new source of acculturative stress, requiring other forms of support in meeting the challenges of a new civilization as well as cultural and religious challenges (Terelak, Borkowska, 2007).

4.3.4.5 Cultural institutions and organization of leisure time

In the era of an excess of free time, entire societies in countries with a high level of civilization play a huge role in coping with the stress of boredom. A famous American sociologist from the State University of California - T.M. Kando (1980), in the 1980s reviewed the world literature on the relationship between culture and free time. Taking into account two criteria of literary classification: idealistic perspective vs. realistic perspective, and the problem of free time vs. mass culture, he divided the literature of the subject into four sections: (1) An idealistic view of free time - the authors define free time idealistically like e.g. ancient Greeks or supporters of the contemporary idea of Olympism do; (2) A realistic view of free time - the authors define free time in terms of recreation, e.g. mass sports, tourism, clubs; (2) A realistic view of free time - the authors define free time in terms of recreation.; (3) Idealistic approach to mass culture - the authors criticize mass culture and support the so-called higher elite culture, e.g. theater, classical music; (4) Realistic approach to mass culture - the authors emphasize the value of mass culture, also from the economic point of view, the so-called show business. Free time in the modern world is not a person's individual matter, but also a sociological and economic category. A 20-hour week of work in wealthy countries can lead to excess of free time which may be a cause of stress. Symptoms of so-called weekend or Sunday neurosis are known as a result of a lack of skills or the ability to organize time outside work, especially in so-called technocratic societies. The solution to this problem is therefore a matter for the cultural development of a give country or region of the world (European culture, Far Eastern culture, African culture, etc.) and for the cultural policies of the government or its agendas. The differences in the approach to the definition of free time and mass culture can be reflected in a country's cultural systems. Another important factor shaping the level of consumption of cultural goods is the economic factor, both at the national level and at the level of the economic status of individual citizens, especially in the case of the so-called *high culture*, which includes a network of such cultural branches as classical music, ballet and professional dance, theater, cinema, art galleries, literature, professional sports, etc. To a lesser extent, the economic crisis affects the so-called *low culture*, which is largely of a commercial nature: newspapers and magazines, books, comic books, cinema, television, Internet, radio, video, sports and tourism. The psychological significance of mass culture as institutional support in a situation of excess of free time is obvious.

Signum temporis of the early 21st century, is the widespread availability of social networking sites, which created through an interactive website, bring together people of common interests or those interested in tastes of others. Users of these portals spend a lot of time communicating via chats, instant messaging services, lists, blogs, Internet forums, etc. A characteristic feature of this type of social communication is speed, mass range and anonymity, but also the risk of being easily "addicted" which is a new source of stress, requiring support in the form of psychotherapy (Rus, Tiemensma, 2018).

The impact of this communication culture on the development of personalities of individuals and societies is debatable (Berry, Ataca, 2007). However, this is a separate issue that goes beyond institutional forms of support in stress situations. The issue of the excess of free time in old age has been omitted, as this problem can only be solved systematically through healthcare institutions (so-called retirement homes) in addition to an ad hoc solution within the scope of local communities (e.g. pensioners' clubs, establishment of the university of the third age).

4.3.4.6 Healthcare institutions

Healthcare system is a derivative of the political system and the level of wealth of the state, but also of social sensitivity. In general, all healthcare systems are geared to providing assistance in the event of a crisis caused by illness or old age.

The development of a network of general and specialized hospitals, outpatient clinics and institutions of a general practitioner, social assistant and psychotherapist is the result of a planned social policy at national or local level. However, certain healthcare standards, including the definition of health, are the preserve of international institutions, in this case the World Health Organization (WHO) as a UN agency.

On a plaque, yellowed over several decades, placed at the entrance to the former Internal Diseases Clinic of Professor Julian Aleksandrowicz in Cracow there is an inscription: "The clinic does not only heal, but also teaches how to live and stay healthy." This inscription is not only a therapeutic indication, but also a preventive aspect of healthcare systems, highlighting the deep sense of prevention as a means of protection against life stress (e.g. rules of life, rules of rest, occupation health and safety rules, environmental protection).

Too easy access to medical support in the event of illness leads to the abuse of medications (private pharmacies, access to over-the-counter medications, pocket first aid kits for any event, etc.), a harmful phenomenon which takes the form of addiction to medications.

A coherent system of social and medical services for people with disabilities is of particular importance. This institutional support in life crisis situations has its international dimension (e.g. UN's Department of Economics and Social Affairs, International Association for the Rehabilitation of the Physically Disabled), national (Ministry of Health and Central Association of Cooperatives of Physically Disabled in Poland, Polish Association for Struggle with Disability, Polish Association of the Blind, etc.) (Hulek, ed., 1991) and local (e.g. rehabilitation centers, integration schools, clubs for young people with disabilities, sports, student and entertainment clubs) (Terelak, 1973). A separate and an important problem of institutional crisis intervention is the system of psychiatric prevention and treatment. This concerns, on the one hand, the state of psychiatric culture in a given country (e.g. in Poland there has been a discussion on the law on mental health for many years), the model of psychiatry itself (e.g. biological vs. humanistic) (Jankowski, 1970), the state and development of a network of psychiatric hospitals and mental health clinics, and, on the other hand, the mental hygiene movement, work of various types of mental health associations or associations aimed at fighting with addictions to: nicotine, alcohol, drugs, etc. (e.g. alcoholics anonymous, juvenile alcoholics clubs, Monar - Society for the Prevention of Drug Addiction), as well as ad hoc crisis intervention activities of various secular and religious institutions (private psychoanalysts, crisis hotlines, schools of relaxation, etc.). Professor Kazimierz Dąbrowski (1997), the creator of mental hygiene and the president of the Polish Mental Hygiene Association of many years, saw crisis support in the following institutions: family and school (e.g. marriage and family counseling); mental health clinics (physician, psychologist, pedagogue); mental hygiene institutes; mental hygiene clinics for healthy people; clinics for children with educational difficulties and mental disorders; general medicine institutions; medical and educational institutions; general sanatoriums and sanatoriums for cases of neurosis, psychoneurosis, states of increased mental stimulation and states on borderline psychoneurosis and psychosis or the so-called schizoneurosis; psychiatric hospitals; prisons.

It should be stressed that various types of lobbies organized in companies of higher social utility are an important stimulus for state institutions and programs in the field of crisis intervention and healthcare.

A separate issue that should be considered from the standpoint of the crisis support systems presented so far is care for the elderly and the disabled. The forms of such care result from the social and political system of the state, its economic system, as well as the general social culture, personal moral sensitivity and sense of responsibility. An example of such sensitivity and moral responsibility on the part of the state is Norway, which on the one hand, offers many forms of voluntary services aimed at caring for lonely and elderly people. 5–6 volunteers who specialize in e.g. washing, feeding, reading books, going for a walk, shopping care for a single person. On the other hand, local and national authorities are responsible for the economic care of older people. Psychological research shows that institutional solutions alone, even the exemplary ones, do not reduce existential fear of loneliness and social isolation (Gierveld, Tilburg, Dykstra, 2006). Supporting institutional forms with various informal initiatives from outside of the closed environment of social protection institutions, such as contact with family, visiting friends, hobby clubs, active participation in cultural life, significantly alleviate the stress of loneliness.

An example of the discussion on the support provided by the state to meet multiple needs, including very intimate needs of the disabled, was one of the 14 films presented at the 4th Belgrade International Film Festival For and By People with Disabilities (June 5–7, 2013) entitled *The Last Taboo* by an American director Alexander Freeman. The film concerned the sexuality of people with disabilities. One of the controversial forms of social support used to help people with disabilities meet their sexual needs is the so-called sexual assistant, specially trained by the *InSebe* foundation. They provide services which in several European countries (e.g. Switzerland, the Netherlands) are paid for by public health insurance funds because they consider that sexual needs are natural in adults.

The consequences of a lack of support or access to it in a situation of solitude and social isolation are the cause of committing suicide (Holt-Lustadt et al., 2015). This is also confirmed by studies conducted by A. Steptoe, an epidemiologist at the University College in London (2013). In 2004–2012 conducted studies on a sample of 6.5 thousand elderly people over the age of 52 who stayed in a state of social isolation (nursing homes), 26 % of which attempted to commit suicide. The author of the study points out that solitude is more stressful than social isolation itself.

In conclusion, the main areas of crisis intervention are complementary, their scope and effectiveness depend to a large extent on social, political, economic and cultural factors. As the above suggests, institutional support in a crisis situation is diversified in different parts of the world and a person, as an individual, is often doomed to drastically limited support or lack thereof, which makes their psychological situation difficult and the person remains lonely among people. Sociological concepts of stress of alienation and anomie indicate that social alienation leads not only to a difficult personal situation (e.g. suicide), but often to a difficult social situation (e.g. deviancies, criminal behavior, acts of terrorism, revolutionary actions). Only a few positive and negative effects of institutional social support in a crisis situation can be mentioned. Among the positive effects are: 1) preventive support (reducing insecurity and anxiety, using good examples, solving problems, restraint, etc.); 2) support in coping with stress (achieving a favorable situation, generating sympathy, providing helpful information, etc.); 3) support for lifestyle change (principles of life hygiene, positive attitude to mental health, creative compliance with social norms, etc.). Among the negative effects of social support are: 1) evoking uncertainty and anxiety, developing bad habits related to expecting help without one's own effort, etc.; 2) trauma after failure to cope with stress despite receiving support; 3) reluctance to mental health rules, sense of entitlement.

Thus, social support is not always effective and often depends, apart from the socio-economic and cultural conditions mentioned above, on the characteristics of the individual, their natural stress resistance, the hierarchy of values, the degree of internalization of social norms, etc. The latter skill can be acquired through participation in social life, which in itself can also be regarded as a form of crisis support. Participation in public life (e.g. social organizations, political parties) shapes self-confidence and gives a sense of control (individuals as a strong their group).

Consultation or expertise are an increasingly exposed form of institutional social support in a crisis situation. This includes, i.a.: 1) a "roadmap" for overcoming difficult problems through therapeutic programs; 2) gathering information on the causes of crises (database); 3) facilitating desired behavioral changes; 4) encouraging the expression of feelings and positive attitudes; 5) encouraging the development of self-awareness; 6) discontinuing support when objectives are achieved.

An example of such expertise-based action in case of the need to restructure a company can be e.g. a global reach expert company *Hay International Business Group from Brussels*, founded in the USA by Edward Hey and operating since 1943 in several dozen branches on all continents. The experts provide clients not only with the necessary knowledge on the principles of modern human resources management, but also with specific skills (*management buy-in* trainings).

Finally, it is worth mentioning that apart from institutional and professional forms of social support, natural and non-professional support systems functioning primarily within a family play an important role in a crisis situation. Functions of parental support for children include important preventive life tips, such as: information about the outside world and the threats associated with it; interpreting the world in terms of values (feedback systems); choosing ideologies (e.g. Catholic, Jewish, atheistic family); helping to solve life problems; mediating in conflicts with others; providing concrete support in any difficult situation in life; a refuge of peace and confidence; a point of reference in the identification process; ensuring the process of achieving emotional and social maturity.

Reflecting on the perspectives of social support services and systems in crisis situations, attention should be paid to modern techniques of diagnosing needs of social assistance, which are becoming more and more common due to the development of post-modern technology and information technology (Terelak, 2011). Due to the widespread availability of devices such as computers, mobile phones and satellite TV, as well as the dynamic development of automatics and robotics, we not only avoid a lot of stress, but also are able to develop intellectually and communicate without language barriers with other people. The use of the Internet to provide *on-line* support is already an exemplary and *signum temporis* of the 21st century, known as the Information Age. *Online* support can be understood as contact via e-mail (e.g. exchange of correspondence with a support specialist), chat rooms or instant messengers (text or multimedia conversation in real time at a fixed time) and closed thematic forums on similar issues (as in: Abu Al-Rub, 2006; Caplan, 2003); Rowiński, Gągolewski, 2007). This vision, regardless of the possibility of its implementation in particular countries, can on the one hand bring a new quality of life in the form of reducing many of the stress in everyday life, and on the other hand it can itself generate new sources of stress and areas of threat, even on a global scale (hackers, hate speech, etc.). Therefore, it seems that the issues of life stress as well as the natural and acquired ways to cope with it presented here are and will continue to be relevant. I think that this statement, which provokes a moment of existential reflection, can successfully replace the afterword of this book. Hope and anxiety best reflect the essence of psychological stress that people face in their daily struggles with life (Folkman, 2010). Stress surrounding us is a challenge to which we do not have to give in passively, but we must actively oppose, while minimizing the cost to the individual and society. Minimizing this cost is the wisdom of life. This wisdom, as we have tried to demonstrate, is the sum of individual and civilizational human experiences, and the hope resulting from faith in the sense of one's own individual and species life. This awareness, as shown by the activity of users of Internet forums on coping with life stress patterns, is becoming increasingly widespread and provides information support.

The conclusions of the stress management theory and practice are that it is a particular cognitive and behavioral effort based on an assessment of one's own resources, on one hand and on the other, on the magnitude and/or intensity of the stress stimulus within the scope of three temporal perspectives: the present (threats here and now), the future (challenges) and the past (harm), and access to social support. This is the basis for designing adequate coping strategies. However, not all remedial strategies are effective in solving stress situations and minimizing the effects of stress. That is why people try to fight, for example, against thanatophobia (fear of dying) in two ways - faith or reason - which goes far beyond the scope psychology as an empirical science, but certainly leads to philosophical reflection on the meaning of human existence (Lamiel, 2010).

General conclusions

The first general conclusion from our considerations is as follows: stress is an integral part of our lives and has as many "faces" as the number of people living in the world (past, present and future), and it is largely up to us whether we see it as "eustress", which has an important motivational function, forcing us to make efforts and achieve life goals, or whether we see it as "distress", which distracts us from achieving our goals and comfort of life. The second important for the reader conclusion concerns the ability to cope with stress, which, apart from immunological support of our general immunity, is, on the one hand, the effect of learning how to prevent stress situations, and on the other hand, the access to support of the closest and sympathetic people as well as many state, local and charity institutions, which, apart from instrumental coping by arousing emotions of hope, can change distress into eustress (Małkiewicz, Terelak, (2016). The third significant fact which impairs the rational use of life experience in coping with stress is subjective probability, burdened with the error of logical reasoning and turning to thinking overburdened with various forms of emotion of hope that "someone" or "something" will magically do the coping for us (Kahneman, Tversky, 1972).

Summary

The book's title alludes to the 50th anniversary of the Polish translation of Hans Selye's book entitled The Stress of Life. The earliest knowledge on the topic of stress can be found in the ancient philosophy and medicine where stress was understood in the three following ways, as load (i.e. external pressure), stress (i.e. internal reaction to external pressure) and strain (i.e. disorder or deformation of the subject). In essence, these three notions are just different aspects of the same phenomenon that is commonly referred to as "stress". The last of the above-mentioned aspects is described in Chapter 1 that reviews theories of stress of the 20th century, from biological mechanisms of stress, through medical concepts to contemporary models of psychological stress. This review ends with conclusions that refer to the views of Claude Bernard – a famous French biologist. He stated that a successful management of one's own stress on the cellular level can be regarded as "life wisdom", since unsuccessful management of stress, which is an inherent part of our lives, is paid for by a decrease in or loss of our well-being and/or health. Bernard created the law of "conservation of internal milieu" and put an emphasis on an important existential fact that cells of multicellular organisms conserve their internal milieu despite threats from the external environment. This conservation is attained by physiological and biochemical processes of the organism. Bernard's concept was further developed by Walter B. Cannon – an American physiologist who created the theory of homeostasis. This theory describes different physiological processes that are reregulated by negative feedback loops that enable the preservation of a certain number of physical and chemical parameters at a constant level (e.g. body temperature, osmotic pressure of blood; glucose concentration, carbon dioxide concentration, blood hemoglobin). The principle of homeostasis is very simple and is based on the existence of biological measurement systems and effector systems that act in reciprocal ways.

A continuation of the biological concepts of stress is the theory of General Adaptation Syndrome (GAS) that encompasses non-specific physiological changes induced by harmful stimuli. GAS is composed of three stadia – alarm reaction, resistance and exhaustion. At the same time, this is also a disease model. Medical theories of stress have a holistic nature, i.e. they approach the human being as a whole, as both the subject and the object of stressors. As regards medical history, i.e. the fundamental part of diagnosis, all information that relates to stressful life events is of particular importance. One of the disadvantages of the theories of everyday stressful events is the difficulty of quantitative analysis. Among the medical theories of stress, one should include the so-called theories of life crises that have been appearing since the 1940s. Such theories try to organize "folk" knowledge on crises in our lives and explain their positive or negative roles in the ontogenetic development. The most well-know of these theories is that of G. Caplan's – an American psychiatrist.

Theories of psychological stress, being part of more general theories of behavior, try to explain some of the psychological mechanisms of human behavior in difficult situations when "normal behavior" in not possible. The first, comprehensive psychological theory that fulfils this assumption is the theory of frustration. This theory is based on the analysis of behavior of people who are faced with obstacles that hinder the achievement of goals. Different creators and interpreters of the theory of frustration have different definitions of its core notion. Some put an emphasis on the obstacles (external object that influences the mental status) and others on the reaction to the obstacles (emotional tension, usually unpleasant, associated with a need). Another theory of psychological stress that is worth mentioning is the theory of emotional tension by I.L. Janis. This theory defines stress as the stressor that induces a high level of emotional tension that hinders the normal way of reacting. The model of M.J. Apter differentiates two opposing aspects of stress: stress-tension (discrepancy between the preferred and actual level of motivation) and stress-effort (focused on actions that could reduce stress-tension). The model of cognitive appraisal by R. Lazarus and S. Folkman is based on two psychological mechanisms – primary and secondary cognitive appraisal of the threat. The primary appraisal is a process that decides on the meaning of the transactional reaction; this can be of no importance, have a positive meaning or be stressful. The latter can be viewed in terms of (a) harm, (b) threat and (c) challenge. The first category (harm or loss) refers to a loss or trauma already incurred, the second category (threat) refers to future damages (anticipated) and the third category (challenge) refers to one's own abilities to handle a given stressful situation. Psychological stress refers primarily to challenges that exceed the capabilities (internal or external) of the individual as appraised by them.

The salutogenic theory of disease by A. Antonovsky includes an interesting model of stress that is concentrated on psychological mechanisms of "sense of coherence" based on general resistance resources (GRRs), including physical, biochemical, material, cognitive and emotional resources associated with values, attitudes, interpersonal relations etc. This model explains successful avoidance or overcoming of many different life difficulties. The structure of sense of coherence, being a global orientation that gives a dynamic sense of life, is composed of three beliefs relating to the surrounding world – comprehensibility, manageability and meaningfulness. The model of stress by Hobfoll is known as the Conservation of Resources Theory. This theory assumes that psychological stress is a reaction to the surroundings that contain a) a threat of pure loss of forces, b) real loss of forces, c) lack of forces caused by exploitation resulting from trying to attain and protect resources.

The evolution of the notions of stress clearly shows how people who do not have an "inborn species enemy", as opposed to animals, still react to stressful situations in an atavistic way with the "fight or flight" reaction. The result is an inadequate and excessive reaction to any stressful stimulus, not only to real stimuli but also to virtual stimuli from the past (harm, loss) and the future (challenge). Moreover, the abilities to cope with stress are not inborn but require prior learning or social support.

Chapter 2 presents sources of stress that reflect numerous, multidirectional relations of people with the broadly-defined physical, biological, social and spiritual environments. Therefore, the sources of stress have been classified as follows: physical (climate, noise, lightening, vibrations, ionizing radiation, hypoxia, gravity – acceleration vs inertia), chronobiologic (circadian rhythms, sudden change of time zone), psychological (deprivation vs overload, disruptions, harms, threats, challenges, etc.) and social (social status, social roles, styles of management, competitiveness, rewards vs. punishments, career, work-home relations, etc.).

In Chapter 3, when describing reaction to stress, four perspective were taken – physiological (EEG, ECG, pulse, respiratory rate, sweating temperature etc.), emotional (arousal, expression, speech, etc.), cognitive (disorders of memory, impairment of cognitive function, etc.) and behavioral (time of psychomotor reaction, visuo-motor coordination, etc.).

Coping with stress is described in Chapter 4 and focuses on two theoretical constructs, namely, resistance to stress and coping with stress. Coping with stress was characterized in the three following forms – process, strategy and style of coping. The styles of coping with stress that are most commonly found in the literature include task-oriented coping, emotion-oriented coping and avoidance-oriented coping. One of the important ways of managing stress is social support, which is defined as interpersonal relations that can help feel and perceive that one is surrounded by people who can be relied upon. Support can also be of emotional nature (experiencing empathy, ability to trust someone, being surrounded by care, friendship), instrumental nature (experiencing help in different life domains and in a concrete way, e.g. borrowing money, help in completing a task) or informational nature (receiving information that could help in coping with tasks and problems). There are no firm opinions on either positive or negative role of social support, since it may in some cases lead to learned helplessness. Apart from individual forms of social support, there are also other forms of institutional support provided primarily by the services of governmental and non-governmental organizations. These forms of support depend mostly on the political systems and political culture of administration in individual countries.

The conclusion from our considerations is as follows: stress is an integral part of our lives and has as many "faces" as the number of people living in the world (past, present and future), and it is largely up to us whether we see it as "eu-stress", which has an important motivational function, forcing us to make efforts and achieve life goals, or whether we see it as "distress", which distracts us from achieving our goals and comfort of life.

List of figures

References

Abu Al-Rub R.F. (2006). Replication and examination of research data on job stress and coworker social support with Internet and traditional samples. "Journal of Nursing Scholarship" 38 (2), 200–204.

Adams, J.S. (1965). Inequity in social exchanges. In: L. Berkowitz (ed.): Advances in experimental social psychology (pp. 267–300). New York: Academic Press.

Akerstedt T., Lindbeck G. (2007). Night shiftwork. In: G. Fink (ed.): Encyclopedia of stress. Second edition (vol. 2, 917–920). New York: Academic Press.

Alderman B.L., Arent S.M., Landers D.M., Rogers T.J. (2007). Aerobic exercise intensity and time of stressor administration influence cardiovascular responses to psychological stress. "Psychophysiology" 44 (5), 759–766.

Allison R.A. (2007). Trauma and memory. In: G. Fink (ed.): Encyclopedia of stress. Second edition (vol. 3, s. 765–767). New York: Academic Press.

Ando M. (2002). Relationships among mental health, coping styles and mood. "Psychological Reports" 90, 606–612.

Andrews B., Hejdenberg J. (2007). Stress in university students. In: G. Fink (ed.): Encyclopedia of stress. Second edition (vol. 3, s. 612–614). New York: Academic Press.

Andrzejuk, A. (2006). Uczucia i sprawność: Związek uczuć i sprawności w " Summa Theologiae" św. Tomasz z Akwinu. (Emotions and condition: The connection between emotions and condition in St. Thomas Aquinas's "Summa Theologiae"). Warszawa: NAVO.

Ano G.G., Vasconvelles E.B. (2005). Religious coping and psychological adjustment to stress: A meta-analysis. "Journal of Clinical Psychology" 61 (4), 461–480.

Antonovsky A. (1979). Health, stress and coping. San Francisco: Jossey-Bass Publishers.

Antonovsky A. (1993). The structure and properties of the sense of coherence scalę. "Social Science and Medicine" 36 (6), 725–733.

Antonucci T.C., Lansford J.E., Ajrouch K.J. (2007). Social support. In: G. Fink (ed.): Encyclopedia of stress. Second edition (vol. 3, s. 538–542). New York: Academic Press.

Appley, M.H., Trumbull, R. (1967). Psychological stress: Issues in research. New York: Appleton-Century-Crofts.

Apter, M.J., Svebak, S. (1984). Stress from Reversal Theory perspective. In: C.D. Spielberger and J. Strelau (eds.): Stress and anxiety (vol. 12). New York: Hemisphere-McGraw Hill.

Arnold L.E., Lindsay R.L. (2007). Attention-deficit hyperactivity disorder and the stress response. In: G. Fink (ed.): Encyclopedia of stress. Second edition (vol. 1, s. 271–276). New York: Academic Press.

Assanangkornchai S., Tangboonngam S., Sam-Angsri N., Edwards J.G. (2007). A Thai community's anniversary reaction to a major catastrophe. "Stress and Health" 23, 43–50.

Avis N.E. (2007). Menopause and stress. In: G. Fink (ed.): Encyclopedia of stress. Second edition (vol. 2, s. 703–706). New York: Academic Press.

Bakker A.B., Heuven E. (2006). Emotional dissonance, burnout, and in-role performance among nurses and policy officers. "International Journal of Stress Management" 13 (4), 423–440.

Balducci C., Alfano V., Fraccaroli F. (2009). Relationships between mobbing at work and MMPI-2 personality profile, posttraumatic stress symptoms, and suicidal ideation and behavior. "Violence and Victims" 24 (1), 52–67.

Bańka A. (1992). Percepcja stresu bezrobocia przez pracowników świadczących profesjonalnie pomoc bezrobotnym. (The perception of the stress of unemployment by employees providing professional support to the unemployed). "Przegląd Psychologiczny" 35 (4), 509–522.

Barna M. (2017). Autism spectrum disorder. Many questions, few answers. "Discover Magazine" 38 (6), 62–65.

Barnett, R.C., Hyde, J.S. (2001). Women, men, work, and family: An Expansionist Theory. "American Psychologist", 56 (10), 781–796.

Baumeister R. F., Vohs K. D. (2004). Handbook of self-regulation: Research, theory, and applications. New York: Guilford Press.

Beck, J.S. (1995). Cognitive Theory: Basics & Beyond. New York: Guilford. ISBN: 0-89862-847-4.

Beck F., Godin W. (1951). Russian and the extraction of confession. New York: Viking Press.

Bedard-Gilligan M., Jaeger J., Echiverri-Cohen A., Zoellner L.A. (2012). Individual differences in trauma disclosure. "Journal of Behavior Therapy and Experimental Psychiatry" 43, 716–723.

Bednard M., Greif J.L., Buckley T.C. (2004). International publication trends in the traumatic stress literature. "Journal of Traumatic Stress" 17 (2), 97–101.

Belloc, N.B., Breslow, L. (1972). Relationship of physical health status and health practices. "Preventive Medicine", 1, 409–421.

Bergiannaki J.D., Psarros C., Varsou E., Paparrigopoulos T., Soldatos C.R. (2003). Protracted acute stress reaction following an earthquake. "Acta Psychiatry Scandinavia" 107, 18–24.

Berkman L.F. (2007). Social networks and social isolation. In: G. Fink (ed.): Encyclopedia of stress. Second edition (vol. 3, s. 523–527). New York: Academic Press.

Berry J.W. (1997). Immigration, aculturation, and adaptation. "Applied Psychology: An International Review" 46, 5–74.

Berry J.W., Ataca B. (2007). Cultural factors in stress. In: G. Fink (ed.): Encyclopedia of stress. Second edition (vol. 1, s. 672–678). New York: Academic Press.

Bettelheim, B. (1979). Surviving and other essays. New York: Vintage Books.

Bexton W.H., Heron W., Scott T.H. (1954). Effects of decreased variation in sensory environment. "Canadian Journal of Psychology" 8, 70–76.

Biela A. (red.) (1984). Stres psychologiczny w sytuacji kryzysu. (Psychological stress in a crisis situation). Lublin: Towarzystwo Naukowe KUL.

Biernacki M., Bicka-Capała M., Tarnowski A. (2007). Teoretyczne i metodologiczne problemy badania obciążenia na przykładzie metody subiektywnego obciążenia pracą. (Theoretical and methodological problems of researching strain, based on the example of the subjective workload method). "Polski Przegląd Medycyny Lotniczej" 13 (4), 465–479.

Bifulco A. (2007). Familial patterns of stress. In: G. Fink (ed.): Encyclopedia of stress. Second edition (vol. 2, s. 1–6). New York: Academic Press.

Binsted K., Basner M., Bedwell W., Wu P. (2016). Investigations at Hi-SEAS into team function and performance on long duration exploration missions. Conference: NASA 2016 Human Research Program Investigators' Workshop at: Galveston, Texas, USA. Projects: HI-SEAS.

Blackwood D., Knight H. (2007). Genetic predisposition to stressful conditions. In: G. Fink (ed.): Encyclopedia of stress. Second edition (vol. 2, s. 141–145). New York: Academic Press.

Blake M. J. (1967). Relationship between circadian rhythm of body temperature and introversion/ex-traversion. "Nature" 215, 896–897.

Blatteis C.M. (2007). Thermal stress. In: G. Fink (ed.): Encyclopedia of stress. Second edition (vol. 3, s. 723–726). New York: Academic Press.

Blythe, B.J., Erdhal, J.C. (1986). Using stress inoculation to prepare a patient for open-heart surgery. "Health and Social Work", 11 (4), 265–274.

Bolino M.C., Turnley W.H. (2005). The personal costs of citizenship behavior: The relationship between individual initiative and role overload, job stress, and work-family conflict. "Journal of Applied Psychology" 90 (4), 740–748.

Borland R.C., Rogers A.S., Nicholson A.N., Pascoe P.A., Spencer M.B. (1986). Performance overnight in shift workers operating a day-night schedule. "Aviation, Space and Environmental Medicine" 57 (3), 241–249.

Boski P. (1994). Psychological analysis of a culture: Stability of core Polish values in the homeland and among immigrants. "Polish Psychological Bulletin" 25 (4), 257–282.

Bronstein I., Montgomery P., Dobrowolski S. (2012). PTSD in asylum-seeking male adolescents from Afghanistan. "Journal of Traumatic Stress" 25, 551–557.

Bryant R.A., Harvey A.G. (2002). Delayed-onset posttraumatic stress disorder: A prospective evaluation. "Australian and New Zealand Journal of Psychiatry" 36, 2005–2009.

Buckey J.C. (2006). Space physiology. New York: Oxford University Press.

Buckley T.C., Blanchard E.B. (2007). Motor vehicle accidents, stress effects of. In: G. Fink (ed.): Encyclopedia of stress. Second edition (vol. 2, s. 764–767). New York: Academic Press.

Burke R.J., Matthiesen S. (2004). Workaholism among Norwegian journalists: Antecedents and consequences. "Stress and Health" 20, 301–308.

Burker E.J., Evon D.M., Sedway J.A., Egan T. (2005). Religious and non-religious coping in lung transplant candidates: Does adding God to the picture tell us more? "Journal of Behavioral Medicine" 28 (6), 513–518.

Byrd R. E. (1938). Alone. New York: G.P. Purtmon's Sons.

Cacioppo J.T., Cacioppo S., Boomsma D.I. (2014). Evolutionary mechanisms for loneliness. "Cognition and Emotion" 28 (1), 3–21.

Cannon W.B. (1932). The wisdom of the body. Hardcover, New York: W.W. Norton & Company, Inc.

Caplan G. (1964). Principles of preventive psychiatry. New York: Tavistock Publications.

Caplan S.E. (2003). Preference for on line social interaction: A theory of problematic Internet use and psychosocial well-being. "Communication Research" 30 (6), 625–648.

Carver, C.S., Scheier, M.F. (1994). Situational Coping and Coping Dispositions in a Stressful Transaction. "Journal of Personality and Social Psychology", 66 (1), 184–195.

Carver, C.S., Scheier, M.F., Weitraub, J.K. (1989). Assessing Coping strategie. A Theoretically Based Approach. "Journal of Personality and Social Psychology", 56 (2), 267-283.

Charney D. (2004). Psychological mechanisms of resilience and vulnerability: Implications for successful adaptation to extreme stress. "American Journal of Psychiatry" 161, 195–216.

Chlewiński, Z. (1982). Rola religii w funkcjonowaniu osobowości (The role of religion in the functioning of personality), W: Z. Chlewiński (red.): Psychologia religii (Psychology of religion) (s. 61–76). Lublin: Towarzyst wo Nauko we KUL.

Chou F.H, Wu H.C., Chou P., Su C.Y., Tsai K.Y., Chao S.S., Chen M.C., Su T.T., Sun W.J., Ou-Yang WC. (2007). Epidemiologie psychiatrie studies on post-disaster impact among Chi-Chi earthquake survivors in Yu-Chi, Taiwan. "Psychiatry and Clinical Neurosciences" 61 (4), 370–378.

Christensen J.M., Talbot J.M. (1986). A review of the psychological aspects of space flight. "Aviation, Space and Environmental Medicine" 57 (3), 203–212.

Colquhoun, W.P. (ed.) (1971): Biological rhythms and human performance (s. 39–107). London: Academic Press.

Comer J.S., Kendall P.C. (2007). Terrorism: The psychological impact on youth. "Clinical Psychology: Science and Practice" 14 (3), 178–212.

Convertino V.A. (2007). Space, health risk of. In: G. Fink (ed.): Encyclopedia of stress. Second edition (vol. 3, s. 548–554). New York: Academic Press.

Cooper C.L., Dewe P. (2004). Stress: A brief history. Boston: Blackwell.

Cooper C.L., Payne R. (Eds.) (1978). Stress at work. New York: John Wiley & Sons.T.

Cox T., Leeka S., Ivanov I., Kortum E. (2004). Work, employment and mental health in Europe. "Work and Stress" 18 (2), 179–185.

Crockett L.J., Iturbide M.I., Stone T.R.A., Mcginley M., Raffaelli M., Carlo G. (2007). Acculturative stress, social support, and coping: Relations to psychological adjustment among Mexican American college students. "Cultural Diversity and Ethnic Minority Psychology" 13 (4), 347–355.

Cullen J.C., Hammer L.B. (2007). Developping and testing a theoretical model linking work – family conflict to employee safety. "Journal of Occupational Health Psychology" 12 (3), 266–278.

Czartoszewski J.W. (2004). Filozofia systemu zarządzania środowiskiem wg PN-EN ISO14001:1998. (The philosophy of the environmental management system according to PN-EN ISO14001:1998). "Studia Ecologiae et Bioethicae" 2, 501–516.

Dąbrowski K. (1964). O dezintegracji pozytywnej. Szkic teorii rozwoju psychicznego człowieka poprzez nierównowagę psychiczną, nerwowość,: nerwice i psychonerwice. (On positive disintegration. A draft of the theory of mental development of a person through mental instability, nervousness, neuroses and psychoneurosis). Warszawa: PZWL.

Dąbrowski, K. (1997). Wprowadzenie do higieny psychicznej (Introduction to mental hygiene). Warszawa: Wydawnictwa Szkolne i Pedagogiczne.

Davoren M., Mccauley D. (2007). Work-related stress. “Psychiatrie Bulletin” 31 (8), 316–317.

Dermerouti E., Mostert K., Bakker A.B. (2010). Burnout and work engagement: A thorough investigation of the independency of both constructs. “Journal of Occupational Health Psychology” 15 (3), 209–222.

Deve P., Trenberth L. (2004). Work stress and coping: Drawing together research and practice. “British Journal of Guidance and Counseling” 32 (2), 143–156.

Dewe P., O’driscoll M., Cooper C. (2010). Coping with work stress: A review and critique. Hoboken: John Wiley & Sons.

Dixon N.F. (1987). Our own worst enemy. London: J. Cape.

Djurkovic N., Mccormack D., Casimir G. (2005). The behavioral reactions of victims to different types of workplace bullying. “International Journal of Organization Theory and Behavior” 8 (4), 439–445.

Dobson M. (2007). Combat stress reaction. In: G. Fink (ed.): Encyclopedia of stress. Second edition (vol. 1, s. 524–528). New York: Academic Press.

Dohrenwend B.S., Dohrenwend B.P. (1982). Some issue in research on stressful live events. In: T. Milton, C. Green, R. Meagher (eds.): Handbook of clinical health psychology (s. 91–102). New York: Plenum Press.

Dollard J., Doob L.W., Miller N.A., Mower O.H., Sears R.R. (1939). Frustration and aggression. New Haven: Yale University Press.

Dołęga J.M. (2004). Filozofia sozologii systemowej (Philosophy of systemic sozology). “Studia Ecologiae et Bioethicae” 2, 519–560.

Domaszuk J., Terelak J. (1982). Zależności między tolerancją przyspieszeń a stanem emocjonalnym pilotów. (Relationship between the tolerance of the forces occurring during accelerations and the emotional state of pilots). “Medycyna Lotnicza” 75 (2), 17–20.

Donate A. P. G., Marques L. M., Lapenta O. M., Asthana M. K., Amodio D., Boggio P. S. (2017). Ostracism via virtual chat room—Effects on basic needs, anger and pain.” PloS one”, 12 (9), e0184215.

Dougall A.L., Baum A. (2007). Three Mile Island, stress effects of. In: G. Fink (ed.): Encyclopedia of stress. Second edition (vol. 3, s. 735–737). New York: Academic Press.

Dunnette M.D., Hough L.M. (Eds.) (1990). Handbook of industrial and organizational psychology. Second edition (vol. 1). Palo Alto: Consulting Psychologists Press, Inc.

Dyson R., Renk K. (2006). Freshmen adaptation to university life: Depressive symptoms, stress coping. “Journal of Clinical Psychology” 62 (10), 1231–1244.

Earls J.H. (1969). Human adjustment to an exotic environment. "Archivum of General Psychiatry" 20, 117–123.

Edelman, R.J., Hardwick, S. (1986). Test anxiety, past performance and coping strategies. "Personalityand Individual Differences", 7 (2), 255–257.

Edwards J.A., Cockerton T., Guppy A. (2007). A longitudinal study examining the influence of work and non-work stressors upon well-being: A multi-group analysis. "International Journal of Stress Management" 14 (3), 294–311.

Eliade. M. (1993). Sacrum, mit, historia. Wybór esejów (Sacrum, myth, history. Selection of essays). Wyd. III. Warszawa: Państwowy Instytut Wydawniczy.

Ellis. A. (1991). The revised ABC's of rational-emotive therapy (RET). "Journal of Rational-Emotive and Cognitive-Behavior Therapy", 9(3):139–172. DOI: 10.1007/BF01061227

Emmons, R.A. (2005). Emotion and Religion, [in:] R.F. Paloutzian, C.L. Park (Eds.), Handbook of the Psychology of Religion and Spirituality, New York: The Guilford Press.

Endler N.S., Parker J.D.A., (1994). Assessment of multidimensional coping: task, emotion and avoidance strategies. "Psychological Assessment" 6 (1), 50–60.

Enns M.W., Cox B.J., Clara I.P. (2005). Perfectionism and neuroticism: A longitudinal study of specific vulnerability and diathesis-stress models. "Cognitive Therapy and Research" 29 (4), 463–478.

Epstein, S. (1983). Natural healing processes of the mind: Graded stress inoculation as an inherent coping mechanism, In: D. Meichenbaum and M.E. Jaremko (Eds.): Stress reduction and prevention (pp. 39–66). New York: Plenum Press.

Erikson E.H. (1968). Identify youth and crisis. New York: Norton.

Fąfrowiccz M., Marek T. (1999). Werońska koncepcja źródeł stresu (The Verona concept of sources of stress).. In: J.F. Terelak (red.): Źródła stresu. Teoria i badania (Sources of stress. Theory and research) (s. 13–22). Warszawa: Wyd. ATK.Farrington D.P., Callagher B., Morley L., Ledger R.J., West D.J. (1986). Unemployment, school leaving, and crime. "British Journal of Criminology" 26 (4), 335–356.

Feeny N.C., Stines L.R., Foa E.B. (2007). Posttraumatic stress disorder – clinical. In: G. Fink (ed.): Encyclopedia of stress. Second edition (vol. 3, s. 135–140). New York: Academic Press.

Fenz W.D., Jones G.B. (1972). Individual differences in physiologic arousal and performance in sport parachutists. "Psychosomatic Medicine" XXXIV (2), 1–8.

Figley Ch.R., Nash W.P. (Eds.) (2007). Combat stress injury: Theory, research and management. New York: Routledge Taylor & Francis Group.

Figueira I., Da Luz M., Braga R.J., Cabizuca M., Coutinho E., Mendlowicz M.V. (2007). The increasing internationalization of mainstream posttraumatic stress disorder research: A bibliometric study. "Journal of Traumatic Stress" 20 (1), 89–95.

Fink G. (Ed) (2007). Encyclopedia of stress. Second edition (vol. 1–4). New York: Academic Press.

Fiske D.W., Maddi S.R. (1967). Functions of varied experience, (Third Edition). Homewood: Dorsey Press, Inc.

Folkman S. (2001). Revised coping theory and process of bereavement. In: M.S. Stroebe et al. (eds.): Handbook of bereavement: Consequences, coping, and care (s. 563–584). Washington, DC: American Psychological Association Press.

Folkman S. (2010). Stress, coping, and hope. "Psycho-Oncology" 19, 901–908.

Folkman S., Lazarus R. (1988). Coping as a mediator of emotion. "Journal of Personality and Social Psychology" 54 (3), 466–475.

Ford M.T., Heinen B.A., Langkamer K.L. (2007). Work and family satisfaction and conflict: A meta-analysis of cross-domain relations. "Journal of Applied Psychology" 92 (1), 57–80.

Frankl V.E. (1947). Die Psychotherapie in der Praxis. Vien: Franz Deuticke.

Frazier, S.E. (1989). Mood state changes of women as a function of regular aerobic exercise. "Perceptual and Motor Skills", 68, 283–287.

Fromm E. (1996). Rewolucja nadziei. Ku uczłowieczonej technologii (The revolution of hope: Towards a humanized technology). Poznań: Rebis

Fujita, A. (1975). An experimental study on the theoretical basis on mental training, In: Trabajos Scientificos: III Congresso Mundial de la Sociedad International de Psicologia del Deporte (pp. 238–239). Madrid: Instituto nacional de Educacion Fisica.

Gabriel R., Ferrando L., Cortón E.S., Mingote C., Garcia-Camba E. (2007). Psychopathological consequences after a terrorist attack: An epidemiological study among victims, the general population, and police officers. "European Psychiatry" 22 (6), 339–346.

Galanter, M. (2006). Spirituality and the Helthy mind: Science, Therapy, and the Reed for Personal meaning. Oxford: University Press.

Gall T.L., Charbonneau C., Clarke N.H., Grant K., Joseph A., Shouldice L. (2005). Understanding the nature and role of spirituality in relation to coping and health: A conceptual framework. "Canadian Psychology" 46 (2), 88–104.

Ganley R.M. (1989). Emotion and eating in obesity: A review of the literaturę. "International of Eating Disorders" 8 (3), 343–361.

George O. (2014). TSRI researchers discover new type of neuron that plays key role in nicotine addiction. Public Release: 17-Nov. Scripps Research Institute.

Geus De E.J.C., Stuble J.H. (2007). Aerobic exercise and stress reduction. In: G. Fink (ed.): Encyclopedia of stress. Second edition (vol. 1, s 73–78). New York: Academic Press.

Godorowski K. (1985). Psychologia i psychopatologia hitlerowskich obozów koncentracyjnych. Próba analizy postaw i zachowań w warunkach ekstremalnych obciążeń. (Psychology and psychopathology of Nazi concentration camps. An attempt at the analysis of attitudes and behaviors in extreme load conditions). Warszawa: Wyd. ATK.

Goffman E. (2008). Człowiek w teatrze życia codziennego (Presentation of self in everyday life). Warszawa: Aletheia.

Golden-Kreutz D.M., Thornton L.M., Gregorio S.W., Frierson G.M., Jim H.S., Carpenter K.M., Shelby R.A., Andersen B.L. (2005). Traumatic stress, perceived global stress, and live events: Prospectively predicting quality of life in breast cancer patients. "Health Psychology" 24 (3), 288–296.

Goldstein D.S. (2004). Merging of the Homeostat Theory with the Concept of Allostatic Load (s. 99–112). In: J. Schulkin (ed.): Allostasis and the costs of physiological adaptation. Edinburg: Cambridge University Press.

Golec L. (2002). Nadciśnienie oddechowe. In: W. Kowalski (red.): Medycyna lotnicza (Respiratory hypertension. In: W. Kowalski (ed.): Aviation Medicine) (s. 47–85). Poznań: Wyd. DWL i OP.

Gołuch, D. (2018). Selected temperamental features and the content aspects of emotions in coping with the stress of social exposure. (unpublished doctoral thesis) (Wybrane cechy temperamentalne a treściowe aspekty emocji w radzeniu sobie ze stresem społecznej ekspozycji. (niepublikowana praca doktorska)). Warszawa: UKSW.

Greenhaus J.H., Beutell N.J. (1985). Sources of conflict between work and family roles. "Academy of Management Review" 10, 76–88.

Greenhaus J.H., Powell G.N. (2006). When work and family are allies: A theory of work-family enrichment. "Academy of Management Review" 31, 72–92.

Grinker R.R., Spiegel J.P. (1945). Men under stress. Philadelphia: Blakiston.

Hagihara A., Miller A.S., Tarumi K., Nobutomo K. (2003). Social support has both positive and negative effects on the relationship of work stress and alcohol consumption. "Stress and Health" 19, 205–215.

Hamaoka D., Benedek D., Grieger T., Ursano J. (2007). Crisis intervention. In: G. Fink (ed.): Encyclopedia of stress. Second edition (vol. 1, s. 190–196). New York: Academic Press.

Hamer M., Steptoe A. (2007). Association between physical fitness, parasympathetic control, and proinflammatory responses to mental stress. "Psychosomatic Medicine" 69 (7), 660–666.

Hammer T.H., Saksvik P., Nytr K., Torvatn H., Bayazit M. (2004). Expanding the psychosocial work environment: Workplace norms and work-family conflict as correlates of stress and health. "Journal of Occupational Health Psychology" 9 (1), 83–97.

Hancock P.A., Desmond P.A. (eds.) (2001). Stress, workload and fatigue. Mahwah: Lawrence Erlbaum Associates.

Hancock P.A., Szalma J.L. (eds.) (2008). Performance under stress. Aldershot (England): Ashgate Publishing Lt.

Hansell, N. (1976). The person-in-distress: On the biosocial dynamics of adaptation. New York: Human Sciences Press.

Hawkley L.C., Cacioppo J.T. (2010). Loneliness matters: A theoretical and empirical review of consequences and mechanisms. "Annals of Behavioral Medicine" 40 (2), 218–227.

Hayman J.W., Kurpius S.R., Befort C., Nicpon M.F., Hull-Blanks E., Sollen-Berger S., Huser L. (2007). Spirituality among college freshmen: Relationships to self-esteem, body image, and stress. "Counseling and Values" 52 (1), 55–70.

Hazboun V. (2007). War, suicide and sacrifice. In: G. Fink (ed.): Encyclopedia of stress. Second edition (vol. 3, s. 860–865). New York: Academic Press.

Hebb D.O (1965). Drives and the C.N.S. In: H. Fowler (ed.): Curiosity and exploratory behavior (s. 176–190). New York: Macmillan Co.

Heckman C.J., Olds-Davis T., Cropsey K.L. (2007). Posttraumatic stress disorder treatment in correctional settings: A brief review of the empirical literature and suggestions for future research. "Psychotherapy: Theory, research, practics, training" 44 (1), 46–53.

Henry P.C. (2005). Life stresses, explanatory style, hopelessness, and occupational class. "International Journal of Stress Management" 12 (3), 241–256.

Hermaszewski M. (2009). Ciężar nieważkości. Opowieści pilota kosmonauty (The weight of weightlessness. The tales of a cosmonaut). Kraków: Wyd. Universitas.

Heszen-Niejodek I. (red.) (1989). Polska adaptacja kwestionariusza S. Folkman i R.S. Lazarusa do badania sposobów radzenia sobie ze stresem WCQ (Polish adaptation of the WCQ - a questionnaire by S. Folkman and R.S. Lazarus designed to study ways of coping with stress). Katowice: Wyd. Uniwersytetu Śląskiego.

Hewlett S.A., Luck C.B. (2007). Praca ekstremalna. Niebezpieczny urok 70-godzinnego tygodnia pracy (Extreme Jobs: The Dangerous Allure of the 70-Hour Workweek. “Harvard Business Review” (edycja polska), IV, 46–58).

Hobfoll S. E. (1998). Stress, culture, and community. The psychology and philosophy of stress. Dordrecht, The Netherlands: Kluwer Academic/Plenum Publishers.

Hobfoll S. E. (2002). Social and psychological resources and adaptation. “Review of General Psychology” 6 (4), 307–324.

Hobfoll, S.E. (2001). The influence of culture, community, and the nested-Self in the stress process: advancing conservation of resources theory. “Applied Psychology International Review” 50 (3), 337–369.

Hockey G.R. (2007). Environmental stress, effects on human performance. In: G. Fink (ed.): Encyclopedia of stress. Second edition (vol. 1, s. 940–945). New York: Academic Press.

Hofstede G. (1980). Culture’s consequences: International differences in work-related values (Second edition). Beverly hills: Sage.

Holahan C.J., Moos R.H., Holahan C.K., Brennan P.L., Schutte K.K. (2005). Stress generation, avoidance coping, and depressive symptoms: A 10-year model. “Journal of Consulting and Clinical Psychology” 73 (4), 658–666.

Holen A. (2007). Posttraumatic stress disorder, delayed. In: G. Fink (ed.): Encyclopedia of stress. Second edition (vol. 3, s. 150–152). New York: Academic Press.

Holmes T.H., Rahe R.H. (1967). The social readjustment rating scale. “Journal of Psychosomatic Research” 11, 213–218.

Holt-Lunstad, J., Smith, T.B., Baker, M., Harris, T., Stephenson, D. Loneliness and Social Isolation as Risk Factors for Mortality: A Meta-Analytic Review. Perspectives on Psychological Science, 2015, Vol. 10(2) 227–237.

Hołyst B. (1984). Narkomania a przestępstwo. In: M. Siemiński (red.): Po tej stronie granicy (s. 158–169) (Drug addiction and crime. In: M. Siemiński (ed.): On this side of the border). Warszawa: Wyd. Radio i Telewizja.

Homans G.C. (1961). Social behavior: Its elementary forms. New York: Harcourt, Brace World.

Horowitz M.J. (1993). Stress – response syndromes: A review of posttraumatic stress and ad-justment disorders. In: J.P Wilson, B. Raphael (eds.): International handbook of traumatic stress syndromes (s. 49–60). New York: Premium Press.

Horney K. (1976). Neurotyczna osobowość naszych czasów (The Neurotic Personality of our Time). Warszawa: PWN.

Hsieh TH. (2004). The relationship between employees' personal work standards and perceived work stress. "International Journal of Stress Management" 11 (2), 177–187.

Hulek, A. (red.) (1991). Spójny system służb socjalnych dla inwalidów i innych osób niepełnosprawnych (A coherent system of social services for invalids and other disabled people).Warszawa: Wyd. TWK.

Jacoby R., Keinen G. (2003). Between stress and hope. From a disease-centered to a health-centered perspective. Westport: Praeger.

Jakubik A. (2003). Zespół uzależnienia od Internetu (Internet Addiction Syndrome). "Studia Psychologica" 3 (3), 133–142.

Jamil H., Nassar-Mcmillan S., Lambert R.G. (2007). Immigration and attendand psycho-logical sequelae: A comparison of three waves of Iraqi immigrants. "American Journal of Orthopsychiatry" 77 (2), 199–205.

Janis I.L. (1958). Psychological stress. New York: J. Wiley and Sons, Inc.

Janis I.L. (1982). Groupthink. Boston: Houghton Mifflin.

Jankowski, K. (1970). Psychological aftereffects of prolonged stay in psychiatric hospital. Warsaw: State Sanatorium for Nervous Diseases.

Jaremko M.E. (1984). Stress inoculation training: A generic approach for the prevention of stress-related disorders. "Personnel and Guidance Journal" 5, 544–550.

Jarosz M. (1975). Psychologia i psychopatologia życia codziennego (Psychology and psychopathology of everyday life). Warszawa: PZWL, s. 372.

Jawetz E., Melnick J.L., Adelberg E.A. (1991). Przegląd mikrobiologii lekarskiej (Review of medical microbiology). Warszawa: PZWL.

Jenaro C., Flores N., Arias B. (2007). Burnout and coping in human service practicioners. "Professional Psychology: Research and Practice" 38 (1), 80–87.

Johnstone A., Johnston L. (2005). The relationship between organizational climate, occupational type and workaholism. "New Zealand Journal of Psychology" 34 (3), 181–192.

Joseph S., Linley PA. (2007). Stress, beneficial effects of. In: G. Fink (ed.): Encyclopedia of stress. Second edition (vol. 3, s. 650–653). New York: Academic Press.

Jung, C. G. (1951). Aion: Researches into the Phenomenology of the Self (Collected Works Vol. 9 Part 2). Princeton, N.J.: Bollingen.

Kaczorowski Z. (2002). Dezorientacja przestrzenna (Spatial disorientation). In: W. Kowalski (red.). Medycyna lotnicza (Aviation Medicine) (s. 197–204). Poznań: Wyd. DWL i OP.

Kahn R.L., Byosier Ph. (1992). Stress in organization. In: M.D. Dunnette, L.M. Hough (eds): Handbook of industrial and organizational psychology. Second edition (vol. 3, s. 571–650).

Kahneman, D., Tversky, A. (1972). Subjective probability: A judgment of representativeness: Cognitive Psychology, 3(3), 430–454.

Kampa A., Golda G. (2007). E-leaming i telepraca w kształceniu i rehabilitacji osób niepełnosprawnych. In: J. Kisielnicki (red.): VI Konferencja pt.: "Uniwersytet wirtualny: model, narzędzia, praktyka" (E-learning and teleworking in the education and rehabilitation of disabled people. In: J. Kisielnicki (ed.): 6th Conference: "Virtual University – Model, Tools, Practice") (s. 238–240). Warszawa: Wyd. PJWSTK.

Kando, T.M. (1980). Leisure and popular culture in transition. The C.V. London: Mosby Company.

Karasek, R. A. (1979). Job demands, job decision latitude, and mental strain: Implications for job redesign. Administrative Science Quarterly, 24, 285-308.

Karatuna I. (2015). Targets' coping with workplace bullying: A qualitative study. "Qualitative Research in Organizations and Management: An International Journal" 10 (1), 21–37.

Kaysen, D., Slimpson, T., Dillworth, T., Larmier, M., Gunter, C., Resick, P.A. (2006). Alcohol problems and posttraumatic stress disorder in female crime victims . Journal of Traumatic Stress, 19 (3), 399–403.

Kępiński A. (1972). Psychopatologia nerwic (Psychopathology of neuroses). Warszawa: PZWL.

Kerkhof G.K. (1987). Zmiany przebiegu rytmów okołodobowych człowieka w zależności od chronotypu (Changes in the course of human circadian rhythms depending on the chronotype). "Medycyna Lotnicza" 95 (2), 1–7.

Khatri, P., Blumenthal, A.J. (2007). Exercise. In: G. Fiinkn (Ed.): Encyclopedia of stress. Second Edition (Vol. I, pp. 982–986). New York: Academic Press.

Kinzie J.D. (2007). Refugees, stress in. In: G. Fink (ed.): Encyclopedia of stress. Second edition (vol. 3, s. 338–340). New York: Academic Press.

Kitajew-Smyk L.A. (1989). Psychologia stresu (Stress psychology). Wrocław: Ossolineum.

Klein N. (2016). To zmienia wszystko: kapitalizm kontra klimat (This changes everything: capitalism vs. the climate). Warszawa: Wydawnictwo MUZA SA.

Klein K.E., Wehmann H.M., Hunt B.I. (1972). Desynchronization of body temperature and performance circadian rhythm as a result of outgoing and homegoing transmeridian fights. "Aerospace Medicine" 43 (2), 119–132.

Klein K.E., Wehmann H.M., Hunt B.I. (1980). Significance of circadian rhythms in aero-space operations. NATO AGARD-AG-247.

Klonoff H., Mcdougall G., Clark, C., Kramer, P., Horgan, J. (1976). The neupsycholorvical, psychiatrie, and physical effects of prolonged and severe stress: 30 years later. "The Journal of Neous and Mental Disease" 163 (4), 246–252.

Klukowski, K.S. Skibniewski, F.W. (2013). A Historical look at the biomedical tests conducted by cosmonauts during the orbital flight Soyuz 30 / Salut 6. "Pol J Aviat Med Psychol". 19(3), 17–22.

Kłossowski M. (2002). Zespół długu czasowego (Jet Lag). Przyczyny, objawy, profilaktyka. In: W. Kowalski (red.): Medycyna lotnicza. (Jet Lag. Causes, symptoms, prevention. In W. Kowalski (ed.): Aviation Medicine) (s. 359–364). Poznań: Wyd. DWL i OP.

Kofta M., Szustrowa T. (red.): Złudzenia które pozwalają żyć (Delusions that let us live). Warszawa: Wydawnictwo Naukowe PWN.

Konradt U., Hertel G. (2003). Quality of management by objectives, task-related stressors, and non-task-related stressors as predictor of stress and job satisfaction among teleworkers. "European Journal of Work and Organizational Psychology" 12 (1), 61–79.

Koolhaas J.M. (2007). Aggressive behavior. In: G. Fink (Ed.): Encyclopedia of stress, Second Edition (vol. 1, pp. 89–92). New York: Academic Press.

Kościuch J. (1984). Hierarchie wartości w nerwicach i w psychopatologii oraz ich zmiany pod wpływem psychoterapii (Hierarchy of values in neuroses and psychopathology and changes thereof under the influence of psychotherapy). Warszawa: Wyd. ATK.

Kotarbiński T. (1986). Drogi dociekań własnych. Fragmenty filozoficzne (Methods of self searching. Philosophical fragments). Warszawa: PWN.

Kowalski W. (1982). Adaptacja człowieka do pobytu w Antarktyce (People's adaptation to the conditions in the Antarctic). Warszawa: Wyd. Wojskowy Instytut Medycyny Lotniczej.

Kowalski W. (2002). Kabiny ciśnieniowe. In: W. Kowalski (red.): Medycyna lotnicza. Wybrane zagadnienia (Pressurized cabins, In: W. Kowalski (ed.) Aviation Medicine (s. 30–153). Poznań: Wyd. DWL i OP.

Kozerenko O.P., Terelak J.F., Miksik O. (1991). The problem of man's psychic adaptation under the space-flight conditions. In: K. Boda, V.M. Baranov (eds.): Current trends in cosmic biology and medicine. Ivanka Pri Dunai (CSRF): Slovak Academy of Sciences, vol. II, 91–94.

Kozłowski S. (1986). Granice przystosowania (Limits of adaptation). Warszawa: Wiedza Powszechna.

Kraut R. (2002). Aristotle: Political philosophy. Oxford: Oxford University Press.

Krąpiec, M.A. (2008). Człowiek i kultura (Man and Culture). Lublin: Polskie Towarzystwo Tomasza z Akwinu.

Krebs K. (2007). Stress management, CAM approach. In: G. Fink (ed.): Encyclopedia of stress. Second edition (vol. 3, s. 636–640). New York: Academic Press.

Kristeller J.L. (2007). Meditation and stress. In: G. Fink (ed.): Encyclopedia of stress. Second edition (vol. 2, s. 678–685). New York: Academic Press.

Kristof, A.L. (1996). Person-organization fit: an integrative review of its conceptualizations, measurement, and implications. Personnel Psychology, 49, 1–49.

Krzyżewski K. (1986). O bezużyteczności kategorii "emocji" w wyjaśnianiu zachowania (On the uselessness of the category of "emotions" in explaining behaviors). "Po¬znańskie Studia z Filozofi Nauki (Filozofa - Poznanie - Psychologia)" 10, 275–290.

Küng H. (1997). Weltethos für Weltpolitik und Weltwirtschaft. München.

Kwarecki, K. (1985). Chronobiologia – perspektywy wykorzystania w medycynie. W: Biochemia. Materiały seminaryjne (Chronobiology – perspectives of use in medicine. In: Biochemistry. Seminar Materials (Tom 3). Warszawa: Wyd. Wojskowa Akademia Medyczna (Military Medical Academy).

Kwarecki K., Terelak J. (1980). Medycyna i psychologia kosmiczna (Medicine and space psychology). Warszawa: Wiedza Powszechna.

Kwarecki K., Święcicki W., Kłossowski M., Terelak J., Zużewicz K. (1982). Zdolność do pracy fizycznej i umysłowej w warunkach 24-godzinnej bezsenności oraz pracy zmianowej (Ability to work physically and mentally under conditions of 24 hours sleeplessness and shift work). "Medycyna Lotnicza" 74 (1), 7–14.

Lambert V.A., Lambert CE., Yamase H. (2002). Psychological hardiness, workplace stress and related stress reduction strategies. "Nursing and Health Sciences" 5, 181–184.

Lamiel, J.T. (2010). Why was there no place for personalistic thinking in 20th century psychology? "New Ideas in Psychology", 28, 135–142.

Lazarus R. (1991). Emotion and adaptation. New York: Oxford University Press.

Lazarus R.S. (1993). Coping theory and research: past, present and futurę. "Psychosomatic Medi-cine" 55 (3), 234–247.

Lazarus R.S. (2006). Stress and emotion: A new synthesis. New York: Springer.

Lazarus R.S., Folkman S. (1984). Stress, appraisal and coping. New York: Springer Publishing Co.

Le Bon G. (1986). Psychologia tłumu (Crowd psychology). Warszawa: PWN.

Ledwoch M. (2006). Experience of time depression according to existential psychologists. In: Z. Uchnast (red.): Psychology of time: Theoretical and empirical approaches (pp. 41–48). Lublin: Wydawnictwo KUL.

Le Moal M. (2007). Historical approach and evolution of the stress concept: A personal account. "Psychoneuroendocrinology" 38 (1), 3–9.

Lester D., Walker R.L. (2007). Suicide, psychology of. In: H. Fowler (ed.): Curiosity and exploratory behavior (vol. 3, s. 684–689). New York: Academic Press.

Leuba C. (1965). Toward some integration of learning theory: The concept of optimal stimulation. In: H. Fowler (ed.): Curiosity and exploratory behavior (s. 169–175). New York: Macmillan Co.

Leung L. (2007). Stressful life events, motives for Internet use, and social support among digital kids. "Cyber Psychology and Behavior" 10 (2), 204–208.

Levi, L. (1972). Preventing work stress. Reading, MA: Addison-Wesley.

Lewin K. (1936). Principles of topological psychology. New York: McGraw-Hill.

Leymann H. (1990). Mobbing and psychological terror at workplace. "Violence & Victims" 5 (2), 119–126.

Łodyga O. (2007). Telepraca – możliwości, ograniczenia, uwarunkowania prawne. "E-mentor" 3 (20), 72–74.

Lorenz K.Z. (1962). Zum Tode von Erich von Holst. "Naturwissenschaften" 49 (17), 385–386.

Lorenz K.Z. (1972). Tak zwane zło (On Aggression). Warszawa: PIW.

Łosiak W. (2007). Psychologia emocji (Psychology of emotions). Warszawa: Wydawnictwo Akademickie i Profesjonalne.

Luck S.J. (2005). An introduction to the event-related potential technique. Cambridge: Massachusetts Institute of Technology Press.

Lucksted A., Treichler E. (2017). The role o sense of belonging in self-stigma among people with serious mental illnesses. "Psychiatric Rehabilitation Journal" 41 (2), 149–152.

Lundberg U. (2007). Workplace stress. In: G. Fink (ed.): Encyclopedia of stress. Second edition (vol. 3, s. 871–878). New York: Academic Press.

Łodyga, O. (2007). Telepraca – możliwości, ograniczenia, uwarunkowania prawne (Telecommuting - opportunities, limitations, legal conditions). „E-mentor", 3 (20), 72–74.

Macdonald C.M. (2003). Evaluation of stress debriefing interventions with military populations. "Military Medicine" 168 (12), 961–967.

Maclean P.D. (1990). The Triune brain in evolution: Role in paleocerebral functions. New York: Plenum Press.

Madran H. D., Cakilci E. F. (2018). The relationship between agression and online video game addiction: A study on massively multiplayer online video game players. "Anadolu Psikiyatri Dergisi-Anatolian Journal of Psychiatry" 15 (2), 99–107.

Małkiewicz M., Terelak J.F. (2016). The role of hope in coping: Presentation of Lazarus's approach. Proceedings of the 37th STAR Conference: Stress and Anxiety in a Changing Society, Zagreb, Croatia, July 6th–8th 2016.

Marczak K., Terelak J.F. (2014). Selected personality correlates of behaviors associated with Internet "piracy". "Polish Journal of Aviation Medicine and Psychology" 20 (4), 19–26.

Marks, E., Hornowski, J. (1968). Obserwacje kliniczne wpływu mikrofal na układ nerwowy (Clinical observations of the influence of microwaves on the nervous system). "Neurologia i Neurochirurgia Polska" II (1), 25–29.

Martin R.A., Kuiper N.A., Olgner L.J., Dobbin J. (1987). Is stress always bad? Telic versus paratelic dominance as a stress-moderating variable. "Journal of Personality and Social Psychology" 53 (5), 970–982.

Marx E. (2000). Przełamywanie szoku kulturowego (Overcoming cultural shock). Warszawa: Placet.

Maslach C., Leiter M.P. (2007). Burnout. In: G. Fink (ed.): Encyclopedia of stress. Second edition (vol. 1, s. 368–371). New York: Academic Press.

Matczak A. (1982). Style poznawcze (Cognitive styles). Warszawa: PWN.

Matheny K.B., Aycock D.W., Pugh J.L., Curlette W.L., Cannella K. (1986). Stress coping: A qualitative and quantitative synthesis with implications for treatment. "Counseling of Psychology" 14 (4), 499–549.

Matthews G. (2007). Distress. In: G. Fink (ed.): Encyclopedia of stress. Second edition (vol. 1, s. 838–842). New York: Academic Press.

Medea, E (1966). Father Agostino Gemelli (1878–1959). Archivio di Psicologia, Neurologia et Psichiatria. 27 (2), 98–105.

Mccarty R., Pacak K. (2007). Alarm phase and General Adaptation Syndrome. In: G. Fink (ed.): Encyclopedia of stress. Second edition (vol. 1, s. 119–123). New York: Academic Press.

Mcewen B.S. (2007). Homeostasis. In: G. Fink (ed.): Encyclopedia of stress. Second edition (vol. 2, s. 347–348). New York: Academic Press.

Mcewen B.S., Wingfield J.C. (2007). Allostasis and allostatic load. In: G. Fink (ed.): Encyclopedia of stress. Second edition (vol. 1, s. 135–140). New York: Academic Press.

Mcfarlane A.C., Yehuda R. (1995). Reselience, vulnerability and the course of posttraumatic reactions. In: B.A. van der Kolk, A.C. McFarlane, L. Weisaeth (eds.): Traumatic stress: The effects of overwhelming experience on mind, body, and society. New York: The Guilford Press.

Mcgowan J., Gardner D., Fletcher R. (2006). Positive and negative affective outcomes of occupational stress. "New Zealand Journal of Psychology" 35 (2), 92–98.

McGrath, J.I. (1976). Stress and behavior in organizations, In: M.D. Dunette (Ed.): Handbook of industrial and organizational psychology (pp. 1351–1395). Chicago: Rand McNally.

Mcmillan L.H., O'driscoll M.P, Marsh N.V, Brady E.C. (2001). Understanding workaholism: Data synthesis, theoretical critique, and future design strategies. "International Journal of Stress Management" 8, 69–91.

Mikuliszyn R., Żebrowski M. (2002). Patofizjologia przyspieszeń. In: W. Kowalski (red.): Medycyna lotnicza (Pathophysiology of accelerations), In: W. Kowalski (ed.) Aviation medicine (s. 98–137). Poznań: Wyd. DWL i OP.

Miller S.M. (1987). Monitoring and blunting: Validation of questionnaire to assess styles of information seeking under threat. "Journal of Personality and Social Psychology" 52, 345–353.

Miller P.M., Kreitman N.B., Ingham J.G., Sashidharan S.P. (1989). Self-esteem, life stress and psychiatrie disorder. "Journal of Affective Disorders" 17, 65–75.

Mintzberg H. (1983). Structure in fives: Designing effective organizations. Englewood Cliffs: Prentice-Hall, Inc.

Moskowitz, J.T., Wrubel, J. (2005). Coping with HIV as a chronic illness: A longitudinal analysis of illness appraisals. "Psychology and Health" 20 (4), 509–531.

Nelson R.J., Martin Ii L.B. (2007). Seasonal changes in stress responses. In: G. Fink (ed.): Encyclopedia of stress. Second edition (vol. 3, s. 427–431). New York: Academic Press.

Nielsen M.B., Einarsen S. (2012). Outcomes of exposure to workplace bullying: A metaanalytic review. "Work & Stress" 26 (4), 309–332.

Nieśpiałowski, A., Terelak, J.F. (2016). Obesity related self-esteem and relationship to coping stress. "Polish Journal of Aviation Medicine, Bioengineering and Psychology", 22(2), 18–26.

North C.S., Pfefferbaum B., Tivis L., et al. (2004). The course of posttraumatic stress disorder in a follow-up study of survivors of the Oklahoma City bombing. "Annals of Clinical Psychiatry" 16, 209–215.

Oates, W. (1971). Confessions of a Workaholic: The Facts about Work Addiction. New York: World Publishing Co.

Oberg K. (1960). Culture shock: Adjustment to new cultural environments. "Practical Anthropology" 7, 177–182.

Obuchowski K. (1982). Kody orientacji i struktura procesów emocjonalnych (Orientation codes and the structure of emotional processes). Warszawa: PWN.

O'donnell M.L., Creamer M., Elliot P., Atkin C. (2005). Health costs following motor vehicle accidents: The role of posttraumatic stress disorder. "Journal of Traumatic Stress" 18 (5), 557–561.

O'donnell M.L., Elliot P., Wolfgang B.J., Creamer M. (2007). Post-traumatic appraisals in the development and persistence of posttraumatic stress symptoms. "Journal of Traumatic Stress" 20 (2), 173–182.

O'driscoll M.P. (2013). Coping with stress: A challenge for theory, research and practice. "Stress and Health" 29, 89–90.

Oquendo M.A., Giner L., Mann J.J. (2007). Suicide, biology of. In: H. Fowler (ed.): Curiosity and exploratory behavior (vol. 3, s. 677–683). New York: Macmillan Co.

Paloutzian, R.F., Park, C.L. (2015). Handbook of the Psychology of Religion and Spirituality. Second Edition. New York: The Guilford Press.

Patchen M. (1961). The choice of wage comparisons. Englewood Cliffs: Prentice-Hall, Inc.

Pawłow I.P. (1952). Dwadzieścia lat badań wyższej czynności nerwowej (zachowania się) zwierząt. (Twenty years of research into higher nervous activity (behavior) of animals).Warszawa: PZWL.

Payne, R.J., Jones, J.G. (1987). Measurement and methodological issues in social support, In: S. Kasl, C.L. Cooper (Eds.), Stress and Health: Issues in Research Methodology (pp. 167–205). Chichester: John Wiley & Sons.

Peeters M.C.W., De Jonge J., Janssen P.P., Van Der Linden S. (2004). Work-home interference, job stressors, and employee health in a longitudinal perspective. "International Journal of Stress Management" 11 (4), 305–322.

Pieterse A.L., Carter R.T. (2007). An examination of the relationship between general life stress, racism-related stress, and psychological health among black men. "Journal of Counseling Psychology" 54 (1), 101–109.

Pitman R.K., Altman B., Macklin M.L. (1989). Prevalence of posttraumatic stress disorder in wounded Vietnam veterans. "American Journal of Psychiatry" 146 (5), 667–669.

Posner M.I. (1994). Attention: The mechanisms of consciousness. "Proceedings of National Academy of Science USA" 91, 7398–7403.

Primack B. A., Shensa A., Sidani J. E., Whaite E. O., Vi Lin L., Rosen D., Millerer E. (2017). Social media use and perceived social isolation among young adults in the US. "American Journal of Preventive Medicine" 53(1), 1–8.

Rahe R.H. (2007a). Combat, acute reactions to. In: G. Fink (ed.): Encyclopedia of stress. Second edition (vol. I, s. 529–532). New York: Academic Press.

Rahe R.H. (2007b). Coping and stress: A lens and filter model. In: G. Fink (ed.): Encyclopedia of stress. Second edition (vol. 3, s. 574–578). New York: Academic Press.

Raut N.B., Singh S., Subramanyam A.A., Pinto C., Kamath R.M., Shanker S., Reichenberg A. (2014). Study of loneliness, depression and coping mechanisms in elderly. "Journal of Geriatric Mental Health" 1 (1), 20–27.

Reykowski J. (1966). Funkcjonowanie osobowości w warunkach stresu psychologicznego (Functioning of personality in conditions of psychological stress). Warszawa: PWN.

Reykowski J. (1977). Spontaniczna agresja i spontaniczne czynniki ją hamujące (Spontaneous aggression and spontaneous factors inhibiting it). "Przegląd Psychologiczny" 2, 204–228.

Rhoads J., Pearman T., Rick S. (2007). Clinical presentation and therapeutic interventions for posttraumatic stress disorder post-Katrina. "Archives of Psychiatric Nursing" 21 (5), 249–256.

Richman, J.A., Wislar, J.S., Flaherty, J.A., Fendrich, M., Rospenda, K.M. (2004). Effects on alcohol use and anxiety of the September 11, 2001, attacks and chronic work stressors: A longitudinal cohort study. "American Journal of Public Health", 94 (11), 2010–2015.

Robbins B.E. (2000). Typology of workaholics with implications for counselors. "Journal of Addictions, and Offender Counseling" 21, 34–48.

Robinson R., Mitchell J., Murdoch R. (1995). The debate of psychological debriefings. "Australasian Journal of Emergency Care" 2, 6–7.

Rose S., Bisson J. (1998). Brief psychological interventions following trauma: A systematic review of the literature. "Journal of Traumatic Stress" 11, 697–710.

Rowiński, T., Gąglewski, M. (2007). Preferencje i postawy wobec pomocy on line (Preferences and attitudes towards online help). „Studia Psychologica", 5 (7), 195–210.

Rus H. M., Tiemensma J. (2018). Social media as a shield: Facebook buffers acute stress. "Physiology & Behavior" 185, 46–54. doi:10.1016/j.physbeh.2017.12.021.

Ruth G., Orly B. (2007). Job insecurity, stress and gender: The moderating role of gender ideology. "Community, Work and Family" 10 (3), 341–355.

Rydstedt L.W., Devereux J., Furnham A.F. (2004). Are lay theories of work stress related to distress? A longitudinal study in the British workforce. "Work and Stress" 18 (3), 245–254.

Rydzyński Z. (1975). Zdrowie psychiczne w siłach zbrojnych (Mental health in the armed forces). Warszawa: Wyd. MON.

Sarol Z., Skibniewski F., Śliwak T. (1974). Badania czynności układu krążenia i oddechowego w czasie lotu (In-flight cardiovascular and respiratory tests). "Lekarz Wojskowy" 8, 613–620.

Schachter S. (1980). Nonpsychological explanations of behavior. In: L. Festinger (ed.) Retrospective on Social Psychology (pp. 131–157). New York: Oxford University Press.

Schaufeli W.B., Bakker A.B., Van der Heijden F.M.M.A., Prins J.T. (2009). Workaholism among medical residents: It is the combination of working excessively and compulsively that counts. "International Journal of Stress Management" 16 (4), 249–272.

Schein E.H. (1958). The Chinese indoctrination program for prisoners of ear: A study of attempted "Brainwashing". In: E.E. Maccoby, T.M. Newcomb and E.L. Hartley (eds.) Readings in social psychology (Third edition) (s. 311–334). New York: Holt, Rinehart and Winston, Inc.

Scherer K.R. (1993). Studying the emotion-antecedent appraisal process: An expert system approach. "Cognition and Emotion" 7 (3/4), 325–355.

Schneider F.M., Zwillich B., Bindl M.J., Hopp F.R., Reich S., Vorderer P. (2017). Social media ostracism: The effects of being excluded online. "Computers in Human Behavior" 73, 385–393.

Schnurr P.P., Hayes A.F., Lunney C.A., Mcfall M., Uddo M. (2006). Longitudinal analysis of the relationship between symptoms and quality of life in veterans treated for posttraumatic stress disorder. "Journal of Consulting and Clinical Psychology" 74 (4), 707–713.

Schultz, J.H. (1956). Das autogene Training. Stuttgart: Thieme Verlag.

Schwarzer R., Taubert S. (2002). Tenacious goal pursuits and striving toward personal rowth: Proactive coping. In: E. Frydenberg (ed.): Beyond coping: Meeting goals, visions and challenges (s. 19–35). London: Oxford University Press.

Seligman, M.E. (2006). Learned optimism: How to change your mind and your life. New York: Vintage.

Selye H. (1936). A syndrome produced by diverse noxious agents. "Nature" vol. 138, July 4, p. 32.

Selye H. (1956). The stress of life. Toronto: McGraw3-Hill Book Company, Inc.

Selye H. (1974). Stress without distress. Philadelphia: J. B. Lippincott Co.

Selye H. (1975). Stress and distress. New York: J.B. Lippincott Co.

Selye H. (1980a). Stress and a holistic view of health for the nursing profession. In: K.E. Claus, J.T. Bailey (eds.): Living with stress and promoting well-being. London: The CV Mosby Co.

Selye H. (1980b). The stress concept today. In: I.L. Kutash, L.B. Shlesinger et al. (eds.): Handbook of stress and anxiety. San Francisco: Jossey-Bass.

Sęk, Helena (1996). Wypalenie zawodowe. Psychologiczne mechanizmy i uwarunkowania (Occupational burnout. Psychological mechanisms and conditions). Poznań: Zakład Wydawniczy K. Domke.

Shurley J.T. (1960). Profound experimental sensory isolation. "American Journal of Psychiatry" 117, 539–545.

Siek, S., Kowalski, J., Terelak, J., Walewska, I. (1986). The influence of practicing Yoga on the dimensions of anxiety and aggression. "Biology of Sport", 3 (3–4), 207–213.

Sies H., Joness D. (2007). Oxidative stress. In: G. Fink (ed.): Encyclopedia of stress. Second edition (vol. 3, s. 45–49). New York: Academic Press.

Skevington S.M. (2007). Quality of life. In: G. Fink (Ed.): Encyclopedia of stress. Second edition (vol. 3, s. 317–319). New York: Academic Press.

Smith R., Morgan J., Monks C. (2017). Students' perceptions of the effect of social media ostracism on wellbeing. "Computers in Human Behavior" 68, 276–285.

Smolicz T., Terelak J.F. (2002). The new face of terrorism. Proceedings of the 25th Jubilee European Association for Aviation Psychology Conference: Safety, Systems and Peaple in Aviation, 16–20th 2002, Warsaw.

Snyder C.R. (2000). Handbook of hope. Theory, measures and applications. Laurence, San Diego: Academic Press.

Solomon Z., Horesh D. (2007). Changes in diagnostic criteria for PTSD: Implications from two prospective longitudinal studies. "American Journal of Orthopsychiatry" 7 (2), 182–188.

Solomon Z., Mikulincer M. (2007). Posttraumatic intrusion, avoidance and social functioning: A 20-year longitudinal study. "Journal of Consulting and Clinical Psychology" 75 (2), 316–324.

Sołżenicyn A.I. (2008). Archipelag GUŁag: 1918–1956. Tom 1–3 (The Gulag Archipelago 1918–1956. Volume 1–3). Warszawa: Rebis Dom Wydawniczy.

Sosnowski T., Zimmer K. (red.) (1993). Metody psychofizjologiczne w badaniach sychologicznych (Psychophysiological methods in psychological research). Warszawa: PWN.

Spaulding R.C., Ford C.V. (1972). The "Pueblo" incident: Psychological reactions to the stresses of imprisonment and repatriation. "American Journal of Psychiatry" 129 (1), 49–58.

Speckhard A. (2007). Suicide terrorism, genesis of. In: G. Fink (ed.): Encyclopedia of stress. Second edition (vol. 3, s. 667–676). New York: Academic Press.

Spence J.T., Robbins A.S. (1992). Workaholism: Definition, measurement, and preliminary results. "Journal of Personality Assessment" 58 (1), 160–178.

Stein N.L., Leventhal B., Trabasso T. (red.) (1990). Psychological and biological approaches to emotion. Hillsdale: Lawrence Erlbaum Associates.

Steptoe, A., Shankar, A., Demakakos, P., Wardle, J. (2013). Social isolation, loneliness, and all-cause mortality in older men and women. Proceedings of the National Academy of Sciences, USA, 110, 5797–5801. doi:10.1073/pnas.1219686110

Strelau J., (1995). Temperament and stress: Temperament as moderator of stressors, emotional states, coping, and costs. In: C.D. Spielberger, I.G. Sarason (eds.). Stress and emotion: Anxiety, anger, and curiosity (T. 15, pp. 215–254). Washington: Hemisphere.wwwed.

Suri R., Altshuler L. (2007). Menstrual cycles and stress. In: G. Fink (ed.): Encyclopedia of stress. Second edition (vol. 2, s. 706–711). New York: Academic Press.

Surtees P., Wainwright N. (2007). Life events and health. In: G. Fink (ed.): Encyclopedia of stress. Second edition (vol. 2, s. 599–607). New York: Academic Press.

Sutherland V.J. (2007). Understimulation/boredom. In: G. Fink (ed.): Encyclopedia of stress. Second edition (vol. 3, s. 794–796). New York: Academic Press.

Swieżawski, S. (1956). Objaśnienia: Św. Tomasz z Akwinu, Traktat o człowieku (Explanations: Saint. Tomasz fro z Aquin, Traktat about a man). Poznań.

Szmigielski S. (1974). Chronobiologia. Rytmy biologiczne człowieka (Chronobiology. Biological rhythms of man). Warszawa: PWN.

Szymanik A., Terelak J.F. (2015). Sense of humor and coping stress among young pilots. "Polish Journal of Aviation Medicine and Psychology" 21 (3), 13–21, 123.

Taft C.T., Kaloupek D.G., Schumm J.A., Marshall A.D., Panuzio J., King D.W., Keane T.M. (2007). Posttraumatic stress disorder symptoms, physiological reactivity, alcohol problems and aggression among military veterans. "Journal of Abnormal Psychology" 116 (3), 498–507.

Taylor, F.W. (1919). The Principles of Scientific Management. New York & London: Harper & Brothers Publishers, pp. 144.

Taylor M.J. (2007). Hypothermia. In: G. Fink (ed.): Encyclopedia of stress. Second edition (vol. 2, s. 428–438). New York: Academic Press.

Teilhard de Chardin P. (1967). Człowiek: Struktura i kierunki ewolucji grupy zoologicznej ludzkiej (Human: Structure and directions of evolution of the human zoological group). Warszawa: Instytut Wydawniczy PAX.

Terelak, J. (1973). Rehabilitacja psychiczna studentów inwalidów na przykładzie klubu „IKAR" (Mental rehabilitation of disabled students on the example of the "IKAR" club". „Zdrowie Psychiczne", 92 (14), 31–39.

Terelak J. (1976). Alpha index and personality traits in pilot. "Aviation Space and Environmental Medicine" 47 (2), 133–136.

Terelak J.F. (1982a). Introspekcje antarktyczne. Diariusz III Wyprawy Antarktycznej Polskiej Akademii Nauk (Antarctic introspection. Diariusz III Antarctic Expedition of the Polish Academy of Sciences). Warszawa: Wyd. MON.

Terelak J.F. (1982b). Człowiek w sytuacjach ekstremalnych. Izolacja antarktyczna (Man in extreme situations. Antarctic isolation). Warszawa: Wyd. Mon.

Terelak J.F. (1989). Trends in Poland in space psychology research. "Aviation, Space and Environmental Medicine" 60 (4), 352–360.

Terelak J.F., Zjawisko blackout – granica życia i śmierci (2002). In: W. Bołoz i Maria Ryś (red.): Między życiem a śmiercią. Uzależnienia, eutanazja, sytuacje graniczne (Th blackout phenomenon - life and death limit (2002). In: W. Bołoz and Maria Ryś (ed.): (Between life and death. Addictions, euthanasia, boundary situation) (s. 266–276). Warszawa: Wyd. UKSW.

Terelak J.F. (2005a). Stres organizacyjny (Organizational stress). Warszawa: Wyd. WSM SIG.

Terelak J.F. (2005b). Psychologia organizacji i zarządzania (Organization and management psychology). Warszawa: Difin.

Terelak, J.F. (red.) (2007). Stres zawodowy: Charakterystyka psychologiczna wybranych zawodów stresowych (Psychological characteristics of selected stressful profession). Warszawa: Wyd. UKSW.

Terelak J.F. (2011). Człowiek w sytuacji pracy w okresie ponowoczesności (Man in a post-modern work situation). Warszawa: Wyd. UKSW.

Terelak J.F. (2015). Psychologia kierowców pojazdów drogowych: Teoria i stan badań. (Psychology of road vehicle drivers: Theory and state of research). Warszawa: Wyd. UKSW.

Terelak J.F. (2016). Człowiek w Kosmosie: Bariery adaptacyjne z perspektywy astronautycznej (Man in space: Adaptive barriers from an astronaut perspective. Adaptive barriers from an astronaut perspective). "Studia Philosophiae Christianae" 52 (3), 111–129.

Terelak J.F., Borkowska A. (2007). Emigracja konsumpcyjna jako źródło dobrostanu psychicznego na przykładzie Polaków przebywających w

Kanadzie (Consumption emigration as a source of mental well-being, based on the example of Poles living in Canada). "Studia Psychologica" 5 (7), 101–122.

Terelak J.F., Jasiński T., (1999). Przyspieszenie +Gz jako źródło stresu. In: J.F. Terelak (red.): Źródła stresu: Teoria i badania (Acceleration +Gz as a source of stress. In: J.F. Terelak (ed.) Sources of stress: theory and research). (s. 90–116), Warszawa: Wyd. ATK.

Terelak, J.F., Kluczyńska, Sylwia, Płeć psychologiczna a style radzenia sobie ze stresem u kobiet – ofiar przemocy ze strony partnera. Przegląd Psychologiczny, 2007, 50 (1), 45–64.

Terelak J.F., Łozinska-Sheridan K.A. (2011). Adaptacja kulturowa kwestionariuszy (Cultural adaptation of questionnaires: "Work-Family Enrichment Scale" D.S. Carlson, K M. Kacmar, J.H. Wayne, J.G. Grzywacz, and "Work-Family Conflict Scale" D.S. Carlson, K.M. Kacmar, L.J. Willis). "Przegląd Psychologiczny" 54 (2), 117–139.

Terelak J., Maciejczyk J. (1989). Some indicators of level of adjustment to extreme conditions of existence in the Arctic and Antarctic. "Polish Psychological Bulletin" 20 (3), 207–213.

Terelak J.F., Przychodzka K. (2015). Hazard perception and anxiety in novice and experienced parachutists. "Polish Journal of Aviation Medicine and Psychology" 21 (4), 14–20.

Terelak J., Ruta A. (1982). Stymulacyjny mechanizm adaptacji człowieka do sytuacji deprywacji sensorycznej (The stimulation mechanism of human adaptation to a situation of sensory deprivation). "Postępy Astronautyki" 15 (4), 19–28.

Terelak-Subramanian J. (2002). Bezrobocie. Przyczyny powstania i sposoby zwalczania. Niepublikowana praca dyplomowa (Unemployment. Reasons for occurrence and ways to fight it. Unpublished thesis). Warszawa: MBI SGGW.

Terelak, J.F., Szewczyk, A. (2013). Differential diagnosis of subjective workload and styles of coping with stress among aircraft crewmembers. Polish Journal of Aviation Medicine and Psychology. 19(4), 11–18.

Terelak J.F., Tarnowski A. (1999). Trudność zadania jako źródło stresu. In: J.F. Terelak (red.): Źródła stresu. Teoria i badania (The difficulty of a task as a source of stress. In: J.F. Terelak (ed.): Sources of stress. Theory and research) (pp. 142–168). Warszawa: Wyd. ATK.

Terelak J.F., Truszczyński O. (1992). Stres w długotrwałym locie kosmicznym ((Stress in lengthy space flight). "Przegląd Psychologiczny" XXXV (1), 91–100.

Terelak J.F., Truszczyński O. (1999). Hipoksja jako źródło stresu (Hypoxia as a source of stress). In: J.F. Terelak (red.): Źródła stresu: Teoria i badania

(In: J.F. Terelak (ed.): Sources of stress: Theory and research) (s. 117–141). Warszawa: Wyd. ATK.

Terelak J.F., Turlejski J., Szczechura J., Rożyński J., Cieciura M. (1985). Dynamics of simple arithmetic task performance under Antarctic isolation. "Polish Psychological Bulletin" 16 (2), 123–128.

Thelwall M. (2017). TensiStrength: Stress and relaxation magnitude detection for social media texts. "Information Processing & Management" 53 (1), 106–121.

Theorel T. (2007). Psychosomatic medicine. In: G. Fink (ed.): Encyclopedia of stress. Second edition (vol. 3, s. 296–306). New York: Academic Press.

Thompson J. (2007). Nuclear warfare, threat of. In: G. Fink (ed.): Encyclopedia of stress. Second edition (vol. 2, s. 937–940). New York: Academic Press.

Tomaszewski T. (1984). Ślady i wzorce (Traces and patterns). Warszawa: WSiP.

Torbjörn A., Göran K, Mats G. (2007). Sleep and sleepiness in relation to stress and dis-placed work. "Physiology and Behavior" 92 (1–2), 250–255.

Tuchweber B., Bois P. (2007). Selye, Hans. In: G. Fink (ed.): Encyclopedia of stress. Second edition (vol. 3, s. 448–450). New York: Academic Press.

Turski B. (2002). Oddziaływanie wibracji na człowieka we współczesnym środowisku (The impact of vibrations on people in today's environment). In: W. Kowalski (red.): Medycyna lotnicza. Wybrane zagadnienia (In: W. Kowalski (ed.): Aviation Medicine) (s. 213–236). Poznań: Wyd. DWL i OP.

Tyszkowa, M. (1977). Osobowość i funkcjonowanie jednostki w sytuacjach społecznej ekspozycji. „Przegląd Psychologiczny", XX, 3, 437–447.

Uchnast Z. (red.) (2006). Psychology of time: Theoretical and empirical approaches. Lublin: Wyd. KUL.

Van Kaam, A. L. (1969). Existential foundations of psychology. Garden City–New York: Image Books.

Vaernes R.J. (2007). Pressure, effects of extreme high and low. In: G. Fink (ed.): Encyclopedia of stress. Second edition (vol. 3, s.184–194). New York: Academic Press.

Van Cauter E. (2007). Sleep loss, jet lag, and shift work. In: G. Fink (ed.): Encyclopedia of stress. Second edition (vol. 3, s. 504–506). New York: Academic Press.

Villani D., Riva F., Riva G. (2007). New technologies for relaxation: The role of presence. "International Journal of Stress Management" 14 (3), 260–274.

Voge, V.M., Goldberg, G. (1986). Effectiveness of biofeedback/relaxation therapy on student naval aviators, In: Abstracts of papers: XXIV International Congress of Aviation and Space Medicine (pp. 188–189). Beograd (Jugoslavia), 13–18 Oct. 1986.

Wallace, R.K., Silver, J., Mills, P.J., Dillbeck, M.C., Wagoner, D.E. (1983). Systolic blood pressure and long-term practice of the TM and TM-idhi program: Effects of TM on systolic blood pressure. "Psychosomatic Medicine", 45 (1), 41–46.

Walster, E., Walster, G., Berscheid, E. (1978). Equity: Theory and research. Boston: Allyn Bacon.

Watterhouse, J., Minores, D., Watterhause, M. (1993). Twój zegar biologiczny. Jak żyć z nim w zgodzie? (Your biological clock. How to live with him in harmony?). Warszawa: KiW.

Wegmann H.M., Klein K.E., Conrad B., Esser P. (1983). A model for prediction of resynchronisation after time-zone flights. "Aviation, Space and Environmental Medicine" 54 (6), 524–527.

Weigel, R.R. (1988). Coping witht economic stress: Implications for helping professionals. "Lifestyles:Fammily and Economic".9 (4), 367–382.

Werka T. (1997). Stres i ból. In: J. Zagrodzka, T. Górska, A. Grabowska (red.): Mózg a zachowanie (Brain and behavior). (pp. 252–268). Warszawa: Wydawnictwo Naukowe PWN.

Wernick, R.L., Jaremko, M.E., Taylor, P.W. (1981). Pain management in severely burned adults: A test of stress inoculation. "Journal of Behavioral Medicine", 4, 103–109.

Wessley S., Rose S., Bisson J. (1998). A systematic review of brief psychological intervention (debriefing) for the treatment of immediate related symptoms and the prevention of posttraumatic stress disorder (PTSD) (Cochrane Review). The Cochrane Library. Issue 3. UK: Oxford.

Whitehead D.L., Steptoe A. (2007). Prison. In: G. Fink (ed.): Encyclopedia of stress. Second edition (vol. 3, s. 217–222). New York: Academic Press.

Whitehouse W.G., Orne E.C., Orne M.T. (2007). Relaxation techniques. In: G. Fink (ed.): Encyclopedia of stress. Second edition (vol. 3, s. 345–350). New York: Academic Press.

WHO – Expert Comittee on Drug Dependence, 16 Raport, Geneva 1969 i 18 Raport of WHO, Geneva 1970.

Wickens C.D. (1991). Processing resources and attention. In: D.L. Damos (ed.): Multiple-task performance (s. 3–34). London: Taylor and Francis.

Wiederhold B. K. (2016). Social media sites, part 1: The dark side. "Cyberpsychology, Behavior, and Social Networking" 19 (3), 157. doi:10.1089/cyber.2016.29027.bkw.

Wojtkowiak M. (2002). Przyspieszenia udarowe (Impact acceleration.). In: W. Kowalski (ed.): Medycyna lotnicza (Aviation Medicine) (pp. 142–153). Poznań: Wyd. DWL i OP.

Wolf W., Levordashka A., Ruff J., Kraaijeveld S., Lueckmann J.M., Williams K. D. (2015). Ostracism Online: A social media ostracism paradigm. "Behavior Research Methods" 47, 361–373. http://dx.doi.org/10.3758/s13428-014-0475-x.

Yates A.J. (ed.) (1965). Frustration and confict: Enduring problems in psychology. London: D. Van Nostrand Co., Inc.

Zaleski Z. (2007). Psychologia wsparcia dla nowej Europy (Psychology of support for a new Europe). Lublin: Wyd. Tow. Nauk. KUL.

Zani A., Proverbio A.M. (eds.) (2003). The cognitive electrophysiology of mind and brain (pp. 259–274). San Diego: Academic Press.

Polish Contemporary Philosophy and Philosophical Humanities
Edited by Jan Hartman

Vol. 1 Roman Murawski: Logos and Máthēma. Studies in the Philosophy of Mathematics and History of Logic. 2011.

Vol. 2 Cezary Józef Olbromski: The Notion of *lebendige Gegenwart* as Compliance with the Temporality of the "Now". The Late Husserl's Phenomenology of Time. 2011.

Vol. 3 Jan Woleński: Essays on Logic and its Applications in Philosophy. 2011.

Vol. 4 Władysław Stróżewski: Existence, Sense and Values. Essays in Metaphysics and Phenomenology. Edited by Sebastian Kołodziejczyk. 2013.

Vol. 5 Jan Hartman: Knowledge, Being and the Human. Some of the Major Issues in Philosophy. Translated by Ben Koschalka. 2013.

Vol. 6 Roman Ingarden: Controversy over the Existence of the World. Volume I. Translated and annotated by Arthur Szylewicz. 2013.

Vol. 7 Jan Hartman: Philosophical Heuristics. Translated by Ben Koschalka. 2015.

Vol. 8 Roman Ingarden: Controversy over the Existence of the World. Volume II. Translated and annotated by Arthur Szylewicz. 2016.

Vol. 9 Tomasz Kubalica: Unmöglichkeit der Erkenntnistheorie. Leonard Nelsons Kritik an der Erkenntnistheorie unter besonderer Berücksichtigung des Neukantianismus. 2017.

Vol. 10 Renata Ziemińska: The History of Skepticism. In Search of Consistency. 2017.

Vol. 11 Jan Woleński: Logic and Its Philosophy. 2018.

Vol. 12 Wielslaw Gumula: On Property and Ownership Relations. 2018.

Vol. 13 Andrzej Zaporowski: Action, Belief, and Community. 2018.

Vol. 14 Andrzej Bator / Zbigniew Pulka (eds.): A Post-Analytical Approach to Philosophy and Theory of Law. 2019.

Vol. 15 Krzysztof Śleziński: Towards Scientific Metaphysics. Volume 1: In the Circle of the Scientific Metaphysics of Zygmunt Zawirski. Development and Comments on Zawirski's Concepts and their Philosophical Context. 2019.

Vol. 16 Krzysztof Śleziński: Towards Scientific Metaphysics. Volume 2: Benedykt Bornstein's Geometrical Logic and Modern Philosophy. A Critical Study. 2019.

Vol. 17 Jan Felicjan Terelak: Eustress and Distress: Reactivation. 2019.

www.peterlang.com

www.ingramcontent.com/pod-product-compliance
Ingram Content Group UK Ltd.
Pitfield, Milton Keynes, MK11 3LW, UK
UKHW041447071026
15587UKWH00010B/545

9 783631 775349